Springer Climate

Series Editor

John Dodson, Institute of Earth Environment, Chinese Academy of Sciences, Xian, China

Springer Climate is an interdisciplinary book series dedicated to climate research. This includes climatology, climate change impacts, climate change management, climate change policy, regional climate studies, climate monitoring and modeling, palaeoclimatology etc. The series publishes high quality research for scientists, researchers, students and policy makers. An author/editor questionnaire, instructions for authors and a book proposal form can be obtained from the Publishing Editor.

Now indexed in Scopus® !

Asta Mikalauskienė • Dalia Štreimikienė •
Ignas Mikalauskas

Climate Change and Responsible Consumption

From Crisis to Conscious Consumer Choices

Springer

Asta Mikalauskienė
Kaunas Faculty
Vilnius University
Kaunas, Lithuania

Ignas Mikalauskas
Kaunas Faculty
Vilnius University
Kaunas, Lithuania

Dalia Štreimikienė
Mykolas Romeris University
Vilnius, Lithuania

ISSN 2352-0698 ISSN 2352-0701 (electronic)
Springer Climate
ISBN 978-3-032-16217-5 ISBN 978-3-032-16218-2 (eBook)
https://doi.org/10.1007/978-3-032-16218-2

This Springer imprint is published by the registered company Springer Nature Switzerland AG
The registered company address is: Gewerbestrasse 11, 6330 Cham, Switzerland

Preface

In an era defined by the escalating challenges of climate change, resource depletion, and social inequality, the intertwined concepts of sustainability and responsible consumption have moved from the periphery to the center of global discourse. This book embarks on a comprehensive exploration of these critical issues, tracing their evolution from scientific understanding and policy formation to the individual and collective actions that shape the future development. It argues that addressing the climate crisis is not merely a technical or political challenge, but a profound societal transformation that requires a deep understanding of our consumption patterns and the values that underpin them.

The book begins with a firm grounding in the science of climate change. The initial chapters analyze the complex interplay between natural climate variability and the unprecedented impact of human activities since the Industrial Revolution. By examining the data on rising global temperatures, greenhouse gas concentrations, and their cascading effects on our planet's systems, the book establishes a clear and urgent case for action. It moves from the global to the regional, highlighting policy frameworks such as those developed by the European Union, which serve as crucial examples of how coordinated efforts can help to address this global challenge.

The book traces the historical development of responsible consumption idea from environmental movements of the 1960s to the establishment of the United Nations' Sustainable Development Goals. This historical perspective reveals a growing recognition that environmental protection, economic prosperity, and social well-being are not competing interests but are, in fact, deeply interconnected. Central to this integrated approach is the concept of responsible consumption—a mindful and ethical engagement with the goods and services that constitute daily lives of all individuals. The book delves into the multifaceted nature of responsible consumption, examining it from environmental, economic, social justice, and ethical perspectives.

A unique contribution of this work is its analysis of how global crises have served as powerful, albeit painful, catalysts for change. Through a compelling examination of pivotal moments—from the 1973 Oil Crisis and the 2008 Global Financial Crisis to the recent disruptions of the COVID-19 pandemic and the Russo-Ukrainian War—the book demonstrates how moments of profound disruption can shatter established norms and open new pathways for behavioral and structural change. These crises have repeatedly forced societies to confront their vulnerabilities and to question their dependence on unsustainable systems.

Ultimately, this book is a call for a more conscious and deliberate approach to a responsible consumption. It contends that while the climate change challenges are immense, the capacity for behavioral change is equally significant. Based on the scientific evidence, historical analysis, and a deep exploration of consumer behavior, it offers readers a nuanced understanding of the path toward a more sustainable and equitable world. It is a journey that begins with knowledge, is guided by a sense of shared responsibility, and is ultimately realized through the transformative power of our individual and collective choices.

Kaunas, Lithuania Asta Mikalauskienė
Vilnius, Lithuania Dalia Štreimikienė
Kaunas, Lithuania Ignas Mikalauskas

Competing Interests The authors have no competing interests to declare that are relevant to the content of this manuscript.

Contents

Chapter 1
Climate Change and Policies to Mitigate Climate Change

Abstract Climate change has become one of the defining global challenges of our time. The warming of the planet is no longer a distant threat but an observable and measurable process that is already transforming natural systems and human life. This chapter discusses the underlying causes and consequences of climate change, paying particular attention to the interplay between natural factors and human-induced activities. While natural processes such as volcanic eruptions, solar radiation cycles, and orbital variations have always influenced the Earth's climate, the rapid increase in greenhouse gas emissions caused by industrialization, energy production, and land-use change has accelerated global warming to unprecedented levels. The chapter explains how carbon dioxide, methane, and other gases intensify the greenhouse effect and disturb the planet's energy balance. Using data and figures, it illustrates long-term trends in temperature rise, sea-level increase, and greenhouse gas concentrations, revealing their cumulative effects on ecosystems and societies. The text also introduces the main indicators used to monitor climate change, including surface temperature, ocean conditions, and land cover alterations. Furthermore, the chapter highlights the European Union's approach to climate mitigation and adaptation, reflecting its policy evolution toward a sustainable, low-carbon future. By linking scientific understanding with policy frameworks, the discussion underlines that addressing climate change requires not only technological and economic adjustments but also strong political commitment and international cooperation. Ultimately, the chapter argues that climate change mitigation is not just an environmental necessity but a shared responsibility for humanity's long term well-being.

1.1 Problems of Climate Change

Climate change is a significant challenge for planet Earth. Scientists agree that the planet is warming faster than ever. Skeptics of climate change fail to provide evidence or deny the rising temperature of the atmosphere.

A. Mikalauskienė et al., *Climate Change and Responsible Consumption*, Springer Climate, https://doi.org/10.1007/978-3-032-16218-2_1

Figure 1.1 shows the change in global average land and sea temperature compared to the 1961–1990 average temperature.

Climate change skeptics try to question climate change itself as a phenomenon and present only factual statements that, in one or another area, at some point, the temperature is lower or higher than usual (Škiudas et al., 2020). They also try to explain the phenomenon of climate change with the natural cyclical development of the natural environment. In this case, an attempt is made to prove that, for example, an unusually hot summer repeats itself every certain period, and there is no need to worry because the next period of the natural cycle will already be a cooler summer. It should be noted that, undoubtedly, the climate has changed and the temperature of the atmosphere has changed due to natural processes not related to human activity, such as volcanic eruptions, meteorite dust, etc. At the same time, the concentration of carbon dioxide in the atmosphere has also changed over the millennia due to natural causes. However, there is no evidence that global warming can be caused solely by natural variations in the natural environment (Trenberth & Fasullo, 2013; Marotzke & Forster, 2015). And so theories about natural climate change are scientifically unfounded. Nevertheless, natural drivers of climate change cannot be ruled out.

The distribution of solar radiation reaching the Earth's surface depends on the planet's orbit, and a very small change in the orbit can result in the distribution of solar radiation across the entire planet. Fluctuations in the tilt of the Earth's axis of rotation can have a profound effect on climate. Hence, the known ice ages and interglacial periods and the theory describing the effect of the Earth's orbital parameters on the planet's climate, also known as the Milankovitch cycle (Caccamo & Magazù, 2021).

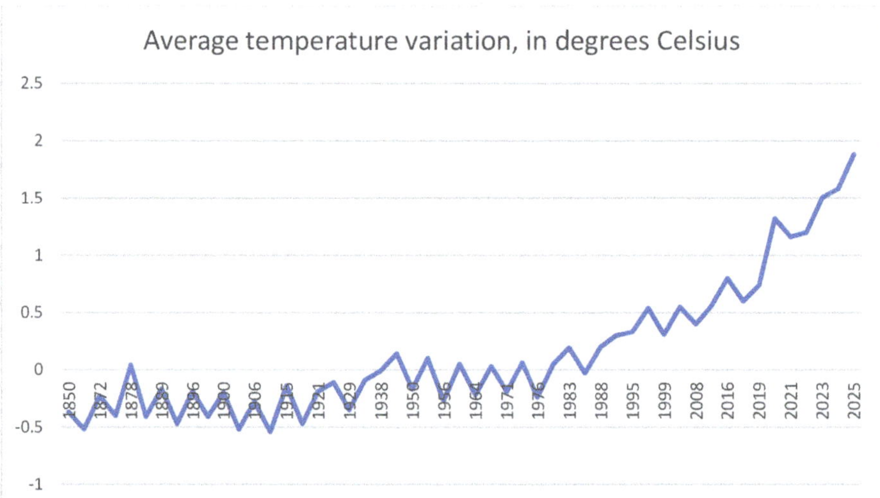

Fig. 1.1 Average temperature variation. Source: Created by authors according to https://ourworldindata.org/co2-and-other-greenhouse-gas-emissions

The Earth's surface is surrounded by a layer of atmosphere that protects our planet from the dangerous and destructive rays of the Sun. The atmospheric layer also protects all the inhabitants and plants of the planet from cosmic cold, so the state of the atmosphere is vital for the entire Earth and its life systems. The Earth itself absorbs about 70% of Sun rays and about 30% reflects them. The surface of the planet, heated by the Sun's rays reaching the Earth, returns the heat to the atmosphere in the form of infrared rays. The upper layers of the troposphere and the stratosphere radiate energy into space unhindered, so the energy balance is established on the scale of the entire planet. Under normal conditions, the Earth absorbs as much of the Sun's energy as it radiates back into space. Very similar or even the same physical processes take place in a simple greenhouse, where the greenhouse gas is glass or plastic that protects the plants in the greenhouse from the harmful effects of the environment. This is how the concept of the "greenhouse effect" appeared, which is also applied to determining the state of the Earth. If the atmosphere did not create a greenhouse effect, the average annual air temperature on our planet at the surface of the Earth would be only −18 °C, and now it is +15 °C. Thus, the thermal result of the greenhouse effect in the lower troposphere is plus 33 °C. The first signs of the greenhouse effect appeared more than 3 billion years ago, when a sufficient mass of the atmosphere was formed. Later, the concentration of GHGs in the atmosphere changed continuously, and the Earth's climate changed along with it. As the greenhouse effect (due to the increasing concentration of greenhouse gases in the atmosphere) increases, the temperature of the lower troposphere continuously rises.

Volcanoes can also affect climate change. During large explosive eruptions, huge amounts of volcanic gases, aerosol droplets, and ash enter the stratosphere (Stenchikov, 2021). However, a volcanic eruption can have an impact on the climate only when the ash mass is thrown to a height greater than 15 km. Coarse ash particles settle quickly on the Earth's surface, while fine ash particles that have entered the stratosphere can circulate there for a very long time. In addition, when a volcano erupts, not only ash is thrown into the stratosphere, but also small chemical compounds that react with water vapor both in the reservoir and in the stratosphere can last for several years. These compounds absorb or scatter the Sun's rays, and less heat reaches the Earth's surface. Thus, the impact of volcanic eruptions on climate change is a relevant issue, but scientists do not have reliable methods to predict the frequency and extent of volcanic eruptions in the future (Cooper et al., 2018).

Figure 1.2 presents a climate change diagram that combines the natural drivers of climate change and the human-induced factors that have led to the rapid and dangerous climate change process at present.

However, most scientists unanimously agree that climate change is caused by human activities, which began to accelerate at a great rate after the Industrial Revolution. As a result of human activities, the average temperature of the atmosphere began to rise rapidly, which caused such climate changes, which are often not only harmful, but also disastrous for the world's flora, fauna, and people (Škiudas et al., 2020). Not only that, the rapid pace of industrialization, by releasing harmful pollutants into the atmosphere, contributed to the change in the chemical

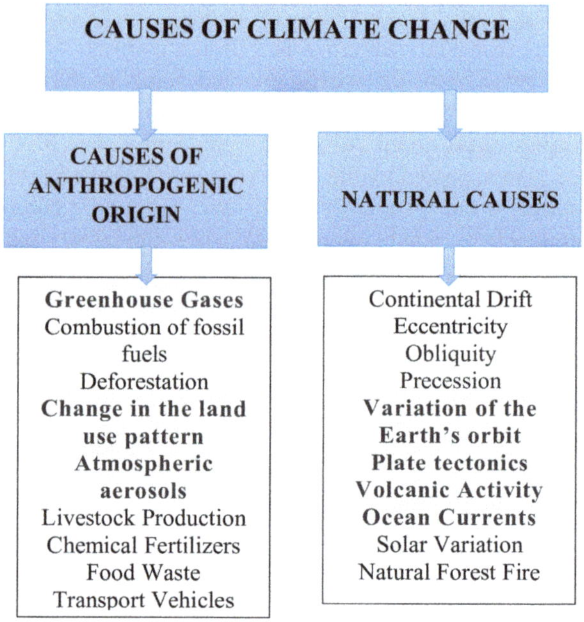

Fig. 1.2 The main causes of climate change. Source: Created by authors

composition of the atmosphere and the strengthening of the greenhouse effect. Human activity does not affect only one component of greenhouse gases—the amount of water vapor (Balevičius et al., 2007). However, as the troposphere warms, water vapor also increases, so positive feedback occurs.

Human activities emit four main greenhouse gases: carbon dioxide (CO_2), methane (CH_4), nitrous oxide (N_2O), and halocarbons (a group of gases containing fluorine, chlorine, and bromine). In 2020, 74.4% of greenhouse gases were carbon dioxide, 17.3% were methane, 6.2% were nitrous oxide, and 2.1% were halocarbons (IPCC, 2007, 2013).

1. Carbon dioxide (CO_2)—mostly from burning fossil fuels (oil, natural gas, coal). It is also produced by burning solid waste and wood. How long these gases persist in the atmosphere is difficult to determine, as they are not destroyed over time, but simply move between different parts of the ocean, the atmosphere, and the land system. For example, much of the carbon dioxide is absorbed by the oceans, but much of it remains in the atmosphere for thousands of years.

Figure 1.3 displays the progression of carbon dioxide emissions resulting from fossil fuel combustion for energy and cement production. It is important to note that land-use change is not accounted for in this figure. The diagram clearly shows the rapid increase in carbon dioxide emissions observed since 1950, which is directly related to industrial development and other anthropogenic activities.

Figure 1.4 displays the regional distribution of CO_2 emissions. Until the twentieth century, carbon dioxide emissions were concentrated in Europe and the United

States. In 1900, approximately 90% of CO2 emissions originated from Europe or the United States. The share of these regions did not decrease to more than 85% until 1950. However, the last decades have brought changes. These changes are linked to the rapid industrialization of China, which once again confirms that one important cause of CO2 emissions, and hence of the acceleration of climate change, is human activity. Today, Europe and the United States account for less than a third of carbon dioxide emissions.

2. Methane (CH4) is generated by agricultural and livestock activities, organic waste decomposition in landfills, and the transportation of petroleum products, natural gas, and coal. It typically remains in the atmosphere for approximately 13 years. Methane is highly effective as a greenhouse gas. Over 100 years, and without accounting for climate feedback mechanisms, one metric ton of methane would contribute to 28 times more warming compared to one metric ton of CO2 (Saunois et al., 2020; Myhre et al., 2013).

The diagram below (Fig. 1.5) shows the trends in methane emissions in the top-emitting countries. It is worth noting that methane emissions have been rising strongly in China since 1995, which, as with carbon dioxide, is linked to the country's particularly rapid industrialization and industrial development.

It can be seen that most of the methane is emitted by the agriculture and livestock sectors and is directly linked to human activities. Only one-fifth of all methane gases released into the atmosphere is of natural origin, with humans responsible for the rest. Figure 1.6 shows a graph of methane emissions by sector.

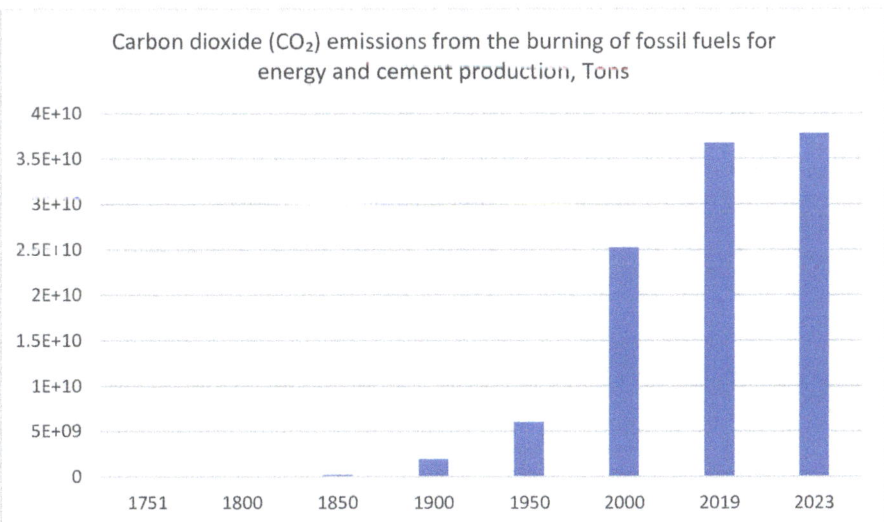

Fig. 1.3 Carbon dioxide (CO2) emissions from the combustion of fossil fuels for energy and cement production. Source: Created by authors according to Global Carbon Project (2021), Andrew and Peters (2021)

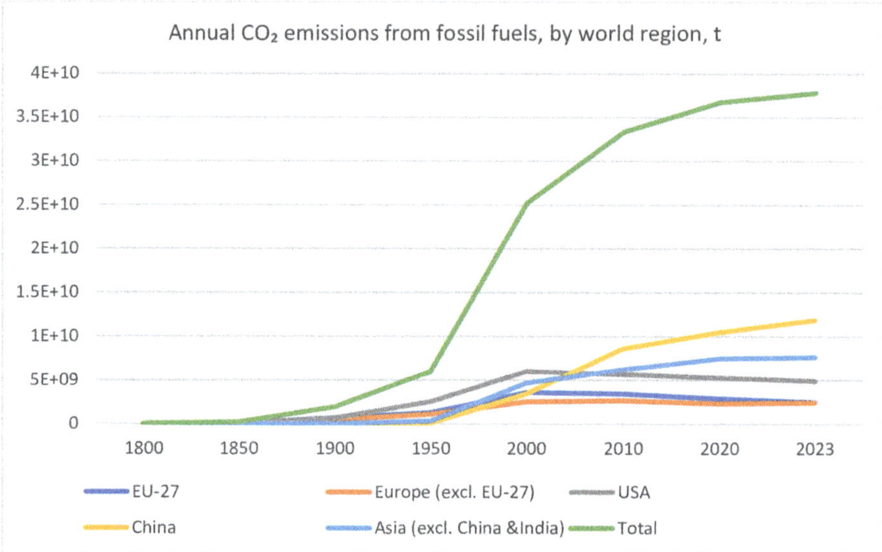

Fig. 1.4 Annual CO2 emissions from fossil fuels, by world region. Source: Created by authors according to Global Carbon Budget - Global Carbon Project (2021). https://ourworldindata.org/grapher/annual-co-emissions-by-region

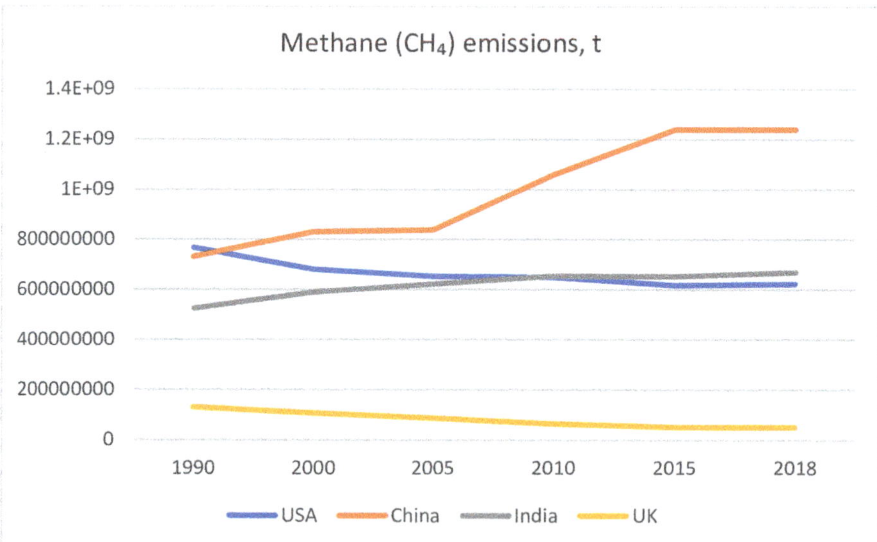

Fig. 1.5 Annual methane emissions. Source: Created by authors according to CAIT (2024) https://ourworldindata.org/greenhouse-gas-emissions

3. Nitrous oxide ($N2O$)—produced by industrial activities, the burning of fossil fuels and solid waste, and the chemical industry. In industrialized countries, nitrous oxide accounts for around 6% of greenhouse gases (Fig. 1.7). It absorbs heat almost 300 times more than carbon dioxide. Since the beginning of the Industrial Revolution, the concentration of nitrous oxide in the atmosphere has increased by almost 16%. The average atmospheric lifetime of the gas is about 120 years.
4. Halogenated carbohydrates (fluorinated greenhouse gases)—gases containing fluorine and other chemicals. These gases are emitted from industrial development, households, and other commercial activities. The average lifetime of the gases in the atmosphere ranges from a few weeks to thousands of years. They are the only greenhouse gases that do not occur naturally but are the result of human activity.

The concentration of these gases in the atmosphere increases over time as they accumulate. The Industrial Revolution has seen an increase in all of these gases, which has been attributed to human activity. Between 1990 and 2015, emissions of these gases associated with anthropogenic activities increased by 43%. Carbon dioxide emissions have increased by 51%. This gas is very "tight," as it can trap heat up to 22,000 times more efficiently than $CO2$. Fluorinated greenhouse gases can persist in the atmosphere for thousands of years.

Scientists recommend taking a holistic approach to analyzing the causes of climate change, as the process of climate change itself is complex and involves different processes, practices, and parties involved in the process. Prof. Arūnas Bukantis, PhD, Head of the Department of Hydrology and Climatology at Vilnius University, recommends that the causes of climate change should not only be divided into natural and anthropogenic causes but also into external and internal causes (Balevičius et al., 2007). According to the professor, external causes of climate change include (Balevičius et al., 2007):

1. *Astronomical:*

   The intensity of solar and galactic irradiance,
   The shape of the Earth's orbit and the parameters of the Earth's orbital motion,
   The inclination of the Earth's axis to the orbital plane,
   The speed of the Earth's rotation on its axis

2. *Geophysical:*

   The Earth's gravitational and magnetic fields,
   Tectonics and mountain building,
   Lithospheric plate drift,
   Volcanism,
   Geothermal heat.

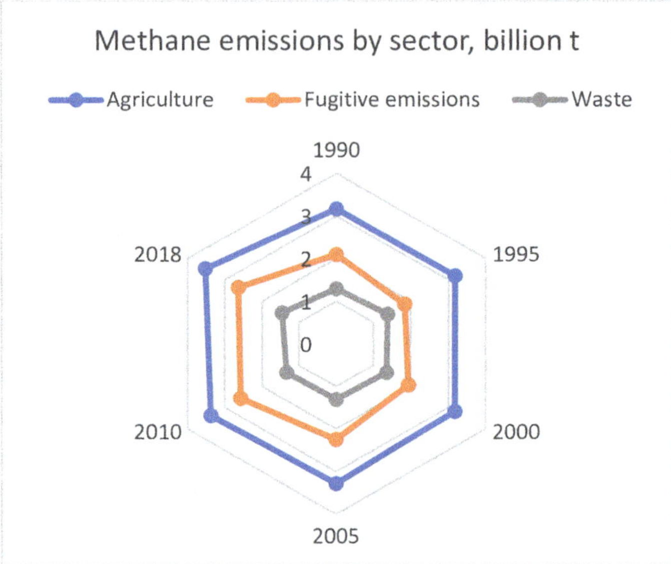

Fig. 1.6 Methane emissions by sector. Source: created by authors according to https://www.climatewatchdata.org/data-explorer/historical-emissions

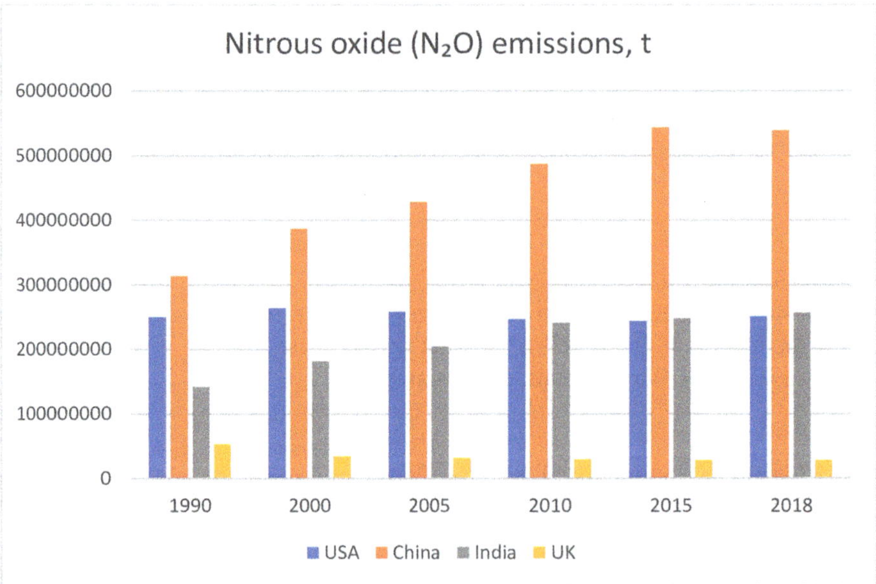

Fig. 1.7 Nitrous oxide (N2O) emissions. Source: Created by authors according to https://www.climatewatchdata.org/data-explorer/historical-emissions

Internal causes of climate change:

- Atmospheric gas composition and aerosol content,
- Terrestrial relief and the structure of the land surface,
- Ocean chemistry and salinity,
- Characteristics of the hydrological cycle,
- Changes in atmospheric and ocean circulation.

A closer look at the studies that have been carried out to identify the causes of climate change shows that, at the present day, it is unlikely that all the causes of climate change have been identified. The different impacts of various external and internal factors on climate are difficult, sometimes impossible, to model because of their variability. As a result, global causes of climate change are often reinforced by regional causes and vice versa. Regional and global causes (factors) of climate change can reinforce, weaken, or neutralize each other.

It is also worth noting that climate variations are long-term and relatively slow, but against this background, there may be several random climate forcings that influence short-term climate changes. The latter are easy to observe, but can easily be confused with global climate change events.

A changing climate affects a wide range of natural processes and becomes highly variable. Climate variability should be interesting not only to climatologists but also to geologists, geographers, biologists, and other specialists. Since the economic and social situation of countries depends on the effects of climate change, explaining the causes of climate change is also of interest to strategic planners.

The factors that determine the intensity of greenhouse gas emissions can be grouped:

1. The structure of the economy. In the early stages of industrialization, the industrial sector accounted for the largest share of gross domestic product (GDP). Meanwhile, energy needs grew rapidly. In the later stages (best described as post-industrialization), the industrial sector's share of GDP declined, while the share of the service sector increased. These shifts in the structure of the economy reduced the growth in energy needs. In developed countries, the industrial sector is actually a relatively small component of the economy (typically 25% of GDP or less), with the service sector accounting for around 60–70% of GDP. In developing countries, the share of the services sector is much lower, while industry is by far the more important sector and accounts for the largest share of GDP.
2. Industrial structure. In the industrial sector, the development of industries from material-intensive to science-intensive technologies plays a major role, leading to higher living standards. This leads to a reduction in energy intensity.
3. Needs saturation. In general, it is possible to assume that energy needs are finite and that one day people's energy needs will be fully satisfied. The evidence that such a limit has already been reached or will be reached is not very strong, but intuitively it seems likely.

Climate change is seen by scientists as a strong market external effect (Fig. 1.8).

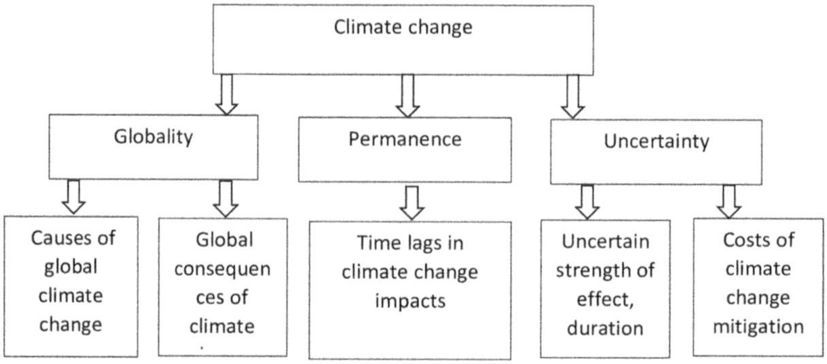

Fig. 1.8 Climate change as a result of externalities. Source: Created by authors

Climate change has a global impact, as the causes and consequences are observed worldwide. It is important to note that the effect of 1 ton of greenhouse gases on climate warming is the same, regardless of where the emissions originated from. This is due to the dispersion of these gases in the atmosphere, and local climate changes are dependent on the global climate system.

The impacts of climate change are permanent and persistent. Once in the atmosphere, some greenhouse gases stay there for thousands of years, which means that their effects are long-lasting and permanent. Moreover, the climate system responds very slowly to changes in atmospheric concentrations of greenhouse gases, and the environmental, economic, and social impacts of climate change have an even longer time lag. The impacts of climate change are currently being experienced and will continue to be experienced for a long time to come.

The severity of climate change impacts remains uncertain, regardless of technological development or the evolution of civilization. It is important to acknowledge the high degree of uncertainty surrounding climate change. The duration of these effects is also unclear, and the costs of mitigating them cannot be predicted. The severity, type, and duration of climate change impacts, as well as the costs of mitigation, are uncertain. Therefore, methods used to assess these risks must account for the large uncertainties. It is evident that without specific and timely measures, climate change will have an extremely severe impact on the global economy.

The Intergovernmental Panel on Climate Change (IPCC) has concluded that human influence is the primary cause of global warming, supporting the scientists' findings (IPCC, 2013).

Addressing climate change is important for several compelling reasons. The main reasons are shown in Fig. 1.9.

Climate change poses a significant threat to the planet's ecosystems, societies, and economies, making it a critical global issue.

Firstly, rising global temperatures result in more frequent and severe weather events such as hurricanes, droughts, floods, and heatwaves, leading to loss of life, displacement of populations, and destruction of infrastructure. Secondly, climate change exacerbates food and water insecurity by altering precipitation patterns,

Environmental Impact

- Climate change threatens the stability and health of ecosystems worldwide. It leads to habitat loss, species extinction, disruptions in food chains, and alterations in natural landscapes, endangering biodiversity and the functioning of ecosystems essential for human survival.

Human Health

- Climate change exacerbates various health risks, including heat-related illnesses, respiratory diseases from air pollution, vector-borne diseases, and waterborne diseases. Rising temperatures and extreme weather events can also affect mental health and well-being, posing significant challenges to public health systems.

Economic Consequences

- Climate change has far-reaching economic impacts, affecting sectors such as agriculture, tourism, fisheries, and insurance. Extreme weather events and environmental degradation lead to crop failures, property damage, loss of livelihoods, increased healthcare costs, and disruptions in global supply chains, imposing substantial economic burdens on communities and nations.

Social Justice

- Climate change disproportionately affects vulnerable populations, including low-income communities, indigenous peoples, women, children, and marginalized groups. They often have limited resources and capacities to adapt to climate impacts, exacerbating existing social inequalities and widening the gap between the rich and poor.

Global Security

- Climate change acts as a threat multiplier, exacerbating existing social, political, and economic tensions. It can lead to resource scarcity, migration, conflicts over water and land, and political instability, posing risks to global peace and security.

Food and Water Security

- Climate change disrupts agricultural productivity, alters growing seasons, and affects water availability, leading to food and water insecurity. This poses risks to global food systems, exacerbates hunger and malnutrition, and increases the vulnerability of communities reliant on agriculture for their livelihoods.

Extreme Weather Events

- Climate change intensifies the frequency and severity of extreme weather events, such as hurricanes, droughts, floods, and wildfires, causing widespread devastation to communities, infrastructure, and ecosystems.

Global Cooperation

- Addressing climate change requires international cooperation and collective action. It necessitates commitments from all countries to reduce greenhouse gas emissions, transition to renewable energy sources, and support adaptation efforts, underscoring the importance of diplomacy and collaboration on a global scale.

Future Generations

- The impacts of climate change will be felt by future generations. Failing to take action now would compromise their ability to meet their needs and enjoy a safe, prosperous, and sustainable future.

Ethical Responsibility

- As stewards of the planet, humans have a moral and ethical responsibility to protect the environment and ensure the well-being of all living beings, both current and future generations. Addressing climate change is not only a matter of self-interest but also a moral imperative to preserve the Earth's ecosystems and safeguard the diversity of life.

Fig. 1.9 The main reasons to pay attention to climate change. Source: Created by authors

reducing crop yields, and disrupting freshwater supplies, posing risks to agricultural productivity and food distribution systems. Thirdly, melting polar ice caps and glaciers contribute to rising sea levels, threatening coastal communities with inundation, erosion, and saltwater intrusion, exacerbating risks for millions of people living in low-lying areas. Fourthly, climate change impacts biodiversity and ecosystems, leading to species extinction, habitat loss, and disruptions to ecological balance, jeopardizing ecosystem services vital for human well-being.

Fifthly, climate-related health risks increase due to air pollution, heat-related illnesses, the spread of vector-borne diseases, and decreased access to clean water and sanitation, disproportionately affecting vulnerable populations. Sixthly, economic losses escalate as extreme weather events damage infrastructure, disrupt supply chains, reduce agricultural productivity, and increase healthcare costs, imposing a substantial burden on national economies and global financial systems. Seventhly, climate change exacerbates social inequalities, as marginalized communities bear the brunt of its impacts, facing disproportionate risks and limited access to resources, services, and opportunities for adaptation and resilience. Eighthly, conflicts over dwindling natural resources such as water and arable land escalate in regions facing heightened climate-related pressures, leading to social unrest, displacement, and migration. Ninthly, addressing climate change requires international cooperation, as it transcends national boundaries and necessitates collective action to reduce greenhouse gas emissions, adapt to unavoidable impacts, and build resilience.

Finally, failure to mitigate climate change would lead to irreversible and catastrophic consequences, including widespread environmental degradation, loss of biodiversity, food and water crises, forced migration, and socio-economic instability, posing existential threats to human civilization and future generations. Therefore, urgent and concerted efforts are essential to address the complex challenges posed by climate change and the transition toward a sustainable, resilient, and equitable future for all.

1.2 Climate Change Indicators

The indicators that need to be assessed in each case, as part of an ongoing analysis of the evolving situation of a country or a region, are very important to identify the most important aspects, to see the country's, the region's, or the world's problems.

The Secretariat of the United Nations Framework Convention on Climate Change (UNFCCC) plays a crucial role in developing climate change indicators. It coordinates the activities of various subsidiary institutions to ensure the implementation of the Framework Convention, the Kyoto Protocol, and the Paris Agreement. The Secretariat collects, evaluates, and organizes information on countries' efforts to combat climate change. The United Nations Framework Convention on Climate Change (UNFCCC) organizes the annual international Conference of the Parties (COP), which is the main global climate change negotiating event. The COP provides updates on the progress of climate negotiations, country statements, press releases, and various reports.

Climate change indicators reflect the UNFCCC and its processes, offering a global perspective. These indicators originate from official sources and are not sourced by the Secretariat from the Internet or other unreliable channels. Collaborating with the World Meteorological Organization (WMO), the UNFCCC supplies information through its climate status reports, although no specific indicator list has been formalized. Additionally, the IPCC is tasked with delivering a comprehensive assessment report, utilized to track progress in climate change mitigation efforts. Multiple institutions provide varying sets of climate indicators.

There are two common types of indicators: those describing the current state and historical trends of the climate system, often termed lag indicators, and those examining future impacts, risks, and adaptation, referred to as baseline indicators. (Swedish International Development Cooperation Agency, 2010):

1. Historical indicators, also known as lagging indicators, involve identifying a concise selection of critical climate indicators to report on past climate change. Surface temperature alone is deemed insufficient as it provides an incomplete representation of the Earth's energy balance. A more comprehensive array of indicators would offer a more nuanced depiction and encompass the entire spectrum of physical climate changes observed over the past 150 years.
2. Forward-looking indicators, or future indicators, are essential for guiding the management of climate change and its societal impacts. They aid in evaluating whether policymakers are implementing appropriate measures for mitigation and adaptation. Engaging a diverse community, which includes social and economic experts, is crucial in establishing a comprehensive set of future indicators. These indicators will play a vital role in informing decision-making processes aimed at addressing the challenges posed by climate change.

Climate indicators, as well as sustainable development indicators, need to meet certain general requirements for indicators. The desirable characteristics of climate indicators are:

- relevance;
- usefulness;
- simplicity;
- universality;
- representativeness;
- sensitivity;
- permanence;
- quantification;
- length of data time sequences.

Relevance is manifested through the clarity and comprehensibility of the indicator for all kinds of audiences. Not surprisingly, several indicators have a very clear national dimension, and in some cases a national dimension as well, which adds to the relevance of the indicator.

Usefulness is understood as the characteristic of an indicator that makes it possible not only to illustrate changes that are taking place but also to make decisions based on these indicators.

Simplicity—a characteristic of an indicator that ensures that both the indicator itself and the decisions based on it can be understood not only by practitioners but also by the general public, thus ensuring that mitigation policy can be implemented with the participation of a wide range of people from all segments of society and that decisions are transparent.

Universality means that the values of the indicators should not depend on the specific characteristics of a country or region, its level of economic development, or culture.

Representativeness must ensure that the analyzed indicators adequately represent the aspect of climate change being analyzed and assessed.

Sensitivity—a characteristic of an indicator that enables timely detection and assessment of changes and timely decisions to address problems.

Permanence is understood as the characteristic of an indicator that ensures that its values will remain substantially unchanged after some minor methodological changes or changes to the structure of the databases. It is clear that sensitivity and stability are in some sense opposite characteristics, and it is therefore important to reconcile as far as possible the following requirements when selecting indicators.

Regarding future indicators, the Paris Agreement outlines a mitigation objective alongside the goal of temperature increase limitation. It is imperative to promptly reduce global greenhouse gas (GHG) emissions, recognizing that developing nations may require more time than developed ones to reach peak emissions, aiming for equilibrium in the latter half of the century between anthropogenic emissions and removals via sinks. Consequently, the primary indicator under the Paris Agreement is greenhouse gas concentration in the atmosphere. However, to comprehensively monitor the carbon cycle, indicators encompassing land-use and oceanic changes are crucial. Indicators about climate change mitigation and socio-economic factors serve to gauge countries' progress in decarbonizing global and national energy supply systems.

December 2016 The World Meteorological Organization meeting in December 2016 discussed and agreed indicators in the following groups (World Meteorological Organization, 2017):

- temperature and energy;
- the composition of the atmosphere;
- the ocean;
- cryosphere;
- land-use/vegetation change;
- extremes and human impacts.

Different categories of indicators are available, with some evaluating environmental factors like air or water quality, or the state of forests. In contrast, others measure the political or organizational response to these issues, such as the existence of environmental legislation (yes/no; year), the presence of environmental/climate change strategy/action plan (yes/no; year), or the frequency of environmental assessments conducted by a partner (Swedish International Development Cooperation Agency, 2010). A combination of indicators that monitor environmental trends and changes alongside those assessing government (policy and administrative) actions is often the most effective approach.

There are instances where a specific indicator can effectively measure multiple facets of development, with the environment (including climate change) being just one aspect. Moreover, improving environmental conditions alone may not suffice to achieve the desired outcomes. Take, for instance, the under-five mortality rate, which not only reflects access to healthcare but also correlates with factors like education, research, gender equality, access to nutrition, and even access to clean water and adequate sanitation. While enhancing access to water and sanitation is crucial, it's evident that all these aspects must synergize to achieve the overarching objective of reducing under-five mortality, as illustrated in this example.

If the cooperation strategy references environmental aspects, encompassing climate, ecosystems, natural resources, pollution, and disasters, whether as an objective, a dialogue topic, or a dedicated sector, it is essential to ensure that this is mirrored in the choice of indicators. The environment isn't merely a sectoral concern; it's also a cross-cutting issue that must be integrated across all sectors. Consequently, indicators related to the environment, climate change, and disaster risk reduction (DRR) should be identified where applicable and feasible, spanning impact, outcome, and output levels within all outcome hierarchies. Typically, the overarching development objective outlined in a cooperation strategy aligns with the impact level, while sector-specific objectives are often at the output and outcome levels.

Global climate conditions are established through climate indicators, drawing on data available year-round. These indicators often depend on multi-source or community estimates, leading to delays in compiling final data records, which means that not all indicators are presented here. For a more comprehensive understanding of the global climate in 2020, additional insights can be gleaned from the World Meteorological Organization (WMO) Statement on the State of the Global Climate.

In a global context, 2020 ranked among the top three warmest years ever recorded. Certain regions, particularly in the Arctic and northern Siberia, saw temperatures soaring more than 6 °C above the norm. However, in the latter part of the year, the eastern Pacific region registered temperatures below the average, attributed to the cooler La Niña phenomenon.

Next, we will discuss global indicators of climate change.

Annual surface temperature change (see Fig. 1.10) is an indicator showing the average change in surface temperature between 1961 and 2021, using 1951–1980 as a base temperature.

The annual change in surface temperature is a crucial indicator of climate change, providing valuable insights into the warming of the Earth's atmosphere. The importance of this indicator is shown in Fig. 1.11.

In summary, tracking annual surface temperature changes is essential for monitoring global warming trends, assessing climate-related risks, guiding policy decisions, and raising public awareness about the urgent need for climate action to mitigate the impacts of climate change.

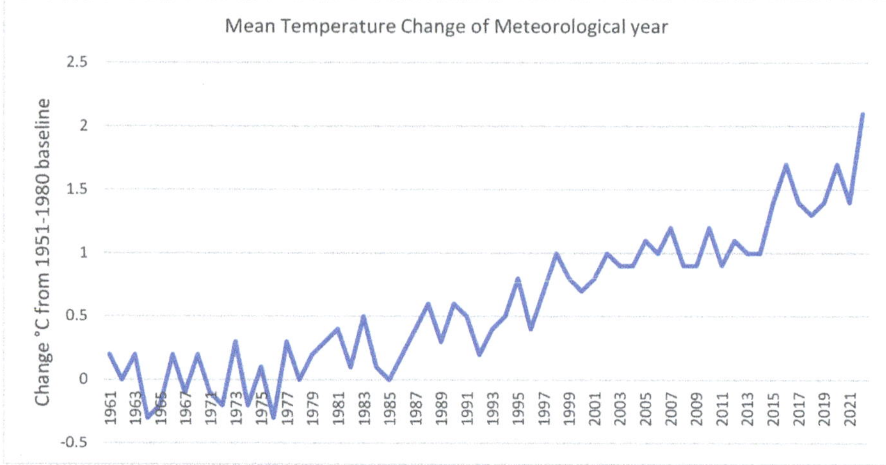

Fig. 1.10 Mean temperature change of meteorological year. Source: Created by authors according to https://climatedata.imf.org/pages/climatechange-data

Concentrations of Greenhouse Gases

Greenhouse gas levels, including CO2, CH4, and N2O, in the atmosphere have surged to their highest levels on record since satellite monitoring began in 2003. Preliminary evaluations from the European State of the Climate report for 2020 suggest that although the growth rate of CO2 has slightly decelerated compared to prior years, CH4 levels have escalated more swiftly. These variations are linked to the modest decrease in emissions associated with the COVID-19 pandemic and warmer temperatures, which amplify the release of CO2 and CH4 from land surfaces.

Atmospheric carbon dioxide levels have been rising steadily since the 1960s (Fig. 1.12). In 2021, atmospheric carbon dioxide levels peaked at 416.45 ppm, compared to 1960 levels of around 316.91 ppm. Carbon dioxide emissions are mainly due to human activities such as the burning of fossil fuels and deforestation and are a major contributor to climate change.

Human economic growth and population expansion have led to unparalleled levels of greenhouse gases (GHGs) in the Earth's atmosphere. Water vapor (H2O), carbon dioxide (CO2), methane (CH4), nitrous oxide (N2O), and fluorinated gases are all adding to the greenhouse effect, being emitted into the atmosphere in significant quantities every day. The figure below illustrates the trajectory of global greenhouse gas emissions (Fig. 1.13).

Concentrations of greenhouse gases (GHGs) are critical indicators of climate change, offering essential insights into the drivers of global warming and the Earth's changing atmospheric composition.

The importance of concentrations of greenhouse gases as a climate change indicator is shown in Figs. 1.14 and 1.15.

Monitoring concentrations of greenhouse gases is fundamental to understanding the drivers and impacts of climate change, informing policy decisions, and raising

Fig. 1.11 The value of the annual change in surface temperature. Source: Created by authors

public awareness about the urgent need for climate action to mitigate its effects and build a sustainable future.

Average Sea Level Change

This indicator provides an estimate of global sea level rise based on satellite radar altimetry measurements. These measurements are acquired by assessing the duration it takes for a radar pulse to travel from the satellite to the sea surface and return.

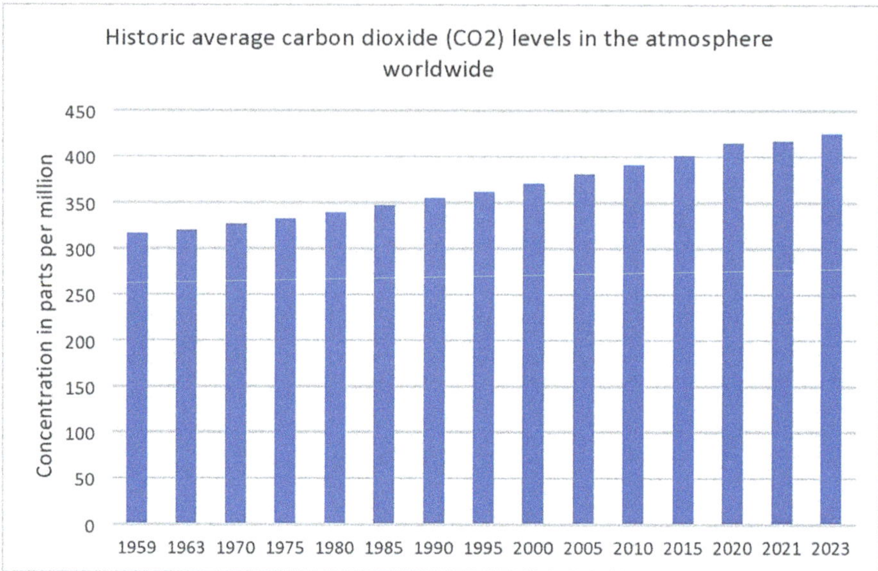

Fig. 1.12 Historic average carbon dioxide (CO2) levels in the atmosphere worldwide. Source: Created by authors according to https://www.statista.com/statistics/1091926/atmospheric-concentration-of-co2-historic/

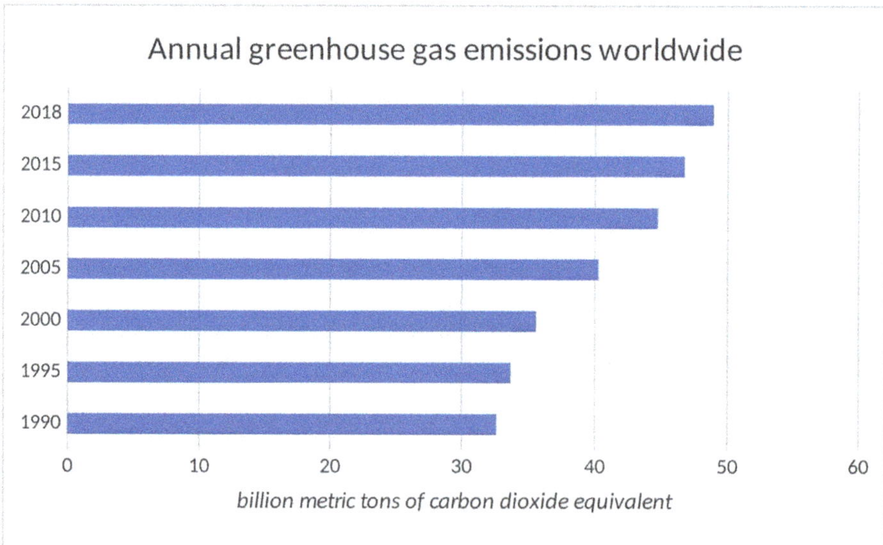

Fig. 1.13 Annual greenhouse gas emissions worldwide. Source: Created by authors according to https://www.statista.com/statistics/1285502/annual-global-greenhouse-gas-emissions/

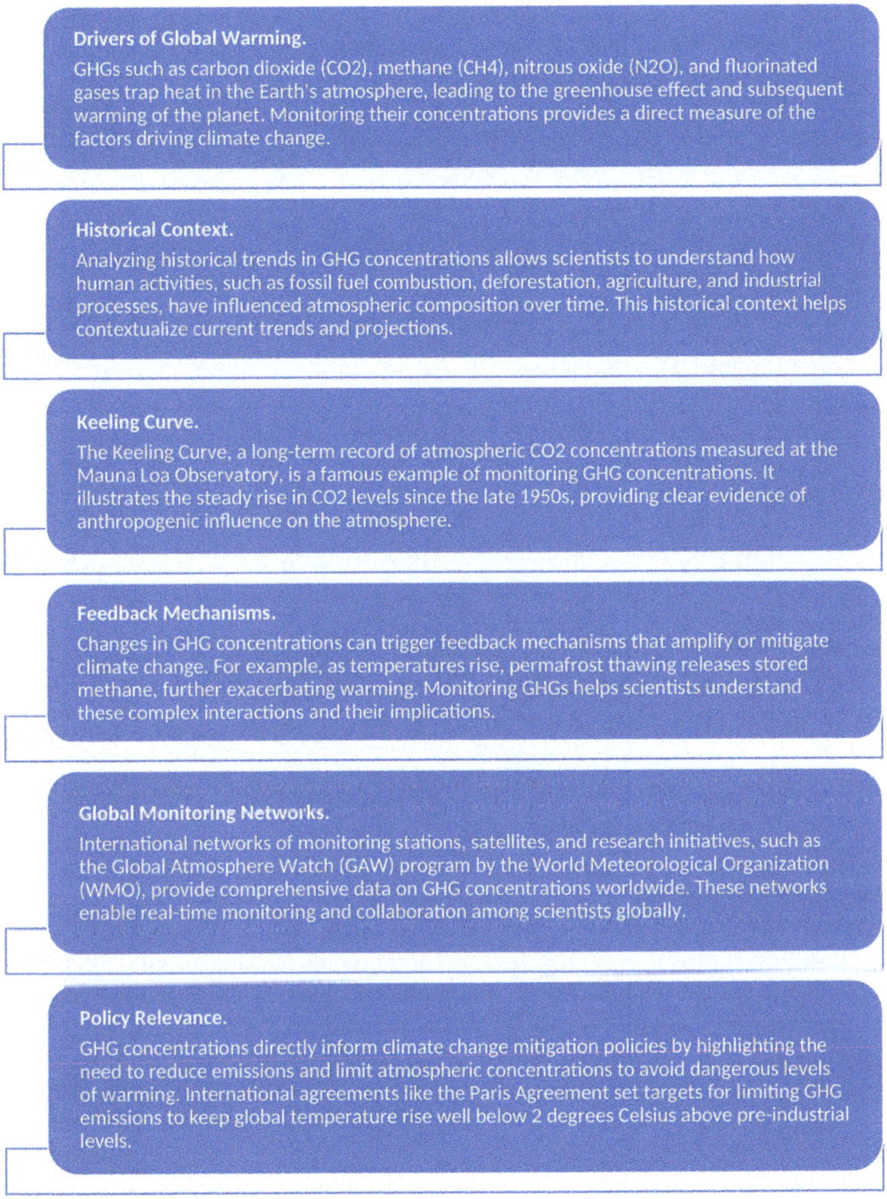

Fig. 1.14 The importance of concentrations of greenhouse gases as a climate change indicator. Source: Created by authors

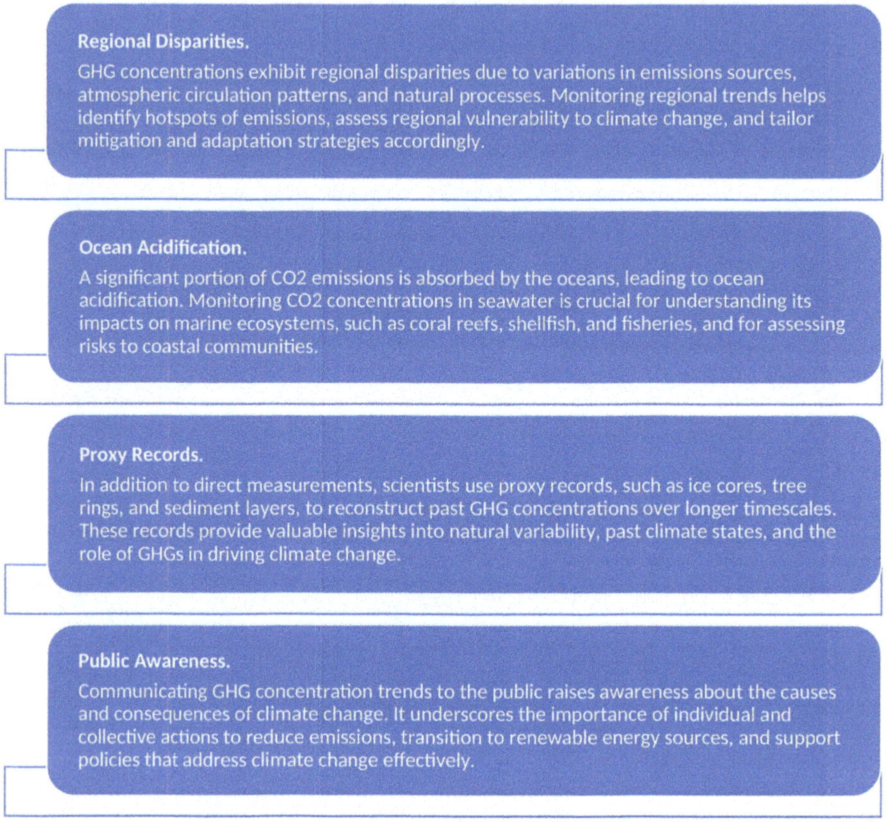

Fig. 1.15 The importance of concentrations of greenhouse gases as a climate change indicator. Source: Created by authors

Global average sea level rise rate since 1993 month of January until 2020 May according to the chosen location (in millimeters per year) is presented in Fig. 1.16.

The average sea level change serves as a crucial indicator of climate change, reflecting the impact of global warming on the Earth's oceans. Rising sea levels result from the thermal expansion of seawater due to warming temperatures and the melting of ice caps and glaciers. Monitoring sea level change provides valuable insights into the rate and magnitude of global warming and its consequences. It helps assess the vulnerability of coastal communities to flooding, erosion, and saltwater intrusion, highlighting the urgent need for adaptation measures. Furthermore, sea level rise exacerbates the risks posed by extreme weather events, such as storm surges and coastal flooding, threatening infrastructure, economies, and ecosystems along coastlines worldwide. Addressing sea level rise requires concerted efforts to reduce greenhouse gas emissions, mitigate climate change impacts, and enhance resilience in vulnerable coastal areas.

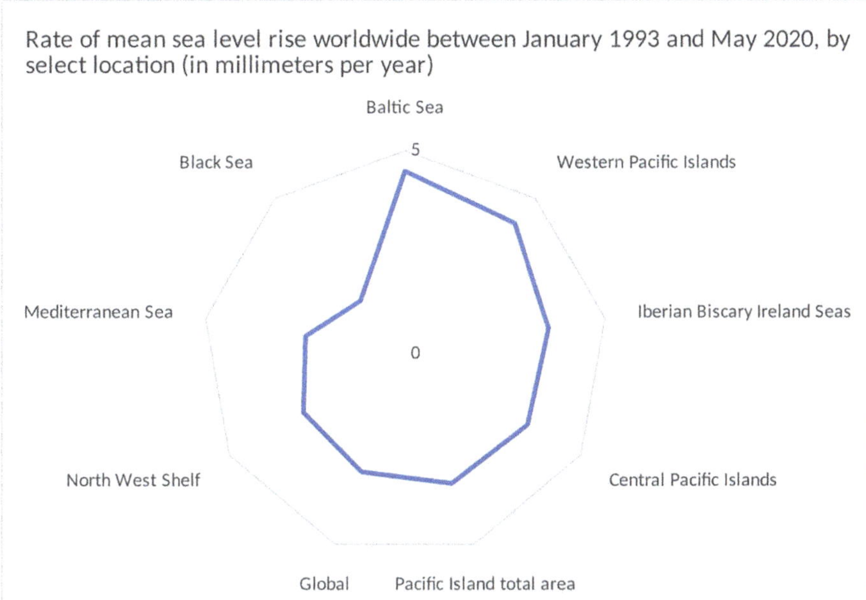

Fig. 1.16 Global average sea level rise rate since 1993 month of January until 2020 May according to the chosen location. Source: Created by authors, according to https://www.statista.com/statistics/1336120/sea-level-rise-by-location/

Sea Ice

Arctic sea ice has reached its second lowest extent on record, while the Antarctic sea ice extent was close to the average annual minimum (National Centre for Atmospheric Research Staff, 2017). Sea ice concentration serves as an indicator of climate change at high latitudes and has significant social and environmental implications. It is a critical boundary condition for atmospheric models, including those used in atmospheric reanalysis, and serves as a benchmark for coupled climate models. As a result, several methods have been developed to estimate sea ice concentrations (Wickham et al., 2021).

The most widely used datasets for sea ice climate research are derived from passive microwave instruments such as SMMR, SSMI, SSMIS, AMSR-E, and AMSR-2 deployed on various satellite platforms. The algorithms applied to microwave brightness temperatures use different channel combinations to correct for weather, satellite drift, and other factors in different ways. Users of sea ice data should be familiar with the different algorithms and their characteristics, the different spatial footprints of satellite instruments and channels, and the methods for integrating data from different sources into long-term datasets. The table and links below serve as a starting point for understanding and accessing relevant datasets, with a focus on long-term datasets rather than near-real-time products (National Centre for Atmospheric Research Staff, 2017).

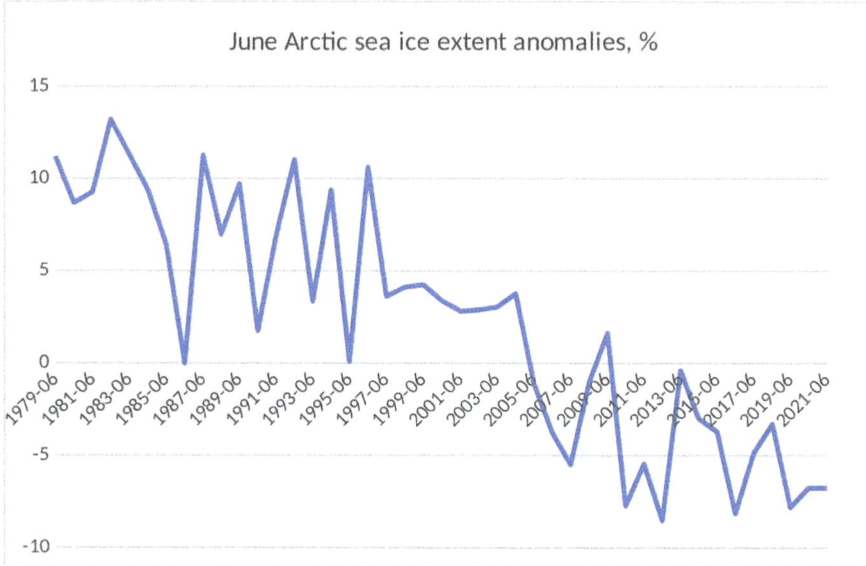

Fig. 1.17 June Arctic sea ice extent anomalies. Source: EUMETSAT OSI SAF Sea Ice Index v2.1. Credit: Copernicus Climate Change Service/ECMWF/EUMETSAT. https://climate.copernicus.eu/sea-ice-cover-june-2021

In June 2021, Arctic sea ice extent was below average, marking the eighth lowest on record according to satellite data, surpassing June values observed over the past 5 years (see Fig. 1.17). The sea ice cover in the Laptev Sea showed below-average levels due to persistent and elevated temperatures. Meanwhile, the Antarctic sea ice extent remained close to the overall average, although notable regional variations were observed. Similar to May, sea ice concentrations were predominantly above average in the Bellingshausen-Amundsen Sea, Indian Ocean, and Western Pacific sectors, while below-average concentrations were noted in the northern Weddell and northern Ross Seas.

Figure 1.18 depicts a time series showing the monthly average anomalies of Antarctic sea ice extent for all June months spanning from 1979 to 2021. These anomalies are expressed as a percentage relative to the average June extent recorded during the period 1991–2020.

In June 2021, the extent of Antarctic sea ice closely approached the 1991–2020 average of 14.0 million km^2, standing only 0.1 million km^2 (1%) above the June average. This marginal positive anomaly contrasted with five consecutive years of negative anomalies observed in June, particularly evident in the years 2017–2019 (refer to Fig. 1.18).

Sea ice serves as a critical indicator of climate change, offering insights into the Earth's changing climate system. Its importance lies in various aspects:

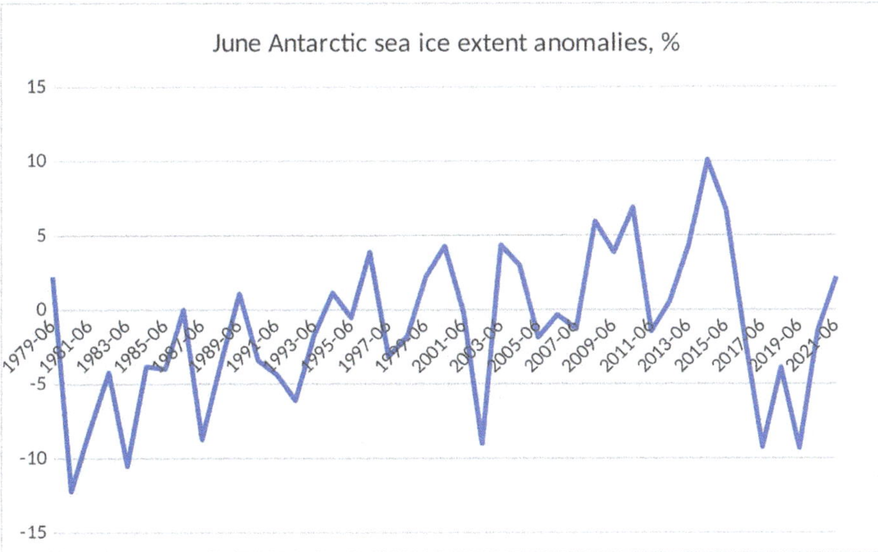

Fig. 1.18 June Antarctic Sea ice extent anomalies. Source: Created by authors according to https://climate.copernicus.eu/sea-ice-cover-june-2021

- Sea ice extent and thickness are sensitive indicators of temperature changes in polar regions. Monitoring these parameters provides crucial data on the rate and extent of global warming.
- Declining sea ice extent, particularly in the Arctic, reflects the unprecedented warming of the Earth's atmosphere and oceans, driven primarily by human activities such as greenhouse gas emissions.
- Sea ice loss contributes to positive feedback loops, amplifying climate change by reducing the Earth's albedo—the reflectivity of the planet's surface—resulting in more solar energy absorption and further warming.
- Sea ice plays a vital role in regulating global climate patterns by influencing ocean circulation and atmospheric circulation systems, impacting weather and climate patterns worldwide.
- The decline in sea ice has profound ecological implications, affecting marine ecosystems, biodiversity, and the distribution of species dependent on ice habitats, such as polar bears, seals, and Arctic marine mammals.
- Sea ice loss threatens the traditional lifestyles and livelihoods of indigenous communities that rely on ice for hunting, transportation, and cultural practices, exacerbating social and economic vulnerabilities.
- The melting of sea ice contributes to sea level rise, albeit to a lesser extent than land-based ice melt. However, it still poses risks to coastal communities and infrastructure worldwide.

- Satellite observations, remote sensing technologies, and field measurements enable scientists to monitor changes in sea ice extent, thickness, and volume accurately, providing valuable data for climate research and modeling.
- Sea ice serves as a natural archive of past climate conditions, offering insights into historical climate variability and long-term climate trends through techniques such as ice core analysis and paleoclimate reconstruction.

Preserving sea ice and mitigating its loss are essential components of climate change mitigation and adaptation strategies. Effective action to reduce greenhouse gas emissions and limit global warming is necessary to safeguard the stability of polar environments and mitigate the far-reaching impacts of sea ice loss on the planet's climate, ecosystems, and societies.

Land Cover and Land Cover Change Indicator

Assessing changes in land surface aids in tracking the effects on ecosystems and biodiversity, crucial for monitoring environmental impacts. Biodiversity loss and the strain on ecosystem services rank among the foremost global concerns. The severity of global biodiversity decline has reached a level recently characterized as "biological destruction" (Wickham et al., 2021).

Land cover has important links to climate regulation. The Earth's ability to release or store carbon influences the amount of CO2 in the atmosphere. These indicators reflect changes in land cover over time, categorizing land cover into types that affect climate, regulate climate, and have a neutral effect. Global land cover data serve as crucial sources of information for comprehending the intricate interplay between human activity and global change.

In the past 20 years, the US Geological Survey, collaborating with other federal agencies, has produced and distributed five versions of the National Land Cover Database products. These resources provide accurate spatial information and reliable data on land cover and changes in land cover over time.

Figure 1.19 shows the evolution of the indicator between 1992 and 2018.

Land cover and land cover change indicators serve as crucial metrics for assessing the impacts of climate change on terrestrial ecosystems. These indicators provide insights into how human activities, such as deforestation, urbanization, and agricultural expansion, alter the Earth's surface and influence climate patterns. Changes in land cover affect surface albedo, carbon storage, and the exchange of energy and water between the land surface and the atmosphere, amplifying or mitigating climate change. Monitoring land cover dynamics helps identify areas of vulnerability to climate impacts, such as increased frequency of wildfires, shifts in agricultural productivity, and changes in biodiversity. By understanding the relationship between land cover changes and climate change, policymakers can develop targeted strategies for land-use management, conservation, and adaptation to minimize environmental risks and promote sustainable development.

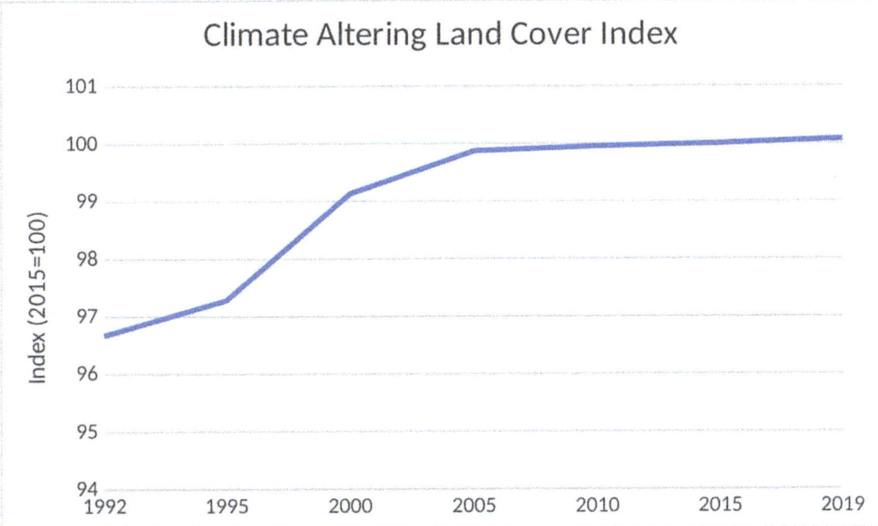

Fig. 1.19 Climate altering land cover index. Source: Created by authors according to https://climatedata.imf.org/pages/climatechange-data

Frequency of Climate-related Disasters

Climate-related disasters, including floods, storms, droughts, and heat waves, are increasingly prevalent globally, with a worrisome connection to climate change. On average, approximately 6800 natural disasters occur worldwide each year.

In 2019, 290 major natural disasters occurred worldwide, which killed 11,694 people, injured 90.638 million people, and caused direct economic losses estimated at 121.856 billion (CRED, 2021). Compared to the average of the last 30 years (1989–2018), the frequency of major natural disasters in 2019 was 10% lower, with 79% fewer deaths, 55% fewer negative impacts, and 7% less direct economic losses (Academy of Disaster Reduction and Emergency Management, 2020). Compared to the 10-year average (2009–2018), the incidence of major natural disasters in 2019 was 14% lower, with 74% fewer deaths, 50% fewer negative impacts, and 28% fewer direct economic losses (Academy of Disaster Reduction and Emergency Management, 2020).

Figure 1.20 shows the number of deaths due to natural disasters in 2019.

In 2021, the Emergency Event Database (EM-DAT) documented 432 catastrophic events attributed to natural disasters globally. These incidents resulted in 10,492 fatalities, impacted 101.8 million individuals, and caused an estimated economic loss amounting to USD252.1 billion.

The number of natural disasters reached 432 in 2021, well above the average number of catastrophic events between 2001 and 2020 (see Table 1.1). The number of natural disasters during this period was 357 (CRED, 2021). The highest number of floods was recorded in 2021 (223 events), which is also above the average number of floods recorded between 2001 and 2020 (163 annual floods) (CRED, 2021).

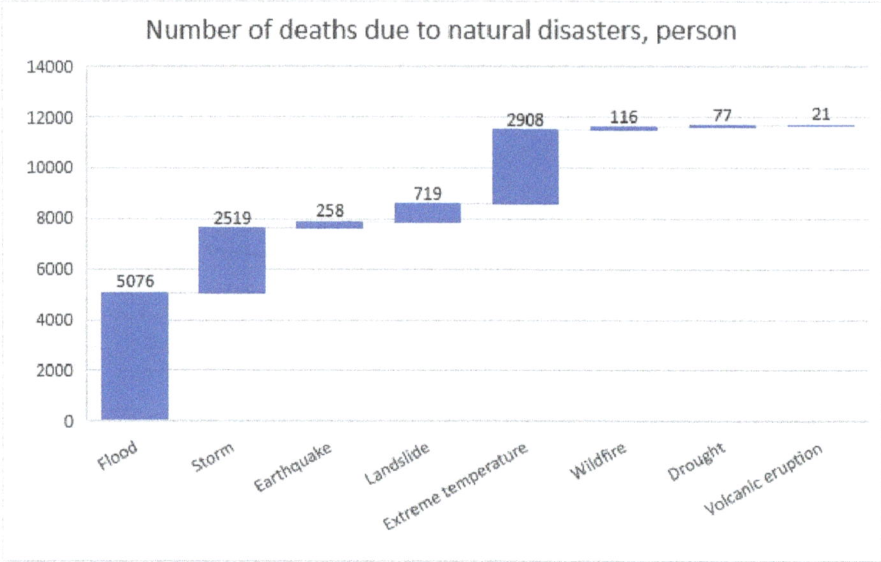

Fig. 1.20 Number of deaths due to natural disasters in 2019 year. Source: Created by authors according to CRED (2021)

Table 1.1 A number of natural disasters

Natural disaster	2001–2020 Average	in 2021
Floods	223	163
Storms	121	102
Heat waves	19	11
Earthquakes	28	27

Source: Created by authors according to CRED (2021)

A closer look reveals that in 2021, the worldwide distribution of climate-related natural disasters on Planet Earth is quite uneven. Figure 1.21 shows the distribution of these events.

Figure 1.22 below shows the frequency of natural disasters from 1980 to 2021.

Climate-related disasters not only result in direct losses of tangible assets like property and infrastructure but also lead to intangible losses such as loss of life and damage to natural and cultural resources. Additionally, they incur indirect losses including reduced output due to diminished productive capital and the diversion of capital toward rebuilding efforts instead of more productive investments like human capital, consequently impacting the country's GDP over the long term. Several studies have endeavored to evaluate both the direct and indirect effects of climate-related disasters on economic growth, often categorizing them based on short-medium (up to 5 years) and long-term (10 years and beyond) timeframes.

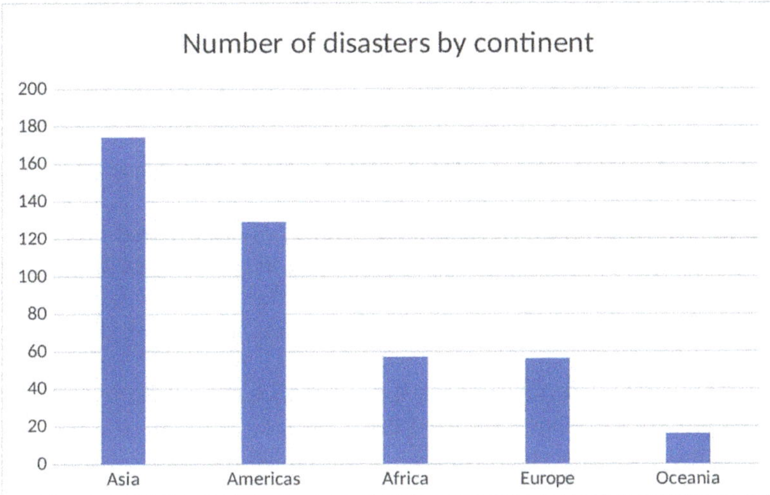

Fig. 1.21 Natural disaster distribution. Source: Created by authors, according to CRED (2021)

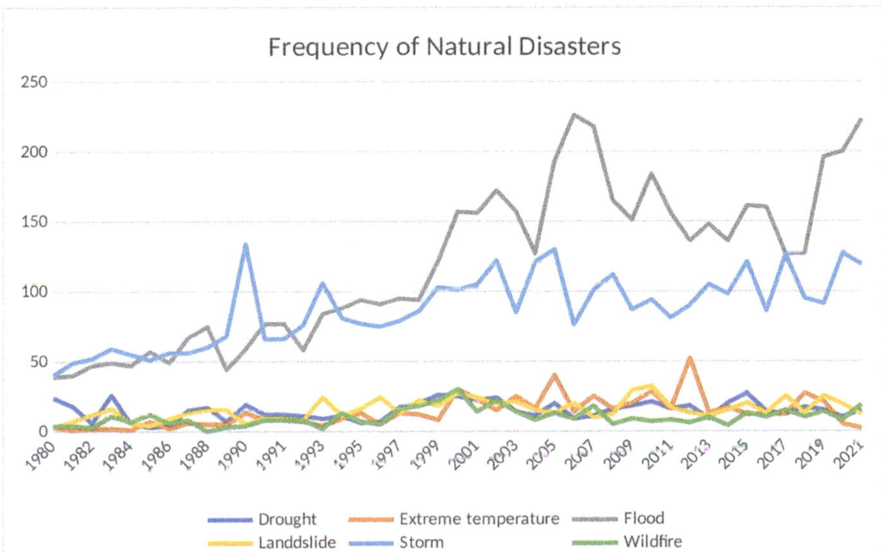

Fig. 1.22 Frequency of natural disasters. Source: Created by authors according to https://climate-data.imf.org/pages/climatechange-data

Warming of the Oceans

In 2021, four of the climate change indicators (greenhouse gases, sea level rise, ocean warming, and ocean acidification) have reached their highest values. It is therefore clear that anthropogenic activities are causing changes in both land and oceans. Such changes have a very serious negative impact on human life and quality of life, on the availability of food and water, and on the economies of countries, causing billions of dollars in losses.

Water covers more than 70% of the Earth's surface and absorbs a large amount of heat, preventing the atmosphere from getting too hot. Normal natural processes (ocean waves, tides, ocean currents) stir the water so that warmer water flows into colder water and vice versa. The oceans therefore play a key role in stabilizing the Earth's climate system.

But while the water naturally mixes, the heat is only transferred from one place to another and doesn't go anywhere. It's important to note that the thermal energy that enters the ocean warms the planet for decades after the heat has directly entered the water. In this case, when the ocean absorbs more heat than it gives off, ocean warming occurs.

Annual global ocean surface temperature anomalies from 1880 to 2021 based on the temperature bias are shown in Fig. 1.23.

The consequences of ocean warming:

- As warming water expands, warming ocean water raises global sea levels.
- As sea levels rise, threats to natural ecosystems increase.
- Threats to coastal populations.
- Thinning sea ice.
- Threat to marine ecosystems..

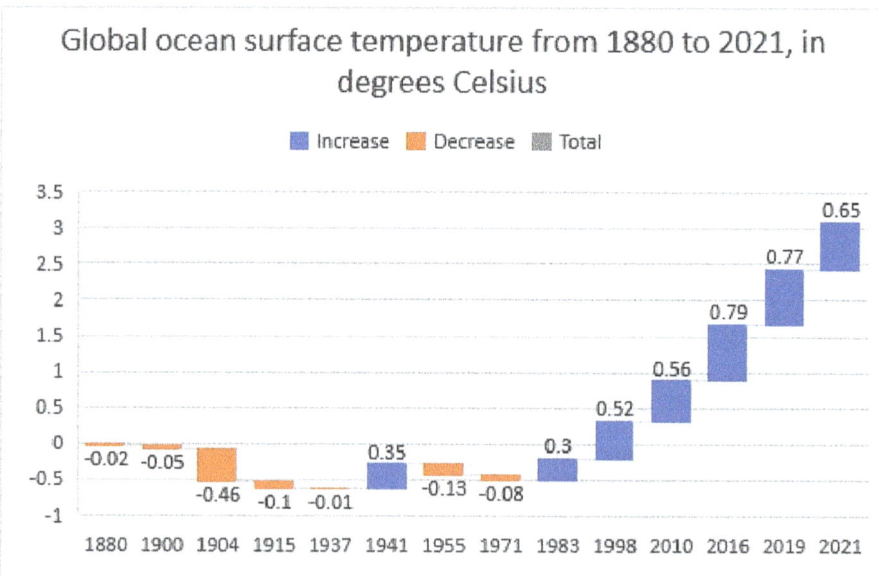

Fig. 1.23 Global ocean surface temperature from 1880 to 2021, in degrees Celsius. Source: Created by authors according to https://www.statista.com/statistics/736147/ocean-temperature-anomalies-based-on-temperature-departure/

Ocean warming also negatively affects people who depend on fishing and ocean-related activities for survival.

The warming of the oceans is a critical indicator of climate change, offering profound insights into the Earth's changing climate system. As oceans absorb over 90% of the excess heat trapped by greenhouse gases, monitoring ocean temperatures provides a direct measure of the planet's energy imbalance. Rising ocean temperatures lead to thermal expansion, contributing significantly to global sea level rise, with implications for coastal communities and ecosystems worldwide. Warming oceans impact marine biodiversity, coral reefs, and fisheries, disrupting marine ecosystems and threatening food security. Understanding ocean warming trends is essential for assessing climate change impacts, informing adaptation strategies, and mitigating the risks posed by rising temperatures to marine life and coastal infrastructure.

Acidification of the Oceans

As previously noted, carbon dioxide levels in the atmosphere have surged since the Industrial Revolution, leading to significant alterations in ocean chemistry. The ocean currently absorbs approximately 30% of the CO2 emissions discharged into the atmosphere. This absorption process initiates a sequence of chemical reactions, culminating in heightened concentrations of hydrogen ions, thereby augmenting water acidity and depleting carbonate ions. The decline in carbonate ions adversely impacts the behavior of non-calcifying organisms, posing a threat to the entire marine food web.

The global average change in ocean pH from 1985 to 2020 is shown in Fig. 1.24.

The acidification of the oceans is a critical indicator of climate change, with far-reaching implications for marine ecosystems and global carbon cycling. As carbon dioxide (CO2) levels rise in the atmosphere due to human activities, a significant portion is absorbed by the oceans, leading to chemical reactions that lower seawater pH levels and increase acidity.

This process, known as ocean acidification, disrupts the carbonate chemistry balance in seawater, hindering the ability of marine organisms to form calcium carbonate structures such as shells and skeletons. Acidification threatens the survival of calcifying organisms like corals, mollusks, and certain plankton species, which play essential roles in marine food webs and ecosystem functioning.

Furthermore, acidification impacts marine biodiversity, with cascading effects on fisheries, coastal economies, and livelihoods dependent on marine resources. Acidification also disrupts marine ecosystems' ability to regulate carbon dioxide levels, potentially exacerbating climate change by reducing the ocean's capacity to absorb atmospheric CO2. Monitoring ocean acidification provides critical data on the rate and extent of carbon uptake by the oceans, helping scientists understand the Earth's carbon cycle and its interactions with the climate system. Ocean acidification serves as a warning sign of the anthropogenic perturbation of marine environments and underscores the need for urgent action to mitigate carbon emissions and limit global warming.

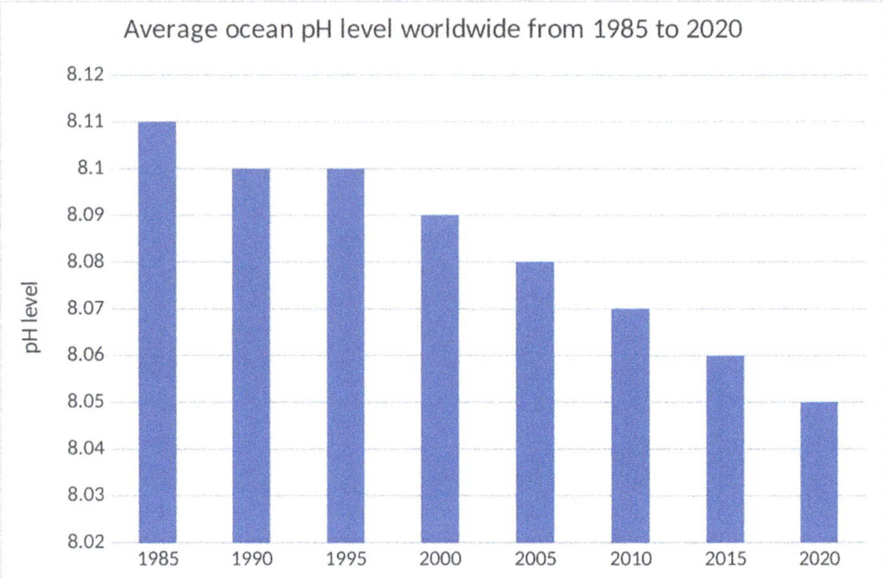

Fig. 1.24 Average ocean pH level worldwide from 1985 to 2020. Source: Created by authors according to https://www.statista.com/statistics/1338869/average-global-ocean-ph/

Mitigating ocean acidification requires concerted efforts to reduce CO2 emissions, transition to renewable energy sources, and promote sustainable land and ocean management practices. Additionally, adaptation strategies may involve enhancing the resilience of marine ecosystems through habitat protection, restoration, and the development of carbon-neutral technologies.

Addressing ocean acidification is essential not only for safeguarding marine biodiversity and ecosystem services but also for ensuring the resilience and sustainability of coastal communities and economies in the face of climate change. By understanding and mitigating the impacts of ocean acidification, we can work toward a more sustainable future for both marine ecosystems and human societies.

1.3 EU Climate Change Mitigation Targets

Modern climate change and its related challenges pose significant obstacles to the global economy. Since its establishment, the European Union (EU) has been actively engaged in international efforts to mitigate climate change, starting with the adoption of the United Nations Framework Convention on Climate Change in 1992. The EU's existing mitigation policy framework ranks among the most advanced globally (Torney, 2018; Wurzel et al., 2019; Oberthür & Dupont, 2021). Despite the EU's dedication to combatting climate change and its esteemed leadership position, it confronts a significant obstacle: effectively addressing the escalating magnitude and dynamics of the climate crisis. The EU's endeavors to stabilize climate change are evident yet insufficient, particularly in light of Europe's historical contributions to climate change and its current obligations in the global mitigation endeavor (Dubash, 2020; Gheuens & Oberthür, 2021; IPCC, 2023; ESABCC, 2023). It is important to underline that mitigation measures globally must be continuously combined with cutting-edge green technologies (innovation) and the latest scientific research (IPCC, 2023). This means pushing for even higher targets and, as a result, strengthening policy measures.

Since 1990, the EU has regularly updated its climate change policy but remains behind in achieving ambitious targets (Dubash, 2020; Gheuens & Oberthür, 2021). In other words, EU policymakers have found themselves in a sort of closed circle, with a constant drive to strengthen mitigation targets and broaden the range of climate policy actions (Kulovesi & Oberthür, 2020). The query revolves around whether the European Green Deal, unveiled in 2019, signifies a fresh, more dynamic, and effective phase of EU climate governance that transcends sluggish, incremental policy advancement.

The European Green Deal is an ambitious EU policy strategy to transform the EU economy into a more sustainable entity, with the aim of making the EU the world's first climate-neutral continent by 2050. This initiative involves reducing greenhouse gas emissions, fostering growth through the adoption of green technologies, and ensuring that the transition is equitable and inclusive, leaving no one behind (European Commission, 2019). In addition to managing climate change, this strategy highlights the importance of meeting a wide range of environmental objectives, including reducing pollution, protecting biodiversity, and restoring ecosystems (European Commission, 2019). In other words, the strategy becomes one of the key policy pillars and the basis for a growth model.

The transition to a low carbon economy, as outlined in the European Green Deal, will require significant investment. Therefore, in addition to the regulatory and sectoral measures outlined in the European Green Deal, adequate funding must be mobilized through both public and private channels. The EU has established specific targets for the allocation of funds to climate action within its primary budgetary instruments—the Multiannual Financial Framework (2021–2027) and the Recovery Fund. Additionally, the EU has implemented frameworks to facilitate Member State support, ensuring they receive the necessary economic assistance to drive change. In terms of private capital, various systems to invite investments and strategies for sustainable financing have been initiated.

The European Green Deal, the European Climate Change Act, and Investment

The European Commission has outlined a comprehensive framework of policies and measures for the transformation of the EU economy and resource efficiency in the European Green Deal Communication (European Commission, 2019). Reducing greenhouse gas emissions, combating climate change, halting biodiversity loss, and tackling environmental pollution are the overarching goals of this plan (see Fig. 1.25). The European Green Deal also serves as the EU's commitment to the United Nations 2030 Agenda and the Sustainable Development Goals.

Fig. 1.25 Directions for Europe's Green Deal. Source: European Commission (2019)

Currently, the strategy of the European Green Deal is being executed through a combination of legislative and non-legislative instruments, with the following objectives in focus:

- The legislative aspect of the European Green Deal includes a bold political commitment to achieve climate neutrality by 2050. This would make the European Union the first climate-neutral continent. To turn this commitment into action, the European Commission has introduced the European Climate Change Act. This will be proposed in March 2020 and formally adopted in July 2021. This law sets legally binding emission reduction targets for the EU by 2030 and outlines a detailed action plan to achieve these targets, with the ultimate goal of climate neutrality by 2050 (European Commission, 2020h).
- The European Green Deal prioritizes the development of renewable energy sources, decarburization efforts, and the reduction of greenhouse gas emissions to ensure a broad supply of clean, affordable, and secure energy. It also aims to tackle energy poverty and ensure affordable prices by promoting an integrated, interconnected, and digitally advanced electricity sector. To achieve these goals, the proposed Regulation implementing the European Energy Infrastructure Guidelines aims to promote the use of renewable energy sources, increase

sectoral integration, and modernize cross-border energy infrastructure within the EU, while setting sustainability criteria for new projects (European Commission, 2020e). In addition, the Commission's strategy for a climate-neutral Europe seeks to position pure hydrogen as a viable alternative to carbon-based fuels and envisages the deployment of hydrogen electrolysis plants across Europe (European Commission, 2020b).

- Decarburization initiatives are driving efforts to promote a sustainable industry. The European Commission's Circular Economy Action Plan, outlined in 2020, introduces measures to prolong product lifecycles, thereby curbing the consumption of raw materials (European Commission, 2020c). Additionally, the new Industrial Strategy for Europe, also unveiled by the Commission in 2020, proposes strategies to bolster a more digitally adept and climate-neutral European industrial sector (European Commission, 2020d). In addition, the European Commission's 2020 proposal for a regulation on batteries and battery waste aims to strengthen the circular economy by improving the recycling of industrial, automotive, and portable batteries, while reducing their environmental impact and addressing social responsibility concerns throughout the battery life cycle (European Commission, 2020g.
- Efforts toward more efficient building usage are emphasized through initiatives such as the European Commission's "A Renovation Wave for Europe," introduced in 2020. This plan delineates strategies for decarbonizing central heating and cooling systems, advocating for building renovations while offering incentives for digitalization and fostering job creation and economic growth throughout the building renovation supply chain (European Commission, 2020e). Furthermore, the revision of the Construction Products Regulation, recently undertaken by The European Parliament and The Council in 2021, aims to establish safety standards and delineate environmental prerequisites for construction products, thereby contributing to sustainability in construction (The European Parliament & The Council, 2021a).
- The focus on sustainable mobility aims to mitigate greenhouse gas emissions from the transport sector, which presently contributes approximately 25% of the EU's total greenhouse gas emissions (European Commission, 2020i). Guided by the Sustainable and Smart Mobility Strategy "A European Future for Transport," introduced by the European Commission in 2020, the objective is to revolutionize the sector and reduce greenhouse gas emissions by 90% by 2050 (European Commission, 2020f). As part of this strategy, the Commission is in the process of revising the Directive on the deployment of alternative fuels infrastructure (European Commission, 2021e). This revision seeks to establish a comprehensive network of zero- and low-emission transport infrastructure across Europe by facilitating the deployment of charging and refueling stations. Additionally, the Commission is updating the Regulation on the development of the European transport network (European Commission, 2021a) to enhance the sustainability of all transportation modes, improve infrastructure efficiency, and expand the availability of alternative fuels.

- To mitigate environmental pollution, the European Commission has unveiled an EU Action Plan titled "Towards Zero Air, Water, and Soil Pollution" (European Commission, 2021b). This plan advocates for the integration of pollution prevention measures across all EU policies and aims to establish specific targets for reducing pollution levels by 2030.
- Preserving biodiversity and fostering a sustainable food supply system are key objectives achieved through action plans aimed at promoting biodiversity and ecosystems, greening urban areas, minimizing pesticide usage, and advocating for higher-quality, sustainable food production (The European Parliament & The Council, 2017).
- The Farm to Fork Strategy (European Commission, 2020a) focuses on reducing waste and food waste and greening food production.

The initiatives detailed in the European Green Deal encompass various economic sectors, spanning transport, energy, agriculture, construction, and industry. Special emphasis is placed on specific sub-sectors, including but not limited to iron and steel, cement, textiles, information and communication technologies, and chemicals (Dormido et al., 2022). A key milestone in this strategy was the publication of the proposed European Climate Change Act (European Commission, 2020h), which established a political commitment to achieve climate neutrality in the European Union economy by 2050, with the aim of achieving net zero greenhouse gas emissions.

The European Climate Law (The European Parliament & The Council, 2021d) solidifies this commitment and provides the legal framework for its implementation. To reach a balance between greenhouse gas emissions and removals within the EU, and to attain negative net emissions from 2050 onward, the law sets an interim target of a 55% reduction in emissions by 2030 compared to 1990 levels—a binding target. Additionally, the law introduces regulations to ensure ongoing progress toward the objectives outlined in the Paris Agreement (The Council of the European Union, 2016), mandating the European Commission to establish climate change targets for 2040. The Commission is tasked with presenting a proposal, along with a report and guidelines, for further reducing greenhouse gas emissions between 2030 and 2050.

The European Climate Change Scientific Advisory Panel established by the Act has several tasks. These include analyzing the latest scientific findings from IPCC reports, providing scientific advice, publishing reports on EU measures, and raising awareness of climate change and its impacts. The European Environment Agency selects 15 members to serve on the Panel for a 4-year term, ensuring they possess diverse expertise and professional backgrounds in climate and environmental science.

Member States are also required to establish their advisory bodies to provide specialized scientific advice and to engage in dialogue on climate and energy issues with local authorities, civil society, businesses, investors, and other stakeholders. In addition, the law requires Member States to submit their 30-year strategy to the Commission, to be updated by 1 January 2029 and every 10 years thereafter, with interim updates every 5 years if necessary (European Commission, 2020h).

With the European Climate Change Law coming into force in July 2021, the European Commission has put forward an initial package of 16 legislative and policy proposals aimed at achieving the goals set out in the European Green Deal. The Climate Change Act aims to revise and modernize the European Union's key legislative frameworks in line to achieve at least a 55% net reduction in greenhouse gas emissions by 2030. Known as "Fit for 55," this comprehensive package includes interlinked and complementary measures in the areas of climate, energy, land use, transport, and taxation.

Concerning the regulation of greenhouse gas emissions through existing legal frameworks, the European Commission has proposed enhancements to the European Union's Emissions Trading Scheme, entailing the incorporation of new sectors, a further reduction in the overall emissions cap, and an augmentation in the annual reduction percentage. Member States are advised to allocate all proceeds from emissions trading to climate and energy initiatives. Conversely, sectors not covered by the scheme, such as buildings, road and inland maritime transport, agriculture, waste management, and small industry, are mandated to establish more stringent individual emission reduction targets for each Member State, considering their economic circumstances and current capacities, as per the Effort Sharing Regulation. In addition, regarding the removal of carbon dioxide from the atmosphere, the Land Use and Forestry Regulation defines the European Union's target for the absorption of carbon dioxide by natural sinks and sets national targets for Member States, which are not only strengthened but also extended to 2035. These initiatives encompass road, air, and maritime transport.

The aim of the amendment to the Energy Taxation Directive (European Commission, 2021c) is to update the European Union's energy and climate policy by abolishing the old taxes and low tax rates that have encouraged the use of fossil fuels. The energy taxation system is designed not only to protect and improve the single market, but also to support sustainability objectives by introducing effective incentive measures. The European Commission is also proposing a Carbon Border Adjustment Mechanism, which would tax a range of imported products according to their carbon emissions. This aims to avoid situations where the EU's mitigation efforts create an imbalance in the distribution of carbon dioxide, thus guaranteeing that Europe's emission reduction efforts contribute effectively to global emissions reductions.

The European Commission has additionally suggested establishing a Social Climate Fund aimed at alleviating the financial burden of measures required for achieving climate neutrality, particularly for the most vulnerable socio-economic segments. This fund would be sustained by earmarking 25% of the revenues obtained from the European Union's greenhouse gas emission allowance scheme, particularly from fuels utilized in road transport and construction.

In December 2021, the European Commission presented two comprehensive groups of proposals focusing on "energy and climate" and "efficient and sustainable mobility" as integral parts of the ambitious European Green Deal. The initial package comprises numerous legislative proposals designed to align with the objectives of the "Fit for 55" initiative, aimed at reshaping the European Union's natural gas market to facilitate decarbonization efforts and enhancing the adoption of green hydrogen by fostering an efficient market environment. Moreover, the package encompasses a strategy aimed at curbing methane emissions.

The European Union's ambitious targets outlined in the European Green Deal will necessitate substantial investments. Europe is estimated to require approximately €390 billion in other investments annually throughout this decade to fulfill its climate change, energy, and transport objectives, along with roughly €130 billion to address other environmental targets (European Commission, 2022). To relieve this transition, the European Commission introduced the Sustainable Europe Investment Plan early in 2020 as a pivotal component of the Green Deal for Europe. This plan comprises a blend of legislative and policy measures with the overarching goals of:

- Mobilizing financial resources is a key aspect, with initial estimates indicating a target of €1 trillion by 2030 sourced from the European Union's long-term budget and other public funding avenues, alongside leveraging private investment through programs like InvestEU as part of the intermediate financing facility (The European Parliament & The Council, 2021b). Furthermore, all economic endeavors are expected to align with environmental objectives, with investment channels directly supporting these objectives identified based on science-based criteria, as outlined in the Taxonomy Regulation adopted on 18 June 2020. (European Parliament and the Council, 2020; The European Parliament & The Council, 2021d)
- To streamline investment decision-making in both private and public sectors, it's essential to institute a system aimed at simplifying the process. This involves creating a comprehensive disclosure procedure for financial institutions and other organizations. Such a procedure ensures that investors have access to the requisite sustainability information, enabling them to make more informed and responsible investment decisions efficiently. (European Commission, 2023; The European Parliament & The Council, 2023, 2024)
- Offer assistance to public establishments and project organizers in establishing robust implementation strategies for sustainable plans. The European Investment Bank has pledged to allocate 50% of the fund toward advancing sustainable investment and has emerged as a pivotal collaborator in executing the "InvestEU" initiative. This diverse toolkit has been specifically crafted to empower companies, market stakeholders, and financial intermediaries in making informed sustainable investment choices, thereby averting the unsustainable utilization of financial assets (European Commission, 2021d; The European Parliament & The Council, 2021c, 2023).

In July 2020, European Heads of State touched an agreement to allocate 30% of the European Union's new long-term budget, the Multiannual Financial Framework 2021–2027, to climate action. Concurrently, a similar percentage of the Green Climate Fund for Environmental Recovery (GCERF) was earmarked for climate action. Under the GCERF, it was mandated that a minimum of 37% of expenditure under retrieval and flexibility measures in Member States' national recovery and resilience plans should be directed toward investments and reforms geared toward climate change-related sustainable initiatives. Addressing climate change and environmental degradation represents a shared challenge, albeit with varied starting points across regions and Member States. Accompanying the Sustainable Europe Investment Plan, the Just Transition Mechanism is designed to assist regions heavily dependent on carbon-intensive industries in transition. Moreover, it aims to help vulnerable individuals by facilitating their access to vocational retraining programs and employment opportunities in emerging sectors of the economy.

To help Member States access the necessary European Union support to meet the objectives outlined in the European Green Deal, the Guidelines on State aid for climate, environment, and energy for 2022 were published on 18 February 2022. These guidelines broaden the range of investments and technologies that Member States can support in line with the European Green Deal and the initiatives outlined in the "Fit for 55" package. This includes support for initiatives to reduce and eliminate greenhouse gas emissions, including the promotion of renewable energy sources, improving the energy efficiency of buildings, facilitating the purchase of electric vehicles, and developing infrastructure for charging or recharging electric vehicles.

The EU's climate change goals are ambitious, driving the creation of a comprehensive legislative package and an innovative policy approach. With these measures, the European Union is poised to meet internationally agreed-upon targets effectively. Prioritizing energy efficiency and a diverse energy mix is vital to dissociate economic growth from energy usage. Concurrently, the scale and caliber of investments, along with the requisite financing, are pivotal to aligning sustainability aims with sustainable long-term economic expansion.

The European Union (EU) has set more ambitious climate change mitigation targets to combat global warming and its associated impacts. Some of the key targets are shown in Fig. 1.26.

The EU is promoting a circular economy model aimed at reducing resource use, waste generation, and emissions. This involves measures to improve resource efficiency, promote recycling and reuse, and minimize the environmental impact of products throughout their lifecycle.

The circular economy holds significant importance in the European Union's (EU) efforts to address climate change, offering a holistic approach to resource management and sustainable development:

- The circular economy aims to maximize resource efficiency by reducing waste, reusing products and materials, and recycling resources at every stage of their lifecycle. By minimizing resource extraction and consumption, the circular economy helps mitigate greenhouse gas emissions associated with the production and disposal of goods.
- Transitioning to a circular economy model reduces the environmental impact of industrial processes, lowering emissions of greenhouse gases and pollutants. By keeping materials and products in use for longer and minimizing waste

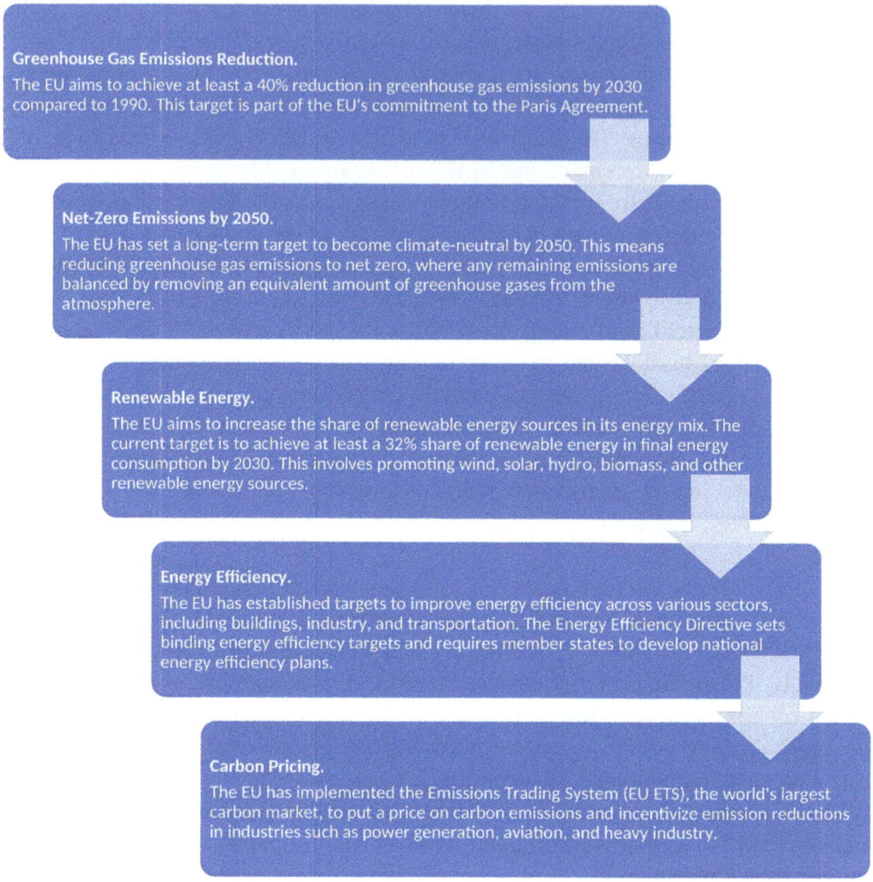

Fig. 1.26 Key climate change mitigation targets in the EU. Source: Created by authors

generation, the circular economy contributes to decarbonizing key sectors such as manufacturing, construction, and transportation.

- The circular economy promotes innovative approaches to waste management, emphasizing waste prevention, reuse, and recycling. This reduces the need for landfilling and incineration, which emit greenhouse gases and other pollutants, while also conserving valuable resources and reducing environmental degradation.
- Reusing and recycling materials requires less energy compared to extracting raw materials and manufacturing new products from scratch. By closing the loop on materials and promoting circular supply chains, the circular economy helps conserve energy and reduce the carbon footprint of industrial processes.
- Transitioning to a circular economy creates new opportunities for job creation and economic growth in sectors such as recycling, remanufacturing, repair, and waste management. By promoting green innovation and entrepreneurship, the

circular economy fosters a more resilient and sustainable economy while supporting the transition to a low-carbon society.

- The circular economy enhances resilience to climate change impacts by promoting resource diversification, reducing reliance on finite resources, and building adaptive capacity in communities and industries. By closing material loops and promoting circularity, the circular economy helps mitigate the environmental risks and vulnerabilities associated with climate change.
- The EU has integrated circular economy principles into its climate change and environmental policies, recognizing the synergies between circularity and climate action. Initiatives such as the European Green Deal and the Circular Economy Action Plan aim to accelerate the transition to a circular economy while achieving climate neutrality by 2050.
- The EU's commitment to the circular economy positions it as a global leader in sustainable development and climate action. By promoting circularity through international partnerships, cooperation, and knowledge sharing, the EU contributes to global efforts to address climate change and advance the Sustainable Development Goals.

The circular economy is integral to the EU's climate change mitigation and adaptation strategies, offering a holistic approach to resource management, emissions reduction, and sustainable development. By transitioning toward circularity, the EU aims to build a more resilient, resource-efficient, and low-carbon economy that safeguards the planet for future generations.

These targets and policies reflect the EU's commitment to leading global efforts to combat climate change and transition to a sustainable, low-carbon economy. It's essential to note that these targets may evolve as the EU continues to assess progress and align its policies with the latest scientific findings and international agreements.

1.4 Climate Change Mitigation and Adaptation Policies in the EU

The European Union has a united policy that communities around the world must take the most urgent and immediate action to prevent global warming. While it has been established that this can be done both technologically and economically, it is political decisions and the agreement of all parties to take collective action play a key role in this situation. It is estimated that, in economic terms, avoiding global warming would cost the planet around 1% of global GDP. This is not an inconceivably high cost, given that, once global warming has been achieved, mitigating its long-term effects could cost as little as 5% of global GDP, and that the economic impact of further combating or mitigating climate change is comparable to that of the world wars of the twentieth century (Council of the European Union, 2016).

In 1980, the scientific community turned its attention to the worldwide problem of climate change. The United Nations Environment Programme (UNEP) and the

World Meteorological Organization (WMO) recognized an international working group. This was followed by the establishment of the Intergovernmental Negotiating Committee for the Framework Convention on Climate Change, following a proposal at the 1990 session of the United Nations General Assembly. The United Nations Framework Convention on Climate Change (UNFCCC), signed by 155 nations at the Rio Conference in 1992, was ratified by the Lithuanian Seimas on 23 February 1995.

The UNFCCC added a protocol in which developed countries made specific commitments. This Protocol was signed in Kyoto in 1997. The developed countries committed themselves to a reduction of at least 5% in their total greenhouse gas emissions from 1990 levels between 2008 and 2012. This common target for the 15 oldest EU Member States (EU-15) was rephrased into a legally binding target for each Member State. Each country's commitment was based on its specific circumstances and its capacity to reduce emissions. Other European nations that became EU members in 2004 and 2007 pledged to reduce emissions by 6% or 8%. The Kyoto Protocol, signed by then President Valdas Adamkus in 1998, was ratified by the Lithuanian Seimas on November 19, 2002. Lithuania, mirroring the commitments of many nations, aimed to cut greenhouse gas emissions by 8% from 1990 levels by 2008–2012. This effort resulted in a 5% decrease in emissions by 2007 compared to the base year. Overall emissions across all EU-27 states dropped by 12.5% in 2007 compared to 1990 levels.

As the main source of greenhouse gas emissions is the combustion of organic fuels, all climate change mitigation policy decisions and international commitments made in this area have a direct impact on the growth of the energy sector. Greenhouse gas emissions in the energy sector can only be reduced by reducing the volume of organic fuels burned (by increasing energy efficiency in production and consumption) and by changing the composition of the fuels burned in favor of less carbon-intensive fuels.

Legal regulation of climate change in the EU is carried out through participation in international agreements (Table 1.2) and the adoption of EU legislation directly related to climate change mitigation (Table 1.3).

Fighting climate change and reducing greenhouse gas emissions are priorities in EU environmental policy. An analysis of legislation relevant to climate change mitigation is presented below (Table 1.3).

It is worth discussing in more detail some of the above-mentioned legislation and international contracts that have a direct influence on the success of mitigation policies at a global level.

Paris Agreement

On December 12, 2015, the Conference of the Parties to the United Nations Framework Convention on Climate Change (UNFCCC) in Paris approved a groundbreaking legally binding global climate change agreement. This agreement encompasses pledges from 195 developed and developing nations to mitigate greenhouse gas emissions, adapt to climate change, and counter its adverse impacts. The quest for a worldwide accord on climate change traces back to 1992 with the adoption of

Table 1.2 International climate change regulatory agreements in the EU

Date	EU international agreement	Purpose
1993	United Nations Framework Convention on Climate Change	To stabilize greenhouse gas concentrations in the atmosphere at a level that does not lead to risky anthropogenic interactions with the climate scheme.
Signed in 1997, entered into force in 2005 (ratified by the EU in 2002)	Kyoto Protocol First period—2005–2012 Second period (Doha Amendment)—2013–2020	Aim: to control emissions of greenhouse gases: carbon dioxide (CO2), methane (CH4), nitrous oxide (N2O), hydrofluorocarbons (HFCs), sulfur hexafluoride (SF6), perfluorocarbons (PFCs). 37 developed countries have pledged to reduce or limit their emissions to an average of 5% below 1990 levels by 2012. The other ratifying countries have not made explicit commitments.
2014	European Council conclusions on the 2030 strategy for climate and energy policy	A legally binding target of at least a 40% reduction in domestic greenhouse gas emissions from all sectors of the economy by 2030, compared to 1990 levels.
Signed in 2015 Ratified by the EU in 2016	Paris Agreement	Council Decision (EU) 2016/1841 concerning the Paris Agreement affirms alignment with the EU's environmental goals, including the preservation, enhancement, and protection of the environment, safeguarding human health, and endorsing global endeavors to tackle regional or worldwide environmental issues, particularly combatting climate change. The objective is to regulate worldwide greenhouse gas (GHG) emissions and prepare for the inevitable effects of climate change, with the overarching goal of limiting the rise in global average temperature to within 2 °C and striving to achieve a maximum increase of 1.5 °C above pre-industrial levels.

Source: Compiled by authors

the United Nations Framework Convention on Climate Change. The EU's actions in implementing the Paris Agreement are presented in Table 1.4.

The Paris Agreement extends its application beyond the year 2020, superseding the agenda recognized by the 1997 Kyoto Protocol, which outlined the commitments of the Parties until 2020. Previous agreements and initiatives endorsed by the Parties, such as the Warsaw International Mechanism on Loss and Damage from the Effects of Climate Change and the Cancun Adaptation Programme for Adaptation to Climate Change, remain in effect under the agenda of the Paris Agreement.

The Paris Agreement aims to achieve a global average temperature rise of no more than 2 °C above pre-industrial levels of 1.5 °C by 2100. Since the start of the Industrial Revolution, the average global temperature has risen by about 1.15 °C. Two-thirds of this increase has taken place rapidly since 1975, at a rate of around 0.15–0.20 °C per decade. While this may seem small, scientists agree that 2

Table 1.3 EU legislation on climate change mitigation

Date	Act of legislation	Purpose
2003	Directive 2003/87/EC	The EU Emissions Trading Scheme (EU ETS) is implemented as a pivotal component of EU strategy aimed at combating climate change through the cost-effective and efficient decrease of greenhouse gas emissions. Operating on the "cap-and-trade" principle, it establishes a framework for regulating emissions within the EU.
2008	Climate change and energy package to meet targets between 2013 and 2020	The package sets an EU target of a 20% reduction in greenhouse gas emissions by 2020 compared to 1990 levels, with a transition to a 30% reduction target. This transition is conditional on comparable emission reduction efforts by other developed countries and adequate contributions by developing countries according to their responsibilities and capabilities. In addition, the package aims to increase the share of renewable energy by up to 20% and to improve energy efficiency by up to 20%.
2008	Covenant of Mayors	The initiative aims to involve Europe's cities and towns in combating climate change. Signatories to the Pact pledged to meet the EU's environmental and energy targets, including reducing CO2 emissions by at least 20% by 2020. Municipalities were required to develop Sustainable Energy Action Plans, implement energy efficiency and renewable energy measures across their local communities, both in the private and public sectors, and organize annual Energy Days. These endeavors receive support from the European Commission, the Covenant of Mayors Office, and the Supporting Structures.
2009	Directive 2009/28/EC on the promotion of the use of energy from renewable sources.	Ensure that by 2020, energy from renewable sources (biomass, wind, hydroelectric, and solar) in the electricity generation, transport, heating, and cooling sectors represents at least 20% of the EU's total energy consumption.
2009	Regulation 443/2009	Achieve CO2 emissions from new passenger cars of 130 g CO2/km in 2015 and reduce them to 95 g CO2/km by 2021. Regulation 253/2014 of 2014, similar to Regulation 443/2009, applies to newly registered light commercial vehicles.
2009	Directive 2009/31/EC on the geological storage of carbon dioxide	Creates a lawful framework for ecologically friendly geological storage of carbon dioxide, to permanently sequester CO2 in such a way as to avoid as far as imaginable any adverse effects and any risks to the environment and human health, and, where this is not possible, to eliminate such effects and risks.

(continued)

Table 1.3 (continued)

Date	Act of legislation	Purpose
2013	Regulation (EU) No 1293/2013 of the European Parliament and of the Council	The Environment and Climate Action Programme, identified as the LIFE Programme, was established for the period spanning from January 1, 2014, to December 31, 2020. Its main objective is to catalyze environmental policy, with the following overarching goals: Facilitating the evolution to a climate-resilient, low-carbon, and resource-efficient economy, safeguarding and enhancing environmental quality, and halting biodiversity loss, which includes backing the Natura 2000 network and combating ecosystem degradation; Enhancing the growth, execution, and implementation of Union environmental and climate rules and regulations, as well as expediting and advocating for the incorporation and mainstreaming of environmental and climate goals into other Union policies and practices across the public and private sectors, including by enhancing the capacity of these sectors; Promoting enhanced environmental and climate domination at all stages, including through increased engagement of public society, NGOs, and limited stakeholders; Supporting the execution of the 7th Environmental Action Programme.
2014	Regulation 517/2014	Its objective is to safeguard the environment through the lessening of fluorinated greenhouse gas (GHG) emissions, establishing regulations concerning the containment, utilization, collection, and elimination of such gases, as well as stipulating conditions for the market placement of particular products and equipment containing these gases.
2014	Climate and energy policy strategy	The strategy outlines measures and targets aimed at enhancing the competitiveness, security, and sustainability of the EU's economy and energy system.

Source: Compiled by authors

degrees mark the threshold at which climate change could become unmanageable and the planet could begin to change irreversibly.

To achieve the overall ambition, governments have agreed to choose and scale up the ambition every 5 years in the light of scientific evidence. They also committed to reporting to other countries and the general public on progress toward the targets, transparency, and oversight. The global situation will be assessed every 5 years. Advancements toward achieving the long-term objective will be monitored via a comprehensive transparency and accountability framework.

The EU and other developed nations will persist in supporting developing countries in dropping greenhouse gas emissions and increasing resilience against climate change effects. Encouragement is extended to other nations to voluntarily contribute to such aid. The global community plans to amplify support for climate change adaptation efforts in developing nations moving forward. Developed countries affirm their dedication to mobilizing $100 billion annually by 2025. The EU pledges to sustain assistance from developed nations for the ensuing century, while a fresh collective target will be established for 2025.

Table 1.4 EU actions to implement the Paris Agreement

Date	Actions	Actions/documents adopted
30 November–11 December 2015	21st Conference of the Parties to the United Nations Framework Convention on Climate Change (UNFCCC) (COP 21) and 11th Meeting of the Parties to the Kyoto Protocol (CMP 11)	Representatives from 150 countries engage in discussions for a novel global accord on climate change, aiming for a binding international agreement.
12th December 2015	The Paris Agreement has been reached	A fresh global consensus on climate change is achieved.
17 December 2015	European Council meeting	European Council conclusions regarding a climate-resilient energy union were drafted and presented. (20)
15 February 2016	Foreign Affairs Council meeting	Action Plan on Climate Change Diplomacy has been adopted (21)
21 April 2016	The signing of the Paris Agreement	The EU signs the Paris Agreement.
30 September 2016	The Environment Council	Decision taken to proceed with ratification at EU level (22)
5 October 2016	The EU formally ratifies the Paris Agreement	The delegates from the Presidency of the Council and the European Commission have officially submitted the ratification documents to the Secretary-General of the UN, who serves as the custodian of the Agreement.
4 November 2016	The Paris Agreement enters into force	The Paris Agreement becomes effective 30 days after meeting the conditions for ratification, which require as a minimum 55 countries collectively responsible for no less than 55% of global greenhouse gas emissions. These conditions were fulfilled on October 4.
5 March 2017	Council of the EU Council assumptions on EU climate and energy diplomacy	The Council approves conclusions on EU climate and energy diplomacy in line with the implementation of the EU's global strategy. These conclusions outline various actions and shared priorities for 2017. (23)
10 October 2017	Council of the EU Council conclusions on climate finance in the preparation of COP 23	The Economic and Financial Affairs Council adopts conclusions on climate finance. The EU is committed to increasing its public finance contributions in the coming years. The conclusions call for the involvement of a wider range of donors.
6–17 November 2017	UN Climate Change Conference (COP 23)	This has resulted in tangible advancements regarding the Paris Work Programme and the Implementation Guidelines for the Paris Agreement have been established. The EU and its Member States have expressed their commitment to depositing the instruments of ratification for the Doha Amendment to the Kyoto Protocol no later than the end of 2017.

(continued)

Table 1.4 (continued)

Date	Actions	Actions/documents adopted
26 February 2018	Foreign Affairs Council conclusions on climate diplomacy	The Council reaffirmed that the EU would continue to play a leading role in global climate action. It also recognized the impact of climate change on international security and stability (24)
2018	EU Council conclusions on climate change	The EU has set new targets to enhance renewable energy consumption to 32% by 2030 and to achieve a 32.5% improvement in energy efficiency. Additionally, reforms have been introduced for the EU Emissions Trading Scheme (EU ETS), along with emission reduction targets for sectors not previously covered by the EU ETS. Furthermore, the EU's climate and energy policy strategy now encompasses land use, land-use change, and forestry. This multifaceted approach demonstrates the EU's commitment to fostering low-carbon and climate-resilient growth, effectively decoupling economic growth from emissions (25).
3–14 December 2018	UN Climate Change Conference (COP 24)	The conference adopts the Katowice Climate Change Package, which sets out how the Paris Agreement must be implemented to make it transparent and equitable for all. The package sets out the essential procedures and mechanisms that will ensure the Paris Agreement's enforceability.
8 November 2019	Council conclusions on climate finance (preparation for COP 25)	In grounding for the UN Climate Change Conference (COP 25), the Economic and Financial Affairs Council has adopted conclusions regarding the financing aspects of combating climate change. The EU and its Member States maintain their position as the world's largest source of public climate finance. Their combined contributions amounted to €20.4 billion in 2017 and increased to €21.7 billion in 2018. The latest figure underscores the EU's commitment to augment its international financial support for climate change to €100 billion. Presently, the EU's contribution to climate change efforts surpasses $100 billion annually, aligning with the target established for developed countries by both 2020 and 2025. (26).

(continued)

Table 1.4 (continued)

Date	Actions	Actions/documents adopted
5 March 2020	Strategy adopted by the EU Council	EU Environment Ministers, representing both the EU and its Member States, approve a long-term development strategy aimed at achieving a low greenhouse gas emission EU.
10–11 December 2020	The European Council	A binding target for the EU entails achieving at least a 55% reduction in greenhouse gas emissions compared to 1990 levels by 2030.
17 December 2020	Council of the EU Regulation	A regulation is approved outlining the EU's multiannual financial framework spanning the period from 2021 to 2027.
18 December 2020	Paris Agreement	The Council has filed a report with the secretariat of the United Nations Framework Convention on Climate Change (UNFCCC) detailing the binding nationally determined contributions (NDCs) for the EU and its member states.
5 October 2021	Council of the EU Conclusions	The Council approves conclusions on climate finance, aiming to fulfill the global commitment to mobilize €100 billion annually by 2025. Additionally, the Council establishes a target of USD 100 billion by 2025 to assist developing countries in addressing the impacts of climate change.
29 October 2021	Council of the EU	The Council has endorsed the distribution of climate finance for the year 2020. Collectively, the EU and its Member States have committed €23.39 billion in climate finance for this year, to aid developing countries in mitigating greenhouse gas emissions and adapting to the impacts of climate change.
13 November 2021	United Nations Climate Change Conference (COP26)	The conference made significant progress on promises under the Paris Agreement but also left room for further work to meet the 1.5 °C maximum warming target. Some important outcomes of COP26: —Developed countries pledged to increase climate finance to reach €100 billion in the coming years. The EU agreed to set a target of USD1 billion for climate change in the next few years, —A global commitment to reduce methane emissions by 30% by 2030 was confirmed, —A declaration on forests and land use, —The finalization of the Paris Rulebook on implementation aspects of the Paris Agreement.

Source: Compiled by authors

The Paris Agreement delineates a comprehensive worldwide strategy designed to advance the implementation of the United Nations Framework Convention on Climate Change. Its primary goal is to bolster the worldwide answer to the challenges posed by climate change within the framework of sustainable development and endeavors to alleviate poverty.

Overall, the Paris Agreement's key highlights can be summarized as follows:

- A long-term target for global average temperature increase limits to ensure that this reduces the risks and effects of climate change;
- Agreed on commitments and actions by countries to reduce their GHG emissions;
- Agreed to report on countries' actions and implementation of targets to ensure transparency and oversight and to set more ambitious targets;
- The decision was made to enhance resilience to the adverse impacts of climate change, promote adaptation measures, and encourage low-emission development to safeguard food production.
- Agreed to ensure that funding is aligned with the trajectory of GHG emission reductions and climate-resilient development.

The Covenant of Mayors

The Intergovernmental Panel on Climate Change has confirmed the swift onset of climate change, primarily caused by human economic activities, especially the utilization of fossil fuels for energy generation. On March 9, 2007, the EU enacted the Energy for a Changing World package, requiring EU Member States to achieve a 20% decrease in carbon dioxide emissions by 2020. This reduction is to be attained through a concurrent 20% improvement in energy efficiency and a corresponding 20% increase in the adoption of renewable energy sources.

The EU Committee of the Regions has spearheaded efforts to ensure the involvement of communities in achieving climate change goals. It has initiated multilevel governance by bringing together local and regional actors to make significant contributions to climate change mitigation objectives. In 2008, the European Commission launched the Covenant of Mayors, aiming to engage local authorities and their communities, alongside national governments, in addressing and mitigating climate change challenges. This political initiative empowers local and regional authorities to enact concrete climate change mitigation policies through action plans, investments in mitigation measures, and community involvement.

In 2015, the Commission launched a new Covenant of Mayors on Climate Change and Energy, which sets out three main orientations:

1. Climate change mitigation.
2. Adaptation to climate change.
3. Reliable, sustainable, and affordable energy for everyone.

The new Covenant of Mayors also sets out a vision for the movement: to accelerate the decarbonization of their territories and regions, to strengthen the adaptive capacity of their communities to cope with the inevitable consequences of climate change, and to bring reliable, sustainable, and affordable energy to every citizen.

The European Covenant of Mayors represents a thriving movement with over 10,000 signatories, driving voluntary commitments and impactful local initiatives for over a decade. Leveraging their collective experience in multilevel cooperation, these signatories unite diverse territories to advance climate action.

The achievement of the initiative lies in the transformation of territories and societies in the context of climate change, creating resilient and efficient territories and communities that will be able to successfully adapt and cope with climate change in the future. Such transformation does not have to be top-down, as only communities themselves know their strengths and weaknesses best, and local government is the closest to the community members and has a high level of trust.

The effective implementation of the Covenant of Mayors within local government necessitates an adjustment of its administrative framework and reliance on departments equipped with the necessary expertise. Executing the Sustainable Energy Strategy is a multifaceted and time-intensive endeavor, demanding meticulous planning and ongoing oversight. This undertaking mandates collaboration and synchronization among various departments of the local authority, spanning environmental, land use, economic, social, infrastructure, mobility, financial, and procurement domains. It's imperative to embed the incorporation of renewable energy technologies into the broader initiatives of relevant municipal departments, ensuring their seamless incorporation into the overall strategic planning of the local authority.

The Covenant of Mayors on Climate and Energy brings together thousands of local authorities who have voluntarily committed to climate and energy targets. By becoming a formal member of the Covenant of Mayors, cities commit to developing a Sustainable Energy (and Climate Change) Action Plan within 2 years, outlining concrete steps to meet the 2020 or 2030 targets. Cities are required to submit monitoring reports every 2 years after the adoption of their action plan setting out their mitigation and adaptation objectives, which verifies progress toward the targets. The emission inventory is updated every 4 years to ensure that progress in reducing emissions and energy consumption is monitored. By signing the Covenant of Mayors, cities demonstrate their initiative and commitment to achieving the goals of increasing EVE, promoting the use of RES, and reducing greenhouse gas (GHG) emissions. Municipalities join the Covenant of Mayors for several reasons:

- International recognition.
- Visibility.
- Opportunity to contribute to EU climate and energy policy.
- Access to funding for climate change and energy projects in their region.
- Sharing of best practices, joint learning, and participation in various events.
- Consultation on decision-making.
- Opportunity to assess oneself in a global context through continuous monitoring of decision-making.
- Opportunity to meet the expectations of the community you represent in the field of climate change and energy policy.

It is an open and democratic initiative with a growing number of participants and positive feedback from community members.

Climate and Energy Policy Strategy

The EU Commission presented its Climate and Energy Strategy on 22 January 2014. It is a Communication setting out the EU's climate and energy policy strategy for 2020–2030 (European Commission, 2014). The Strategy aims to launch a debate on how to pursue policies in these areas beyond 2020 when the current Strategy expires.

The strategy endorsed by EU leaders underscores the ongoing advancement toward a low-carbon economy and reaffirms the EU's commitment to global climate negotiations. Its focal point is establishing an energy framework that ensures affordable energy access for consumers, bolsters security for EU energy providers, curtails reliance on energy imports and greenhouse gas emissions, and fosters opportunities for green growth and job creation. At its core, the strategy includes a binding objective to slash the EU's greenhouse gas emissions by a minimum of 40% below 1990 levels by 2030, with a reformed and efficient EU Emissions Trading System (ETS) identified as a pivotal tool in attaining this target.

Renewable energy is pivotal in the shift toward a competitive, secure, and sustainable energy framework. Figure 1.27 portrays the share of renewable energy in the overall final energy usage within the EU-27. Resources like wind, solar, hydropower, ocean energy, geothermal, biomass, and biofuels provide effective substitutes for fossil fuels, assisting in curbing greenhouse gas emissions. Furthermore, they aid in broadening energy-sourcing avenues and diminishing reliance on unpredictable fossil fuel markets.

Initially established on 23 April 2009 through the co-decision procedure, the original Renewable Energy Directive set a target for the EU to derive 20% of its energy consumption from renewable sources by 2020. Additionally, it mandated that 10% of transport fuels in all Member States originate from renewable sources.

The Directive also delineated a range of mechanisms accessible to Member States for achieving these goals, encompassing support schemes, guarantees of origin, collaborative projects, and partnerships with both other Member States and third countries. Additionally, it set forth criteria to ensure the sustainability of biofuels.

EU leaders agree on a target to increase the proportion of renewable energy to a minimum of 27% of EU energy consumption by 2030.

Energy efficiency stands as a fundamental pillar of the 2030 Strategy. With an indicative target of achieving 27% energy savings by 2030 (as outlined in Directive 2009/28/EC), the EU emphasizes the importance of optimizing energy usage. The evolution of primary energy consumption levels across EU countries is depicted in Fig. 1.28, showcasing the region's progress in this regard.

It is also useful to show primary energy consumption—the distance to the 2030 target. This distance is shown in Fig. 1.29.

The objective should be economically viable and take into full account the efficacy of the EU Emissions Trading Scheme (ETS) in achieving overarching climate change goals. Covering almost 40% of total greenhouse gas emissions, the EU ETS governs emissions from key industrial sectors like electricity and heat generation, cement production, iron and steel manufacturing, oil refining, and aviation.

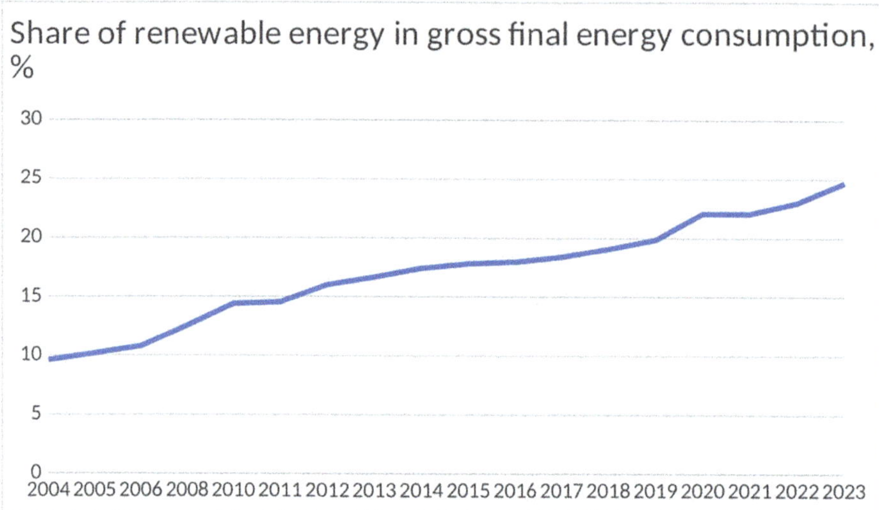

Fig. 1.27 Share of renewable energy in gross final energy consumption in EU-27. Source: Created by authors according to Eurostat, https://ec.europa.eu/eurostat/databrowser/view/sdg_07_40/default/line?lang=en

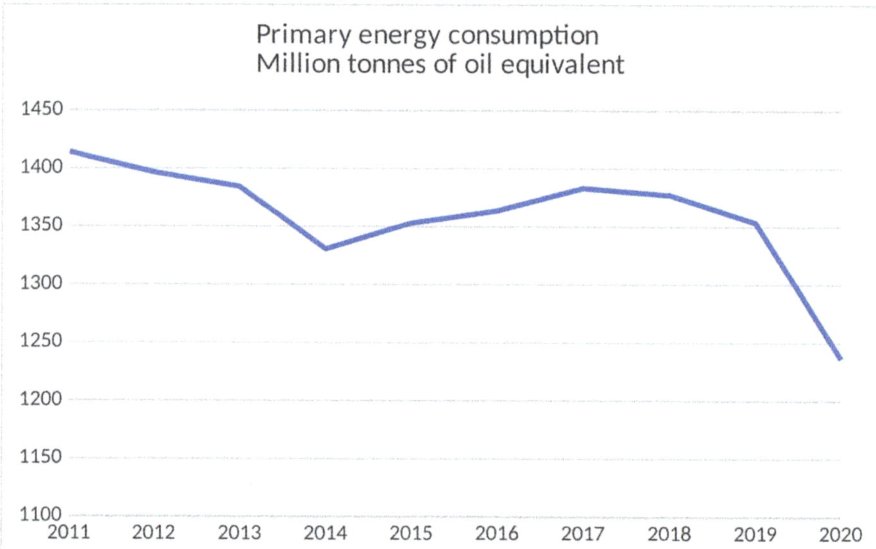

Fig. 1.28 Primary energy consumption in EU countries. Source: Created by authors according to Eurostat https://ec.europa.eu/eurostat/databrowser/view/NRG_IND_EFF__custom_2635909/default/table?lang=en

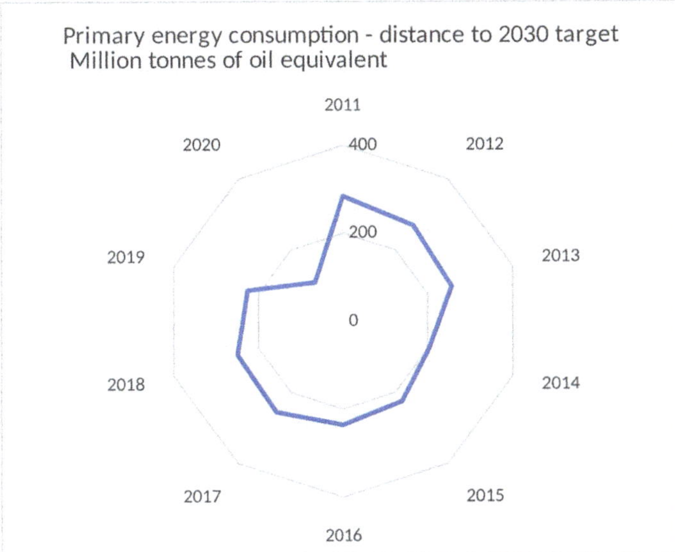

Fig. 1.29 EU primary energy consumption target for 2030. Source: Created by authors according to Eurostat https://ec.europa.eu/eurostat/databrowser/view/NRG_IND_EFF__custom_2635954/default/line?lang=en

Although the EU ETS has shown reasonable performance in recent years, aligning with the EU's ambitious commitments under the Paris Agreement to reduce greenhouse gas emissions by at least 40% by 2030, reforms to the EU ETS for the post-2020 period were enacted in 2018. These reforms, integrated into the EU ETS Directive, include additional provisions expected to facilitate participating countries in meeting their targets within the stipulated timeframe.

The revised EU ETS Directive includes fresh provisions aimed at addressing the risk of carbon leakage and implementing a cross-sectoral correction factor to mitigate this risk. For instance, 57% of allowances will be auctioned, with a potential 3% reduction if the cross-sectoral correction factor is implemented. Revised rules for free allowance allocation will align more closely with actual production volumes, and benchmarks for allocation will be updated accordingly.

Industries facing a higher risk of moving production outside the EU will be granted their full allocation free of charge, whereas those with a lower risk will receive 30% of their allocation free of charge. The gradual phasing out of free allocation for the latter sectors will begin after 2026, except for the district heating sector.

The new Directive also includes provisions for an initial reserve for new entrants to retain unused allowances from the current 2013–2020 period, along with 200 million allowances allocated to the market stability reserve. A maximum of 200 million tons of new allowances will be allocated to the reserve for allowance allocation, with any unused allowances from the period 2021–2030 returned to the Market Stability Reserve.

According to the revised EU ETS Directive, Member States will maintain the authority to compensate for indirect CO2-related expenses in compliance with State aid regulations, with enhanced reporting and transparency measures in place.

Given the varying impacts and patterns of climate change across Europe's regions, most adaptation initiatives will be managed at the regional or local level. The EU strategy seeks to complement these efforts by providing guidance and funding, promoting knowledge development, sharing information, and integrating adaptation considerations into relevant EU policies.

The EU has enacted ambitious legislation across various policy areas to honor its international climate change commitments, with binding emission reduction targets set for key sectors of the economy to significantly curb greenhouse gas emissions. As of 2017, the EU had already achieved a nearly 22% reduction in emissions compared to 1990 levels, reaching its 2020 emissions reduction goal 3 years ahead of schedule.

In December 2020, aligning with the EU's dedication to bolstering its climate objectives in adherence to the Paris Agreement, EU leaders approved a binding target for the EU to slash its net domestic greenhouse gas emissions by a minimum of 55% below 1990 levels by 2030. This target surpasses the EU's former goal of a 40% reduction in greenhouse gas emissions by 2030.

In April 2021, a preliminary agreement on a European climate law, establishing a 2030 emissions reduction target in legislation, was reached by the Council and Parliament. Subsequently, EU ministers adopted the agreement in June 2021.

In its December 2019 conclusions, the European Council underlined that moving toward climate neutrality will offer significant opportunities:

- for economic growth,
- markets,
- to create more jobs,
- develop technology.

EU leaders also emphasized the importance of establishing a supportive framework to ensure that the transition to a low-carbon economy is not only cost-effective but also socially equitable and fair. The recently introduced Just Transition Mechanism aims to provide tailored support to regions and sectors facing specific challenges during the climate transition.

Moreover, leaders underscored the necessity of mainstreaming climate action across all policy sectors and reiterated the EU's steadfast commitment to fulfilling its obligations. They emphasized the significant role of both public and private investment in steering the EU toward a transformative trajectory. In this context, it was highlighted that the EU's forthcoming long-term budget will play a substantial role in financing climate action initiatives.

With the adoption of the EU's long-term budget for 2021–2027 and the establishment of the Next Generation EU instrument, it was mandated that at least 30% of total expenditure be allocated to projects aimed at addressing climate-related issues.

Implementing climate change mitigation and adaptation policies in the European Union (EU) is of utmost importance for several compelling reasons:

- Global Leadership. As a major economic and political entity, the EU has a responsibility to lead by example in addressing climate change. Its actions can influence global efforts to mitigate greenhouse gas emissions, transition to renewable energy, and adapt to climate impacts.
- Commitment to International Agreements. The EU is committed to international agreements such as the Paris Agreement, which aims to limit global warming to well below 2 °C above pre-industrial levels. Implementing climate policies demonstrates the EU's commitment to fulfilling its obligations under these agreements.
- Protection of Environment and Ecosystems. Climate change poses significant threats to the environment and biodiversity. Mitigation and adaptation policies help protect ecosystems, safeguard biodiversity, and preserve natural resources for current and future generations.
- Public Health and Well-being. Climate change impacts human health through increased heatwaves, air pollution, waterborne diseases, and food insecurity. Mitigation policies that reduce air pollution and greenhouse gas emissions contribute to improving public health and well-being.
- Economic Stability and Resilience. Climate change poses risks to economies and financial systems through extreme weather events, disruptions to supply chains, and impacts on industries such as agriculture, tourism, and insurance. Implementing adaptation measures and transitioning to a low-carbon economy enhances economic stability and resilience.
- Innovation and Job Creation. Climate action stimulates innovation and creates new opportunities for green technologies, renewable energy, energy efficiency, and sustainable infrastructure. Investing in clean energy and green jobs fosters economic growth and competitiveness in the global market.
- Social Equity and Justice. Climate change disproportionately affects vulnerable communities, exacerbating social inequalities and injustices. Implementing climate policies that prioritize the needs of these communities and ensure equitable access to resources and opportunities is essential for social cohesion and justice.
- Security and Stability. Climate change can exacerbate conflicts over natural resources, trigger migration, and destabilize regions, posing risks to global security and stability. Implementing climate policies reduces these risks by addressing the root causes of climate-related vulnerabilities and promoting cooperation and resilience.

- Preservation of Cultural Heritage. Climate change threatens cultural heritage sites, traditions, and cultural practices. Implementing adaptation measures helps protect cultural heritage from erosion, flooding, and other climate impacts, preserving the rich cultural diversity of Europe.
- Long-Term Sustainability. Ultimately, implementing climate change mitigation and adaptation policies is essential for ensuring the long-term sustainability of the EU's economy, environment, and society. By taking decisive action now, the EU can build a resilient, low-carbon future that benefits both current and future generations.

Climate change and policies to mitigate it are crucial for safeguarding the environment, public health, and economic stability. Mitigation efforts aim to reduce greenhouse gas emissions, which helps to minimize the disruption of ecosystems, protect biodiversity, and mitigate the impacts of extreme weather events. Implementing climate policies promotes the transition to renewable energy sources, enhances energy security, and stimulates innovation and job creation in the clean energy sector. Addressing climate change is essential for meeting international commitments such as the Paris Agreement and advancing sustainable development goals, including poverty reduction and social equity. Ultimately, mitigation policies play a vital role in shaping a resilient, sustainable future for current and future generations.

Conclusions

1. Climate change refers to significant and long-term alterations in global or regional climate patterns, primarily attributed to human activities such as burning fossil fuels, deforestation, and industrial processes. The main driver of climate change is the emission of greenhouse gases, such as carbon dioxide (CO2), methane (CH4), and nitrous oxide (N2O), which trap heat in the Earth's atmosphere, leading to a rise in temperatures.

The consequences of climate change are wide-ranging and include rising global temperatures, more frequent and severe weather events like hurricanes, droughts, floods, and wildfires, as well as disruptions to ecosystems, agriculture, and water resources. Melting ice caps and glaciers contribute to rising sea levels, threatening coastal communities and habitats.

Addressing climate change requires international cooperation and comprehensive strategies to reduce greenhouse gas emissions, transition to renewable energy sources, improve energy efficiency, protect ecosystems, and adapt to the changes already underway. The urgency of action is highlighted by scientific consensus and increasing evidence of the tangible impacts of climate change on societies and ecosystems worldwide.

2. Climate change indicators are crucial for monitoring and understanding the evolving state of the Earth's climate system. These indicators provide valuable

information about trends, patterns, and impacts associated with climate change. The importance can be:

- Tracking changes. Climate change indicators allow scientists to track changes in various aspects of the climate system over time, such as temperature, precipitation, sea level rise, and greenhouse gas concentrations. This tracking helps identify trends and patterns, providing evidence of climate change and its impacts.
- Informing policy. Indicators serve as essential tools for policymakers, providing scientific evidence to inform decision-making processes related to climate change mitigation and adaptation strategies. By understanding how different indicators are changing, policymakers can develop effective policies to address climate change at local, national, and global levels.
- Assessing impacts. Climate change indicators help assess the impacts of climate change on natural ecosystems, human societies, economies, and public health. By monitoring indicators such as changes in biodiversity, extreme weather events, crop yields, and heat-related illnesses, stakeholders can better understand the vulnerabilities and risks associated with climate change and develop strategies to mitigate them.
- Communicating science. Indicators provide tangible and easily understandable metrics for communicating the science of climate change to the public, policymakers, and other stakeholders. Visual representations of indicators, such as maps, graphs, and charts, help convey complex scientific concepts in a clear and accessible manner, raising awareness and facilitating informed decision-making.
- Guiding adaptation. Climate change indicators play a crucial role in guiding adaptation efforts by identifying areas and sectors most vulnerable to climate impacts. By understanding which indicators are changing and how they affect different regions and sectors, communities can develop adaptive strategies to minimize risks, enhance resilience, and protect livelihoods.

Climate change indicators are essential tools for monitoring, understanding, and responding to the complex challenges posed by climate change, helping to inform policies, guide adaptation efforts, and build resilience in the face of a changing climate.

3. Climate change mitigation and adaptation policies are of paramount importance in the European Union (EU) due to several key reasons:

   - Mitigation policies aim to reduce greenhouse gas emissions, which in turn help mitigate the impacts of climate change, such as extreme weather events, sea-level rise, and disruptions to ecosystems. Adaptation policies focus on enhancing resilience to these impacts, protecting lives, livelihoods, and infrastructure.

- The EU is committed to international agreements such as the Paris Agreement, which aims to limit global warming to well below 2 °C above pre-industrial levels, with efforts to limit it to 1.5 °C. Mitigation policies are crucial for the EU to fulfill its obligations under these agreements.
- Transitioning to a low-carbon economy presents economic opportunities, including job creation in renewable energy sectors, energy efficiency improvements, and the development of green technologies. Mitigation policies such as carbon pricing and renewable energy targets stimulate innovation and investment in these sectors.
- Mitigation policies reduce the EU's dependence on fossil fuels, enhancing energy security and reducing vulnerabilities to fluctuations in global energy markets. Renewable energy sources and energy efficiency measures contribute to diversifying the energy mix and increasing resilience to supply disruptions.
- Climate change poses significant threats to ecosystems and biodiversity. Adaptation policies help safeguard ecosystems by preserving habitats, restoring degraded areas, and promoting sustainable land and water management practices. This is essential for maintaining ecosystem services vital for human well-being.
- Climate change impacts human health through increased heatwaves, air pollution, and the spread of vector-borne diseases. Mitigation policies that reduce air pollution and promote active transportation and sustainable urban planning contribute to improving public health and well-being.
- Climate change disproportionately affects vulnerable communities, exacerbating existing social inequalities. Mitigation and adaptation policies should prioritize the needs of these communities, ensuring equitable access to resources and opportunities and fostering social cohesion and resilience.
- The EU plays a crucial role in global efforts to address climate change. By implementing ambitious mitigation and adaptation policies, the EU demonstrates leadership and promotes international cooperation to tackle this global challenge effectively.

4. Implementing climate change mitigation and adaptation policies in the EU is imperative due to its global leadership role and commitment to international agreements like the Paris Agreement. These policies are crucial for protecting the environment, biodiversity, and natural resources, as well as safeguarding public health and well-being from the impacts of climate change. Economic stability and resilience are enhanced through the transition to a low-carbon economy, fostering innovation, job creation, and social equity. Climate action is essential for ensuring security, stability, and the preservation of cultural heritage in the face of climate-related risks and vulnerabilities. Ultimately, these policies contribute to the long-term sustainability of the EU's economy, environment, and society, benefiting both current and future generations.

References

Academy of Disaster Reduction and Emergency Management. (2020). *2019 Global Natural Disaster Assessment Report*. https://www.preventionweb.net/files/73363_2019globalnaturaldisasterassessment.pdf

Andrew, R. M., & Peters, G. P. (2021). *The Global Carbon Project's fossil CO2 emissions dataset* [Data set]. Zenodo. https://doi.org/10.5281/zenodo.5569235.

Balevičius, A., et al. (2007). *Global environmental change*. Educational book. 299 p. Vilnius University. ISBN 978-9955-668-77-0.

Caccamo, M. T., & Magazù, S. (2021). On the breaking of the Milankovitch cycles triggered by temperature increase: The stochastic resonance response. *Climate 2021, 9*, 67. https://doi.org/10.3390/cli9040067

CAIT. (2024). *Climate Data Explorer via Climate Watch*. https://www.climatewatchdata.org/data-explorer/historical-emissions

Cooper, C., Swindles, G., Savov, et al. (2018). Evaluating the relationship between climate change and volcanism. *Earth-Science Reviews, 177*, 238–247. ISSN 0012-8252. https://doi.org/10.1016/j.earscirev.2017.11.009

Council of the European Union. (2016). *European climate diplomacy after COP21 - Council conclusions*. https://data.consilium.europa.eu/doc/document/ST-6061-2016-INIT/en/pdf

CRED. (2021). *Disasters in numbers*. CRED. https://cred.be/sites/default/files/2021_EMDAT_report.pdf

DIRECTIVE 2009/28/EC OF THE EUROPEAN PARLIAMENT AND OF THE COUNCIL of 23 April 2009 on the promotion of the use of energy from renewable sources and amending and subsequently repealing Directives 2001/77/EC and 2003/30/EC. https://eur-lex.europa.eu/legal-content/EN/TXT/PDF/?uri=CELEX:32009L0028&from=LT

Dormido, L., Garrido, I., L'Hotellerie-Fallois, P., & Santillán, J. (2022). Climate change and sustainable growth: International initiatives and European policies. *BANCO DE ESPAÑA*, 1–38.

Dubash, N. K. (2020). Revisiting climate ambition: The case for prioritizing current action over future intent. *Wiley Interdisciplinary Reviews: Climate Change, 11*(1), e622. https://doi.org/10.1002/WCC.622

ESABCC. (2023). *Scientific advice for the determination of an EU-wide 2040 climate target and a greenhouse gas budget for 2030-2050* (pp. 1–110). European Scientific Advisory Board on Climate Change. https://doi.org/10.2800/609405

European Commission. (2014). *Apie Europos Sąjungos politiką. Klimato politika*. Europos Sąjungos leidinių biuras. https://doi.org/10.2775/85728. https://vbplatforma.org/uploaded_files/library/143799902665_publication-climate-action-2014_lt.pdf

European Commission. (2019). Communication from the Commission to the European Parliament, the European Council, the Council, the European Economic and Social Committee and the Committee of the Regions: the European Green Deal. COM(2019)(640 final), 1–24. https://eur-lex.europa.eu/legal-content/EN/TXT/?uri=CELEX:52019DC0640

European Commission. (2020a). Communication from the Commission to the European Parliament, the Council, the European Economic and Social Committee and the Committee of the Regions: A farm to fork strategy for a fair, healthy and environmentally-friendly food system, COM/2020/381 final. https://eur-lex.europa.eu/legal-content/EN/TXT/?uri=CELEX%3A52020DC0381

European Commission. (2020b). Communication from the Commission to the European Parliament, the Council, the European Economic and Social Committee and the Committee of the Regions: A hydrogen strategy for a climate-neutral Europe, COM/2020/301 final. https://eur-lex.europa.eu/legal-content/EN/TXT/?uri=CELEX%3A52020DC0301

European Commission. (2020c). Communication from the Commission to the European Parliament, the Council, the European Economic and Social Committee and the Committee of the Regions: A new Circular Economy Action Plan for a cleaner and more competitive Europe, COM/2020/98 final. https://eur-lex.europa.eu/legal-content/EN/TXT/PDF/?uri=CELEX:52020DC0098

European Commission. (2020d). Communication from the Commission to the European Parliament, the Council, the European Economic and Social Committee and the Committee of the Regions: A New Industrial Strategy for Europe, COM/2020/102 final. https://eur-lex.europa.eu/legal-content/EN/TXT/?uri=CELEX%3A52020DC0102

European Commission. (2020e). Communication from the Commission to the European Parliament, the Council, the European Economic and Social Committee and the Committee of the Regions: A Renovation Wave for Europe - greening our buildings, creating jobs, improving lives, COM/2020/662 final. https://eur-lex.europa.eu/legal-content/EN/TXT/PDF/?uri=CELEX:52020DC0662

European Commission. (2020f). Communication from the Commission to the European Parliament, the Council, the European Economic and Social Committee and the Committee of the Regions: Sustainable and Smart Mobility Strategy – putting European transport on track for the future, COM/2020/.

European Commission. (2020g). Proposal for a Regulation of the European Parliament and of the Council concerning batteries and waste batteries, repealing Directive 2006/66/EC and amending Regulation (EU) No 2019/1020, COM/2020/798. https://eur-lex.europa.eu/legal-content/EN/TXT/PDF/?uri=CELEX:52020PC0798

European Commission. (2020h). Proposal for a REGULATION OF THE EUROPEAN PARLIAMENT AND OF THE COUNCIL establishing the framework for achieving climate neutrality and amending Regulation (EU) 2018/1999 (European Climate Law). COM (2020) (80 final), 1–46. https://doi.org/10.1017/CBO9781107415324.004

European Commission. (2020i). *Sustainable & smart mobility strategy*. https://commission.europa.eu/strategy-and-policy/priorities-2019-2024/european-green-deal/transport-and-green-deal_en

European Commission. (2021a). Commission staff working document Evaluation of the Regulation (EU) No. 1315/2013 on Union Guidelines for the development of a trans-European transport network. SWD(2021) 118 final. https://eur-lex.europa.eu/legal-content/EN/TXT/?uri=CELEX%3A52021SC0117

European Commission. (2021b). Communication from the Commission to the European Parliament, the Council, the European Economic and Social Committee and the Committee of the Regions: Pathway to a Healthy Planet for All, EU Action Plan: "Towards Zero Pollution for Air, Water and Soil" C. https://eur-lex.europa.eu/legal-content/EN/ALL/?uri=COM%3A2021%3A400%3AFIN

European Commission. (2021c). Proposal for a Council Directive restructuring the Union framework for the taxation of energy products and electricity (recast), COM/2021/563 final.

European Commission. (2021d). Proposal for a Regulation of the European Parliament and of the Council on European green bonds, COM/2021/391 final. https://eur-lex.europa.eu/legal-content/EN/TXT/?uri=CELEX%3A52021PC0391

European Commission. (2021e). Proposal for a Regulation of the European Parliament and of the Council on the deployment of alternative fuels infrastructure, and repealing Directive 2014/94/EU of the European Parliament and of the Council, COM/2021/559 final. https://eur-lex.europa.eu/legal-content/en/TXT/?uri=CELEX%3A52021PC0559

European Commission. (2022). Information from European Union Institutes, Bodies, Offices and Agencies. COMMUNICATION FROM THE COMMISSION Guidelines on State aid for climate, environmental protection and energy 2022 (2022/C 80/01). Official Journal of the European Union. https://eur-lex.europa.eu/legal-content/EN/TXT/?ur

European Commission. (2023). COMMISSION STAFF WORKING DOCUMENT IMPACT ASSESSMENT REPORT Accompanying the documents Proposal for a Council Directive on Business in Europe: Framework for Income Taxation (BEFIT) and Proposal for a Council Directive on Transfer Pricing SWD/2023/308 final. SWD(2023).

European Parliament and the Council. (2020). Regulation (EU) 2020/852 of the European Parliament and of the Council of 18 June 2020 on the establishment of a framework to facilitate sustainable investment, and amending Regulation (EU) 2019/2088 (Text with EEA relevance). Official Journal of the European Union. http://data.europa.eu/eli/reg/2020/852/oj

Gheuens, J., & Oberthür, S. (2021). EU climate and energy policy: How myopic is it? *Politics and Governance, 9*(3), 337–347. https://doi.org/10.17645/pag.v9i3.4320

Global Carbon Budget - Global Carbon Project. (2021). The Global Carbon Budget dataset is available at https://doi.org/10.18160/gcp-2021 and https://doi.org/10.5281/zenodo.5569235.

Global Carbon Project. (2021). *Supplemental data of Global Carbon Project 2021 (1.0)* [Data set]. Global Carbon Project. https://doi.org/10.18160/gcp-2021.

IPCC. (2007). *Climate Change 2007: The Physical Science Basis. Contribution of Working Group I to the Fourth Assessment Report of the Intergovernmental Panel on Climate Change* [Solomon, S., D. Qin, M. Manning, Z. Chen, M. Marquis, K.B. Averyt, M. Tignor and H.L. Miller (eds.)]. Cambridge University Press.

IPCC. (2013). *Climate Change 2013: The Physical Science Basis. Contribution of Working Group I to the Fifth Assessment Report of the Intergovernmental Panel on Climate Change*. 1535 pp., Cambridge University Press.

IPCC. (2023). *Climate Change 2023: Synthesis Report. Contribution of Working Groups I, II and III to the Sixth Assessment Report of the Intergovernmental Panel on Climate Change* (pp. 1–186). https://doi.org/10.59327/IPCC/AR6-9789291691647

Kulovesi, K., & Oberthür, S. (2020). Assessing the EU's 2030 Climate and Energy Policy Framework: Incremental change toward radical transformation? *Review of European, Comparative and International Environmental Law, 29*(2), 151–166. https://doi.org/10.1111/REEL.12358

Marotzke, J., & Forster, P. M. (2015). Forcing, feedback and internal variability in global temperature trends. *Nature, 517*, 565–570. https://doi.org/10.1038/nature14117

Myhre, G., Shindell, D., Bréon, F.-M., Collins, W., Fuglestvedt, J., Huang, J., Koch, D., Lamarque, J. F., Lee, D., Mendoza, B., Nakajima, T., Robock, A., Stephens, G., Takemura, T., & Zhang, H. (2013). Anthropogenic and Natural Radiative Forcing. In *Climate Change 2013: The Physical Science Basis. Contribution of Working Group I to the Fifth Assessment Report of the Intergovernmental Panel on Climate Change* [Stocker, T.F., D. Qin, G.-K. Plattner, M. Tignor, S.K. Allen, J. Boschung, A. Nauels, Y. Xia, V. Bex and P.M. Midgley (eds.)]. Cambridge University Press.

National Centre for Atmospheric Research Staff. (2017). *The Climate Data Guide: Sea Ice Concentration data: Overview, comparison table and graphs*. https://climatedataguide.ucar.edu/climate-data/sea-ice-concentration-data-overview-comparison-table-and-graphs

Oberthür, S., & Dupont, C. (2021). The European Union's international climate leadership: Towards a grand climate strategy? *Journal of European Public Policy, 28*(7), 1095–1114. https://doi.org/10.1080/13501763.2021.1918218

Saunois, M., Stavert, A. R., Poulter, B., Bousquet, P., Canadell, J. G., Jackson, R. B., et al. (2020). The global methane budget 2000–2017. *Earth System Science Data, 12*(3), 1561–1623.

Škiudas, K., Kubilius, A., & Urbanavičius, J. (2020). *Climate change caused by human activity: Causes, consequences, possibilities*. European Public Policy Institute. Vilnius. ISSN 2669-1744.

Stenchikov, G. (2021). The role of volcanic activity in climate and global changes. In *Climate change* (pp. 607–643). https://doi.org/10.1016/B978-0-12-821575-3.00029-3
Swedish International Development Cooperation Agency. (2010). Environmental and climate change indicators. Global issues. Guidance at country and sector level. Sida, 2011. https://cdn.sida.se/publications/files/sida61411en-environmental-and-climate-change-indicators.pdf
The Council of the European Union. (2016). International Agreements. COUNCIL DECISION (EU) 2016/1841 of 5 October 2016 on the conclusion, on behalf of the European Union, of the Paris Agreement adopted under the United Nations Framework Convention on Climate Change. Official Journal of the European Union. https://eur-lex.europa.eu/legal-content/EN/TXT/?uri=OJ%3AL%3A2016%3A282%3ATOC
The European Parliament & The Council. (2017). Regulation (EU) 2017/625 of the European Parliament and the Council. On official controls and other official activities performed to ensure the application of food and feed law, rules on animal health and welfare, plant health and plant protection product. Official Journal of the European Union. https://eur-lex.europa.eu/eli/reg/2017/625/oj
The European Parliament & The Council. (2021a). Consolidated text: Regulation (EU) No 305/2011 of the European Parliament and of the Council of 9 March 2011 laying down harmonised conditions for the marketing of construction products and repealing Council Directive 89/106/EEC (Text with EEA relevance)T. https://eur-lex.europa.eu/eli/reg/2011/305/2021-07-16
The European Parliament & The Council. (2021b). Regulation (EU) 2021/523 of the European Parliament and of the Council of 24 March 2021 establishing the InvestEU Programme and amending Regulation (EU) 2015/1017. Official Journal of the European Union. http://data.europa.eu/eli/reg/2021/523/oj
The European Parliament & The Council. (2021c). Regulation (EU) 2021/1056 of the European Parliament and of the Council of 24 June 2021 establishing the Just Transition Fund PE/5/2021/REV/1. Official Journal of the European Union. http://data.europa.eu/eli/reg/2021/1056/oj
The European Parliament & The Council. (2021d). REGULATION (EU) 2021/1119 OF THE EUROPEAN PARLIAMENT AND OF THE COUNCIL of 30 June 2021 establishing the framework for achieving climate neutrality and amending Regulations (EC) No 401/2009 and (EU) 2018/1999 ('European Climate Law'). Official Journal of the European Union. http://data.europa.eu/eli/reg/2021/1119/oj
The European Parliament & The Council. (2023). Regulation (EU) 2023/2631 of the European Parliament and of the Council of 22 November 2023 on European Green Bonds and optional disclosures for bonds marketed as environmentally sustainable and for sustainability-linked bonds. Official Journal of the European Union. http://data.europa.eu/eli/reg/2023/2631/oj
The European Parliament & The Council. (2024). Consolidated text: Regulation (EU) 2019/2088 of the European Parliament and of the Council of 27 November 2019 on sustainability-related disclosures in the financial services sector (Text with EEA relevance)Text with EEA relevance. Official Journal of the European Union. https://eur-lex.europa.eu/legal-content/EN/TXT/?uri=CELEX%3A02019R2088-20240109&qid=1707735580277
Torney, D. (2018). Follow the leader? Conceptualising the relationship between leaders and followers in polycentric climate governance. *Environmental Politics, 28*(1), 167–186. https://doi.org/10.1080/09644016.2019.1522029
Trenberth, K. E., & Fasullo, J. T. (2013). An apparent hiatus in global warming? *Earth's Future, 1*, 19–32. https://doi.org/10.1002/2013EF000165
Wickham, et al. (2021, May). Thematic accuracy assessment of the NLCD 2016 land cover for the conterminous United States. *Remote Sensing of Environment, 257*, 112357. https://doi.org/10.1016/j.rse.2021.112357

World Meteorological Organization. (2017). *Indicators of Climate Change*. Prepared by the GCOS Secretariat, WMO. https://library.wmo.int/doc_num.php?explnum_id=3418
Wurzel, R. K. W., Liefferink, D., & Torney, D. (2019). Pioneers, leaders and followers in multi-level and polycentric climate governance. *Environmental Politics, 28*(1), 1–21. https://doi.org/10.1080/09644016.2019.1522033

Chapter 2
Climate Change and Responsible Consumption

Abstract Sustainable development has become a cornerstone of global policy and academic discourse in the twenty-first century. It addresses the complex challenge of balancing economic growth, social well-being, and environmental protection. As the world faces escalating ecological degradation, inequality, and resource depletion, the urgency for sustainable solutions has intensified. The emergence of global environmental awareness in the 1960s and 1970s laid the foundation for the current sustainability movement. Influential works, such as Rachel Carson's Silent Spring, and high-profile events, including the Cuyahoga River fire and the Santa Barbara oil spill, triggered widespread public concern. These developments catalyzed the creation of environmental regulations, institutions, and advocacy movements. The Brundtland Report (1987) was a pivotal milestone, introducing the formal definition of sustainable development and highlighting the need for integrated approaches. Since then, international summits have further institutionalized the concept, leading to the establishment of global development frameworks.

In 2015, the United Nations adopted the 2030 Agenda for Sustainable Development, comprising 17 Sustainable Development Goals (SDGs). These goals provide a comprehensive and universal roadmap for addressing interconnected global challenges.

This chapter explores the theoretical foundations, evolution, principles, and critiques of sustainable development. It also analyzes the structure and relevance of the SDGs in advancing global sustainability. Through a multidisciplinary lens, the chapter examines how sustainable development serves as a strategic framework for harmonizing ecological, social, and economic priorities. Particular attention is given to the integration principle, intergenerational equity, and the precautionary approach. By tracing the historical development of the sustainability discourse, the chapter highlights how global consensus has been shaped by science, policy, and social movements. Finally, it underscores the importance of addressing implementation barriers to ensure that the promise of sustainable development translates into tangible outcomes.

A. Mikalauskienė et al., *Climate Change and Responsible Consumption*, Springer Climate, https://doi.org/10.1007/978-3-032-16218-2_2

2.1 Sustainable Development and Sustainable Development Goals

Sustainable development is a comprehensive and forward-thinking approach that aims to balance different, and often competing, needs against an awareness of the environmental, social, and economic limitations we face as a society. The foundational principle of sustainable development is to meet the needs of the present without compromising the ability of future generations to meet their own needs.

Table 2.1 presents various definitions of sustainable development.

Sustainable development is a holistic approach aimed at meeting the needs of the present without compromising future generations' ability to meet their own needs. It involves balancing economic growth, social inclusivity, and environmental stewardship. Key principles include minimizing environmental degradation, conserving natural resources, and enhancing human well-being. It emphasizes a dynamic process where communities adapt to social and environmental changes while ensuring a good quality of life.

Sustainable development seeks to integrate economic, social, and environmental dimensions into decision-making processes. It focuses on improving human life quality within the Earth's carrying capacity and ensuring equitable access to resources. The approach encourages proactive measures to prevent environmental harm and supports governance systems that promote sustainability. It aims to create a balanced relationship between human development and environmental sustainability. International frameworks like the UN SDGs guide sustainable development by setting comprehensive goals for global development. Ultimately, sustainable development is about achieving long-term prosperity for all, through responsible and inclusive growth.

Sustainable development represents a comprehensive and long-term approach to societal progress that seeks to reconcile economic growth, environmental protection, and social equity. It is based on the principle of meeting the needs of the present without compromising the ability of future generations to meet their own needs. This concept underscores the necessity of aligning human development with ecological limits and the equitable distribution of resources.

Over the decades, the understanding of sustainable development has evolved through interdisciplinary perspectives and international policy frameworks. Early conceptualizations highlighted the importance of resource conservation and environmental stewardship, while more recent interpretations emphasize systemic integration across economic, environmental, and social dimensions.

Sustainable development calls for the transformation of production and consumption patterns, the responsible management of natural resources, and inclusive economic systems. It promotes resilience and adaptability in the face of global challenges such as climate change, biodiversity loss, and socio-economic disparities. In this context, sustainability is not merely an environmental issue but a multidimensional agenda requiring cross-sectoral collaboration and long-term vision.

Table 2.1 Definitions of sustainable development

	Definition	Author
1.	Development that meets the needs of the present without compromising the ability of future generations to meet their own needs.	Report of the World Commission on Environment and Development: Our Common Future (1987).
2.	Sustainable development refers to a transformative process where resource use, investment strategies, technological innovation, and institutional evolution are aligned in a way that strengthens the capacity to meet human needs and ambitions—both now and in the future.	Report of the World Commission on Environment and Development: Our Common Future (1987).
3.	Sustainable development is an approach to development that looks to balance different, and often competing, needs against an awareness of the environmental, social, and economic limitations we face as a society.	UK Government
4.	Sustainable development involves improving the quality of human life while living within the carrying capacity of supporting ecosystems.	World Conservation Strategy
5.	Sustainable development is the development that minimizes environmental degradation and that meets the needs of present generations without compromising the ability of future generations to meet their needs.	Munasinghe
6.	Sustainable development is a form of development that takes into account the protection of the environment, the prudent use of natural resources, and the enhancement of human well-being.	OECD
7.	Sustainable development involves carefully managing and preserving natural resources, while guiding technological and institutional transformations in a way that secures the ability to meet human needs—both today and for generations to come.	FAO
8.	Sustainable development seeks to create a balance between the economic, social, and environmental dimensions of development.	World Bank
9.	Sustainable development is the guiding principle for long-term global development, consisting of three interdependent pillars: economic growth, social inclusivity, and environmental sustainability.	United Nations
10.	Sustainable development is the use of resources to meet human needs while preserving the environment so that these needs can be met not only in the present but also for future generations.	US EPA
11.	Sustainable development is a comprehensive and integrated approach to improving the well-being of people and the environment, now and in the future.	UNESCO

Source: Created by authors

A pivotal moment in the institutionalization of sustainable development was the adoption of the 2030 Agenda for Sustainable Development by the United Nations in 2015. This global agenda introduced the Sustainable Development Goals (SDGs)—a set of 17 interlinked objectives designed to guide countries in addressing key global challenges by 2030. The SDGs integrate priorities such as poverty eradication, quality education, gender equality, clean energy, climate action, and responsible consumption and production.

Each goal is accompanied by specific targets and indicators, encouraging nations to monitor progress and align policy efforts accordingly. Importantly, the SDGs emphasize the interdependence of environmental sustainability, economic prosperity, and social inclusion, recognizing that progress in one area often reinforces advancements in others.

Ultimately, sustainable development under the SDG framework aims to foster inclusive, resilient, and equitable societies, where economic growth does not come at the expense of environmental integrity or social justice. By advancing integrated strategies and reinforcing global partnerships, the SDGs serve as both a roadmap and a call to action for achieving sustainability at all levels of governance and society.

Historical Context of Sustainable Development

The concept of sustainable development has evolved, with roots tracing back to ancient civilizations that practiced sustainable agriculture and resource management. However, the modern understanding of sustainability began to take shape in the mid-twentieth century as the environmental impacts of industrialization became increasingly evident. Historical stages of the concept of sustainable development are presented in Fig. 2.1

Early environmental awareness (1960s–1970s) (Fig. 2.1). The 1960s and 1970s marked a significant shift in public awareness and concern for environmental issues. This period, often referred to as the birth of the modern environmental movement,

Fig. 2.1 Historical stages of the concept of sustainable development. Source: Created by authors

was characterized by growing recognition of the detrimental impacts of industrialization, pollution, and unchecked resource exploitation on the environment and human health. The confluence of scientific discoveries, influential publications, and grassroots activism during this time laid the foundation for contemporary environmental policies and sustainable development initiatives.

- *Rachel Carson's "Silent Spring" (1962).* One of the most influential works of this era was Rachel Carson's book "Silent Spring," published in 1962 (Carlson, 1962). Carson, a marine biologist and conservationist, highlighted the adverse effects of pesticides, particularly DDT, on wildlife, ecosystems, and human health. Her meticulous research and compelling narrative galvanized public opinion and sparked widespread environmental activism. "Silent Spring" is credited with launching the environmental movement and leading to policy changes, including the eventual ban on DDT in the United States. In Rachel Carson's book "Silent Spring," DDT refers to dichloro-diphenyl-trichloroethane, a synthetic chemical compound used as an insecticide. DDT was widely employed during and after World War II to control mosquito populations and prevent the spread of malaria, as well as to protect crops from agricultural pests. While it was highly effective in killing insects, DDT had significant and far-reaching environmental and health consequences that were largely unrecognized or ignored at the time.

The publication of "Silent Spring" in 1962 had a profound impact on public awareness and policy regarding environmental protection. It led to increased scrutiny of pesticide use, significant changes in laws and regulations, and the eventual ban of DDT in many countries, including the United States in 1972. Carson's work is often credited with helping to launch the modern environmental movement and inspiring the creation of key environmental institutions, such as the U.S. Environmental Protection Agency (EPA).

Overall, DDT in "Silent Spring" symbolizes the broader issue of human impact on the environment and the urgent need for more responsible and informed approaches to managing natural resources and protecting ecosystems.

- *The Cuyahoga River Fire (1969).* The Cuyahoga River in Cleveland, Ohio, became infamous for catching fire in 1969 due to the high levels of industrial pollution and flammable waste in the water. This event, though not the first of its kind, drew national attention and became a symbol of the severe environmental degradation caused by industrial activities. The Cuyahoga River fire highlighted the urgent need for environmental regulation and cleanup efforts, contributing to the establishment of the Environmental Protection Agency (EPA) and the passage of the Clean Water Act in the United States (Cronin, 2019).
- *The Santa Barbara Oil Spill (1969).* In 1969, a massive oil spill off the coast of Santa Barbara, California, released over 3 million gallons of crude oil into the Pacific Ocean. The spill caused extensive damage to marine and coastal ecosystems and killed thousands of seabirds, fish, and marine mammals. The disaster drew widespread media coverage and public outrage, underscoring the environmental risks of offshore oil drilling and prompting stricter regulations on oil and gas industries.

Legislative and institutional responses in this period:

1. Formation of environmental organizations. The heightened environmental awareness of the 1960s and 1970s led to the creation and growth of numerous environmental organizations. Groups such as the Sierra Club, the Natural Resources Defense Council (NRDC), and Greenpeace emerged as powerful advocates for environmental protection, mobilizing public support and influencing policy decisions.
2. Establishment of Earth Day (1970). Earth Day, first celebrated on April 22, 1970, was a landmark event in the environmental movement. Organized by Senator Gaylord Nelson and environmental activist Denis Hayes, Earth Day brought together millions of people across the United States in a unified call for environmental protection. The event's success demonstrated the widespread public concern for environmental issues and helped to build momentum for subsequent legislative action.
3. Creation of the U.S. Environmental Protection Agency (EPA) (1970). In response to growing environmental concerns, President Richard Nixon established the Environmental Protection Agency in December 1970. The EPA was tasked with consolidating federal environmental programs and enforcing environmental laws. Its creation marked a significant step toward systematic environmental regulation and protection in the United States.

The early 1970s saw the enactment of several key pieces of environmental legislation in the United States, including:

- *The Clean Air Act (1970).* This act aimed to control air pollution by setting emissions standards for industries and motor vehicles.
- *The Clean Water Act (1972).* This act focused on reducing water pollution and protecting water quality through comprehensive regulations and enforcement mechanisms.
- *The Endangered Species Act (1973).* This act provided legal protection for threatened and endangered species and their habitats, aiming to prevent extinction and promote recovery.

On a global scale, this period is associated with the United Nations Conference on the Human Environment (Stockholm Conference) (1972), and Club of Rome, and "The Limits to Growth" (1972). The Stockholm Conference, held in 1972, was the first major international gathering focused on environmental issues. It brought together representatives from 113 countries and resulted in the Stockholm Declaration, which outlined principles for environmental sustainability and emphasized the need for international cooperation. The conference also led to the establishment of the United Nations Environment Programme (UNEP), which plays a key role in coordinating global environmental efforts. In 1972, the Club of Rome, a global think tank, published "The Limits to Growth," a report based on computer simulations that predicted the consequences of continued economic and population growth on the planet's finite resources. The report warned of potential ecological and economic collapse if current trends persisted, sparking debate and raising awareness about the need for sustainable development practices.

The early environmental awareness of the 1960s and 1970s was a transformative period that brought environmental issues to the forefront of public consciousness and policy agendas. Influential publications, environmental disasters, grassroots activism, and legislative actions during this time laid the groundwork for modern environmentalism and sustainable development. The legacy of this era continues to shape contemporary efforts to protect the environment and promote sustainability, highlighting the enduring importance of balancing economic, social, and environmental considerations for the well-being of present and future generations.

Brundtland Report (1987) (Fig. 2.1). The concept of sustainable development was formally introduced by the World Commission on Environment and Development (WCED), also known as the Brundtland Commission, in its 1987 report titled "Our Common Future." The report defined sustainable development as development that meets the needs of the present without compromising the ability of future generations to meet their own needs. The Brundtland Report emphasized the interconnectedness of economic development, environmental sustainability, and social equity, laying the groundwork for integrating these dimensions into policy and practice.

United Nations Earth Summit (1992) (Fig. 2.1). The 1992 United Nations Conference on Environment and Development (UNCED), also known as the Earth Summit, held in Rio de Janeiro, further cemented the principles of sustainable development. The summit resulted in key documents such as the Rio Declaration on Environment and Development and Agenda 21, a comprehensive plan of action for sustainable development.

Millennium Development Goals (MDGs) (2000) (Fig. 2.1). In 2000, the United Nations adopted the Millennium Development Goals (MDGs), which set specific targets for reducing poverty, improving health and education, and ensuring environmental sustainability by 2015. The MDGs provided a focused framework for global development efforts.

Sustainable Development Goals (SDGs) (2015) (Fig. 2.1). Building on the MDGs, the United Nations launched the Sustainable Development Goals (SDGs) in 2015 as part of the 2030 Agenda for Sustainable Development. The 17 SDGs are a comprehensive and ambitious set of goals that address a wide range of global challenges, including poverty, inequality, climate change, environmental degradation, peace, and justice.

The concept of sustainable development, while gaining prominence in recent decades, is rooted in historical practices of resource management and environmental awareness. Ancient civilizations often implemented forms of sustainable agriculture, forestry, and water use that reflected an implicit understanding of ecological limits. However, the contemporary formulation of sustainable development emerged in response to the profound environmental and social transformations induced by industrialization in the twentieth century.

A significant shift in environmental consciousness occurred during the 1960s and 1970s, a period marked by growing public concern over pollution, resource depletion, and the ecological consequences of unchecked economic growth. This era witnessed the birth of the modern environmental movement, propelled by scientific discoveries, critical publications, and civil society activism.

One of the most influential contributions of this period was Rachel Carson's seminal work *Silent Spring* (1962), which exposed the detrimental effects of synthetic pesticides—particularly DDT—on ecosystems and human health. Carson's rigorous documentation and compelling narrative galvanized public opinion, leading to regulatory reforms and laying the groundwork for environmental advocacy on a global scale.

Several high-profile environmental disasters further underscored the urgency of regulatory action. In 1969, the Cuyahoga River in Cleveland, Ohio, caught fire due to industrial pollution, becoming a potent symbol of environmental neglect. The same year, the Santa Barbara oil spill off the California coast released millions of gallons of crude oil into the ocean, devastating marine ecosystems and provoking widespread public outrage.

These events catalyzed the formation of environmental institutions and policies. The U.S. Environmental Protection Agency (EPA) was established in 1970 to coordinate federal environmental efforts, while key legislative acts—including the Clean Air Act (1970), Clean Water Act (1972), and Endangered Species Act (1973)—set important precedents in environmental governance.

Globally, the United Nations Conference on the Human Environment (Stockholm, 1972) marked a turning point by recognizing environmental protection as a shared international responsibility. The conference resulted in the Stockholm Declaration, which articulated foundational principles for environmental management and led to the creation of the United Nations Environment Programme (UNEP).

In the same year, the Club of Rome released *The Limits to Growth*, a report based on systems modeling that projected severe ecological and economic consequences if global trends in population growth, industrialization, and resource use continued unabated. Though controversial, the report stimulated widespread debate and brought sustainability issues into the realm of international policy discourse.

The Brundtland Report, officially titled *Our Common Future* and published in 1987 by the World Commission on Environment and Development (WCED), provided a definitive articulation of sustainable development. It emphasized the interdependence of economic development, social equity, and environmental sustainability, and introduced the now widely accepted definition of sustainable development. The report also called for global cooperation to integrate these dimensions into policymaking and development strategies.

Subsequent global summits continued to advance the sustainable development agenda. The Earth Summit in Rio de Janeiro (1992) produced critical frameworks such as the Rio Declaration on Environment and Development and Agenda 21, laying out a comprehensive plan of action for sustainable development in the twenty-first century.

In 2000, the United Nations adopted the Millennium Development Goals (MDGs), a focused set of targets aimed at reducing poverty, improving health and education, and promoting environmental sustainability by 2015. Building upon their legacy, the Sustainable Development Goals (SDGs) were launched in 2015 as part of the 2030 Agenda for Sustainable Development, providing an integrated and far-reaching blueprint for global development across 17 goals and 169 targets.

This historical trajectory highlights a gradual but significant evolution from environmental awareness to an integrated sustainability paradigm. The consolidation of environmental, economic, and social objectives into global governance structures reflects a growing recognition that sustainable development is essential for long-term human and planetary well-being.

Key Principles of Sustainable Development, according to Filgueira et al. (2020), Liu et al. (2020), Pisano et al. (2020); von Wehrden et al. (2020), Wals and Peters (2020), are shown in Fig. 2.2.

Let us expand on the first principle of sustainable development—integration. Integration is a foundational principle of sustainable development, emphasizing the necessity of considering economic, social, and environmental dimensions holistically. This principle recognizes that these dimensions are interdependent and that sustainable development can only be achieved through policies and actions that simultaneously address all three areas. Key aspects of integration are shown in Fig. 2.3.

The benefits and challenges of the integration principle of sustainable development can be seen in Table 2.2.

The principle of integration is crucial for achieving sustainable development, as it ensures that economic growth, social equity, and environmental protection are pursued together. By adopting holistic decision-making, promoting policy coherence, fostering cross-sectoral collaboration, and maintaining a long-term perspective, societies can better navigate the complex challenges of sustainable development and create resilient and thriving communities for future generations.

The next principle of sustainable development is Intergenerational Equity. Intergenerational equity is a core principle of sustainable development that emphasizes fairness and justice between present and future generations. It involves ensuring that the decisions and actions of the current generation do not compromise the ability of future generations to meet their own needs. This principle is rooted in ethical considerations and seeks to balance the use and conservation of resources over time. Key aspects of intergenerational equity are shown in Fig. 2.4.

Intergenerational equity emphasizes fairness and justice between present and future generations by ensuring sustainable use of resources. It calls for responsible management and conservation of natural resources, like forests and water, to maintain their availability over time (Oliver, 2003). Protecting the environment from degradation is crucial to preserving ecosystem services and biodiversity for future generations (IPCC, 2018). This principle also seeks to promote economic and social stability by creating conditions that support sustainable growth, social inclusion, and poverty reduction (World Bank, 2018). Ensuring equitable access to resources

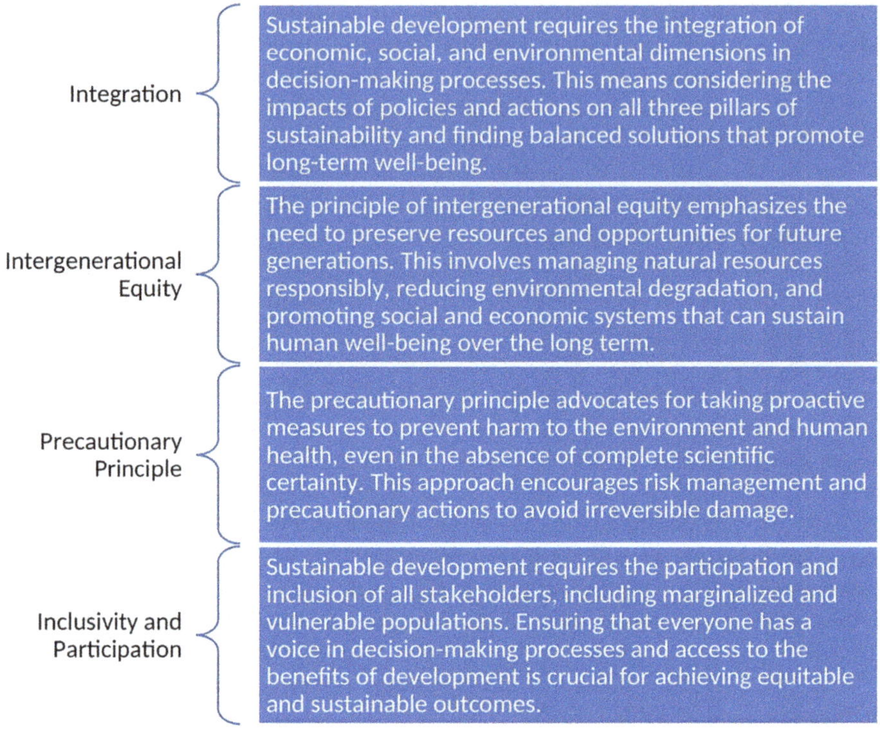

Fig. 2.2 Key principles of sustainable development. Source: Created by authors

across generations includes natural resources, technological advancements, and economic opportunities (IRENA, 2019).

Intergenerational equity advocates for long-term planning to avoid short-term decisions that could harm future generations (Jacobs, 2016). Sustainable practices in areas like agriculture and energy use are necessary to maintain environmental and economic health (Tilman et al., 2011). Addressing current inequities in resource distribution is vital to achieving fairness for future generations (Stiglitz, 2012). This principle challenges the prioritization of immediate gains over long-term sustainability, requiring a shift toward policies that support environmental and social well-being (UNFCCC, 2015). Overall, intergenerational equity ensures that the actions of today do not compromise the prospects of tomorrow's generations, promoting a sustainable and just world for all.

It is also possible to distinguish this principle's benefits and challenges (see Table 2.3).

Intergenerational equity is a fundamental principle of sustainable development that seeks to ensure fairness and justice between present and future generations. By prioritizing resource conservation, environmental protection, economic and social stability, and equitable access to resources, societies can promote sustainable development and safeguard the well-being of future generations. Addressing the

Holistic Decision-Making

Integration requires a comprehensive approach to decision-making that considers the potential impacts on the economy, society, and environment. This holistic perspective ensures that policies do not disproportionately favor one dimension at the expense of the others.

For example, urban development projects should not only focus on economic growth but also on social inclusivity and environmental sustainability (Hák, Janoušková, & Moldan, 2016).

Policy Coherence

Policy coherence is critical to integration. It involves aligning policies across different sectors to ensure they support and reinforce each other rather than working at cross-purposes.

An example of policy coherence is aligning energy policies with environmental regulations to promote the use of renewable energy sources while reducing carbon emissions (OECD, 2019).

Cross-Sectoral Collaboration

Effective integration often requires collaboration between various sectors and stakeholders. This includes governments, businesses, civil society, and international organizations working together to achieve common goals.

Collaborative platforms and partnerships, such as those seen in sustainable urban planning, bring together diverse expertise and resources to create more sustainable and resilient cities (United Nations, 2015).

Long-Term Perspective

A long-term perspective is essential for integration, as sustainable development aims to meet the needs of present and future generations. Policies should be designed with foresight, considering their long-term impacts on all three dimensions.

Strategic planning processes, such as those used in climate change adaptation strategies, often incorporate scenario planning and risk assessments to ensure sustainability (European Commission, 2020).

Fig. 2.3 Key aspects of integration principle of sustainable development. Source: Created by authors

challenges of short-term interests, economic pressures, and inequities in resource distribution is essential for achieving intergenerational equity.

The third principle of sustainable development precautionary principle advocates for taking proactive measures to prevent harm to the environment and human health, even in the absence of complete scientific certainty. This approach encourages risk management and precautionary actions to avoid irreversible damage (Fig. 2.5).

The precautionary principle emphasizes taking preventive action in the face of uncertainty to avoid potential harm to human health and the environment. It advocates for proactive risk management by implementing measures even when scientific evidence about potential risks is inconclusive (Raffensperger & Tickner, 1999; Harremoës et al., 2001). This principle shifts the burden of proof to proponents of an activity to demonstrate its safety, rather than requiring opponents to prove harm (Tickner, 2003).

It promotes preventive action before harm occurs, rather than reacting after the fact, which is particularly crucial in environmental policy and public health (Kriebel et al., 2001). Recognizing scientific uncertainty is a key aspect, encouraging caution in decision-making when potential risks are not fully understood (O'Riordan &

Table 2.2 Benefits and challenges of the integration principle of sustainable development

Benefit	Explanation	Example
Benefits of the integration principle		
Enhanced resilience	Integrated approaches can enhance the resilience of communities and ecosystems by addressing vulnerabilities and promoting adaptive capacities across different sectors.	For instance, integrated water resource management (IWRM) combines water, land, and related resources management to maximize economic and social welfare without compromising the sustainability of vital ecosystems (GWP, 2000).
Efficient resource use	By considering economic, social, and environmental impacts together, integrated approaches can lead to more efficient and sustainable resource use.	Integrated energy planning, for example, optimizes energy production and consumption patterns to reduce waste and improve efficiency (IRENA, 2018).
Balanced development	Integration helps ensure balanced development that promotes economic prosperity, social equity, and environmental protection.	Sustainable tourism initiatives often exemplify this balance by promoting local economic development while preserving cultural heritage and natural landscapes (UNWTO, 2018).
Challenges of the integration principle		
Institutional silos	One of the main integration challenges is the existence of institutional silos, where different departments or organizations operate independently without sufficient coordination.	Breaking down these silos requires strong leadership, effective communication, and mechanisms for interdepartmental and intersectoral collaboration (UNDP, 2017).
Conflicting interests	Conflicting interests among stakeholders can hinder integrated approaches. Economic priorities, social needs, and environmental concerns can sometimes be at odds, making it difficult to find mutually agreeable solutions.	Mediating these conflicts often requires negotiation, compromise, and the development of innovative solutions that address multiple interests (Meadowcroft, 2007).
Resource constraints	Implementing integrated approaches can be resource-intensive, requiring investment in new technologies, infrastructure, and capacity-building.	Ensuring adequate funding and resources for integrated projects is essential, particularly in developing countries where financial and technical capacities may be limited (World Bank, 2015).

Source: Created by authors

Resource Conservation

Intergenerational equity calls for the responsible management and conservation of natural resources to ensure their availability for future generations. This includes sustainable practices in agriculture, forestry, fisheries, and energy use.

For example, sustainable forestry practices aim to balance tree harvesting with reforestation efforts to maintain forest ecosystems and resources for future use (Brown et al., 2017).

Environmental Protection

Protecting the environment from degradation is essential to preserving ecosystem services and biodiversity, which are vital for the well-being of future generations. Efforts to reduce pollution, mitigate climate change, and protect natural habitats are critical components of this aspect

The Paris Agreement on climate change is an example of an international effort to address intergenerational equity by limiting global warming and reducing greenhouse gas emissions (UNFCCC, 2015).

Economic and Social Stability

Ensuring economic and social stability involves creating conditions that support sustainable economic growth, social inclusion, and poverty reduction. This helps future generations inherit a world with opportunities for prosperity and well-being.

Investments in education, healthcare, and infrastructure are necessary to build resilient and thriving communities (World Bank, 2018).

Equitable Access to Resources

Intergenerational equity requires that access to resources is distributed fairly across generations. This includes not only natural resources but also technological advancements, knowledge, and economic opportunities.

Policies promoting renewable energy sources ensure that future generations have access to sustainable and clean energy options (IRENA, 2019).

Fig. 2.4 Key aspects of the intergenerational equity principle of sustainable development. Source: Created by authors

Cameron, 1994). The principle also includes cost-effectiveness, balancing the economic feasibility of preventive measures with their potential to prevent significant harm (Sandin, 1999).

Benefits of the precautionary principle (see Table 2.4) include protecting human health and the environment from potentially catastrophic impacts (Gollier & Treich, 2003) and fostering sustainable practices by encouraging the development of safer technologies (Kriebel et al., 2001). It can enhance public trust by showing a commitment to safeguarding public interests and addressing uncertainties transparently (Graham, 2004).

The precautionary principle is a fundamental aspect of sustainable development, emphasizing the need to take proactive measures to protect health and the environment in the face of scientific uncertainty. By promoting preventive action, managing risks, and balancing costs and benefits, this principle supports the development of safer and more sustainable practices. Addressing the challenges of implementing the precautionary principle requires careful consideration of innovation, economic implications, and effective stakeholder engagement.

Table 2.3 Benefits and challenges of the intergenerational equity principle of sustainable development

Benefit	Explanation	Example
Benefits of the intergenerational equity principle		
Sustainable resource use	By prioritizing the long-term availability of resources, intergenerational equity promotes sustainable resource use, ensuring that future generations can enjoy the same or improved quality of life as the present generation.	Practices such as sustainable agriculture help maintain soil health and productivity over the long term (Tilman et al., 2011).
Reduced environmental impact	Emphasizing environmental protection reduces the risk of environmental degradation, which can have severe consequences for future generations. This includes mitigating the effects of climate change and preserving biodiversity.	Efforts to reduce carbon footprints and enhance carbon sequestration contribute to long-term environmental sustainability (IPCC, 2018).
Enhanced social cohesion	Promoting equity across generations can enhance social cohesion and stability by reducing inequalities and fostering a sense of shared responsibility for the future.	Policies that address social determinants of health, such as education and economic opportunities, can improve long-term social outcomes (Marmot, 2015).
Challenges of the intergenerational equity principle		
Short-term interests	One of the main challenges is the prevalence of short-term interests and gains, which often take precedence over long-term sustainability. Political and economic systems frequently prioritize immediate benefits, sometimes at the expense of future well-being.	Overcoming this challenge requires a shift in mindset and policymaking toward long-term planning and sustainability (Jacobs, 2016).
Economic pressures	Economic pressures, such as the need for rapid development and growth, can lead to the overexploitation of resources. Balancing economic development with sustainable practices is a persistent challenge.	Implementing green economy strategies can help align economic activities with sustainability goals (UNEP, 2011).
Inequities in resource distribution	Existing inequities in resource distribution can complicate efforts to achieve intergenerational equity. Addressing these inequities requires targeted policies and interventions to ensure fair access and opportunities for all generations.	Social policies aimed at reducing poverty and enhancing economic inclusion are crucial for achieving intergenerational equity (Stiglitz, 2012).

Source: Created by authors

Risk Management

The precautionary principle calls for the proactive management of potential risks. This involves taking preventive measures when an activity raises threats of harm to human health or the environment, even if some cause-and-effect relationships are not fully established scientifically (Raffensperger & Tickner, 1999).

For example, restrictions on the use of genetically modified organisms (GMOs) in agriculture are often based on precautionary measures due to uncertainties about their long-term impacts on health and ecosystems (Carr & Levidow, 2000).

Environmental Protection

The principle advocates for taking action to prevent harm before it occurs, rather than waiting for scientific certainty. This shifts the burden of proof to proponents of an activity to demonstrate its safety, rather than requiring opponents to prove harm (Harremoës et al., 2001).

In environmental policy, this approach can be seen in the regulation of chemicals and pollutants, where precautionary measures are taken to limit exposure to substances suspected of being harmful (EEA, 2013).

Scientific Uncertainty

Recognizing and addressing scientific uncertainty is central to the precautionary principle. It underscores the importance of caution when there is a lack of conclusive evidence about potential risks (O'Riordan & Cameron, 1994).

This approach is particularly relevant in the context of emerging technologies and environmental changes, where long-term effects are not yet fully understood (UNESCO, 2005).

Cost-Effectiveness

The precautionary principle also considers the cost-effectiveness of preventive measures. It promotes actions that are economically feasible while providing a safeguard against potential risks (Sandin, 1999).

Balancing the costs and benefits of precautionary actions ensures that measures are practical and sustainable over the long term.

Fig. 2.5 Key aspects of the precautionary principle of sustainable development. Source: Created by authors

Sustainable development requires the participation and inclusion of all stakeholders, including marginalized and vulnerable populations. Ensuring that everyone has a voice in decision-making processes and access to the benefits of development is crucial for achieving equitable and sustainable outcomes. *Inclusivity and participation* are fundamental principles of sustainable development that emphasize the active involvement and equitable consideration of all stakeholders in decision-making processes. These principles ensure that diverse voices are heard and that the benefits and responsibilities of development are shared fairly. Key aspects of the inclusivity and participation principle of sustainable development are shown in Fig. 2.6.

Inclusivity and participation in sustainable development involve engaging a wide range of stakeholders, especially marginalized groups, to ensure diverse perspectives are considered in decision-making processes. Equitable participation requires addressing barriers such as language and socio-economic status to provide all

Table 2.4 Benefits and challenges of the precautionary principle of sustainable development

Benefit	Explanation	Example
Benefits of the precautionary principle		
Protection of health and the environment	By prioritizing preventive action, the precautionary principle helps protect human health and the environment from potential harm that might not yet be fully understood. This proactive stance can prevent catastrophic outcomes (Gollier & Treich, 2003).	For instance, early action to mitigate climate change, even amid scientific uncertainties, helps protect ecosystems and communities from severe impacts (IPCC, 2014).
Promotion of sustainable practices	Implementing the precautionary principle encourages the adoption of sustainable practices that minimize risk and promote long-term well-being. This approach supports the development of safer technologies and products (Tickner, 2003).	Sustainable agriculture practices that avoid potentially harmful pesticides are an example of this principle in action, promoting health and environmental sustainability (Kriebel et al., 2001).
Enhanced public trust	Applying the precautionary principle can enhance public trust in regulatory and decision-making processes. It demonstrates a commitment to protecting public interests and addressing concerns about potential risks (Graham, 2004).	Transparent and precautionary approaches in policymaking can build confidence in governmental and institutional actions.
Challenges of the precautionary principle		
Balancing innovation and precaution	One of the main challenges is balancing the need for innovation with the caution advocated by the precautionary principle. Overly stringent application of the principle can potentially stifle technological and economic development (Sunstein, 2005).	Finding a balance that allows for innovation while ensuring safety is critical to sustainable development.
Economic costs	The precautionary principle can involve significant economic costs, particularly when it leads to the restriction or banning of technologies and products. Assessing the cost-effectiveness of precautionary measures is essential to ensure that they are sustainable (Manson, 2002).	Policymakers must weigh the potential costs of precautionary actions against the benefits of preventing harm.
Scientific and political controversies	The application of the precautionary principle can be contentious, with debates over the interpretation of scientific data and the appropriate level of precaution. These controversies can complicate decision-making processes (Foster et al., 2000).	Effective communication and stakeholder engagement are necessary to navigate these challenges and build consensus.

Source: Created by authors

community members with equal opportunities to contribute. Transparency and accountability are crucial for building trust, involving mechanisms like public consultations and participatory budgeting (Fung, 2006; Wampler, 2007). Collaborative decision-making fosters ownership and commitment by co-creating solutions with

Stakeholder Engagement

Engaging a wide range of stakeholders, including marginalized and vulnerable groups, in decision-making processes is crucial for achieving sustainable development. This involves recognizing and valuing the perspectives and knowledge of different communities (Reed, 2008).

Effective stakeholder engagement can lead to more comprehensive and accepted solutions, as it incorporates diverse views and expertise. For instance, involving local communities in conservation projects can improve outcomes by leveraging indigenous knowledge (Berkes, 2009).

Equitable Participation

Ensuring equitable participation means providing all stakeholders with equal opportunities to contribute to and benefit from development initiatives. This includes addressing barriers such as language, education, and socioeconomic status that might prevent some groups from participating fully (Arnstein, 1969).

Tools like participatory rural appraisal (PRA) can help facilitate more inclusive participation by using methods that are accessible and understandable to all community members (Chambers, 1994).

Transparency and Accountability

Transparency in decision-making processes is essential for building trust and accountability. Providing clear, accessible information about policies, decisions, and their impacts enables stakeholders to make informed contributions and hold decision-makers accountable (Fung, 2006).

Mechanisms such as public consultations, participatory budgeting, and citizen advisory committees can enhance transparency and accountability in governance (Wampler, 2007).

Collaborative Decision-Making

Collaborative decision-making involves working together with stakeholders to co-create solutions. This approach fosters ownership and commitment to sustainable development initiatives, as stakeholders feel their input directly influences outcomes (Ansell & Gash, 2008).

Examples include community based natural resource management (CBNRM) programs, which empower local communities to manage resources sustainably (Fabricius et al., 2001).

Fig. 2.6 Key aspects of the inclusivity and participation principle of sustainable development. Source: Created by authors

stakeholders, enhancing the effectiveness and acceptance of initiatives. Despite challenges (Table 2.5) like power dynamics and resource constraints, inclusive and participatory approaches lead to more effective, equitable, and resilient outcomes.

Inclusivity and participation are essential for achieving sustainable development that is fair, effective, and resilient. By engaging diverse stakeholders, ensuring equitable participation, promoting transparency and accountability, and fostering collaborative decision-making, these principles help to create more inclusive and sustainable communities. Addressing the challenges of power dynamics, resource constraints, and coordination complexity is crucial for realizing the full benefits of these principles.

Sustainable development, while widely endorsed as a vital global goal, faces numerous challenges and criticisms that complicate its implementation and effectiveness. These challenges (Table 2.6) span across economic, social, political, and

Table 2.5 Benefits and challenges of the inclusivity and participation principle of sustainable development

Benefit	Explanation	Example
Benefits of the inclusivity and participation principle		
Enhanced effectiveness and efficiency	Inclusive and participatory processes often lead to more effective and efficient outcomes, as they incorporate local knowledge and address the specific needs and priorities of different groups.	For example, involving farmers in the design and implementation of agricultural projects can lead to more practical and sustainable farming practices.
Social equity and justice	These principles promote social equity and justice by ensuring that all groups, particularly the marginalized and disadvantaged, have a voice in development processes. This helps to reduce inequalities and distribute the benefits of development more fairly (Cornwall, 2008).	Programs that prioritize women's participation in decision-making have been shown to improve outcomes in areas such as health, education, and economic development (Agarwal, 2010).
Building social capital	Inclusivity and participation help build social capital by fostering networks of trust, reciprocity, and cooperation among stakeholders. Strong social capital enhances community resilience and the capacity to address collective challenges.	Community-driven development projects often succeed because they build on the strengths and capacities of local networks (Mansuri & Rao, 2004).
Challenges of the inclusivity and participation principle		
Power dynamics and inequality	Power dynamics and existing inequalities can hinder genuine participation. Dominant groups may overshadow the voices of marginalized communities, leading to unequal influence in decision-making processes (Cooke & Kothari, 2001).	Addressing these power imbalances requires deliberate strategies to empower marginalized groups and ensure their meaningful participation (Gaventa, 2006).
Resource and capacity constraints	Effective participation requires resources and capacity, which may be limited in some contexts. Ensuring that all stakeholders can participate meaningfully often involves investing in capacity-building and providing necessary resources.	Capacity-building initiatives, such as training and education programs, can enhance the ability of marginalized groups to engage in participatory processes (Kumar, 2002).
Complexity of coordination	Coordinating inclusive and participatory processes can be complex and time-consuming, requiring careful planning and management. Balancing the diverse interests and perspectives of stakeholders can be challenging.	Successful coordination often involves establishing clear processes and mechanisms for dialogue, negotiation, and conflict resolution.

Source: Created by authors

Table 2.6 Challenges of sustainable development

Economic challenges	
Balancing economic growth and sustainability	Achieving sustainable development often requires reconciling economic growth with environmental preservation. Critics argue that the pursuit of economic growth can lead to resource depletion and environmental degradation, counteracting sustainability goals.
	The tension between immediate economic benefits and long-term environmental sustainability remains a significant obstacle, with some arguing for a redefinition of economic success beyond GDP.
Financing sustainable development	Securing adequate funding for sustainable development initiatives is a persistent challenge. Many developing countries struggle to finance projects that align with sustainability goals due to limited financial resources and competing priorities.
	Innovative financing mechanisms, such as green bonds and sustainability-linked loans, have been proposed, but their implementation and effectiveness are still evolving.
Social challenges	
Inequality and social inclusion	Addressing social inequality is crucial for sustainable development, yet it remains a significant hurdle. Marginalized groups often lack access to the benefits of development, exacerbating disparities.
	Ensuring inclusive participation in decision-making processes is essential, but power imbalances and systemic barriers can limit the effectiveness of such efforts.
Cultural and local contexts	Sustainable development strategies must be tailored to local contexts, considering cultural, social, and environmental factors. One-size-fits-all approaches are often ineffective and can lead to resistance from local communities.
	Engaging local stakeholders and integrating indigenous knowledge into development plans can enhance relevance and acceptance.
Political challenges	
Governance and policy coherence	Effective governance is critical for implementing sustainable development policies. However, fragmented governance structures and lack of policy coherence can undermine efforts.
	Coordination across different levels of government and sectors is necessary to ensure that policies are aligned and mutually reinforcing.
Political will and leadership	The success of sustainable development initiatives often hinges on political will and leadership. Without strong commitment from political leaders, sustainability goals can be deprioritized or ignored.
	Political instability and changing administrations can also disrupt the continuity of sustainability programs.
Environmental challenges	
Climate change and environmental degradation	Climate change poses a severe threat to sustainable development, exacerbating environmental degradation and increasing the frequency of extreme weather events.
	Mitigating climate change requires global cooperation and significant reductions in greenhouse gas emissions, which have proven challenging to achieve.

(continued)

Table 2.6 (continued)

Biodiversity loss	Biodiversity loss, driven by habitat destruction, pollution, and overexploitation of resources, undermines ecosystem services essential for human well-being.
	Conservation efforts are often insufficiently funded and can conflict with development objectives, creating a need for integrated approaches that balance conservation and development.

Source: Created by authors according to Biermann (2021), CBD (2021), Hickel (2020), IPCC (2021a, 2021b), Jackson (2021), Jordan et al. (2020)

environmental dimensions, reflecting the complexity of balancing diverse needs and objectives.

The challenges and criticisms of sustainable development reflect the complexity and multifaceted nature of achieving global sustainability. Addressing these challenges requires innovative solutions, inclusive approaches, and strong political commitment. By recognizing and navigating these obstacles, the international community can make meaningful progress toward a more sustainable future.

The essential elements of the critique of sustainable development are presented in Figs. 2.7 and 2.8.

The Sustainable Development Goals (SDGs) are a collection of 17 global goals set by the United Nations in 2015 as part of the 2030 Agenda for Sustainable Development. These goals are a universal call to action to end poverty, protect the planet, and ensure that all people enjoy peace and prosperity by 2030. The SDGs are:

1. Eradicating poverty. Eliminate poverty in every form and in all regions of the world.
2. Ending hunger. Eliminate hunger by ensuring food security, improving nutrition, and advancing sustainable agriculture.
3. Health and Well-being. Promote health and well-being for individuals of all ages through access to quality healthcare and healthy living conditions.
4. Inclusive education. Guarantee equitable, high-quality education and encourage opportunities for lifelong learning for everyone.
5. Gender equality. Ensure equal rights and opportunities for women and girls and empower them in all spheres of life.
6. Water and sanitation access. Provide sustainable and universal access to safe water and sanitation services.
7. Sustainable energy for all. Guarantee affordable, clean, and modern energy access for everyone.
8. Inclusive economic growth and decent jobs. Support inclusive, sustainable economic development and ensure access to decent, productive employment for all.
9. Resilient industry and innovation. Develop robust infrastructure, promote sustainable industrialization, and encourage technological innovation.
10. Reducing inequality. Narrow social and economic disparities both within and between nations.
11. Sustainable urban development. Create inclusive, safe, resilient, and environmentally sustainable urban and rural communities.

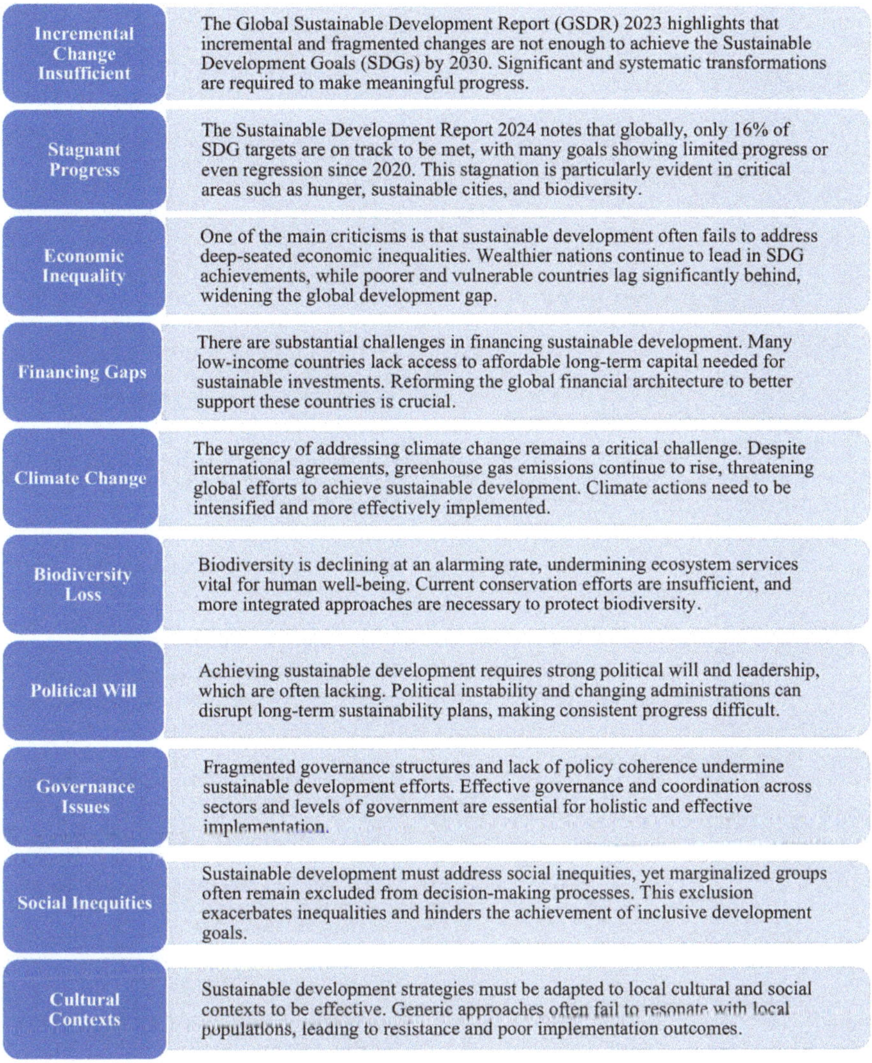

Fig. 2.7 Elements of the critique of sustainable development (1). Source: Created by authors according to UN Sustainable Development Report (2024), IPCC (2021a, 2021b), WWF (2022a, 2022b), Lehmann et al. (2021), Filipowicz (2023), UN (2021)

12. Sustainable consumption and production. Promote responsible use and production of resources to minimize environmental impact.
13. Climate response. Take immediate and effective action to address climate change and its consequences.
14. Marine ecosystems. Protect ocean and marine ecosystems and use marine resources sustainably.

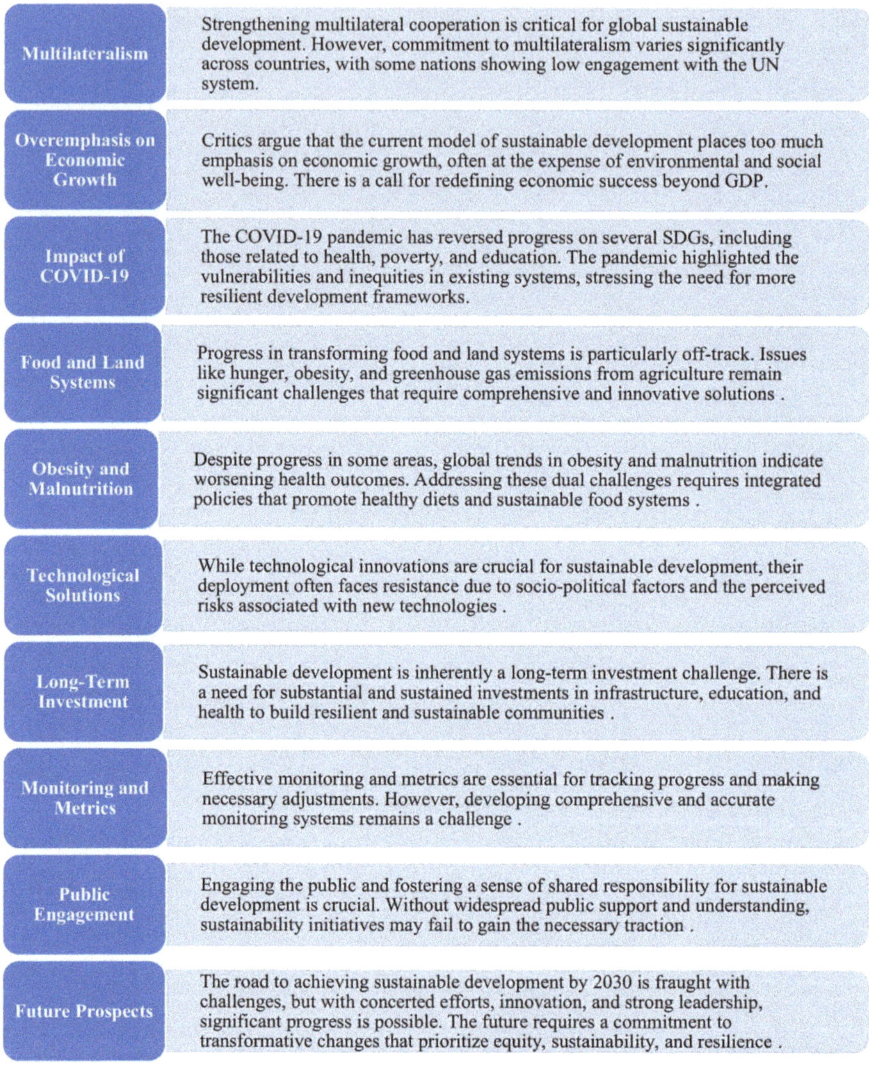

Fig. 2.8 Elements of the critique of sustainable development (2). Source: Created by authors according to UN Sustainable Development Report (2024), IPCC (2021a, 2021b), WWF (2022a, 2022b), Lehmann et al. (2021), Filipowicz (2023), UN (2021)

15. Land ecosystems and biodiversity. Safeguard and restore terrestrial ecosystems, sustainably manage forests, and combat land degradation and biodiversity loss.
16. Peace and strong institutions. Promote peaceful, just, and inclusive societies, ensure universal access to justice, and strengthen accountable institutions.
17. Global partnerships. Enhance international cooperation and mobilize global partnerships to support the achievement of sustainable development goals.

The SDGs are crucial in addressing climate change and promoting responsible consumption. SDG 12 focuses directly on ensuring sustainable consumption and production patterns. This goal aims to do more and better with less, increasing net welfare gains from economic activities by reducing resource use, degradation, and pollution. It involves engaging consumers in sustainable consumption practices, promoting resource and energy efficiency, and sustainable infrastructure, and providing access to basic services, green and decent jobs, and a better quality of life for all.

SDG 13 calls for urgent action to combat climate change and its impacts. This goal emphasizes the need to integrate climate change measures into national policies, strategies, and planning. It also highlights the importance of improving education, awareness, and human and institutional capacity on climate change mitigation, adaptation, impact reduction, and early warning.

Accelerating progress toward the Sustainable Development Goals (SDGs) requires a multifaceted approach, integrating policy reforms, financial innovations, technological advancements, and enhanced global cooperation. Several strategies to accelerate SDG progress are shown in Table 2.7.

Accelerating progress toward the SDGs requires an integrated approach that combines strong political commitment, innovative financing, technological advancements, global cooperation, inclusive participation, and targeted efforts to reduce inequalities. By adopting these strategies, the international community can make significant strides toward achieving the SDGs and creating a sustainable and equitable future for all.

Understanding sustainable development and the SDGs is foundational to tackling climate change and fostering responsible consumption. These goals provide a comprehensive framework that integrates economic, social, and environmental dimensions, ensuring a balanced approach to development that can support both current and future generations. By aligning efforts with the SDGs, we can make significant progress toward a sustainable and resilient future.

2.2 Sustainable Consumption

Sustainable consumption involves utilizing goods and services in a way that satisfies essential needs and enhances quality of life, while reducing the consumption of natural resources, limiting toxic substances, and minimizing waste and pollution throughout their entire life cycle—ensuring that future generations can also meet their own needs. This concept is integral to sustainable development as it seeks to balance economic growth, environmental protection, and social well-being. Some definitions of sustainable consumption are shown in Table 2.8.

As we can see from Table 2.8, sustainable consumption involves the use of goods and services that respond to basic needs and improve the quality of life while minimizing the use of natural resources, toxic materials, and waste production to prevent jeopardizing the needs of future generations. It is an essential aspect of sustainable

Table 2.7 Strategies to accelerate SDG progress

Strengthening political will and governance	
Policy coherence and integration	Governments need to ensure that policies across various sectors are aligned and support the SDGs. This involves breaking down silos between different departments and creating integrated strategies for sustainable development
Political leadership	Strong leadership and commitment from political leaders are essential to prioritize and sustain efforts toward achieving the SDGs. This includes embedding the SDGs into national development plans and policies.
Innovative financing mechanisms	
Mobilizing resources	Increasing financial resources through innovative mechanisms like green bonds, sustainability-linked loans, and global taxation can provide the necessary funds for sustainable development projects
Reforming financial architecture	There is a need to reform the global financial system to facilitate access to affordable, long-term capital for low-income and lower-middle-income countries, allowing them to invest in sustainable infrastructure and services
Technological and scientific advancements	
Leveraging technology	Utilizing advanced technologies such as renewable energy, smart agriculture, and digital solutions can drive sustainable development. Investments in research and development are crucial for creating and scaling up these innovations
Science-based policymaking	Integrating scientific evidence into policymaking ensures that decisions are based on the best available knowledge, promoting effective and efficient solutions
Enhancing global cooperation and partnerships	
Strengthening multilateralism	Enhanced global cooperation and stronger support for multilateral institutions like the United Nations are necessary to address transnational challenges and ensure coordinated efforts toward the SDGs
Public-private partnerships	Engaging the private sector through partnerships can mobilize additional resources and expertise, fostering innovation and scaling up sustainable development initiatives
Empowering communities and ensuring inclusivity	
Inclusive participation	Ensuring that all stakeholders, especially marginalized and vulnerable groups, are actively involved in decision-making processes enhances the relevance and acceptance of sustainable development initiatives
Education and capacity-building	Investing in education and capacity-building programs empowers communities to participate effectively in sustainable development and adapt to changes
Addressing social and economic inequities	
Reducing inequalities	Targeted policies to reduce economic and social inequalities are essential for achieving the SDGs. This includes measures to improve access to education, healthcare, and economic opportunities for disadvantaged groups
Social protection systems	Strengthening social protection systems can mitigate the impacts of economic shocks and ensure that vulnerable populations are not left behind

Source: Created by authors according to Sustainable Development Report (2024), UN (2021), Kamruzzaman (2020), Independent Group of Scientists (2023), Stevenson et al. (2021), UNDP (2020), Smith and Watson (2022)

Table 2.8 Definitions of sustainable consumption

	Definition	Author
1	Sustainable consumption means meeting the needs of present generations without compromising the ability of future generations to meet their own needs, focusing on the efficiency and sustainability of resource use.	World Commission on Environment and Development (1987)
2	Sustainable consumption and production focuses on enhancing resource and energy efficiency, supporting the development of sustainable infrastructure, and ensuring access to essential services, environmentally responsible employment, and improved living standards for everyone.	United Nations Environment Programme (2021)
3	Sustainable consumption refers to the use of products and services that fulfill fundamental needs and enhance overall quality of life, while significantly reducing the reliance on natural resources and harmful substances, as well as limiting waste and pollutant emissions throughout their entire life cycle—thereby safeguarding the ability of future generations to meet their own needs.	Geissdoerfer et al. (2020)
4	Sustainable consumption encompasses behaviors and choices that aim to reduce individual and collective environmental impacts while enhancing social and economic well-being	Mont and Heiskanen (2021)
5	Sustainable consumption involves the adoption of consumption patterns and behaviors that contribute to reducing environmental impacts and promoting social equity and economic viability.	Verplanken and Roy (2015a, 2015b)
6	Sustainable consumption is about the search for, and the implementation of, a set of policies and practices that support the consumption of goods and services that meet basic needs and improve quality of life while minimizing the use of natural resources and toxic materials as well as the emissions of waste and pollutants.	Jackson (2006)
7	Sustainable consumption seeks to reduce the ecological footprint by altering individual and collective consumption patterns, emphasizing the importance of reducing, reusing, and recycling	Peattie and Collins (2009)
8	Sustainable consumption involves practices and policies that support the purchase and use of products and services that have a minimal impact on the environment and promote social well-being.	Tukker et al. (2008)
9	Sustainable consumption is about changing our consumption habits to reduce environmental impact and ensure that the Earth's resources are preserved for future generations, while also promoting social equity and economic sustainability	European Environment Agency

Source: Created by authors

development that seeks to balance economic growth, environmental protection, and social well-being. Key aspects of sustainable consumption are assumed in Table 2.9.

Sustainable consumption focuses on using goods and services that meet basic needs while minimizing the environmental impact and ensuring social equity. Resource efficiency is a key aspect of promoting the effective use of materials and energy to reduce waste and emissions (Geissdoerfer et al., 2020). Reducing environmental impact involves choosing products with lower carbon footprints and supporting practices like sustainable agriculture and renewable energy. Promoting social equity ensures that consumption patterns benefit all, including marginalized

Table 2.9 Key aspects of sustainable consumption

Resource efficiency	
Definition and importance	Resource efficiency aims to reduce the environmental impact of consumption by using resources more effectively and efficiently. It involves adopting practices that maximize the use of materials and energy while minimizing waste and emissions.
Examples	Energy-efficient appliances, water-saving technologies, and sustainable food production practices are prime examples of resource efficiency. The circular economy model, which focuses on reusing, repairing, refurbishing, and recycling, significantly contributes to resource efficiency
Reducing environmental impact	
Definition and importance	Reducing environmental impact involves making choices that decrease the ecological footprint of consumption activities. This includes selecting products and services with lower carbon footprints and reducing the consumption of high-impact resources such as fossil fuels.
Examples	Choosing renewable energy sources, using public transportation, and consuming locally produced and organic foods can significantly reduce environmental impacts. Promoting sustainable agriculture and reducing food waste are also critical components.
Promoting social equity	
Definition and importance	Sustainable consumption also aims to ensure social equity by promoting fair trade, labor rights, and access to essential services for all people, particularly marginalized and underserved communities.
Examples	Supporting fair trade products that ensure fair wages and working conditions for producers, and initiatives that provide access to clean water and energy in developing regions.
Behavioral change	
Definition and importance	Encouraging behavioral change toward more sustainable lifestyles is crucial for sustainable consumption. It involves raising awareness about the environmental and social impacts of consumption and promoting habits such as reducing, reusing, and recycling.
Examples	Educational campaigns that promote sustainable practices, incentives for using public transport, and social marketing strategies that shift consumer behavior toward sustainable choices.

Source: Created by authors according to Geissdoerfer et al. (2020), Markowski et al. (2023), UNEP (2021)

communities, by supporting fair trade and labor rights (UNEP, 2021). Behavioral change is crucial, encouraging habits like reducing, reusing, and recycling to foster sustainable lifestyles.

The principles of sustainable consumption are designed to guide individuals, businesses, and governments toward practices that meet current needs without compromising the ability of future generations to meet theirs. Key principles of sustainable consumption are shown in Fig. 2.9.

Resource efficiency—Optimize the use of resources to minimize waste and reduce environmental impact. This involves using materials and energy more efficiently in production processes and promoting products that require fewer resources over their lifecycle. *Minimization of waste*—Reduce the amount of waste generated

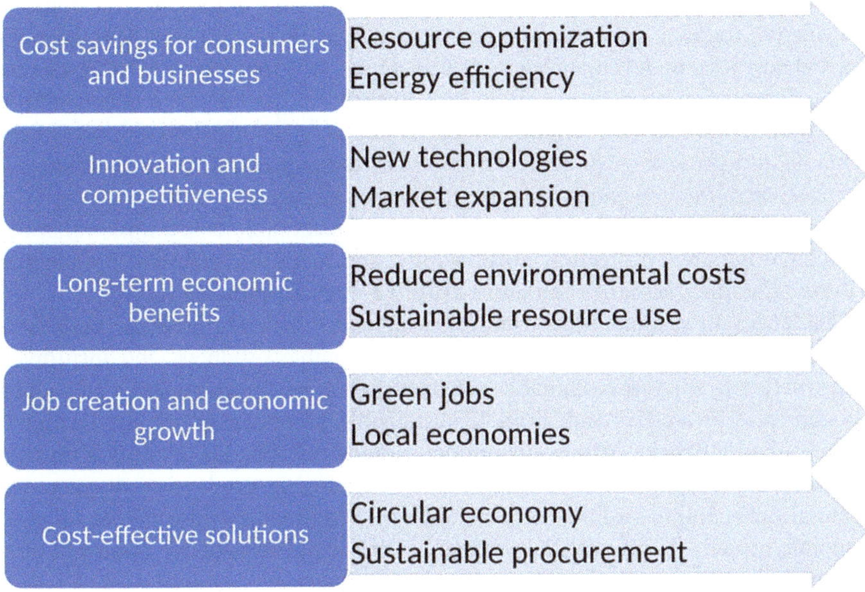

Fig. 2.9 Key principles of sustainable consumption. Source: Created by authors

and promote recycling and reuse. Encouraging practices such as recycling, composting, and the use of biodegradable materials helps minimize waste sent to landfills and reduce pollution. *Protection of natural resources*—Ensure the sustainable use of natural resources to preserve ecosystems and biodiversity. Sustainable consumption supports practices that protect forests, oceans, and other natural habitats, promoting biodiversity and ecosystem health. *Social equity and fair trade*—Promote fairness and equity in consumption patterns, ensuring that all individuals have access to essential resources and fair compensation. Supporting fair trade products ensures that producers in developing countries receive fair wages and work in safe conditions, contributing to social equity. *Consumer education and awareness*—Increase consumer awareness about the environmental and social impacts of their consumption choices. Educating consumers through campaigns, labeling, and public information can help them make more informed and sustainable choices. *Sustainable lifestyles*—Encourage lifestyles that reduce environmental impact and enhance quality of life. Promoting behaviors such as reducing meat consumption, using public transportation, and conserving energy can significantly reduce individual carbon footprints. *Corporate responsibility*—Encourage businesses to adopt sustainable practices in their operations and supply chains. Companies can reduce their environmental impact by implementing sustainable sourcing, reducing waste, and increasing energy efficiency. *Policy support and governance*—Develop and enforce policies that support sustainable consumption and production. Governments can implement regulations and incentives to promote sustainable practices, such as subsidies for renewable energy and penalties for pollution. *Innovation and circular economy*—Foster innovation and adopt circular economy principles to extend the lifecycle of products and materials. Encouraging the development of new technologies and business models that promote reuse, repair, and recycling can drive sustainability. *Transparency and accountability*—Ensure transparency and accountability in the production and consumption of goods and services. Businesses and governments should provide clear information about the sustainability of products and practices, enabling consumers to make informed choices.

These principles help create a framework for sustainable consumption that balances environmental protection, social equity, and economic viability. By adhering to these principles, societies can move toward a more sustainable future.

Challenges to sustainable consumption include a lack of consumer awareness, economic barriers such as higher costs of sustainable products, and insufficient infrastructure to support sustainable practices. Effective communication and education can raise awareness and promote sustainable practices. Economic incentives and subsidies can make sustainable options more accessible. Developing infrastructure like recycling facilities and promoting sustainable production practices are essential for enabling sustainable consumption. Sustainable consumption balances economic growth, environmental protection, and social well-being, contributing to a sustainable future.

Sustainable consumption has its benefits:

1. *Environmental protection*. Environmental protection is a fundamental component of sustainable consumption, focusing on minimizing the negative environmental impacts of consumption patterns and promoting practices that preserve natural resources and ecosystems. This aspect is crucial for maintaining the health of the planet and ensuring the well-being of current and future generations. Key aspects of environmental protection in sustainable consumption are shown in Table 2.10.

Environmental protection through sustainable consumption is vital for preserving natural resources, reducing pollution, conserving biodiversity, and mitigating climate change. These practices not only safeguard the environment but also provide significant health, economic, and social benefits. By adopting sustainable consumption habits, individuals and communities can contribute to a healthier planet and a more sustainable future.

Benefits of environmental protection in sustainable consumption:

- Improved ecosystem health. By reducing pollution and conserving natural resources, sustainable consumption helps maintain healthy ecosystems. This ensures the continued provision of ecosystem services such as clean air, water, and fertile soil, which are essential for human survival and well-being (Geissdoerfer et al., 2020).
- Enhanced public health. Reducing environmental pollutants leads to better public health outcomes. For example, minimizing air and water pollution reduces the incidence of respiratory and waterborne diseases, improving overall community health.

Table 2.10 Key aspects of environmental protection in sustainable consumption

Aspect of environmental protection	Explanation	Example
Reduction in resource depletion	Sustainable consumption practices aim to reduce the excessive use of natural resources, ensuring their availability for future generations. This includes adopting methods that maximize the efficiency of resource use and minimize waste.	The promotion of renewable energy sources like solar and wind power reduces reliance on fossil fuels, thereby conserving finite natural resources.
Decreased pollution and waste	Implementing sustainable consumption practices leads to a significant reduction in pollution and waste. This includes minimizing greenhouse gas emissions, reducing plastic pollution, and lowering toxic waste production.	Using biodegradable packaging materials instead of plastic can significantly reduce the pollution of oceans and landfills. Similarly, adopting zero-waste practices and encouraging recycling and composting can decrease overall waste.
Biodiversity conservation	Sustainable consumption supports biodiversity conservation by reducing habitat destruction and promoting the use of sustainably sourced products. This helps maintain the balance of ecosystems and protects various species from extinction.	Selecting products certified by entities such as the Forest Stewardship Council (FSC) guarantees that the wood and paper materials originate from forests managed in a way that balances environmental protection, social responsibility, and economic viability.
Climate change mitigation	Reducing the environmental impact of consumption contributes to mitigating climate change. This involves lowering carbon footprints through energy-efficient products, reducing meat consumption, and supporting sustainable transportation options.	Electric vehicles (EVs) produce fewer emissions than traditional gasoline-powered cars, contributing to lower greenhouse gas emissions and improved air quality.

Source: Created by authors

- Long-term economic benefits. Sustainable consumption can lead to long-term economic benefits by preventing the costs associated with environmental degradation. Healthy ecosystems provide resources and services that are crucial for economic activities such as agriculture, fishing, and tourism (UNEP, 2021).
- Resilience to environmental changes. Sustainable consumption practices enhance resilience to environmental changes by promoting adaptive and mitigation strategies. Communities that adopt sustainable practices are better prepared to cope with the impacts of climate change and other environmental challenges.

2. *Economic efficiency*. Economic efficiency in the context of sustainable consumption refers to the optimal use of resources to achieve the desired outcomes with minimal waste and cost. It involves making consumption practices not only environmentally sustainable but also economically viable, ensuring long-term

benefits for businesses, consumers, and society. Key aspects of economic efficiency in sustainable consumption are shown in Fig. 2.10.

Using energy-efficient appliances and technologies can lead to significant cost savings on utility bills for consumers and operational costs for businesses. For instance, LED lighting and energy-efficient HVAC systems reduce energy consumption and lower costs. Efficient use of resources in production processes minimizes waste, reducing the cost of raw materials and waste management. This can improve profitability for businesses and lower prices for consumers. Sustainable consumption drives innovation, leading to the development of new technologies and products that can enhance economic competitiveness. Companies investing in green

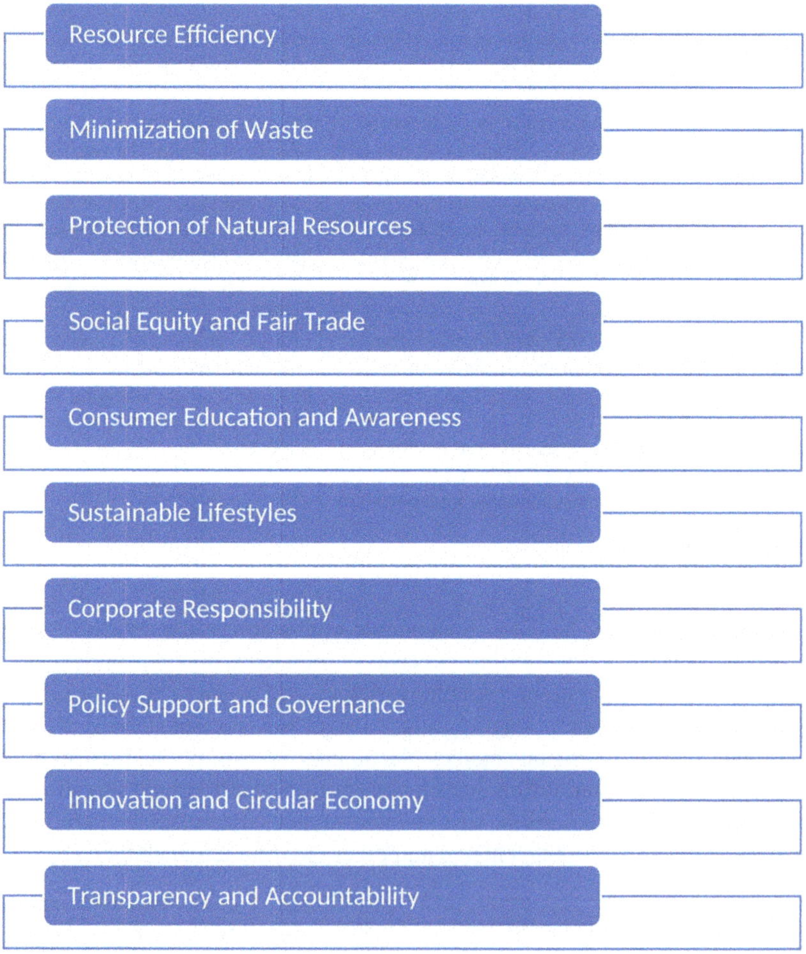

Fig. 2.10 Key aspects of economic efficiency in sustainable consumption. Source: Created by authors

technologies and sustainable products often gain a competitive edge in the market. Businesses that adopt sustainable practices can tap into new markets and consumer segments that prioritize sustainability, thereby expanding their customer base and increasing market share.

Sustainable consumption practices help avoid the costs associated with environmental degradation, such as healthcare costs from pollution-related diseases and the economic impacts of climate change. By ensuring the sustainable use of resources, economic efficiency supports long-term economic stability and growth. This prevents resource scarcity and ensures that resources remain available for future economic activities. The shift toward sustainable consumption creates new job opportunities in green industries such as renewable energy, sustainable agriculture, and waste management. These sectors are growing and contributing to economic development.

Supporting local businesses and producers through sustainable consumption strengthens local economies, fosters entrepreneurship, and promotes economic resilience. Implementing circular economy principles, such as recycling, reusing, and refurbishing, can provide cost-effective solutions for managing resources and waste. This reduces the need for new raw materials and lowers waste disposal costs. Businesses and governments adopting sustainable procurement practices can achieve cost savings through bulk purchasing of sustainable goods and services, which often have lower long-term costs due to their durability and efficiency.

Economic efficiency in sustainable consumption is about achieving optimal resource use to maximize benefits while minimizing costs and waste. It promotes cost savings, drives innovation, supports long-term economic stability, creates jobs, and offers cost-effective solutions. By integrating economic efficiency into sustainable consumption practices, businesses and consumers can achieve financial benefits while contributing to environmental sustainability.

3. *Social well-being.* Social well-being in the context of sustainable consumption involves ensuring that consumption patterns contribute positively to societal health, equity, and quality of life. Sustainable consumption practices aim to create social benefits that extend beyond the individual, fostering community resilience, equity, and overall societal health. Aspects of social well-being in sustainable consumption are shown in Table 2.11.

Social well-being is a critical component of sustainable consumption, encompassing health, equity, community resilience, and education. By promoting practices that improve health outcomes, enhance quality of life, support fair trade, and foster community resilience, sustainable consumption can significantly contribute to societal well-being. Educating consumers and encouraging sustainable behaviors are essential for achieving these benefits.

4. *Strengthening community resilience.* Community resilience refers to the capacity of a community to anticipate, prepare for, respond to, and recover from adverse situations such as economic downturns, environmental changes, and social disruptions. Sustainable consumption practices play a vital role in enhanc-

Table 2.11 Aspects of social well-being in sustainable consumption

Aspect of social well-being		Explanation	Example
Improved health outcomes	Healthier products	Sustainable consumption promotes the use of products that are safer and healthier for consumers. This includes organic foods free from harmful pesticides, non-toxic household products, and clean energy sources that reduce air pollution.	A shift to organic food consumption reduces exposure to chemical pesticides, leading to better health outcomes, such as lower rates of chronic diseases linked to chemical exposure (Smith-Spangler et al., 2012).
Enhanced quality of life	Sustainable living environments	Sustainable consumption includes supporting the development of sustainable communities that provide better living conditions through green spaces, reduced pollution, and access to essential services.	Urban green spaces improve mental health, reduce stress, and enhance overall well-being by providing areas for recreation and social interaction (World Health Organization, 2016).
Social equity and inclusion	Fair trade practices	Sustainable consumption promotes fair trade, ensuring that producers in developing countries receive fair compensation, work in safe conditions, and benefit from sustainable business practices.	Fair trade certification ensures that farmers and workers are paid fair wages, work under safe conditions, and have access to community development funds
Community resilience	Local economic support	Sustainable consumption encourages the support of local businesses and producers, which strengthens local economies and builds community resilience. This reduces dependence on global supply chains and enhances economic stability.	Supporting local farmers' markets not only provides fresh, locally sourced food but also strengthens local economies by keeping money within the community.
Education and awareness	Consumer education	Educating consumers about the environmental and social impacts of their consumption choices empowers them to make more informed decisions that contribute to social well-being.	Educational campaigns about the benefits of recycling and reducing plastic use can lead to widespread behavior changes that benefit the environment and society.

Source: Created by authors

ing community resilience by fostering local economies, promoting social cohesion, improving health outcomes, and ensuring environmental sustainability. Key aspects are shown in Table 2.12.

By supporting local economies, communities become less dependent on global markets and more self-sufficient, which enhances economic stability and reduces vulnerability to global economic fluctuations. Enhanced social cohesion and

Table 2.12 Aspects of community resilience in sustainable consumption

Aspect of community resilience		Definition and importance	Examples and impact
Supporting local economies	Economic stability	Strengthening local economies through sustainable consumption involves prioritizing locally produced goods and services, which helps keep financial resources within the community.	Supporting local farmers' markets, local craftspeople, and small businesses can enhance economic resilience by creating jobs and fostering economic stability. A study on farmers' markets in Canada found that they contribute significantly to local economies by keeping money within the community and supporting local farmers (Feagan & Morris, 2009).
Enhancing social cohesion	Community engagement	Sustainable consumption promotes community engagement by encouraging local initiatives such as community-supported agriculture (CSA) and cooperative businesses.	Community-supported agriculture programs allow consumers to purchase shares in a local farm's harvest, fostering a direct connection between consumers and farmers. This not only supports local agriculture but also builds a sense of community and shared purpose (Brunori et al., 2011).
Environmental stewardship	Resource management	Communities that adopt sustainable consumption practices are more likely to engage in sustainable resource management, which enhances environmental resilience.	Practices such as water conservation, recycling, and the use of renewable energy sources reduce the community's environmental footprint and ensure the sustainability of local resources. For instance, the adoption of community solar projects can provide clean energy while reducing dependence on external energy sources (IPCC, 2021a, 2021b).
Building local capacity	Education and skills development	Sustainable consumption practices often involve educating community members about sustainable practices and building skills that enhance local capacity.	Training programs in sustainable agriculture, renewable energy technologies, and waste management can build local expertise and capacity. Such initiatives not only promote sustainable practices but also create a knowledgeable and skilled workforce that can support the community's resilience (Schultz et al., 2013).

(continued)

Table 2.12 (continued)

Aspect of community resilience		Definition and importance	Examples and impact
Health and well-being	Healthy lifestyles	Promoting sustainable consumption can lead to healthier lifestyles by encouraging the consumption of organic and locally produced foods.	Consuming organic foods reduces exposure to harmful pesticides, while locally produced foods are often fresher and contain fewer preservatives. These practices contribute to better health outcomes and reduce healthcare costs (Smith-Spangler et al., 2012).

Source: Created by authors

community engagement create robust social networks that can mobilize resources quickly and efficiently during crises, leading to faster recovery and greater overall stability. Sustainable consumption practices lead to better resource management and reduced environmental impact, contributing to long-term environmental sustainability and resilience to climate change. Communities practicing sustainable consumption see improved health outcomes due to healthier diets and reduced pollution, which decreases the burden on healthcare systems and enhances quality of life.

Strengthening community resilience through sustainable consumption involves supporting local economies, enhancing social cohesion, promoting environmental stewardship, building local capacity, and improving health and well-being. These practices not only make communities more resilient to economic, social, and environmental disruptions but also contribute to sustainable development goals. By adopting sustainable consumption, communities can create a robust foundation for enduring stability and prosperity.

Overcoming barriers (Table 2.13) to sustainable consumption involves addressing economic, social, and informational challenges that prevent individuals and communities from adopting sustainable practices.

Overcoming barriers to sustainable consumption requires a multifaceted approach that includes raising consumer awareness, addressing economic barriers, developing necessary infrastructure, and encouraging behavioral change. By implementing these strategies, we can promote sustainable consumption practices that benefit both individuals and the planet.

Sustainable consumption is intricately linked to several Sustainable Development Goals (SDGs) (Table 2.14) as it directly and indirectly influences economic, social, and environmental sustainability.

Sustainable consumption is closely linked to achieving the Sustainable Development Goals (SDGs) by promoting resource efficiency, reducing waste, and ensuring equitable access to resources. It supports SDG 1 (No poverty) and SDG 2 (Zero hunger) by encouraging fair trade and local food production, which enhance economic stability and food security. In relation to SDG 3 (Good health and well-being), sustainable consumption promotes healthier lifestyles through the

Table 2.13 Strategies to tackle barriers to sustainable consumption

Challenge	Solutions	
Increasing consumer awareness and education		
Many consumers lack knowledge about the environmental and social impacts of their consumption choices.	Education campaigns	Governments and NGOs can run public awareness campaigns highlighting the benefits of sustainable consumption and the environmental impact of different products
	School curricula	Integrating sustainability topics into school curricula can educate the younger generation about sustainable consumption from an early age
	Product labeling	Clear and informative labeling on products can help consumers make more informed choices. Labels should provide information on the environmental impact, such as carbon footprint, and social aspects, like fair trade certification
Addressing economic barriers		
Sustainable products often cost more than conventional alternatives, making them less accessible to many consumers.	Subsidies and incentives	Governments can provide subsidies and financial incentives to reduce the cost of sustainable products, making them more competitive with conventional options
	Economies of scale	Encouraging the production and consumption of sustainable products can lead to economies of scale, reducing costs over time. This can be achieved through policies that promote green technologies and sustainable practices in industries
	Sustainable financing	Financial institutions can offer favorable loan terms and investment opportunities for businesses and consumers who adopt sustainable practices. Green bonds and sustainability-linked loans are examples of financial instruments that can support sustainable consumption
Developing infrastructure and availability		
Limited infrastructure and availability of sustainable products and services can restrict consumer choices.	Infrastructure investment	Governments and private sectors need to invest in infrastructure that supports sustainable consumption, such as recycling facilities, public transportation, and renewable energy systems
	Local production	Encouraging local production of sustainable goods can reduce transportation emissions and make sustainable products more accessible. Initiatives like community-supported agriculture (CSA) programs can help achieve this
	Retailer partnerships	Partnering with retailers to increase the availability of sustainable products in stores can help consumers make sustainable choices more easily. Retailers can be encouraged to stock more sustainable options through incentives and policy support
Overcoming behavioral resistance		

(continued)

Table 2.13 (continued)

Challenge	Solutions	
Long-standing habits and resistance to change can hinder the adoption of sustainable consumption practices.	Behavioral nudges	Implementing behavioral nudges, such as default options for sustainable products or small incentives for sustainable choices, can influence consumer behavior subtly and effectively
	Community-based initiatives	Engaging communities in sustainability initiatives can create a culture of sustainability and collective action. Community programs and peer influence can help change behaviors and foster sustainable practices
	Policy measures	Governments can implement policies that make sustainable choices easier and less convenient. This can include regulations that phase out unsustainable products, such as single-use plastics, and policies that promote sustainable alternatives

Source: Created by authors according to Schultz et al. (2021), Verplanken and Roy (2015a, 2015b), UNEP (2021), Geissdoerfer et al. (2020), OECD (2022)

consumption of organic and less processed foods. By adopting energy-efficient products and renewable energy sources, it contributes to SDG 7 (Affordable and clean energy) and helps mitigate climate change, addressing SDG 13 (Climate action).

Sustainable consumption also drives economic growth and job creation in green industries, supporting SDG 8 (Decent work and economic growth) and SDG 9 (Industry, innovation, and infrastructure) through innovation and sustainable practices. It fosters the development of sustainable cities and communities (SDG 11) by promoting efficient resource use and reducing waste. By directly addressing the need for responsible consumption and production patterns, it fulfills the aims of SDG 12 (Responsible consumption and production). Furthermore, sustainable consumption practices help protect marine and terrestrial ecosystems, contributing to SDG 14 (Life below water) and SDG 15 (Life on land). Finally, achieving sustainable consumption requires robust partnerships, aligning with SDG 17 (Partnerships for the Goals) to foster collaboration among governments, businesses, and civil society.

Promoting consumer education about sustainable consumption is essential for encouraging environmentally and socially responsible behaviors. There are several strategies to effectively educate consumers (see Fig. 2.11).

Promoting consumer education about sustainable consumption requires a multifaceted approach that includes public awareness campaigns, educational programs, clear product labeling, corporate responsibility, government policies, and behavioral insights. By implementing these strategies, we can empower consumers to make informed choices that contribute to environmental sustainability and social well-being.

Table 2.14 Sustainable consumption link with sustainable development goals

Sustainable development goal	Link with sustainable consumption	Example
SDG 1: No poverty	Sustainable consumption practices can reduce poverty by promoting fair trade, supporting local economies, and ensuring equitable access to resources.	Fair trade initiatives ensure that producers in developing countries receive fair wages, contributing to poverty reduction.
SDG 2: Zero hunger	Sustainable consumption promotes food security and sustainable agriculture, ensuring that food systems are resilient and capable of feeding the growing population.	Supporting local food production and reducing food waste are key components of sustainable consumption that help ensure food availability and affordability
SDG 3: Good health and well-being	Sustainable consumption reduces exposure to harmful substances and promotes healthier lifestyles through the consumption of organic and less processed foods.	Choosing organic foods reduces the intake of pesticides and chemicals, leading to better health outcomes
SDG 7: Affordable and clean energy	Sustainable consumption includes using energy-efficient products and renewable energy sources, which contribute to energy savings and reduce greenhouse gas emissions.	Adoption of solar panels and energy-efficient appliances in households reduces energy consumption and supports cleaner energy initiatives
SDG 8: Decent work and economic growth	Sustainable consumption can drive economic growth by creating green jobs and supporting sustainable business practices.	The growth of the renewable energy sector has created millions of jobs globally, contributing to economic growth and sustainability
SDG 9: Industry, innovation, and infrastructure	Sustainable consumption encourages industries to innovate and adopt sustainable practices, leading to more resilient infrastructure and industrialization.	Circular economy models promote the reuse and recycling of materials, fostering innovation in product design and industrial processes
SDG 11: Sustainable cities and communities	Sustainable consumption supports the development of sustainable cities by promoting efficient resource use, reducing waste, and enhancing the quality of life.	Urban farming and community gardens contribute to local food production and green spaces in cities, promoting sustainability and community engagement
SDG 12: Responsible consumption and production	This SDG is directly focused on ensuring sustainable consumption and production patterns by reducing waste and promoting resource efficiency.	Policies and initiatives that encourage recycling, composting, and sustainable sourcing of materials directly support this goal
SDG 13: Climate action	Sustainable consumption helps mitigate climate change by reducing greenhouse gas emissions and promoting low-carbon lifestyles.	Reducing meat consumption and choosing plant-based diets significantly lowers the carbon footprint associated with food production
SDG 14: Life below water	Reducing plastic use and promoting sustainable seafood consumption protect marine ecosystems and reduce pollution in oceans.	Choosing products with less plastic packaging and supporting sustainable fisheries help preserve marine biodiversity

(continued)

Table 2.14 (continued)

Sustainable development goal	Link with sustainable consumption	Example
SDG 15: Life on land	Sustainable consumption promotes the conservation of terrestrial ecosystems by supporting sustainable agriculture and forestry practices.	Buying FSC-certified wood products ensures that forests are managed sustainably, protecting biodiversity and reducing deforestation
SDG 17: Partnerships for the goals	Achieving sustainable consumption requires collaboration between governments, businesses, and civil society to implement sustainable practices and policies.	Multi-stakeholder partnerships and global initiatives like the United Nations Global Compact foster collaboration and commitment to sustainability goals

Source: Created by authors according to Smith-Spangler et al. (2012), IEA (2021), UNEP (2021), Geissdoerfer et al. (2020), IPCC (2021a, 2021b), WWF (2022a, 2022b)

2.3 Sustainable Production

Sustainable production involves generating goods and services through methods that minimize pollution, preserve energy and natural resources, ensure economic feasibility, and promote safety and well-being for workers, communities, and consumers. It also aims to provide socially meaningful and creatively fulfilling employment for all involved. It is a comprehensive approach that encompasses environmental, economic, and social dimensions of sustainability. According to Sustainability Reporting Guidelines (UNEP, 2017), sustainable production involves the efficient use of natural resources, minimizing waste and pollution, and ensuring that production processes do not harm the environment or human health. According to the Organization for Economic Co-operation and Development (OECD, 2008), sustainable production refers to the manufacture of goods and services through processes that avoid pollution, use energy and natural resources efficiently, remain economically sustainable, and ensure safety and well-being for workers, consumers, and communities, while also offering socially meaningful and creatively satisfying work environments. According to the International Institute for Sustainable Development (IISD, 2019), sustainable production means integrating economic growth, social inclusion, and environmental protection. It is about making production processes more efficient and sustainable, while also ensuring fair labor practices and economic viability.

Sustainable production is defined and evaluated according to three dimensions of sustainable development: environmental, economic, and social (Fig. 2.12).

The environmental dimension includes resource efficiency, waste minimization, and pollution prevention. Resource efficiency in sustainable production involves optimizing the use of resources throughout the production process to minimize waste and environmental impact. It encompasses a range of strategies and practices aimed at achieving the most productive and sustainable use of natural resources.

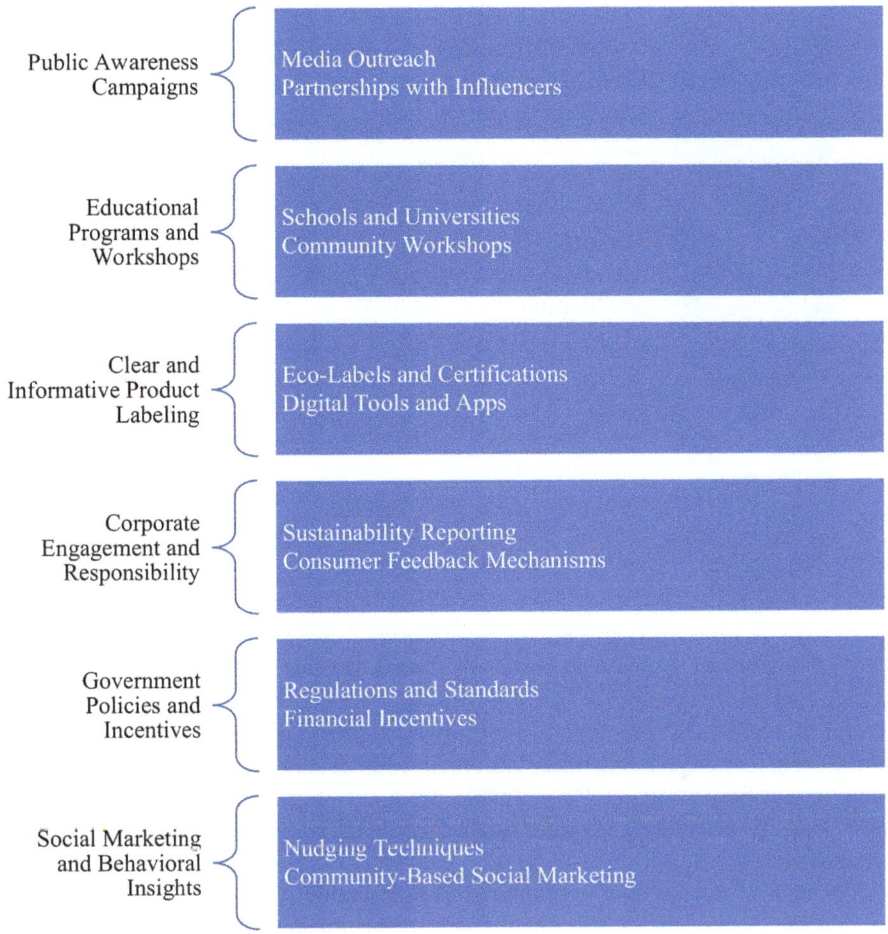

Fig. 2.11 Strategies to effectively educate consumers about sustainable consumption. Source: Created by authors

Resource efficiency refers to using the Earth's limited resources sustainably while minimizing environmental impact. It involves producing more with less by optimizing the use of materials, energy, and water throughout the production cycle. Strategies for achieving resource efficiency are shown in Table 2.15.

The benefits of resource efficiency can be seen in Fig. 2.13. Resource-efficient practices can lead to substantial cost savings by reducing material and energy costs, decreasing waste disposal expenses, and improving process efficiency. Businesses that adopt resource-efficient practices often gain a competitive edge by lowering production costs and improving product quality. Efficient use of resources reduces the extraction and processing of raw materials, thereby minimizing environmental degradation and pollution. Conservation of natural resources helps conserve finite

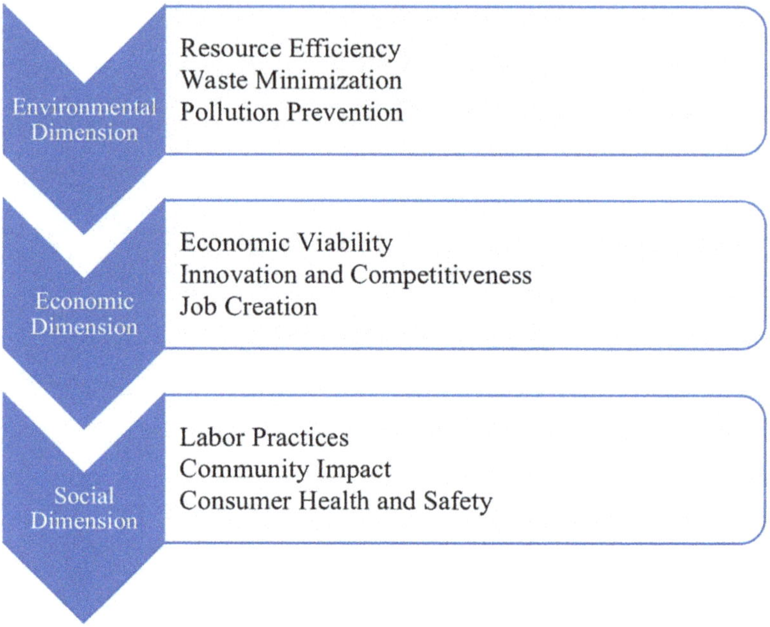

Fig. 2.12 Dimensions of sustainable production. Source: Created by authors

natural resources, ensuring their availability for future generations. The transition to more resource-efficient practices can create jobs in new industries such as recycling, renewable energy, and sustainable product design. Reducing pollution and waste leads to better air and water quality, contributing to improved public health outcomes.

Resource efficiency is a cornerstone of sustainable production, promoting the optimal use of materials, energy, and water to minimize environmental impact and enhance economic viability. By adopting cleaner production, lean manufacturing, energy efficiency, and material efficiency practices, businesses can achieve significant environmental, economic, and social benefits. Overcoming the challenges associated with resource efficiency requires concerted efforts from governments, businesses, and communities to provide the necessary support and incentives.

Processes are designed to minimize waste generation through techniques such as recycling, reuse, and remanufacturing. The aim is to create a circular economy where materials are kept in use for as long as possible. *Waste minimization* is a critical component of sustainable production, focusing on reducing the amount of waste generated during the production process. This strategy not only conserves resources and energy but also minimizes the environmental impact of production activities. Strategies for achieving waste minimization are shown in Table 2.16.

As can be seen from Fig. 2.14, minimizing waste reduces pollution in landfills, water bodies, and the atmosphere, contributing to a cleaner environment. Efficient use of materials conserves natural resources, reducing the need for raw material

Table 2.15 Strategies for achieving resource efficiency

Strategy for achieving resource efficiency	Concept	Example
Cleaner production	Cleaner production involves implementing processes that reduce waste and emissions, increase energy efficiency, and minimize the use of hazardous substances. This proactive approach focuses on preventing pollution at the source rather than dealing with it after it has been created	Adopting closed-loop systems where waste materials are recycled back into the production process rather than being discarded.
Lean manufacturing	Lean manufacturing aims to maximize efficiency by eliminating waste, improving processes, and optimizing resource use. It emphasizes continuous improvement, value stream mapping, and just-in-time production to reduce inventory and resource consumption.	Toyota's production system, which minimizes waste through efficient inventory management and streamlined production processes.
Energy efficiency	Enhancing energy efficiency involves using less energy to perform the same task or produce the same amount of output. This can be achieved through technological upgrades, process improvements, and energy management practices.	Implementing energy-efficient lighting, heating, and cooling systems in manufacturing facilities.
Material efficiency	Material efficiency focuses on optimizing the use of raw materials to reduce waste and improve the lifecycle performance of products. This includes designing products for longer life, using recycled materials, and reducing material input per unit of output.	Designing packaging that uses less material while maintaining functionality, or using recycled metals in production.

Source: Created by authors according to Tang et al. (2024), Sanz-Torro et al. (2025)

extraction and processing. Reducing waste leads to cost savings in raw materials, waste disposal, and energy consumption. Businesses can also save money through improved efficiency and reduced regulatory compliance costs. Recycling and reusing waste materials can create new revenue streams. For example, selling recycled materials or energy generated from waste can add to a company's income. The recycling and waste management industries can create jobs and contribute to economic development. Reducing waste and pollution leads to healthier communities by decreasing exposure to harmful substances and improving air and water quality.

Waste management faces challenges because implementing waste minimization strategies can require significant upfront investment in new technologies and processes. Achieving waste minimization often requires changing long-standing practices and behaviors within organizations and communities, and some materials and processes are more challenging to recycle or reuse due to technical limitations. However, governments can provide grants, subsidies, and tax breaks to support businesses in adopting waste minimization practices, providing education and training to employees and communities can help overcome resistance to change and

Fig. 2.13 Benefits of resource efficiency. Source: Created by authors according to van Ewijk (2018)

build support for waste minimization initiatives, and investing in R&D can help overcome technical barriers by developing new recycling technologies and more efficient production processes.

Waste minimization is a crucial aspect of sustainable production, offering significant environmental, economic, and social benefits. By adopting strategies such as source reduction, recycling and reuse, lean manufacturing, closed-loop systems, sustainable packaging, and energy recovery, businesses can reduce their environmental footprint, save costs, and contribute to a more sustainable future. Overcoming the challenges associated with waste minimization requires a combination of financial incentives, education, and technological innovation.

Sustainable production aims to prevent pollution at its source. This includes reducing emissions of greenhouse gases, toxic chemicals, and other pollutants that can harm the environment and human health. *Pollution prevention* is a critical component of sustainable production, focusing on eliminating or reducing the generation of pollutants at the source rather than managing pollution after it has been created. This approach not only benefits the environment but also enhances economic efficiency and social well-being. Below is an expanded look at pollution prevention, including key strategies, benefits, challenges, and solutions. Strategies for achieving pollution prevention are shown in Table 2.17.

Figure 2.15 shows the benefit of pollution prevention as one of the environmental dimension elements of sustainable production (see Fig. 2.12).

Table 2.16 Strategies for achieving waste minimization

Strategy for achieving waste minimization	Definition	Example
Source reduction	Source reduction entails modifying the design, production, or usage of materials and products to minimize both the volume and hazardous nature of the waste produced.	Designing products with fewer materials, using non-toxic alternatives, and adopting manufacturing processes that generate less waste.
Recycling and reuse	Recycling converts waste materials into new products, while reuse involves using items again for the same or new purposes.	Recycling scrap metal in manufacturing, using recycled paper in packaging, and repurposing waste materials in construction.
Lean manufacturing	Lean manufacturing focuses on eliminating waste in all forms, including defects, overproduction, and unnecessary inventory.	Implementing just-in-time production to reduce excess inventory and adopting 5S methodology to improve workplace organization and efficiency.
Closed-loop systems	Closed-loop systems ensure that waste materials are reintroduced into the production process, creating a circular economy.	Recycling wastewater in manufacturing plants and using by-products from one process as raw materials in another.
Sustainable packaging	Sustainable packaging involves designing packaging materials that reduce environmental impact and waste.	Using biodegradable materials, reducing packaging size, and designing for recyclability.
Energy recovery	Energy recovery involves converting waste materials into usable energy, such as electricity or heat.	Incinerating waste to produce steam for electricity generation and using anaerobic digestion to convert organic waste into biogas.

Source: Created by authors according to Mostaghimi and Behnamian (2023), Utsev et al. (2024)

Preventing pollution at the source reduces emissions of greenhouse gases, toxic chemicals, and other pollutants, contributing to cleaner air and water. Efficient use of raw materials and energy conserves natural resources and reduces the need for resource extraction and processing. Pollution prevention can lead to significant cost savings by reducing raw material and energy consumption, waste disposal costs, and regulatory compliance costs. Process modifications and cleaner technologies often improve production efficiency, leading to increased productivity and profitability. Reducing emissions and waste improves air and water quality, leading to better public health outcomes and enhanced quality of life for communities. Pollution prevention initiatives can create jobs in environmental management, green chemistry, and sustainable production sectors.

However, implementing pollution prevention measures can require significant upfront investment in new technologies and process modifications. Some industries face technical challenges in adopting pollution prevention practices, particularly in

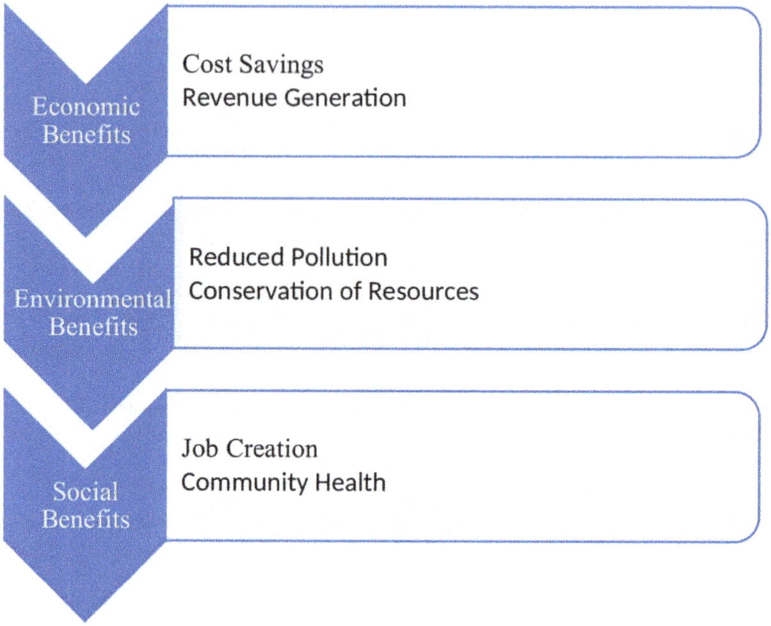

Fig. 2.14 Benefits of waste minimization. Source: Created by authors

complex processes and with hazardous materials, and achieving pollution prevention often requires changing long-standing practices and behaviors within organizations.

Pollution prevention is a proactive approach that focuses on eliminating or reducing the generation of pollutants at the source. By implementing strategies such as source reduction, process modification, green chemistry, energy efficiency, and sustainable materials management, businesses can achieve significant environmental, economic, and social benefits. Overcoming the challenges associated with pollution prevention requires a combination of financial incentives, research and development, and education and training.

Sustainable production integrates economic, environmental, and social objectives to create a production system that is not only environmentally friendly and socially responsible but also economically viable (Fig. 2.12). The economic dimension focuses on ensuring that sustainable practices enhance economic viability, drive innovation and competitiveness, and create value for businesses and society.

Economic viability refers to the ability of a business to operate sustainably while maintaining profitability. For sustainable production to be widely adopted, it must make economic sense for businesses. Ensuring economic viability is crucial because businesses need to remain profitable to continue their operations and invest in sustainable practices. Strategies for achieving economic dimension goals are shown in Table 2.18.

Table 2.17 Strategies for achieving pollution prevention

Strategy for achieving pollution prevention	Definition	Example
Source reduction	Source reduction involves altering production processes, raw materials, and product designs to prevent pollution before it is created.	Substituting toxic raw materials with non-toxic alternatives, redesigning products to use fewer hazardous substances, and implementing cleaner production technologies.
Process modification	Modifying production processes to reduce the generation of pollutants.	Implementing closed-loop systems that recycle water and chemicals within the production process, improving equipment efficiency to reduce emissions, and optimizing process controls to minimize waste.
Green chemistry	Developing chemical products and processes in a way that minimizes or completely avoids the use and creation of hazardous substances.	Developing biodegradable chemicals, using safer solvents, and designing energy-efficient chemical processes.
Energy efficiency	Using energy more efficiently to reduce emissions from energy production and consumption.	Upgrading to energy-efficient equipment, using renewable energy sources, and implementing energy management systems.
Sustainable materials management	Managing materials throughout their lifecycle to minimize environmental impact.	Using recycled materials, designing products for longer lifespans, and implementing take-back programs for end-of life products.

Source: Created by authors according to Awewomom et al. (2024), Salvador and Barros (2019)

Innovation involves developing new products, processes, or technologies that improve efficiency and reduce environmental impact. Competitiveness refers to a business's ability to compete effectively in the market by offering superior value through sustainable practices. Innovation and competitiveness are crucial for the long-term success and growth of businesses. Sustainable production drives innovation by encouraging the development of new technologies and practices that reduce costs and environmental impact (see Table 2.19). Value creation in the context of sustainable production means generating economic value while delivering environmental and social benefits. This holistic approach ensures that businesses thrive while contributing positively to society and the planet. Creating value through sustainable practices aligns business objectives with broader societal goals, fostering long-term sustainability and resilience (see Table 2.16).

The economic dimension of sustainable production encompasses ensuring economic viability, driving innovation and competitiveness, and creating value for businesses and society. By adopting strategies such as enhancing efficiency, investing in renewable technologies, developing eco-friendly products, and engaging

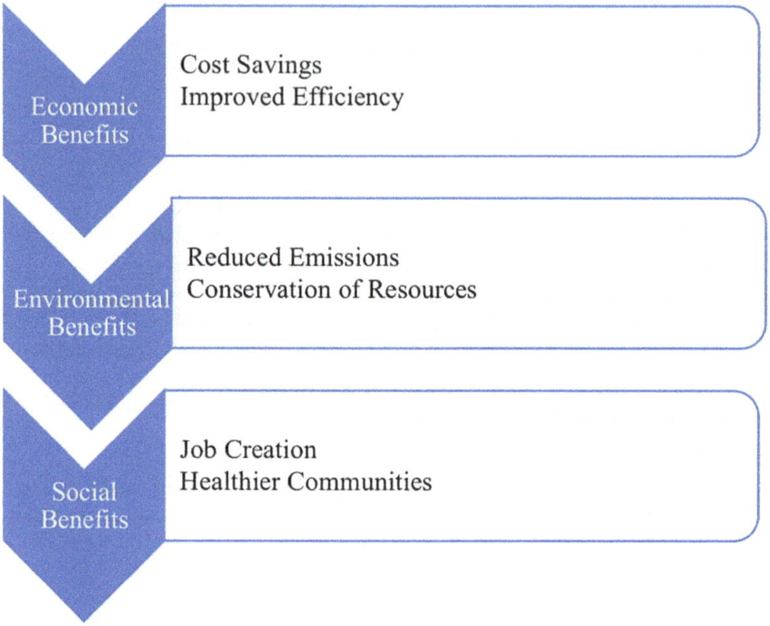

Fig. 2.15 Benefit of pollution prevention. Source: Created by authors

stakeholders, businesses can achieve sustainable growth and contribute to a more sustainable future.

According to Fig. 2.12, the social dimension of sustainable production includes labor practices, community impact, and consumer health and safety (Table 2.19).

The social dimension of sustainable production focuses on ensuring fair labor practices, positively impacting local communities, and protecting consumer health and safety. By adopting ethical labor practices, engaging in community development, and ensuring product safety, businesses can contribute to social sustainability while enhancing their reputation and competitiveness. Sustainable production practices not only benefit the environment and economy but also create a more just and equitable society.

In summary, sustainable production offers a wide array of benefits across environmental, economic, and social dimensions. Some of the key benefits are shown in Fig. 2.16.

Sustainable production provides numerous benefits across environmental, economic, social, and consumer dimensions. By reducing pollution, conserving resources, driving innovation, improving public health, promoting fair labor practices, and supporting community development, sustainable production contributes to a more sustainable and equitable world. Businesses that adopt sustainable practices can enhance their competitiveness, reduce risks, and build stronger relationships with consumers and communities.

Table 2.18 Strategies for achieving the economic dimension goals of sustainable production

Economic viability		
Cost savings through efficiency	Energy and resource efficiency	The adoption of energy-efficient technologies and the efficient use of resources can result in substantial financial savings. For example, implementing energy-saving lighting and optimized HVAC systems can significantly lower energy expenses.
	Waste reduction	Reducing waste not only minimizes environmental impact but also lowers disposal costs and can even generate revenue from recycling programs.
Access to new markets	Sustainable products	There is a growing market for sustainable products. Businesses that adopt sustainable practices can tap into this market, attracting environmentally conscious consumers and gaining a competitive edge
Risk management	Regulatory compliance	Adopting sustainable practices helps businesses comply with environmental regulations, avoiding fines and legal issues. This proactive approach can reduce financial risks associated with regulatory changes
	Reputation management	Engaging in sustainable practices can strengthen a company's public image, increasing its appeal to investors, consumers, and potential employees. A positive reputation, in turn, may contribute to higher sales and expanded investment prospects.
Innovation and competitiveness		
Technological advancements	Renewable energy technologies	Investing in renewable energy sources, such as solar and wind, can reduce energy costs and dependency on fossil fuels, enhancing competitiveness
	Smart manufacturing	Implementing smart manufacturing technologies, such as IoT and AI, can optimize production processes, reduce waste, and improve efficiency
Product innovation	Eco-friendly products	Developing products with lower environmental impacts, such as biodegradable packaging or energy-efficient appliances, meets the growing demand for sustainable goods and can open new markets
	Circular economy models	Adopting circular economy principles, where products are designed for reuse, refurbishment, and recycling, can differentiate a business from its competitors and create new revenue streams
Business model innovation	Service-based models	Shifting from product-based to service-based models, such as leasing or product-as-a-service, can reduce resource consumption and create long-term customer relationships
	Collaborative consumption	Encouraging shared use of products, such as car-sharing or tool libraries, can reduce production demand and increase product utilization rates
Value creation		

(continued)

Table 2.18 (continued)

Stakeholder engagement	Community involvement	Engaging with local communities and stakeholders can help businesses identify and address social and environmental concerns, enhancing their social license to operate
	Employee engagement	Involving employees in sustainability initiatives can boost morale, increase productivity, and attract talent who value corporate responsibility
Sustainable supply chains	Supplier collaboration	Working closely with suppliers to adopt sustainable practices can enhance supply chain resilience, reduce costs, and improve product quality
	Transparency and traceability	Implementing transparent and traceable supply chains ensures that products are sourced responsibly, enhancing brand reputation and customer trust
Long-term investment	Sustainable investments	Investing in sustainable infrastructure, technologies, and practices can yield long-term benefits, including cost savings, risk reduction, and enhanced competitiveness
	Innovation hubs	Establishing innovation hubs and centers for sustainable development can drive continuous improvement and foster a culture of sustainability within the business

Source: Created by authors according to Setyadi et al. (2025)

Sustainable production is closely aligned with the Sustainable Development Goals (SDGs), as it promotes practices that balance economic growth, social inclusion, and environmental protection (Table 2.20).

Sustainable production is integral to achieving the Sustainable Development Goals (SDGs) by promoting practices that balance economic growth, social inclusion, and environmental protection. It contributes to SDG 1 (No Poverty) by creating jobs and supporting fair wages, and to SDG 2 (Zero hunger) by enhancing food security through sustainable agriculture. By reducing pollution and using non-toxic materials, it supports SDG 3 (Good health and well-being). Sustainable production also aids SDG 6 (Clean water and sanitation) by minimizing water pollution and improving water use efficiency. It promotes the use of renewable energy and energy efficiency, aligning with SDG 7 (Affordable and clean energy).

Furthermore, it ensures decent work conditions and economic growth, supporting SDG 8 (Decent Work and economic growth). Sustainable production drives innovation and builds resilient infrastructure, contributing to SDG 9 (Industry, innovation, and infrastructure). It supports sustainable cities by reducing environmental impacts, thus aligning with SDG 11 (Sustainable cities and communities). By promoting resource efficiency and reducing waste, it directly addresses SDG 12 (Responsible consumption and production). Finally, sustainable production practices reduce greenhouse gas emissions, support SDG 13 (Climate action), and protect marine and terrestrial ecosystems, contributing to SDG 14 (Life below water) and SDG 15 (Life on land).

Table 2.19 Social dimension of sustainable production

Labor practices	Fair labor practices	Fair labor practices ensure that workers are treated ethically and fairly. This includes fair wages, reasonable working hours, and the right to collective bargaining.
	Safe working conditions	Safe working conditions involve providing a work environment that minimizes the risk of accidents and health issues. This includes proper training, safety equipment, and adherence to health and safety regulations.
	Non-discrimination and inclusivity	Non-discrimination policies ensure that all workers are treated equally regardless of gender, race, ethnicity, or other characteristics. Inclusivity practices involve creating a diverse and inclusive workplace.
Community impact	Local economic development	Sustainable production practices can stimulate local economies by creating jobs, supporting local suppliers, and investing in community infrastructure.
	Social programs and community engagement	Engaging with local communities and investing in social programs can enhance community well-being. This includes educational programs, healthcare initiatives, and community development projects.
	Environmental stewardship	Companies can positively impact local communities by engaging in environmental stewardship activities, such as protecting local ecosystems and promoting biodiversity.
Consumer health and safety	Product safety	Ensuring that products are safe for consumers and free from harmful substances. This includes rigorous testing and quality control measures.
	Health and wellness	Promoting health and wellness through products that contribute to a healthier lifestyle. This includes providing healthy food options, promoting physical activity, and avoiding harmful additives.
	Transparency and information	Providing clear and accurate information about products, including ingredients, sourcing, and production practices. Transparency helps consumers make informed decisions.

Source: Created by authors

Implementing sustainable practices involves a holistic approach that integrates environmental, economic, and social dimensions. Here are key steps to implement sustainable practices effectively:

1. Assess current practices. Conduct a sustainability audit: evaluate current operations to identify areas where resources are wasted, emissions are high, or social issues are present. (Example: Assess energy use, waste production, water consumption, and labor practices).
2. Set clear goals and objectives. Define sustainability goals: set specific, measurable, achievable, relevant, and time-bound (SMART) goals for sustainability. (Example: Aiming to reduce carbon emissions by 20% within 5 years or achieve zero waste to landfill by 2025).

Environmental Benefits

Reduction in Pollution and Waste
Conservation of Natural Resources
Biodiversity Protection

Economic Benefits

Cost Savings
Innovation and Competitive Advantage
Risk Management

Social Benefits

Improved Public Health
Fair Labor Practices
Community Development

Consumer Benefits

Product Safety and Quality
Transparency and Trust

Fig. 2.16 Some of the key benefits of sustainable production. Source: Created by authors

3. Develop a sustainability strategy. Create a comprehensive plan: develop a strategic plan that outlines the steps needed to achieve sustainability goals, including timelines, resources, and responsible parties. (Example: A strategy that includes energy efficiency upgrades, waste reduction initiatives, and supplier engagement programs).
4. Implement sustainable technologies. Invest in technology: implement technologies that enhance efficiency and reduce environmental impact. (Examples: Installing renewable energy systems (solar panels, wind turbines), upgrading to energy-efficient equipment, and adopting water recycling systems).
5. Optimize resource use. Enhance resource efficiency: use resources more efficiently to minimize waste and reduce costs. (Examples: Implementing lean manufacturing principles, optimizing logistics to reduce fuel consumption, and using materials that have lower environmental impacts).
6. Engage stakeholders. Involve employees and suppliers: engage employees, suppliers, and other stakeholders in sustainability initiatives. (Examples: Conducting training programs, establishing sustainability criteria for suppliers, and involving the community in sustainability projects).
7. Monitor and report progress. Track and communicate: regularly monitor progress toward sustainability goals and report on achievements and areas for improvement. (Examples: Using sustainability metrics, publishing annual sustainability reports, and using tools like the Global Reporting Initiative (GRI) framework).
8. Foster a culture of sustainability. Promote sustainable values: encourage a culture of sustainability within the organization by embedding sustainable practices into daily operations and decision-making. (Examples: Recognizing and

Table 2.20 Sustainable production link with sustainable development goals

Sustainable Development Goal	Link with sustainable consumption	Example
SDG 1: No poverty	Sustainable production can reduce poverty by creating jobs, supporting local economies, and ensuring fair wages and working conditions.	Fair trade practices ensure that workers in developing countries receive fair compensation, which helps lift them out of poverty.
SDG 2: Zero hunger	Sustainable agricultural practices improve food security and ensure sustainable food production systems.	Techniques such as organic farming, crop rotation, and sustainable land management enhance soil fertility and food productivity.
SDG 3: Good health and well-being	Reducing pollution and using non-toxic materials in production processes improves public health.	Companies that adopt green chemistry principles produce fewer harmful emissions, leading to cleaner air and water, which benefits public health.
SDG 6: Clean water and sanitation	Sustainable production minimizes water pollution and promotes efficient water use.	Industries implementing closed-loop water systems can significantly reduce water consumption and pollution, supporting clean water goals.
SDG 7: Affordable and clean energy	Sustainable production promotes the use of renewable energy and improves energy efficiency.	Manufacturing facilities that install solar panels and adopt energy-efficient technologies contribute to the clean energy transition.
SDG 8: Decent work and economic growth	Sustainable production practices ensure decent work conditions, enhance productivity, and support economic growth.	By promoting fair labor practices and investing in employee training, businesses can improve productivity and economic resilience.
SDG 9: Industry, innovation, and infrastructure	Sustainable production drives innovation and fosters the development of resilient infrastructure.	Adopting advanced manufacturing technologies such as IoT and AI can optimize production processes, leading to more resilient and efficient industries.
SDG 11: Sustainable cities and communities	Sustainable production supports the development of sustainable cities by reducing environmental impacts and promoting resource-efficient urban infrastructure.	Urban manufacturing centers that use sustainable practices can help reduce city-wide pollution and waste, contributing to more sustainable urban environments.
SDG 12: Responsible consumption and production	This SDG directly addresses sustainable production by promoting resource efficiency, reducing waste, and encouraging sustainable practices.	Implementing circular economy principles in production processes helps minimize waste and encourages the reuse of materials.
SDG 13: Climate action	Sustainable production practices reduce greenhouse gas emissions and enhance resilience to climate change.	Industries adopting energy-efficient technologies and renewable energy sources contribute to climate change mitigation efforts.

(continued)

Table 2.20 (continued)

Sustainable Development Goal	Link with sustainable consumption	Example
SDG 14: Life below water	Sustainable production reduces marine pollution and promotes the sustainable use of ocean resources.	Companies that manage their waste properly and reduce plastic use help prevent ocean pollution and protect marine ecosystems.
SDG 15: Life on land	Sustainable production practices protect terrestrial ecosystems and promote biodiversity.	Sustainable forestry practices, such as those certified by the Forest Stewardship Council (FSC), help protect forests and their biodiversity.
SDG 17: Partnerships for the goals	Achieving sustainable production requires collaboration among governments, businesses, and civil society.	Multi-stakeholder partnerships and global initiatives like the United Nations Global Compact foster collaboration and commitment to sustainability goals.

Source: Created by authors

rewarding sustainable behaviors, integrating sustainability into corporate values, and encouraging innovation in sustainability).

9. Collaborate and innovate. Partner for innovation: collaborate with other organizations, governments, and research institutions to drive innovation in sustainability. (Examples: Participating in industry-wide sustainability initiatives, joining sustainability-focused consortia, and investing in R&D for sustainable technologies).
10. Ensure compliance and continuous improvement. Stay compliant and adaptive: ensure compliance with environmental regulations and continuously seek ways to improve sustainability practices. (Examples: Staying updated with regulatory changes, conducting regular reviews of sustainability performance, and being open to adopting new sustainable technologies and practices).

Implementing sustainable practices requires a comprehensive and integrated approach. By assessing current practices, setting clear goals, developing a strategic plan, investing in technology, optimizing resource use, engaging stakeholders, monitoring progress, fostering a culture of sustainability, collaborating for innovation, and ensuring compliance, organizations can effectively transition to more sustainable operations.

The implementation of sustainable production principles faces barriers, which are summarized in Table 2.21.

Implementing sustainable production faces several barriers, including high initial costs, lack of technology and expertise, resistance to change, inconsistent regulations, and market competitiveness issues. Overcoming these barriers requires concerted efforts from businesses, governments, and consumers to invest in technology, provide financial incentives, raise awareness, and develop consistent regulations and standards.

Table 2.21 Main barriers across economic, social, technical, and regulatory dimensions

Barrier	Explanation	Impact
Economic barriers		
High initial costs	Implementing sustainable production often requires significant upfront investment in new technologies, infrastructure, and training.	These costs can be a deterrent for businesses, particularly small and medium-sized enterprises (SMEs), which may lack the capital to invest in sustainable practices.
Uncertain return on investment (ROI)	The financial benefits of sustainable production can take time to materialize, and the ROI can be uncertain.	Businesses may be hesitant to invest in sustainability without clear evidence of financial returns.
Technical barriers		
Lack of technology and expertise	Implementing sustainable production requires advanced technologies and technical expertise that may not be readily available.	Businesses may struggle to find or develop the necessary technology and skills to transition to sustainable practices.
Complexity of implementation	Sustainable production involves complex processes and systems that can be difficult to implement and manage.	The complexity can lead to operational challenges and increased costs.
Social barriers		
Resistance to change	Employees and management may resist changes to established practices and routines.	Resistance to change can slow down the implementation of sustainable practices and reduce their effectiveness.
Lack of consumer awareness and demand	Consumers may not be aware of the benefits of sustainable products, leading to lower demand.	Without strong consumer demand, businesses may be less motivated to invest in sustainable production.
Regulatory and policy barriers		
Inconsistent regulations and standards	Inconsistent regulations and standards across regions can create challenges for businesses operating in multiple markets.	Navigating different regulatory environments can increase costs and complexity.
Lack of government support and incentives	Insufficient government support and incentives for sustainable production can make it difficult for businesses to justify the transition.	Without adequate incentives, businesses may not see the financial benefits of sustainable practices.
Market barriers		
Market competitiveness	Sustainable products may be more expensive than conventional alternatives, making them less competitive in the market.	Higher prices can limit market penetration and reduce the potential impact of sustainable production.

(continued)

Table 2.21 (continued)

Barrier	Explanation	Impact
Supply chain challenges	Ensuring sustainability across the entire supply chain can be challenging, particularly for global businesses.	Supply chain issues can undermine efforts to implement sustainable production practices.

Source: Created by authors according to Leal Filho et al. (2022), Burri and Kugler (2023)

2.4 Circular Economy and Responsible Consumption

As businesses and communities increasingly embrace sustainable production, they encounter both opportunities and challenges. Sustainable production involves integrating environmental, economic, and social practices to reduce environmental impact, enhance economic viability, and promote social well-being. This approach plays a critical role in advancing several Sustainable Development Goals (SDGs), including the eradication of poverty (SDG 1), elimination of hunger (SDG 2), promotion of health and well-being (SDG 3), access to clean water and sanitation (SDG 6), provision of affordable and clean energy (SDG 7), support for decent work and economic growth (SDG 8), encouragement of innovation and resilient infrastructure (SDG 9), development of sustainable urban areas (SDG 11), fostering of responsible consumption and production patterns (SDG 12), action against climate change (SDG 13), conservation of marine ecosystems (SDG 14), and protection of terrestrial ecosystems (SDG 15). By aligning business strategies with these goals, companies can drive innovation, improve efficiency, and create a positive impact on society and the environment (Geissdoerfer et al., 2020; UNEP, 2021; OECD, 2022).

However, sustainable production is not without its challenges. High initial costs, technical barriers, resistance to change, and inconsistent regulations can hinder the implementation of sustainable practices. Overcoming these barriers requires concerted efforts from businesses, governments, and consumers to invest in sustainable technologies, provide financial incentives, raise awareness, and develop consistent regulations and standards (World Bank, 2020; IEA, 2021). Despite these challenges, the benefits of sustainable production—such as cost savings, innovation, competitive advantage, improved public health, fair labor practices, and community development—make it a crucial strategy for long-term sustainability and resilience.

As we transition from the concept of sustainable production, it is essential to explore the complementary framework of the circular economy. While sustainable production focuses on optimizing processes to minimize environmental impact, the circular economy takes a more systemic approach. It emphasizes the need to redesign economic systems to be restorative and regenerative by design. This means creating closed-loop systems where products, materials, and resources are reused, remanufactured, and recycled, minimizing waste and reducing the consumption of finite resources.

The circular economy aims to decouple economic growth from resource consumption, thereby fostering a more sustainable and resilient economy. It supports responsible consumption by encouraging consumers to make more sustainable choices and businesses to develop products that are durable, repairable, and recyclable. This paradigm shift not only addresses environmental challenges but also creates economic opportunities, driving innovation and competitiveness in new markets (UNEP, 2021; OECD, 2022). By integrating the principles of the circular economy with sustainable production, businesses can enhance their sustainability efforts, reduce costs, and contribute to a more sustainable future.

Historical overview of the emergence of the circular economy concept:

1. 1960s–1970s—early environmental awareness.

The concept of the circular economy has its roots in the environmental movements of the 1960s and 1970s, when concerns about pollution, resource depletion, and ecological degradation began to gain traction. The publication of Rachel Carson's "Silent Spring" in 1962 highlighted the detrimental effects of pesticides on the environment and sparked widespread environmental awareness. During this period, the notion of "limits to growth" was also explored, notably in the 1972 report by the Club of Rome, which emphasized the unsustainable nature of continuous economic and population growth given finite resources.

2. 1980s—introduction of industrial ecology. In the 1980s, the field of industrial ecology emerged, which examined the flow of materials and energy through industrial systems. This approach sought to optimize resource use and reduce environmental impacts by mimicking natural ecosystems, where waste from one process becomes input for another. The concept of industrial symbiosis, where waste streams from one industry are utilized as resources by another, became a key component of industrial ecology.
3. 1990s—the rise of the circular economy. The term "circular economy" began to take shape in the 1990s, influenced by several key developments:

   - Performance economy. Swiss architect and economist Walter Stahel introduced the concept of the "performance economy" in his 1982 report to the European Commission. He emphasized the importance of extending product life cycles through maintenance, repair, and remanufacturing, which would create jobs and reduce resource consumption.
   - Cradle to cradle. Chemist Michael Braungart and architect William McDonough popularized the "cradle to cradle" design philosophy in their 2002 book "Cradle to Cradle: Remaking the Way We Make Things." This approach advocates designing products with their entire lifecycle in mind, ensuring that all materials can be fully reused or recycled.
   - Natural capitalism. In their 1999 book "Natural Capitalism," Paul Hawken, Amory Lovins, and L. Hunter Lovins argued for a radical shift in the way businesses operate, proposing that economic systems should be designed to mimic natural ecosystems, where waste is minimized, and materials are continuously cycled.

4. 2000s—institutional and policy support. In the 2000s, the circular economy gained further traction with support from institutions and policymakers. The European Union began to integrate circular economy principles into its policies, culminating in the Circular Economy Action Plan launched in 2015, which aimed to "close the loop" of product lifecycles through greater recycling and reuse.
5. 2010s–present—mainstream adoption and global initiatives. The circular economy has continued to gain momentum in the 2010s and beyond, driven by global sustainability goals and increasing recognition of the economic benefits of resource efficiency. Key developments include:
   - Ellen MacArthur Foundation. Founded in 2010, the Ellen MacArthur Foundation has played a pivotal role in promoting the circular economy globally. The foundation has partnered with businesses, governments, and academia to develop circular economy frameworks and drive large-scale change (Ellen MacArthur Foundation, 2021).
   - Global goals. The adoption of the United Nations Sustainable Development Goals (SDGs) in 2015 has further embedded circular economy principles into global sustainability efforts. SDG 12, "Responsible Consumption and Production," directly aligns with circular economy practices (UN, 2015).
   - Corporate adoption. Many multinational corporations have adopted circular economy principles, integrating them into their business models to improve resource efficiency, reduce costs, and meet consumer demand for sustainable products. Companies like IKEA, Unilever, and Patagonia have implemented circular economy strategies, such as product take-back schemes and closed-loop manufacturing processes.

The concept of the circular economy has evolved over several decades, drawing on early environmental awareness, industrial ecology, and various economic theories advocating for resource efficiency and sustainability. Today, it represents a comprehensive approach to creating sustainable economic systems that prioritize long-term resource stewardship and environmental health.

The circular economy is built on several key principles that aim to create a regenerative system in which resources are reused, remanufactured, and recycled, minimizing waste and environmental impact. The key principles of a circular economy are shown in Table 2.22.

The circular economy principles aim to create a sustainable economic system where resources are continuously cycled, waste is minimized, and natural systems are regenerated. By designing out waste, keeping materials in use, using renewable energy, fostering system effectiveness, and supporting local economies, businesses and communities can contribute to a more sustainable and resilient future.

Designing out waste and pollution is a fundamental principle of the circular economy that focuses on eliminating waste at the design stage of products and processes. This principle emphasizes the need to rethink how products are designed, manufactured, and used to prevent waste generation and minimize pollution. By addressing waste and pollution from the beginning, businesses can create more

Table 2.22 Key principles of circular economy

Principle	Example
Design out waste and pollution	
Products and processes should be designed to minimize waste and pollution from the outset. This involves rethinking product design, material selection, and manufacturing processes to ensure that waste is not generated in the first place.	Designing products with fewer parts and materials makes them easier to disassemble and recycle.
Keep products and materials in use	
Extend the lifecycle of products and materials through reuse, repair, refurbishment, and remanufacturing. This principle emphasizes the need to keep resources circulating in the economy for as long as possible.	Implementing product take-back schemes where consumers return used products to the manufacturer for refurbishment or recycling
Regenerate natural systems	
Adopt practices that support and regenerate natural systems, ensuring that human activities contribute positively to the environment. This includes using renewable resources and enhancing biodiversity.	Agricultural practices that restore soil health and increase biodiversity, such as agroforestry and regenerative farming
Use renewable energy	
Transition to renewable energy sources to power production processes, reducing dependency on fossil fuels and minimizing carbon emissions.	Manufacturing facilities powered by solar or wind energy, which reduce greenhouse gas emissions and reliance on non-renewable energy sources
Foster system effectiveness	
Optimize the entire system rather than focusing on individual components. This involves considering the interconnectedness of different sectors and designing solutions that benefit the whole system.	Industrial symbiosis where the waste of one industry becomes the input for another, creating a network of mutually beneficial relationships
Prioritize regenerative resources	
Use resources that are renewable, recyclable, or biodegradable to ensure that the materials used in production can be reintegrated into the environment or reused in other forms.	Utilizing biodegradable packaging materials that can be composted after use, reducing the environmental impact of waste
Promote product as a service	
Shift from product ownership to product as a service, where consumers pay for the service a product provides rather than owning the product itself. This encourages manufacturers to produce durable and maintainable products.	Car-sharing services where users pay for the use of a vehicle rather than owning it, which can reduce the number of cars on the road and the resources needed to produce them
Support local economies and communities	
Strengthen local economies by sourcing materials locally, creating jobs, and supporting local businesses. This reduces transportation emissions and fosters economic resilience within communities.	Encouraging local sourcing of materials and production to boost local economies and reduce the carbon footprint associated with transportation

Source: Created by authors according to UNGC (2021), UNEP (2021), IEA (2021), Ellen MacArthur Foundation (2021)

sustainable products and systems that are efficient and environmentally friendly. Key strategies for designing out waste and pollution are represented in Fig. 2.17.

Designing out waste and pollution is a proactive approach that addresses environmental challenges at their source. By adopting sustainable product design, optimizing processes, using eco-friendly packaging, and implementing pollution prevention technologies, businesses can significantly reduce their environmental impact, enhance economic performance, and contribute to social well-being. This principle is crucial for transitioning to a circular economy and achieving long-term sustainability.

Keeping products and materials in use is a core principle of the circular economy that focuses on extending the lifecycle of products and materials to maximize their value and reduce waste. This involves practices such as reuse, repair, refurbishment,

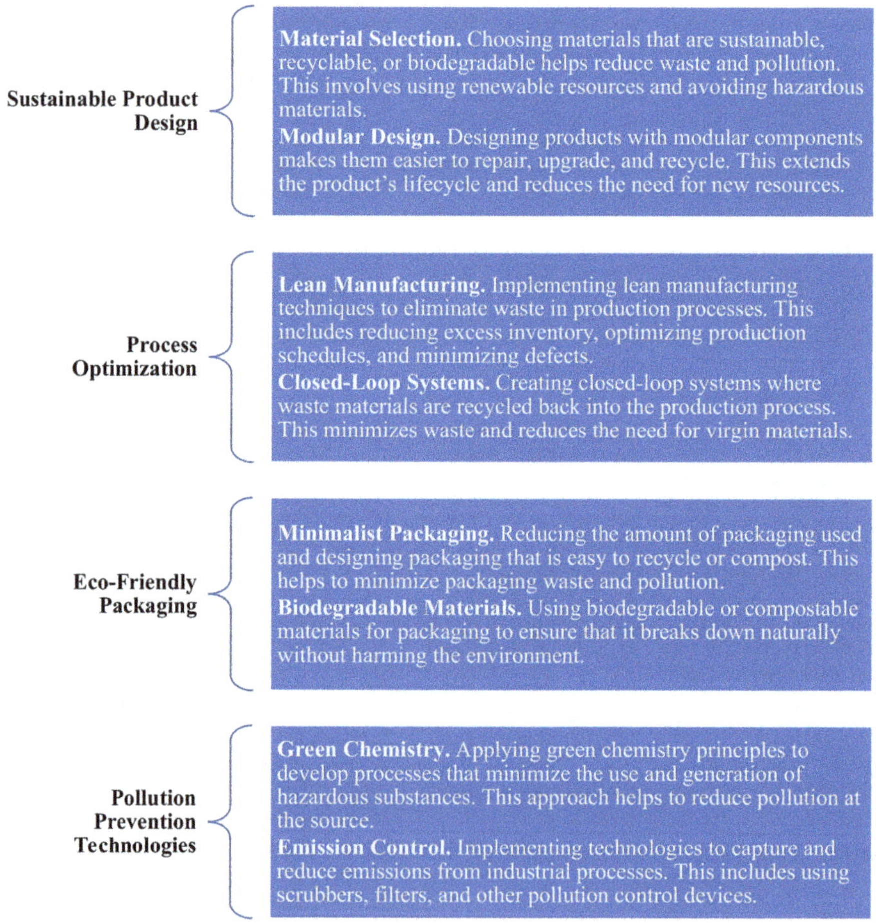

Fig. 2.17 Strategies for designing out waste and pollution. Source: Created by authors according to Hassan and Alashwal (2024)

remanufacturing, and recycling. The goal is to create a closed-loop system where products and materials continuously circulate within the economy, thereby reducing the need for new resources and minimizing environmental impact. Key strategies for keeping products and materials are represented in Fig. 2.18.

Keeping products and materials in use is a critical principle of the circular economy, focusing on maximizing the value of resources and minimizing waste. By adopting strategies such as product life extension, circular business models, material recovery, and eco-design, businesses and communities can significantly reduce their environmental impact, enhance economic resilience, and promote social well-being.

Regenerating natural systems is a vital principle of the circular economy that focuses on restoring and enhancing the health of ecosystems. This principle emphasizes using renewable resources, increasing biodiversity, and adopting practices that

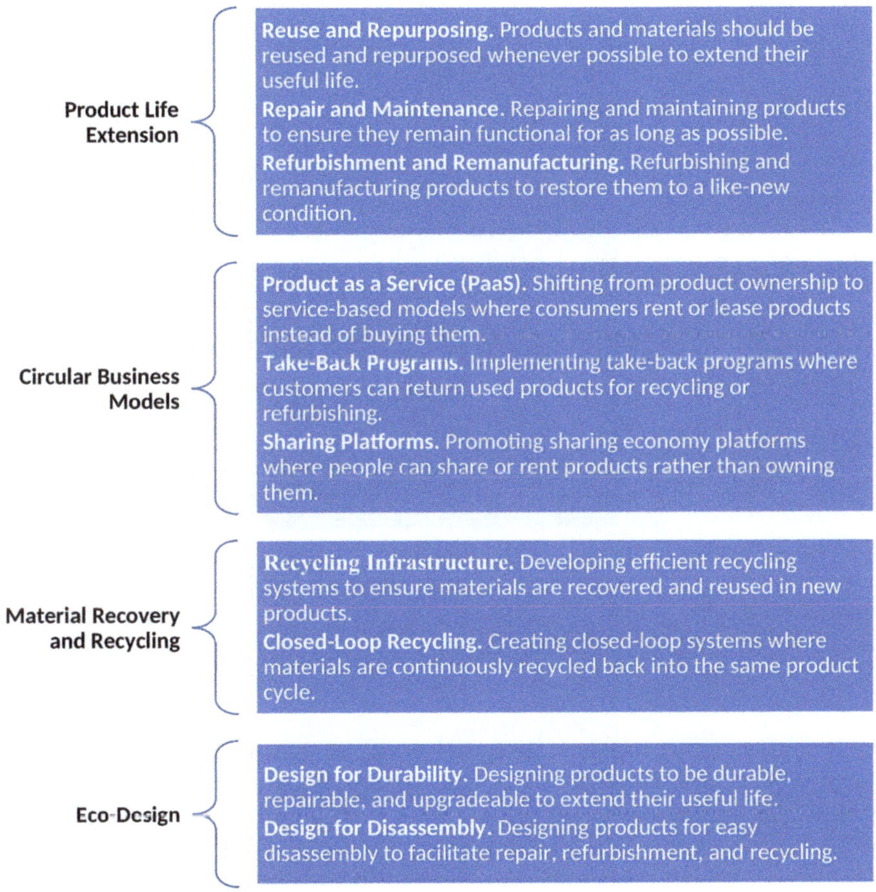

Fig. 2.18 Strategies for keeping products and materials. Source: Created by authors according to Fontana et al. (2021), Haase and Lythje (2022)

contribute positively to the environment. The goal is to create systems that are not only sustainable but also regenerative, ensuring that natural systems can replenish and thrive. Key strategies for regenerating natural systems are represented in Fig. 2.19.

Using this strategy (Fig. 2.19) allows for benefits along the three dimensions of sustainable development (Fig. 2.20).

Regenerating natural systems is a critical principle of the circular economy that focuses on restoring and enhancing the health of ecosystems. By adopting strategies such as using renewable resources, enhancing biodiversity, practicing circular agriculture, managing aquatic systems sustainably, and implementing forest management practices, businesses and communities can create systems that are not only sustainable but also regenerative. These practices contribute to environmental

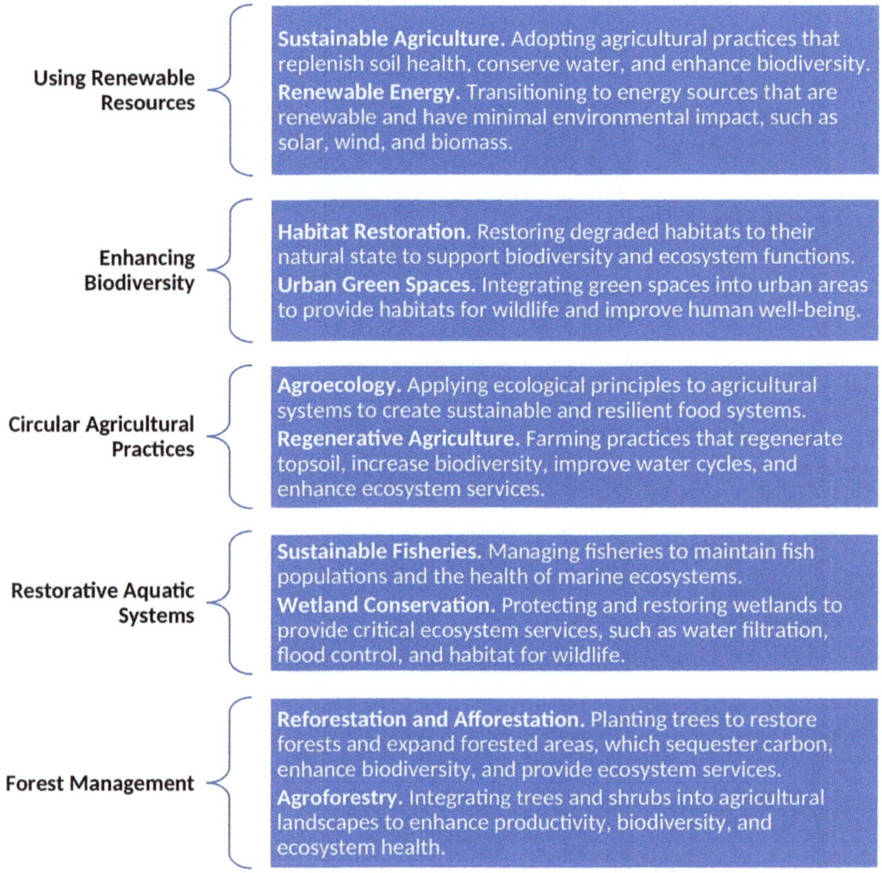

Fig. 2.19 Strategies for regenerating natural systems. Source: Created by authors according to Williams et al. (2024), Toner et al. (2023)

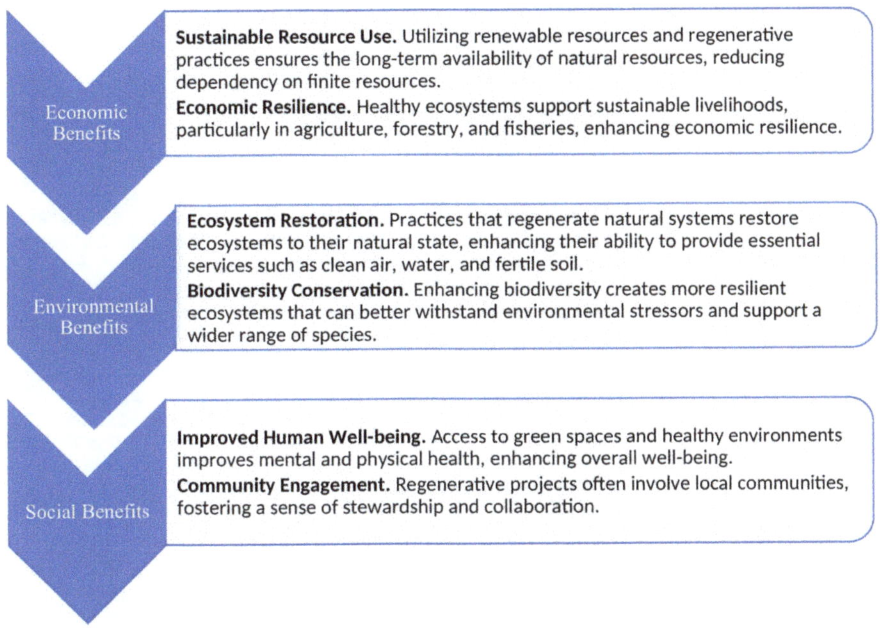

Fig. 2.20 Benefits of regenerating natural systems strategies. Source: Created by authors

health, economic resilience, and social well-being, supporting a more sustainable future.

Using renewable energy is one more principle of the circular economy that focuses on transitioning from fossil fuels to renewable sources of energy such as solar, wind, hydro, and biomass. This shift is essential for reducing greenhouse gas emissions, combating climate change, and creating a sustainable energy system that can support economic growth without depleting natural resources. Key strategies for using renewable energy are represented in Fig. 2.21.

Using renewable energy is a cornerstone of the circular economy, contributing to environmental sustainability, economic resilience, and social well-being. By adopting strategies such as solar and wind energy, hydropower, biomass energy, and geothermal energy, businesses and communities can significantly reduce their environmental footprint, enhance energy security, and create sustainable economic opportunities.

Fostering system effectiveness is the next principle of the circular economy that emphasizes optimizing entire systems rather than individual components. This holistic approach aims to maximize resource efficiency, reduce waste, and create synergies across different sectors. By considering the interconnectedness of various processes and industries, fostering system effectiveness can lead to more sustainable and resilient economic systems. Key strategies for fostering system effectiveness are represented in Fig. 2.22.

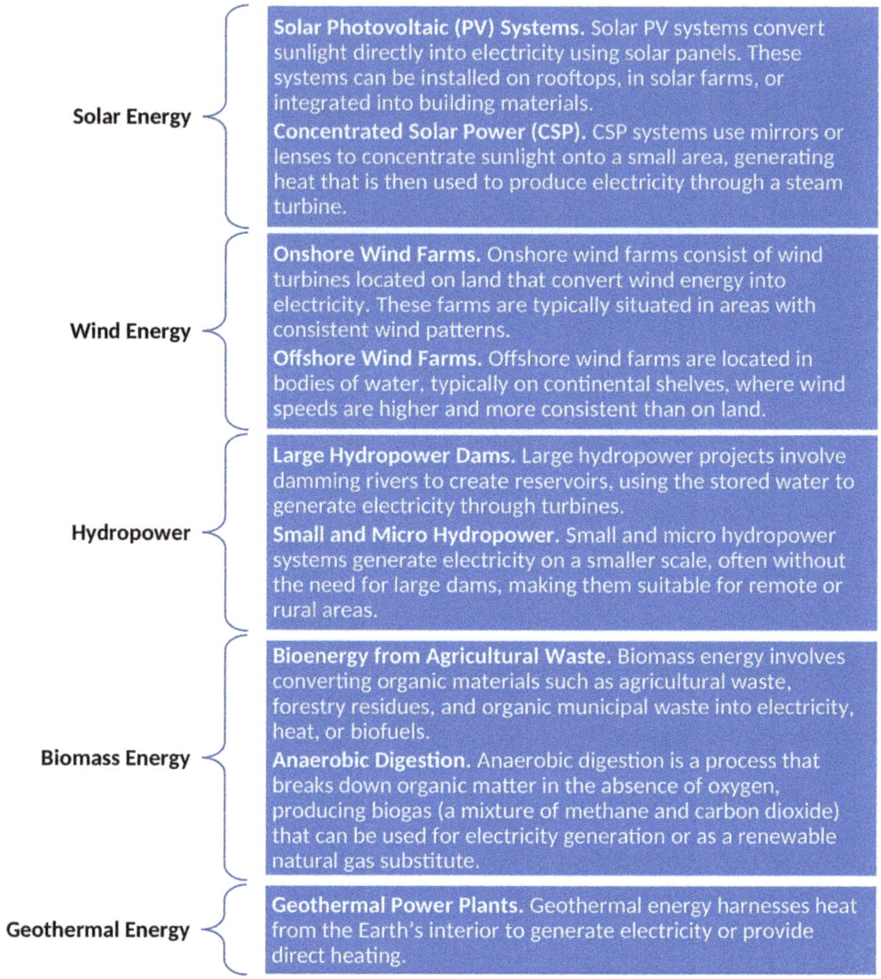

Fig. 2.21 Strategies for using renewable energy. Source: Created by authors

Fostering system effectiveness is essential for achieving the goals of the circular economy. By adopting strategies such as industrial symbiosis, closed-loop supply chains, system-level design, systemic efficiency, and supportive policies, businesses and governments can create more sustainable and resilient economic systems. These approaches not only benefit the environment but also drive economic growth and enhance social well-being.

Prioritizing regenerative resources is a fundamental principle of the circular economy that emphasizes the use of resources that naturally replenish and restore ecosystems. This approach involves choosing materials and energy sources that do not deplete or harm the environment, ensuring long-term sustainability and

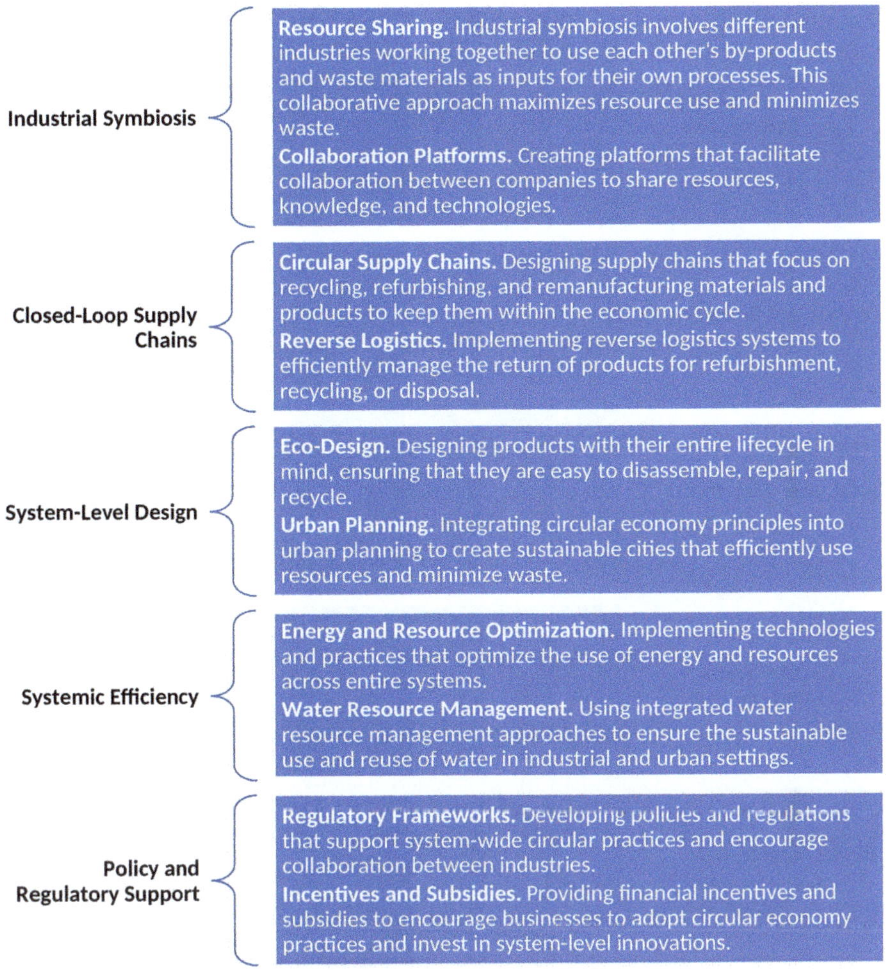

Fig. 2.22 Strategies for fostering system effectiveness. Source: Created by authors

ecological balance. Key strategies for prioritizing regenerative resources are represented in Fig. 2.23.

Prioritizing regenerative resources is essential for creating a sustainable and resilient circular economy. By adopting sustainable agricultural practices, renewable energy sources, sustainable forestry, circular water management, and biodegradable materials, businesses and communities can significantly reduce their environmental impact, enhance economic resilience, and promote social well-being. These practices not only conserve and restore natural resources but also support long-term sustainability and ecological balance.

Product as a Service (PaaS) is one of the circular economy principles and a business model that shifts the traditional ownership of products to a usage-based model.

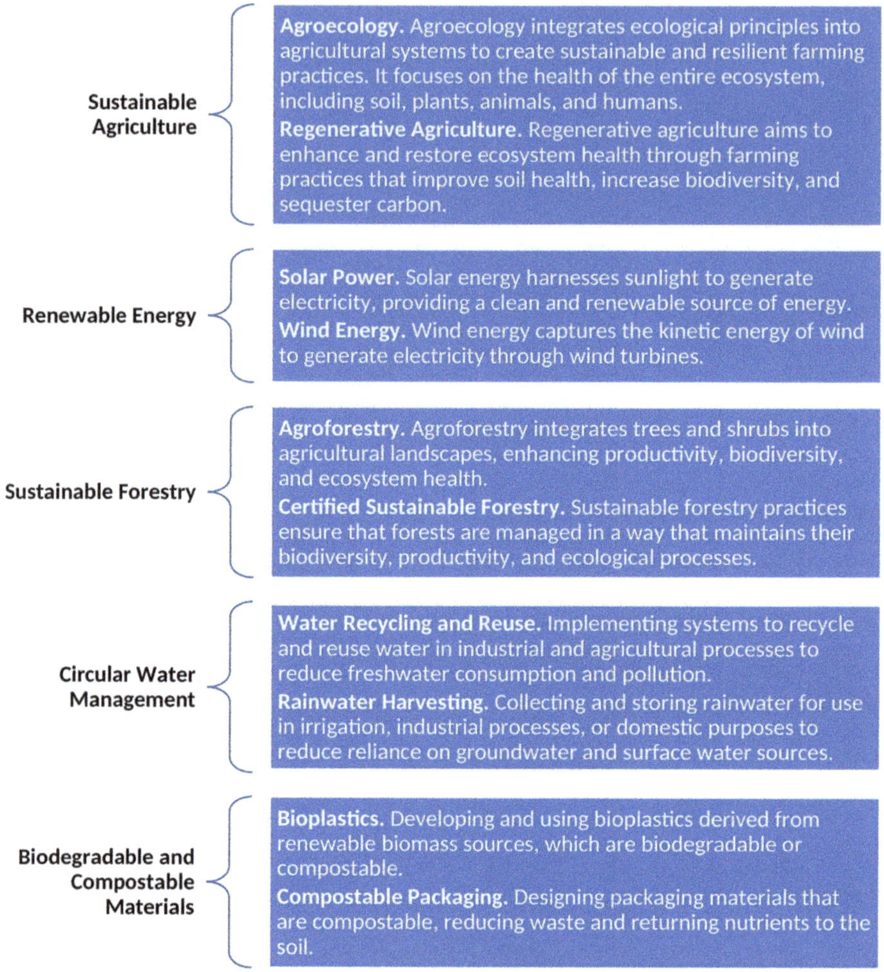

Fig. 2.23 Strategies for prioritizing regenerative resources. Source: Created by authors

Instead of purchasing a product outright, customers pay for the service it provides. This approach can significantly reduce waste, enhance resource efficiency, and promote sustainability by encouraging longer product lifecycles, improved maintenance, and efficient resource use. Key strategies to implement Product as a Service (PaaS) are shown in Fig. 2.24.

Promoting Product as a Service (PaaS) is a transformative approach that aligns with the principles of the circular economy. By adopting strategies such as subscription models, leasing and renting, performance-based models, maintenance and upgrades, and sharing economy platforms, businesses can enhance resource efficiency, reduce waste, and create sustainable economic opportunities. These models

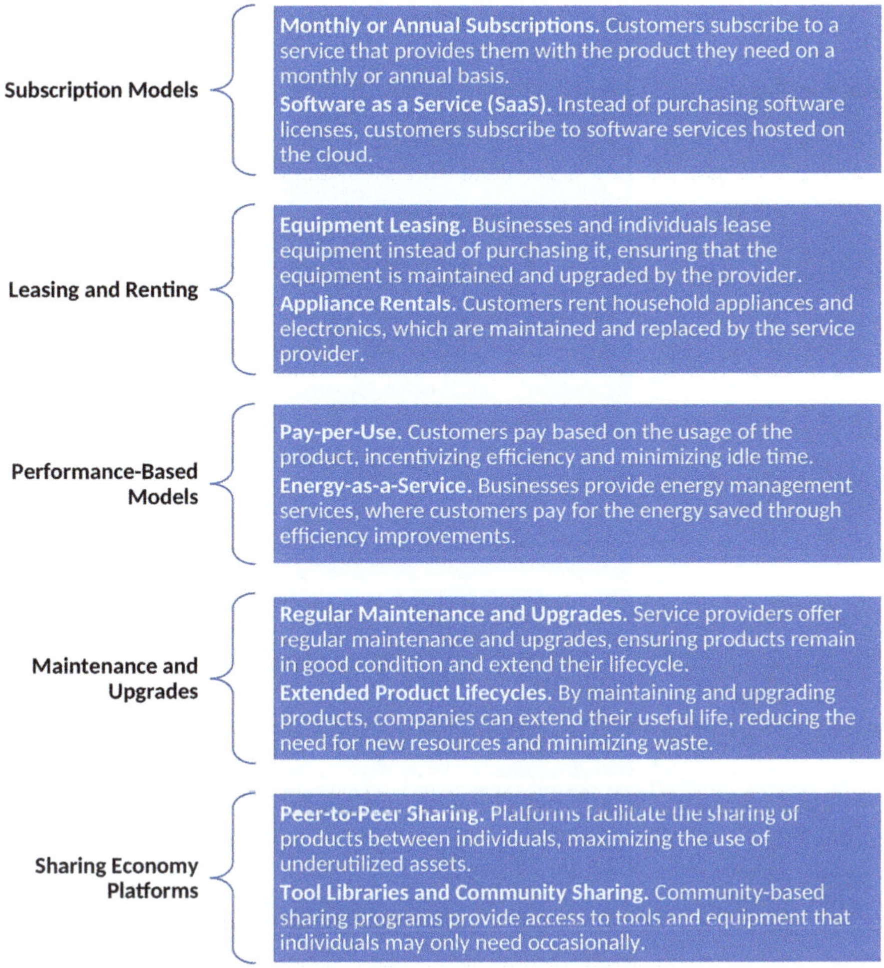

Fig. 2.24 Strategies to implement Product as a Service (PaaS). Source: Created by authors

not only benefit the environment but also provide economic and social advantages, making products and services more accessible and affordable.

Supporting local economies and communities is a vital principle of the circular economy, focusing on fostering economic resilience, social well-being, and environmental sustainability at the local level. This principle encourages sourcing materials locally, investing in local businesses, and engaging with community stakeholders to create a positive impact on local economics and social structures. Key strategies to implement supporting local economies and communities are shown in Fig. 2.25.

Supporting local economies and communities is essential for achieving the goals of the circular economy. By adopting strategies such as local sourcing, investing

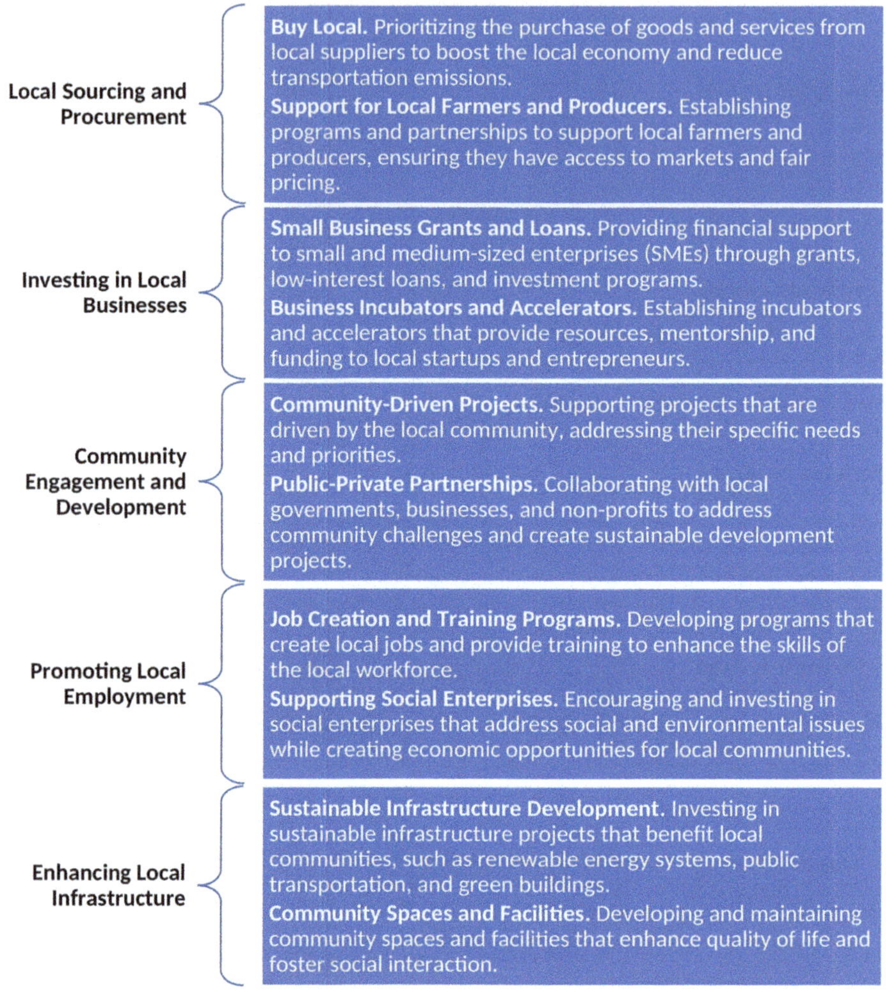

Fig. 2.25 Strategies to implement supporting local economies. Source: Created by authors

in local businesses, engaging with communities, promoting local employment, and enhancing infrastructure, businesses and governments can create more sustainable, resilient, and thriving local economies. These efforts not only benefit the environment but also foster economic growth and social well-being.

The circular economy is built on several core principles aimed at creating sustainable economic systems. Firstly, it emphasizes designing out waste and pollution by optimizing product designs and manufacturing processes. Secondly, it promotes keeping products and materials in use through reuse, repair, refurbishment, and recycling. The third principle is regenerating natural systems by using renewable resources and enhancing ecosystem health. Another key principle is prioritizing regenerative resources to ensure that materials can be continuously cycled back into the economy. It also focuses on using renewable energy to reduce reliance on fossil fuels and minimize environmental impact. The circular economy encourages product-as-a-service models, where consumers pay for the service a product provides rather than owning the product itself. Supporting local economies and communities is another crucial principle, fostering economic resilience and social well-being. Fostering system effectiveness by optimizing entire systems rather than individual components ensures maximum resource efficiency and sustainability. Lastly, it promotes closed-loop supply chains to maintain the continuous circulation of materials within the economy. These principles collectively aim to create a resilient and sustainable economic system that benefits the environment, economy, and society.

Key indicators of a circular economy are metrics that help assess how well an economy is transitioning from a linear model (take, make, dispose) to a circular one (reduce, reuse, recycle). These indicators cover various aspects of resource efficiency, waste management, economic impact, and social benefits. Some key indicators of a circular economy:

- Resource efficiency.
- Waste management.
- Economic impact.
- Social benefits.
- Environmental impact.

The key indicators of a circular economy encompass resource efficiency, waste management, economic impact, social benefits, and environmental impact. Monitoring these indicators helps track progress toward a more sustainable and circular economic model, providing valuable insights for policymakers, businesses, and stakeholders.

The circular economy and the Sustainable Development Goals (SDGs) are closely interconnected and promoting a circular economy in the context of the Sustainable Development Goals (SDGs) is crucial (see Table 2.23).

Promoting a circular economy is essential for achieving the SDGs as it addresses multiple environmental, economic, and social challenges. By fostering resource efficiency, reducing waste, supporting climate action, and creating economic opportunities, the circular economy provides a comprehensive approach to sustainable development. This holistic approach ensures that economic growth is decoupled from resource use and environmental degradation, leading to a more sustainable and resilient future.

Promoting a circular economy is crucial for achieving the Sustainable Development Goals (SDGs) as it maximizes resource efficiency and minimizes waste, contributing directly to SDG 12 (Responsible consumption and production). By extending product lifecycles through reuse, repair, and recycling, the circular economy supports SDG 11 (Sustainable cities and communities) by reducing urban waste and promoting sustainable urbanization. It also helps mitigate climate change (SDG 13) by reducing greenhouse gas emissions through more efficient resource use and waste management.

Table 2.23 Importance of circular economy in the context of SDG

Importance	SDG Link
Resource efficiency	
A circular economy maximizes the value of resources by keeping them in use for as long as possible. This approach reduces the need for new raw materials, which can help conserve natural resources and reduce environmental degradation.	Supports the objectives of SDG 12 (Responsible Consumption and Production) by encouraging the sustainable management and efficient utilization of natural resources.
Waste reduction	
By emphasizing reuse, repair, refurbishment, and recycling, the circular economy significantly reduces waste generation. This not only lessens the burden on landfills but also minimizes pollution.	Supports SDG 11 (Sustainable cities and communities) and SDG 14 (Life below water) by reducing urban waste and marine litter.
Climate action	
Implementing circular economy principles can significantly lower greenhouse gas emissions. For instance, recycling existing materials generally consumes less energy compared to manufacturing products from virgin resources.	Contributes to SDG 13 (Climate action) by mitigating climate change impacts through reduced emissions.
Economic growth and job creation	
The transition to a circular economy can stimulate innovation, create new business opportunities, and generate employment in areas such as recycling, repair, and sustainable product design.	Advances SDG 8 (Decent work and economic growth) by fostering economic growth and creating jobs.
Sustainable industrial practices	
Encouraging industries to adopt circular practices promotes innovation and sustainability in manufacturing processes. This shift can enhance productivity and economic competitiveness while reducing environmental footprints.	Supports SDG 9 (Industry, innovation, and infrastructure) by building resilient infrastructure and promoting inclusive and sustainable industrialization.
Community and social benefits	
A circular economy can enhance social well-being by reducing pollution, improving public health, and fostering a sense of community through shared resources and local initiatives.	Contributes to SDG 3 (Good health and well-being) and SDG 11 (Sustainable cities and communities) by creating healthier living environments and promoting community resilience.
Biodiversity conservation	
Circular economy practices can help protect ecosystems and biodiversity by reducing the extraction of raw materials and minimizing waste and pollution.	Supports SDG 15 (Life on land) and SDG 14 (Life below water) by promoting the sustainable use of terrestrial and marine ecosystems.
Water conservation	
Efficient use and recycling of water within circular systems can help conserve this vital resource, reducing pressure on freshwater supplies.	Aligns with SDG 6 (Clean water and sanitation) by promoting sustainable water management practices.
Strengthening partnerships	

(continued)

Table 2.23 (continued)

Importance	SDG Link
The circular economy fosters cooperation among key stakeholders—such as governments, businesses, and local communities—to develop and implement sustainable solutions.	Advances SDG 17 (Partnerships for the goals) by fostering multi-stakeholder partnerships and enhancing cooperation for sustainable development.

Source: Created by authors

Additionally, the circular economy fosters economic growth and job creation (SDG 8) by stimulating new business models and employment opportunities in recycling, remanufacturing, and sustainable design sectors. By prioritizing renewable resources and reducing dependency on non-renewable materials, it supports SDG 7 (Affordable and clean energy) and SDG 9 (Industry, innovation, and infrastructure), promoting sustainable industrialization and innovation.

The circular economy enhances community resilience and well-being (SDG 3) by reducing pollution and fostering healthier living environments. It also strengthens local economies (SDG 1) through localized production and consumption patterns, reducing poverty and enhancing economic resilience. Furthermore, by promoting sustainable agricultural practices and reducing food waste, the circular economy helps achieve SDG 2 (Zero Hunger) and supports biodiversity conservation (SDG 15).

Lastly, the circular economy encourages multi-stakeholder partnerships (SDG 17), fostering collaboration between governments, businesses, and communities to create sustainable solutions. Overall, it provides a comprehensive approach to sustainability, ensuring economic growth is decoupled from resource depletion and environmental degradation.

Adopting a circular economy faces several significant challenges across various dimensions. Here are some of the biggest challenges:

- Economic and financial barriers: high initial costs and uncertain return on investment (ROI). Transitioning to circular business models often requires significant upfront investments in new technologies, processes, and infrastructure. The financial benefits of circular economy practices can take time to materialize, and the ROI may be uncertain.
- Technical and infrastructural barriers: lack of technology and expertise, and inadequate infrastructure. Implementing circular economy principles often requires advanced technologies and specialized knowledge, which may not be readily available. The current infrastructure for waste management and recycling is often not equipped to handle the complexities of circular systems.
- Regulatory and policy barriers: inconsistent regulations and standards, and lack of government support and incentives. Regulations and standards related to the circular economy can vary widely across regions, creating complexity for businesses operating in multiple markets. Insufficient government support and incentives for circular practices can make it challenging for businesses to justify the transition.

- Market and consumer barriers: market competitiveness and consumer awareness and demand. Circular products can be more expensive than conventional alternatives due to higher production costs. Consumers may not be fully aware of the benefits of circular products or may be unwilling to change their consumption habits.
- Social and cultural barriers: resistance to change and cultural norms and behaviors. Employees and management may resist changes to established practices and routines. Cultural attitudes toward consumption and waste can be deeply ingrained, making it difficult to shift toward circular practices.

Adopting a circular economy faces several significant challenges, including economic and financial barriers, technical and infrastructural barriers, regulatory and policy barriers, market and consumer barriers, and social and cultural barriers. Overcoming these challenges requires concerted efforts from businesses, governments, and consumers to invest in new technologies, provide financial incentives, raise awareness, and develop consistent regulations and standards.

We often use two terms to emphasize consumer behavior in the marketplace: sustainable consumption and responsible consumption. Both concepts aim to reduce the negative impact of consumption on the environment, society, and the economy, but they emphasize different aspects and approaches (see Table 2.24).

While both sustainable and responsible consumption aim to reduce negative impacts, sustainable consumption primarily focuses on the environmental and resource aspects, ensuring that consumption does not exceed the planet's capacity. Responsible consumption broadens this perspective to include ethical and social considerations, ensuring that consumption practices do not harm workers, communities, or future generations.

In practice, there is a significant overlap between the two concepts. For instance, buying locally produced organic food supports both sustainable (reduces carbon footprint and pesticide use) and responsible consumption (supports local farmers and fair trade practices).

Understanding the distinction and interplay between sustainable and responsible consumption helps consumers and policymakers create more holistic approaches to reducing the negative impacts of consumption on the environment, society, and economy. Both concepts are essential for achieving long-term sustainability and ethical consumption practices.

The circular economy plays a crucial role in promoting responsible consumption by emphasizing the sustainable management of resources throughout the lifecycle of products. This approach aligns with the principles of responsible consumption, which focus on ethical, social, and environmental considerations.

Here are key aspects of how the circular economy supports responsible consumption:

1. Minimizing waste and pollution. The circular economy aims to design out waste and pollution by keeping products and materials in use for as long as possible. This includes practices like recycling, refurbishing, and remanufacturing, which help to reduce the environmental footprint of consumption. By reducing waste

Table 2.24 Sustainable and responsible consumption

	Sustainable consumption	Responsible consumption
Definition	Sustainable consumption emphasizes the use of goods and services that fulfill essential needs and enhance well-being, while limiting the depletion of natural resources, the use of hazardous substances, and the generation of waste and pollution. Its overarching aim is to ensure that consumption practices remain within the Earth's ecological boundaries and are viable over the long term.	Responsible consumption emphasizes the ethical and moral aspects of consumption. It involves making choices that not only consider environmental sustainability but also take into account social and economic justice. Responsible consumers are aware of the impact of their consumption on workers, communities, and future generations.
Key aspects	Emphasizes reducing the use of natural resources and increasing the efficiency of resource use. Focuses on minimizing environmental harm, including reducing carbon footprints, pollution, and biodiversity loss. Considers the entire life cycle of products, from production and use to disposal, ensuring sustainability at each stage. Ensures that consumption patterns are economically viable and do not lead to resource depletion or economic instability.	Focuses on the social and ethical implications of consumption, including fair trade, labor rights, and humane treatment of animals. Encourages consumers to be informed about the origins of products, the conditions under which they were made, and their overall impact. Considers how consumption patterns affect local communities and economies. Emphasizes the long-term consequences of consumption choices for future generations.
Examples	Choosing products with minimal packaging. Buying energy-efficient appliances. Supporting renewable energy sources.	Buying fair trade products to support ethical labor practices. Avoid brands known for unethical practices or human rights violations. Supporting local businesses to strengthen local economies.

Source: Created by authors

and promoting the reuse of materials, the circular economy minimizes the negative environmental impacts associated with resource extraction, production, and disposal. This supports responsible consumption by ensuring that products are used more efficiently and sustainably (Ellen MacArthur Foundation, 2021).

2. Ethical and fair practices. Circular economy models often incorporate ethical considerations into their business practices. This includes fair labor practices, ethical sourcing of materials, and ensuring that products are safe for consumers and the environment. By promoting ethical business practices, the circular economy ensures that the consumption of goods does not come at the expense of workers' rights or environmental health. This aligns with responsible consumption principles that prioritize social and ethical impacts.
3. Enhancing consumer awareness. The circular economy encourages transparency and consumer awareness regarding the lifecycle of products. Businesses adopting circular models often provide information about the origins of their materials, the sustainability of their processes, and the environmental impact of their

products. Increased transparency and consumer awareness help consumers make informed choices that reflect their values and priorities. This promotes responsible consumption by empowering consumers to select products that align with their ethical and environmental standards.
4. Supporting local economies. Circular economy practices often involve local sourcing, manufacturing, and recycling, which support local economies and reduce the carbon footprint associated with transportation. By strengthening local economies and reducing reliance on global supply chains, the circular economy fosters community resilience and economic stability. This supports responsible consumption by ensuring that local communities benefit from sustainable economic activities.
5. Encouraging long-term thinking. The circular economy promotes long-term thinking by designing products and systems that are durable, repairable, and upgradable. This contrasts with the linear economy's focus on short-term consumption and disposal. By encouraging long-term thinking and the maintenance of products, the circular economy helps to reduce the frequency of purchases and the associated environmental impacts. This supports responsible consumption by advocating for more sustainable and thoughtful consumption patterns

The circular economy enhances responsible consumption by integrating environmental sustainability, ethical practices, consumer awareness, local economic support, and long-term thinking into the lifecycle of products and services. By doing so, it ensures that consumption patterns contribute positively to society and the environment, aligning with the broader goals of sustainable development and ethical consumption.

Conclusions

1. Sustainable development aims to meet present needs without compromising the ability of future generations to meet their own needs. The Sustainable Development Goals (SDGs) provide a comprehensive framework to address global challenges such as poverty, inequality, climate change, environmental degradation, and peace and justice. The integration of economic, social, and environmental dimensions is crucial for achieving these goals. The SDGs emphasize the importance of inclusive and sustainable economic growth, improved social inclusion, and environmental protection. Policies and practices that support sustainable development are essential for achieving long-term global prosperity and well-being.
2. Sustainable consumption focuses on using products and services that meet basic needs and enhance quality of life while minimizing the use of natural resources, toxic materials, and emissions of waste and pollutants. It involves making informed and ethical choices that reduce environmental impact and promote social equity. Encouraging sustainable consumption patterns is vital for reducing the ecological footprint and supporting sustainable production processes. Consumers play a critical role by choosing products that are durable, repairable, and recyclable, and by reducing waste through practices such as recycling and composting.

3. Sustainable production involves creating goods and services in ways that are economically viable, socially responsible, and environmentally sound. It emphasizes resource efficiency, waste minimization, pollution prevention, and the use of renewable energy sources. By adopting sustainable production practices, businesses can reduce their environmental impact, enhance their competitiveness, and contribute to sustainable economic growth. Key strategies include optimizing resource use, implementing cleaner production techniques, and fostering innovation in sustainable technologies. Sustainable production is essential for achieving SDG 12 (Responsible consumption and production) and other related goals.
4. The circular economy complements responsible consumption by promoting the continuous use of resources through reuse, repair, refurbishment, and recycling. This approach reduces waste, conserves natural resources, and minimizes environmental impacts. Responsible consumption involves making choices that consider ethical, social, and environmental factors, aligning with circular economy principles. Together, they foster sustainable production and consumption patterns that support the achievement of multiple SDGs, including SDG 12 (Responsible consumption and production), SDG 13 (Climate action), and SDG 11 (Sustainable cities and communities). Implementing circular economy practices requires collaboration among governments, businesses, and consumers, supported by effective policies and incentives.

References

Agarwal, B. (2010). *Gender and green governance: The political economy of women's presence within and beyond community forestry*. Oxford University Press. https://doi.org/10.1093/acprof:oso/9780199569687.001.0001

Awewomom, J., Dzeble, F., Takyi, Y. D., et al. (2024). Addressing global environmental pollution using environmental control techniques: A focus on environmental policy and preventive environmental management. *Discover Environment, 2*, 8. https://doi.org/10.1007/s44274-024-00033-5

Biermann, F. (2021). The future of 'environmental' policy in the Anthropocene: Time for a paradigm shift. *Environmental Politics, 30*(1–2), 61–80. https://doi.org/10.1080/09644016.2020.1846958

Brunori, G., Rossi, A., & Malandrin, V. (2011). Co-producing transition: Innovation processes in farms adhering to solidarity-based purchase groups (GAS) in Tuscany, Italy. *International Journal of Sociology of Agriculture and Food, 18*(1), 28–53.

Burri, M., & Kugler, K. (2023, April 20). *Digitization, regulatory barriers and sustainable development*. Trade Law 4.0 Working Paper No 3/2023. Available at SSRN: https://ssrn.com/abstract=4424470 or https://doi.org/10.2139/ssrn.4424470.

Carson, R. (1962). *Silent spring*. Houghton Mifflin Company. 400 p. ISBN-10: 0618249060; ISBN-13: 978-0618249060.

CBD. (2021). *The Post-2020 Global Biodiversity Framework: Targets, indicators, and measurability implications at global and national level*. Convention on Biological Diversity. https://www.cbd.int/doc/c/409e/19ae/369752b245f05e88f760aeb3/wg2020-05-1-02-en.pdf

Cooke, B., & Kothari, U. (Eds.). (2001). *Participation: The new tyranny?* Zed Books. https://doi.org/10.1016/S0738-0593(02)00022-6

Cornwall, A. (2008). Unpacking 'participation': Models, meanings and practices. *Community Development Journal, 43*(3), 269–283. https://doi.org/10.1093/cdj/bsn010

Cronin, J. (2019). The Cuyahoga fire at fifty: A false history obscures the real water crisis that never ceased. *Journal of Environmental Studies and Sciences*. https://doi.org/10.1007/s13412-019-00550-3

Ellen MacArthur Foundation. (2021). *Circular economy*. https://www.ellenmacarthurfoundation.org/global-commitment-2021/overview

Feagan, R., & Morris, D. (2009). Consumer quest for embeddedness: A case study of the Brantford Farmers' Market. *International Journal of Consumer Studies, 33*(3), 235–243. https://doi.org/10.1111/j.1470-6431.2009.00745.x

Filgueira, B. F., Filho, W. L., & Teles, T. (2020). Sustainability and sustainable development: A review of principles and practice. *Journal of Cleaner Production, 273*, 122095. https://doi.org/10.1016/j.jclepro.2020.122095

Filipowicz, K. (2023). The social dimension of sustainable development. In A. Kuźniarska, K. Mania, & M. Jedynak (Eds.), *Organizing sustainable development*. Routledge. https://doi.org/10.4324/9781003379409

Fontana, A., Barni, A., Leone, D., Spirito, M., Tringale, A., Ferraris, M., Reis, J., & Goncalves, G. (2021). Circular economy strategies for equipment lifetime extension: A systematic review. *Sustainability, 13*(3), 1117. https://doi.org/10.3390/su13031117

Foster, K. R., Vecchia, P., & Repacholi, M. H. (2000). Science and the precautionary principle. *Science, 288*(5468), 979–981. https://doi.org/10.1126/science.288.5468.979

Fung, A. (2006). Varieties of participation in complex governance. *Public Administration Review, 66*(s1), 66–75. https://faculty.fiu.edu/~revellk/pad3003/Fung.pdf

Gaventa, J. (2006). Finding the spaces for change: A power analysis. *IDS Bulletin, 37*(6), 23–33. https://doi.org/10.1111/j.1759-5436.2006.tb00320.x

Geissdoerfer, M., Pieroni, M. P. P., Pigosso, D. C. A., & Soufani, K. (2020). Circular business models: A review. *Journal of Cleaner Production, 277*, 123741. https://doi.org/10.1016/j.jclepro.2020.123741

Gollier, C., & Treich, N. (2003). Decision-making under scientific uncertainty: The economics of the precautionary principle. *Journal of Risk and Uncertainty, 27*(1), 77–103. https://doi.org/10.1023/A:1025576823096

Graham, J. D. (2004). *The perils of the precautionary principle: Lessons from the American and European experience*. Heritage Foundation. https://www.heritage.org/government-regulation/report/the-perils-the-precautionary-principle-lessons-the-american-and

GWP (Global Water Partnership). (2000). *Integrated water resources management*. https://www.gwp.org/globalassets/global/toolbox/publications/background-papers/04-integrated-water-resources-management-2000-english.pdf

Haase, L. M., & Lythje, L. S. (2022). User strategies for prolonging product lifetimes: A new starting point for circular conceptual design. *Sustainability, 14*(22), 15133. https://doi.org/10.3390/su142215133

Harremoës, P., Gee, D., MacGarvin, M., Stirling, A., Keys, J., Wynne, B., & Guedes Vaz, S. (2001). *Late lessons from early warnings: The precautionary principle 1896-2000*. European Environment Agency. https://www.researchgate.net/publication/270901778_EEA_Late_Lessons_from_Early_Warnings_The_Precautionary_Principle_1896-2000

Hassan, N. M., & Alashwal, A. (2024). Developing a model for the implementation of designing out waste in construction. *Architectural Engineering and Design Management, 21*(1), 154–170. https://doi.org/10.1080/17452007.2024.2311670

Hickel, J. (2020). The sustainable development index: Measuring the ecological efficiency of human development in the Anthropocene. *Ecological Economics, 167*, 106331. https://doi.org/10.1016/j.ecolecon.2019.05.011

IEA. (2021). *World Energy Outlook 2021*. International Energy Agency. IEA Report. https://www.iea.org/reports/world-energy-outlook-2021
IISD (2019). International Institute for Sustainable Development (IISD), Annual Report 2018–2019 https://www.iisd.org/publications/annual-report/iisd-annual-report-2018-2019
Independent Group of Scientists. (2023). *Global Sustainable Development Report 2023: Times of crisis, times of change: Science for accelerating transformations to sustainable development*. United Nations. https://sdgs.un.org/sites/default/files/2023-09/FINAL%20GSDR%20 2023-Digital%20-110923_1.pdf
IPCC. (2014). *Climate Change 2014: Synthesis report*. Intergovernmental Panel on Climate Change.
IPCC. (2018). *Global warming of 1.5°C*. Intergovernmental Panel on Climate Change. https://www.ipcc.ch/sr15/
IPCC. (2021a). *Climate Change 2021: The physical science basis*. Intergovernmental Panel on Climate Change. https://www.ipcc.ch/report/ar6/wg3/
IPCC. (2021b). *Climate Change 2021: The physical science basis*. Intergovernmental Panel on Climate Change. https://www.ipcc.ch/report/ar6/wg1/
IRENA (International Renewable Energy Agency). (2018). *Planning for the renewable future*. https://www.aler-renovaveis.org/contents/lerpublication/irena_2017_jan_planning_for_the_renewable_future.pdf
IRENA. (2019). *Renewable energy and jobs: Annual Review 2019*. International Renewable Energy Agency. ISBN: 978-92-9260-134-8. https://www.irena.org/-/media/Files/IRENA/Agency/Publication/2019/Jun/IRENA_RE_Jobs_2019-report.pdf?rev=58ac56eaa71242309b0278055747df68
Jackson, T. (2006). *Sustainable consumption*. Earthscan Publications. https://www.routledge.com/The-Earthscan-Reader-on-Sustainable-Consumption/Jackson/p/book/9781844071647
Jackson, T. (2021). *Prosperity without growth: Foundations for the economy of tomorrow* (2nd ed.). Routledge.
Jacobs, M. (2016). Policy making for the long term in advanced democracies. *Annual Review of Political Science, 19*(1), 433–454. https://doi.org/10.1146/annurev-polisci-110813-034103
Jordan, A., Huitema, D., Van Asselt, H., Forster, J., & Berkhout, F. (2020). *Climate change policy in the Anthropocene: Towards a multi-level climate governance approach*. Cambridge University Press.
Kamruzzaman, P. (2020). Exploring the Nexus between participation and empowerment. *Journal of Development Policy and Practice, 5*(1), 32–53. https://doi.org/10.1177/2455133320909926
Kriebel, D., Tickner, J., Epstein, P., Lemons, J., Levins, R., Loechler, E. L., et al. (2001). The precautionary principle in environmental science. *Environmental Health Perspectives, 109*(9), 871–876. https://doi.org/10.1289/ehp.01109871
Kumar, S. (2002). *Methods for community participation: A complete guide for practitioners*. ITDG Publishing.
Leal Filho, W., Salvia, A. L., Vasconcelos, C. R. P., et al. (2022). Barriers to institutional social sustainability. *Sustainability Science, 17*, 2615–2630. https://doi.org/10.1007/s11625-022-01204-0
Lehmann, P., Beck, S., de Brito, M. M., Gawel, E., Groß, M., Haase, A., Lepenies, R., Otto, D., Schiller, J., Strunz, S., et al. (2021). Environmental sustainability post-COVID-19: Scrutinizing popular hypotheses from a social science perspective. *Sustainability, 13*, 8679. https://doi.org/10.3390/su13168679
Liu, J., Mooney, H., Hull, V., Davis, S. J., Gaskell, J., Hertel, T., et al. (2020). Scientific principles for accelerating the sustainable development goals (SDGs). *Science of the Total Environment, 728*, 138196. https://doi.org/10.1016/j.scitotenv.2020.138196
Manson, N. A. (2002). Formulating the precautionary principle. *Environmental Ethics, 24*(3), 263–274. https://home.olemiss.edu/~namanson/Formulating%20the%20PP.pdf
Mansuri, G., & Rao, V. (2004). Community-based and -driven development: A critical review. *The World Bank Research Observer, 19*(1), 1–39.
Markowski, Ł., Kotliński, K., & Ostrowska, A. (2023). Sustainable consumption and production in the European Union—An attempt to assess changes and convergence from the perspec-

tive of Central and Eastern European Countries. *Sustainability, 2023*(*15*), 16485. https://doi.org/10.3390/su152316485
Marmot, M. (2015). *The health gap: The challenge of an unequal world*. Bloomsbury Publishing. https://www.ncbi.nlm.nih.gov/pmc/articles/PMC5837404/
Meadowcroft, J. (2007). Who is in charge here? Governance for sustainable development in a complex world. *Journal of Environmental Policy & Planning, 9*(3–4), 299–314. https://doi.org/10.1080/15239080701631544
Mont, O., & Heiskanen, E. (2021). Promoting sustainable consumption: The case of the European Union. *Sustainability Science, 16*(4), 1073–1087. https://doi.org/10.1007/s11625-021-00939-4
Mostaghimi, K., & Behnamian, J. (2023). Waste minimization towards waste management and cleaner production strategies: A literature review. *Environment, Development, and Sustainability, 25*, 12119–12166. https://doi.org/10.1007/s10668-022-02599-7
O'Riordan, T., & Cameron, J. (1994). *Interpreting the precautionary principle*. Earthscan Publications. Routledge. https://doi.org/10.4324/9781315070490
OECD. (2022). *Financing climate futures: Rethinking infrastructure*. OECD Publishing. https://www.oecd-ilibrary.org/environment/financing-climate-futures_9789264308114-en
Oliver, C. D. (2003). sustainable forestry: what is it? How do we achieve it? *Journal of Forestry, 101*(5), 8–14. https://doi.org/10.1093/jof/101.5.8
Organization for Economic Co-operation and Development (OECD). (2008). *Sustainable manufacturing and eco-innovation*. https://www.oecd.org/content/dam/oecd/en/publications/reports/2010/01/eco-innovation-in-industry_g1ghbd93/9789264077225-en.pdf
Peattie, K., & Collins, A. (2009). Sustainable consumption: The consumer perspective. *Environmental Sciences, 6*(1), 9–18.
Pisano, U., Berger, G., Endl, A., & Sedlacko, M. (2020). Sustainability and sustainable development: Principles, policies, and practices. *Sustainability Science, 15*(4), 1187–1200. https://doi.org/10.1007/s11625-020-00833-y
Raffensperger, C., & Tickner, J. (1999). *Protecting public health and the environment: Implementing the precautionary principle*. Island Press.
Report of the World Commission on Environment and Development: Our Common Future. (1987). https://sustainabledevelopment.un.org/content/documents/5987our-common-future.pdf
Salvador, R., & Barros, M. V. (2019). Pollution prevention and control strategies, implications and challenges. In W. Leal Filho, A. Azul, L. Brandli, P. Özuyar, & T. Wall (Eds.), *Responsible consumption and production. Encyclopedia of the UN Sustainable Development Goals*. Springer. https://doi.org/10.1007/978-3-319-71062-4_99-1
Sandin, P. (1999). Dimensions of the precautionary principle. *Human and Ecological Risk Assessment: An International Journal, 5*(5), 889–907. https://doi.org/10.1080/10807039991289185
Sanz-Torro, V., Calafat-Marzal, C., Guaita-Martinez, J. M., et al. (2025). An integrated approach to resource efficiency, green markets and support measures in SMEs. *International Entrepreneurship and Management Journal, 21*, 84. https://doi.org/10.1007/s11365-025-01098-1
Schultz, P. W., Bator, R. J., Large, L. B., Bruni, C. M., & Tabanico, J. J. (2013). Littering in context: Personal and environmental predictors of littering behavior. *Environment and Behavior, 45*(1), 35–59.
Schultz, P. W., Bator, R. J., Large, L. B., Bruni, C. M., & Tabanico, J. J. (2021). Littering in context: Personal and environmental predictors of littering behavior. *Environment and Behavior, 45*(1), 35–59. https://doi.org/10.1177/0013916511412179
Setyadi, A., Soekotjo, S., Lestari, S. D., Pawirosumarto, S., & Damaris, A. (2025). Trends and opportunities in sustainable manufacturing: A systematic review of key dimensions from 2019 to 2024. *Sustainability, 17*(2), 789. https://doi.org/10.3390/su17020789
Smith, L. T., & Watson, I. (2022). *Decolonizing methodologies: Research and indigenous peoples* (3rd ed.). Zed Books.

Smith-Spangler, C., Brandeau, M. L., Hunter, G. E., Bavinger, J. C., Pearson, M., Eschbach, P. J., Sundaram, V., Liu, H., Schirmer, P., Stave, C., Olkin, I., & Bravata, D. M. (2012). Are organic foods safer or healthier than conventional alternatives?: A systematic review. *Annals of Internal Medicine, 157*(5), 348–366. https://doi.org/10.7326/0003-4819-157-5-201209040-00007

Stevenson, H., Auld, G., Allan, J. I., Elliott, L., & Meadowcroft, J. (2021). The practical fit of concepts: Ecosystem services and the value of nature. *Global Environmental Politics, 21*(2), 3–22. https://doi.org/10.1162/glep_a_00587

Stiglitz, J. E. (2012). *The price of inequality: How today's divided society endangers our future*. W.W. Norton.

Sunstein, C. R. (2005). *Laws of fear: Beyond the precautionary principle*. Cambridge University Press. https://doi.org/10.1017/CBO9780511790850

Tang, X., Wang, Q., Noor, S., Nazir, R., Nasrullah, M. J., Hussain, P., & Larik, S. A. (2024). Exploring the impact of green finance and green innovation on resource efficiency: The mediating role of market regulations and environmental regulations. *Sustainability, 16*, 8047. https://doi.org/10.3390/su16188047

Tickner, J. A. (2003). Precaution and preventive public health policy. *Public Health Reports, 118*(6), 493–497. https://doi.org/10.2190/6NR3-CNU0-TGUV-UMU0

Tilman, D., et al. (2011). Global food demand and the sustainable intensification of agriculture. *Proceedings of the National Academy of Sciences, 108*(50), 20260–20264. https://doi.org/10.1073/pnas.1116437108

Toner, J., Desha, C., Reis, K., Hes, D., & Hayes, S. (2023). Integrating ecological knowledge into regenerative design: A rapid practice review. *Sustainability, 15*(17), 13271. https://doi.org/10.3390/su151713271

Tukker, A., Emmert, S., Charter, M., Vezzoli, C., Sto, E., Andersen, M. M., Geerken, T., Tischner, U., & Lahlou, S. (2008). Fostering change to sustainable consumption and production: An evidence based view. *Journal of Cleaner Production, 16*(11), 1218–1225. https://doi.org/10.1016/j.jclepro.2007.08.015

UN. (2021). *Financing for Sustainable Development Report 2021*. United Nations. https://desapublications.un.org/publications/financing-sustainable-development-report-2021

UN Sustainable Development Report. (2024). https://dashboards.sdgindex.org/chapters

UNDP (United Nations Development Programme). (2017). *Institutional and coordination mechanisms: Guidance note on facilitating integration and coherence for SDG implementation*. https://sustainabledevelopment.un.org/index.php?page=view&type=400&nr=2478&menu=1515

UNDP. (2020). *Human Development Report 2020: The next frontier—Human development and the anthropocene*. United Nations Development Programme. https://hdr.undp.org/content/human-development-report-2020

UNEP. (2011). *Towards a green economy: Pathways to sustainable development and poverty eradication*. United Nations Environment Programme. https://www.unep.org/resources/report/towards-green-economy-pathways-sustainable-development-and-poverty-eradication-10

UNEP. (2021). *Sustainability and circularity in the textile value chain: Global stocktaking*. United Nations Environment Programme. https://www.unep.org/resources/publication/sustainability-and-circularity-textile-value-chain-global-roadmap

UNFCCC. (2015). *The Paris Agreement*. United Nations Framework Convention on Climate Change. https://unfccc.int/kyoto_protocol?gad_source=1&gclid=CjwKCAjwnei0BhB-EiwAA2xuBkrjluhWAP1oDlw6WBlflawlgb3dJTs9s41bcIBgRRoxtqNXM09XnRoCYbkQAvD_BwE

United Nations Environment Programme (UNEP). (2017). *Sustainability Reporting Guidelines*. https://www.unep.org/explore-topics/resource-efficiency/what-we-do/responsible-industry/corporate-sustainability

United Nations Environment Programme (UNEP). (2021). *Emissions Gap Report 2021*. https://www.unep.org/resources/emissions-gap-report-2021

United Nations Global Compact (UNGC). (2021). *UN Global Compact Strategy 2021–2023*.

United Nations. (2015). *Transforming our world: The 2030 Agenda for Sustainable Development.* https://sustainabledevelopment.un.org/post2015/transformingourworld/publication

UNWTO (United Nations World Tourism Organization). (2018). *Tourism for sustainable development in developing countries.* https://www.e-unwto.org/doi/book/10.18111/9789284415496

Utsev, J. T., Imoni, S., Onuzulike, C., Akande, E. O., Orseer, A. M., & Tiza, M. T. (2024). Strategies for sustainable construction waste minimization in the modern era. *Bincang Sains Dan Teknologi, 3*(01), 1–10. https://doi.org/10.56741/bst.v3i01.506

van Ewijk, S. (2018). *Resource efficiency and the circular economy: Concepts, economic benefits, barriers, and policies* [Doctoral dissertation, University College London]. UCL Discovery. https://discovery.ucl.ac.uk/id/eprint/10054117

Verplanken, B., & Roy, D. (2015a). Consumer habits and sustainable consumption. *Frontiers in Psychology, 11*, 1900. In L. Reisch & J. Thogersen (Eds.), *Handbook of research on sustainable consumption.* Edward Elgar. https://doi.org/10.4337/9781783471270.00026

Verplanken, B., & Roy, D. (2015b). Consumer habits and sustainable consumption. In L. Reisch & J. Thogersen (Eds.), *Handbook of research on sustainable consumption* (pp. 243–253). (Elgar Original Reference). Edward Elgar..

von Wehrden, H., Luederitz, C., Leventon, J., Russell, S., & Abson, D. J. (2020). How can science support the 2030 Agenda for Sustainable Development? Four tasks to tackle the normative dimension of sustainability. *Sustainability Science, 15*(4), 1129–1139. https://doi.org/10.1007/s11625-020-00871-6

Wals, A. E., & Peters, M. A. (2020). Sustainable development and participatory action research: A systematic review. *Systemic Practice and Action Research, 33*(4), 399–417. https://doi.org/10.1007/s11213-020-09536-6

Wampler Brian (2007). Participatory Budget in Brazil: Contestation, Cooperation and Accountability (2009). Government and International Affairs Faculty Publications. 29. https://digitalcommons.usf.edu/gia_facpub/29

Williams, B. A., Beyer, H. L., Fagan, M. E., et al. (2024). Global potential for natural regeneration in deforested tropical regions. *Nature, 636*, 131–137. https://doi.org/10.1038/s41586-024-08106-4

World Bank. (2011). *World Development Report 2011: Conflict, security, and development.* © World Bank. http://hdl.handle.net/10986/4389

World Bank. (2015). *World Bank annual report 2015.* https://documents.worldbank.org/en/publication/documentsreports/documentdetail/880681467998200702/world-bank-annual-report-2015

World Bank (2018). *The human capital project.* World Bank.. https://www.worldbank.org/en/publication/human-capital

World Health Organization (WHO). (2016). *Urban green spaces and health: A review of evidence.* Report number: http://www.euro.who.int/en/health-topics/environment-and-health/pages/news/news/2016/11/who-report-shows-urban-green-spaces-deliver-multiple-health-benefits

WWF. (2022a). *Living Planet Report 2022: Bending the curve of biodiversity loss.* World Wide Fund for Nature. https://wwfint.awsassets.panda.org/downloads/embargo_13_10_2022_lpr_2022_full_report_single_page_1.pdf

WWF. (2022b). *Living Planet Report 2022: Bending the curve of biodiversity loss.* World Wide Fund for Nature. https://livingplanet.panda.org/en-US/

Chapter 3
Responsible Consumption

Abstract The idea of responsible consumption has become increasingly important as societies face the combined challenges of environmental degradation, climate change, and social inequality. This chapter discusses what it actually means to consume responsibly and why this concept is central to achieving sustainable development. It begins by outlining how consumption patterns have evolved together with economic growth and how these changes have affected the environment. The chapter then turns to the values and motivations that guide consumer behavior, emphasizing that responsibility involves not only individual awareness but also the broader social and institutional context in which people make choices. Attention is given to the role of education, communication, and access to reliable information in shaping more sustainable habits. The text also explores the contribution of digital technologies that make it easier for consumers to understand product impacts and to participate in sharing or circular economy initiatives. At the policy level, the discussion highlights how the European Union and international frameworks promote responsible consumption through resource efficiency, waste prevention, and support for sustainable business models. Yet, despite growing awareness, progress remains uneven. Economic pressures, convenience, and limited availability of sustainable alternatives often stand in the way of lasting behavioral change. Through this analysis, the chapter argues that responsible consumption cannot rely on moral appeals alone—it requires structural support, market innovation, and a cultural shift toward valuing sufficiency over excess. Ultimately, it suggests that responsible consumption should be seen as an evolving social practice that connects individual choices with collective responsibility for a fair and resilient future.

A. Mikalauskienė et al., *Climate Change and Responsible Consumption*, Springer Climate, https://doi.org/10.1007/978-3-032-16218-2_3

3.1 The Concept of Responsible Consumption

Responsible consumption is a mindful approach to purchasing and using goods and services that considers individual needs and broader societal and environmental impacts. This concept encourages consumers to evaluate the consequences of their choices, prioritizing products that minimize environmental harm, support ethical labor practices, and contribute positively to the local and global community. At its core, responsible consumption is about balancing personal fulfillment with the duty to protect our planet and ensure equitable treatment for all involved in the production and supply chain. By making conscious choices, individuals play an active role in fostering sustainable development and mitigating the adverse effects of overconsumption on resources, ecosystems, and societies.

Here are several perspectives on responsible consumption, each emphasizing different aspects of the concept:

1. Environmental perspective. Responsible consumption is the intentional selection and use of products and services that have minimal impact on natural resources and ecosystems. From this perspective, it involves choosing items that reduce carbon emissions, limit waste, and conserve resources like water, energy, and raw materials. Responsible consumers, therefore, prioritize eco-friendly products, opt for minimal packaging, and make choices that align with environmental sustainability goals, contributing to a healthier planet for future generations.
2. Economic perspective. From an economic standpoint, responsible consumption emphasizes supporting businesses that prioritize ethical and sustainable practices. It involves spending in ways that encourage fair trade, sustainable supply chains, and local economic resilience. This approach also considers the hidden costs of consumption, such as the environmental and social impacts embedded in a product's lifecycle, and favors businesses that mitigate these costs. By choosing responsibly produced goods, consumers can influence market trends and stimulate economic models that value sustainability alongside profitability.
3. Social justice perspective. Through the lens of social justice, responsible consumption is the practice of choosing goods and services that uphold fair labor practices, respect human rights, and foster equitable global trade. This view highlights the need for consumer awareness of working conditions, wages, and treatment of laborers involved in production. It encourages people to consider the human impact of their purchases, opting for brands and products that support social equity, fair wages, and safe working conditions.
4. Ethical and moral perspective. In an ethical framework, responsible consumption is the commitment to act in ways that respect the rights and dignity of all living beings. It involves moral considerations around animal welfare, human health, and the overall societal impact of consumption choices. This perspective urges consumers to think beyond their immediate needs and consider the ethical implications of their consumption patterns, advocating for mindful use of resources, reduced waste, and compassion in the products we support.

5. Personal health and well-being perspective. From a health-conscious angle, responsible consumption includes choosing products that promote individual and community well-being. This might involve selecting items with minimal environmental toxins, natural or organic options, and products that contribute to a healthy lifestyle. It underscores the idea that personal well-being is intertwined with the environment, as healthy consumption habits often lead to healthier communities and ecosystems.

Responsible consumption, from an environmental perspective, emphasizes a conscious approach to selecting products and services that minimize ecological harm and promote the preservation of natural resources. This perspective focuses on understanding the full environmental impact of a product throughout its lifecycle—from raw material extraction to production, distribution, use, and disposal. Responsible consumers seek to lessen their ecological footprint, which includes reducing carbon emissions, conserving water, minimizing waste, and protecting biodiversity. Elements of environmentally responsible consumption are shown in Table 3.1.

The environmental perspective on responsible consumption is about adopting habits and making purchasing decisions that lessen one's impact on the planet. By prioritizing sustainable options, supporting a circular economy, reducing waste, and conserving natural resources, consumers can help foster a healthy environment for present and future generations. This approach underscores that individual actions, when multiplied, can create significant positive change in mitigating climate change, conserving ecosystems, and supporting global sustainability.

From an economic standpoint, responsible consumption focuses on the role consumers play in shaping markets and economic systems through their spending choices. It emphasizes the power of individuals and communities to influence industry practices, supply chain ethics, and local economies by prioritizing goods and services produced through fair, transparent, and sustainable practices. Economically responsible consumption also considers the "hidden costs" of production—such as environmental degradation and social inequities—which are often not reflected in a product's price but have significant long-term impacts. Key elements of economically responsible consumption are shown in Table 3.2.

The economic perspective on responsible consumption emphasizes the power of consumers to reshape the market by prioritizing ethical, sustainable, and locally produced goods. By spending responsibly, individuals can influence corporate behaviors, encourage sustainable innovation, support local economies, and help create a market that values transparency and accountability. This approach aligns individual spending habits with a broader vision of economic resilience, environmental preservation, and social equity, highlighting the potential for economic systems to evolve toward greater sustainability.

From the viewpoint of social justice, responsible consumption is about making choices that respect human rights, promote equity, and foster fair treatment throughout the entire supply chain. This perspective focuses on the social and ethical implications of consumption, emphasizing that consumers have the power to support or

Table 3.1 Elements of environmentally responsible consumption

Elements of environmentally responsible consumption	Definition	Example
Reducing resource consumption	Responsible consumption advocates for minimizing the use of finite resources such as fossil fuels, minerals, and fresh water. Consumers are encouraged to buy only what they need, prioritize items with lower resource demands, and choose options that involve renewable resources wherever possible.	Selecting energy-efficient appliances, using public transportation instead of personal vehicles, or supporting companies that use renewable energy sources reflect responsible choices aimed at conserving resources.
Promoting circular economy practices	The circular economy model focuses on extending the life of products through repair, reuse, recycling, and upcycling, thereby reducing waste and the demand for new resources. Responsible consumers play a role in this by choosing durable goods, purchasing second-hand items, and supporting businesses that design products for longevity and recyclability.	Buying furniture made from reclaimed wood or choosing products with recyclable or biodegradable packaging reduces the strain on ecosystems and landfills.
Reducing carbon footprint	The environmental perspective encourages individuals to consider the carbon footprint associated with the products they consume. This includes choosing goods that require less energy to produce, favoring locally sourced items to reduce transportation emissions, and being mindful of the energy consumed during the usage phase of a product.	Opting for seasonal and local produce, which requires less transportation and refrigeration, thereby lowering carbon emissions.
Minimizing waste and pollution	Responsible consumption calls for minimizing waste by choosing products with minimal or recyclable packaging and supporting zero-waste initiatives. It also encourages the selection of products that have a smaller pollution footprint, such as items produced without harmful chemicals or toxic materials that can harm water and soil ecosystems.	Consumers can support this by using reusable bags, bottles, and containers, avoiding single-use plastics, and being mindful of products with harmful by-products or excessive packaging.

(continued)

Table 3.1 (continued)

Elements of environmentally responsible consumption	Definition	Example
Protecting biodiversity	This aspect involves choosing products that do not contribute to the destruction of ecosystems or the endangerment of species. Responsible consumption encourages support for brands that avoid deforestation, overfishing, and habitat destruction, and that prioritize biodiversity-friendly practices.	Consumers can contribute by avoiding products linked to unsustainable agriculture (e.g., palm oil contributing to deforestation) and supporting certifications like Fair Trade, Rainforest Alliance, or Marine Stewardship Council, which advocate for biodiversity conservation.
Adopting sustainable food choices	The environmental view of responsible consumption also includes sustainable food choices that support both personal health and planetary health. This means favoring plant-based diets, reducing meat consumption, and selecting organic or sustainably farmed products.	Choosing plant-based proteins over meat can significantly reduce water usage and greenhouse gas emissions, as livestock farming is resource-intensive and contributes heavily to methane emissions.

Source: Created by authors according to Çam et al. (2025); Brož et al. (2023); De et al. (2025)

challenge injustices around the world through their purchases. Socially responsible consumption involves choosing products that reflect fair labor practices, ethical sourcing, and equitable access to resources, helping to ensure that everyone involved in the production process is treated fairly and with dignity. Key elements of the social justice perspective on responsible consumption are shown in Table 3.3.

The social justice perspective on responsible consumption highlights the role of consumers in promoting fairness, equity, and ethical treatment in the global economy. Through thoughtful purchasing decisions, individuals can support companies that prioritize fair labor, gender equality, Indigenous rights, and economic justice, fostering a more just and inclusive world. By embracing this perspective, consumers can drive demand for products that reflect their values and help create a more equitable society where the benefits of production and trade are distributed fairly.

From an ethical and moral perspective, responsible consumption goes beyond fulfilling personal needs or desires to considering the broader moral implications of each purchase. This viewpoint encourages consumers to align their choices with core ethical values, such as respect for life, compassion, fairness, and integrity. It involves making decisions that respect the dignity of workers, promote animal welfare, support environmental sustainability, and uphold societal values, all of which reflect a commitment to acting responsibly in a global community. By making ethical consumption choices, individuals can positively influence industries, support humane practices, and contribute to a more compassionate, just world. Key aspects of the ethical and moral perspective on responsible consumption are shown in Table 3.4.

Table 3.2 Elements of economically responsible consumption

Elements of economically responsible consumption	Definition	Example
Supporting ethical and sustainable businesses	One of the core ideas is that consumers have the power to drive demand for ethical businesses, which prioritize fair labor practices, environmentally friendly methods, and transparent supply chains. By choosing products from companies that uphold sustainable and socially responsible values, consumers encourage industries to adopt better practices.	Purchasing fair-trade coffee or clothing from certified ethical brands helps sustain businesses committed to fair wages, safe working conditions, and environmental protection. This ultimately pressures larger corporations to align with these values to remain competitive.
Encouraging local economic resilience	Responsible consumption also involves supporting local businesses and small-scale producers, which contributes to economic resilience by strengthening local economies and reducing dependence on global supply chains. Buying locally produced goods supports community jobs, reduces transportation emissions, and keeps money circulating within the local economy.	Choosing locally sourced produce, crafts, and artisanal products instead of mass-produced items from large corporations. This keeps profits within the community, fosters entrepreneurship, and reduces the carbon footprint associated with long-distance transportation.
Promoting circular economy principles	Economically responsible consumption aligns closely with the circular economy model, which prioritizes resource efficiency, waste reduction, and product longevity. In a circular economy, products are designed to be reusable, repairable, or recyclable, extending their value over time and reducing the need for new raw materials.	Consumers can support this model by choosing second-hand items, leasing or renting goods instead of buying, and selecting brands that offer repair or take-back programs. For instance, purchasing a refurbished smartphone instead of a new one not only saves money but also reduces electronic waste and the demand for resources like rare minerals.
Internalizing external costs	Many traditional market prices do not account for "externalities," or hidden costs like pollution, deforestation, or water depletion caused by production. Responsible consumption encourages consumers to acknowledge these costs and support businesses that work to minimize them or embed these considerations into their pricing.	Products with certifications (like organic or eco-labels) may be more expensive due to the higher cost of sustainable production methods, but they reflect a more accurate price that includes environmental and social responsibility. By choosing these products, consumers signal to the market that they value practices that reduce external costs.

(continued)

Table 3.2 (continued)

Elements of economically responsible consumption	Definition	Example
Empowering consumers with transparency and accountability	Economically responsible consumption relies on transparency, where consumers are informed about the origins, production processes, and environmental impact of the products they purchase. Companies that provide clear and honest information empower consumers to make choices aligned with their values.	Transparency can be encouraged through certifications, sustainability reporting, and corporate social responsibility (CSR) initiatives that provide insights into a company's social and environmental impact. For example, businesses that disclose their carbon footprint or publish an annual sustainability report show accountability, helping consumers make more informed decisions.
Encouraging sustainable innovation and investment	When consumers choose responsibly produced goods, they drive demand for sustainable innovations and technologies that minimize environmental and social harm. This demand encourages companies to invest in eco-friendly production processes, cleaner energy sources, and innovative materials that reduce resource consumption.	The rising demand for electric vehicles has spurred automakers to innovate in battery technology and infrastructure, benefiting both the environment and the economy by creating new industries, jobs, and opportunities for green investment.
Reducing consumption for financial and environmental efficiency	Economically responsible consumption also includes a shift toward minimalism or thoughtful spending, where consumers buy fewer, higher-quality products that last longer. This approach reduces waste and prevents the environmental impacts associated with overproduction while enabling consumers to save and allocate resources efficiently.	By avoiding impulsive purchases and focusing on items with longevity, consumers can reduce their overall expenditures and environmental footprint. This trend, often seen in younger generations, is reshaping industries like fashion and technology, with a shift from fast-fashion and disposable electronics to durable and repairable products.

Source: Created by authors according to Arora and Mishra (2023)

The ethical and moral perspective on responsible consumption encourages individuals to act with compassion, fairness, and respect for all life. It involves making purchasing decisions that align with deeply held values, advocating for human rights, animal welfare, environmental sustainability, and social equity. By choosing products and services that support ethical practices, consumers contribute to a world where business and industry operate with a conscience, striving for justice and respect for all beings. This perspective highlights that consumption is not just an economic act but a moral choice with the power to shape society for the better.

From a personal health and well-being perspective, responsible consumption is about making choices that positively impact one's physical health, mental wellness, and overall quality of life. This perspective emphasizes selecting products that are

Table 3.3 Elements of the social justice perspective on responsible consumption

Elements of the social justice perspective on responsible consumption	Definition	Example
Promoting fair labor practices	A central pillar of socially responsible consumption is the promotion of fair labor practices, which ensure that workers are paid fair wages, provided safe working conditions, and treated with respect. This also includes opposition to exploitative labor practices such as child labor, forced labor, and unsafe working conditions.	By choosing products certified as fair trade or ethically sourced, consumers can support companies that prioritize workers' rights. For example, fair-trade coffee and chocolate offer an alternative to products tied to exploitative labor practices, ensuring fair wages for farmers and better working conditions.
Supporting gender equality and women's empowerment	Social justice in consumption also involves supporting products and companies that work to uplift women and promote gender equality. Many industries, especially in developing countries, rely heavily on female labor, yet women often face discrimination, lower wages, and limited opportunities for advancement.	Some brands directly empower women by providing fair wages, leadership opportunities, and funding for education and healthcare. By choosing to purchase from these companies, consumers can contribute to a more equitable economic landscape. For example, brands that invest in women-led cooperatives or provide career training for women in marginalized communities help promote gender equality.
Ensuring ethical sourcing and fair supply chains	Responsible consumption involves selecting products with ethical supply chains, where raw materials are sourced in ways that respect human rights and environmental standards. This includes supporting companies that source materials without exploiting local communities or depleting resources needed by those who live in the area.	Purchasing diamonds certified as conflict-free, or avoiding minerals mined in unsafe or exploitative conditions, supports ethical sourcing. Many technology companies, for example, are working to ensure that minerals such as cobalt and lithium, crucial to electronics and batteries, are sourced responsibly to avoid supporting exploitative practices.
Advocating for indigenous rights and cultural sensitivity	Socially responsible consumption acknowledges and respects the rights and traditions of Indigenous and local communities. Many consumer goods, such as textiles, crafts, and certain foods, originate from Indigenous cultures and rely on their traditional knowledge. Responsible consumers seek to support these communities by buying directly from artisans or from companies that respect and give back to Indigenous communities.	Purchasing authentic, ethically sourced crafts from Indigenous artisans helps preserve cultural heritage and provides economic support to communities that are often marginalized or exploited by mass production industries.

(continued)

Table 3.3 (continued)

Elements of the social justice perspective on responsible consumption	Definition	Example
Challenging systemic inequities through consumer power	Socially responsible consumption can also challenge systemic inequities embedded in global trade. Large corporations often profit disproportionately, while small-scale producers and workers in lower-income countries receive only a small fraction of the profits. Consumers who prioritize equitable brands and products contribute to more balanced economic systems.	By avoiding goods from companies with a history of unethical practices, such as exploitative wages or environmental abuses, consumers can exert pressure on companies to reform and prioritize fair and ethical practices.
Prioritizing inclusivity and accessibility in products and services	The social justice perspective also values inclusivity in consumer products, supporting companies that design accessible and inclusive products for people of all backgrounds, abilities, and communities. This approach ensures that consumption benefits and represents diverse needs.	Supporting businesses that make products with universal design, such as adaptive clothing for people with disabilities or language options on packaging and services, promotes a market that is fair and accessible to everyone, regardless of their abilities or background.
Reducing exploitation and supporting economic development in marginalized communities	Social justice-oriented consumption emphasizes buying products that contribute to the economic growth and development of marginalized communities. Instead of exploiting cheap labor or resources, companies can contribute to sustainable development by investing in local education, healthcare, and infrastructure in the communities from which they source.	Brands that invest in community development and fair trade practices uplift local economies. For example, some fashion brands partner with artisans in rural communities to provide fair wages and fund local schools or health clinics, helping to break cycles of poverty and foster long-term growth.

Source: Created by authors according to Wahlen and Stroude (2023), Guilbert (2024)

(continued)

free from harmful chemicals, sustainably produced, and conducive to a balanced lifestyle. Responsible consumption under this viewpoint promotes a holistic approach to health, where individual well-being is connected to the wellness of the community and the environment. By prioritizing health-conscious choices, consumers can foster better personal health outcomes while contributing to a sustainable and thriving ecosystem. Key aspects of the personal health and well-being perspective on responsible consumption are shown in Table 3.5.

The personal health and well-being perspective on responsible consumption encourages consumers to prioritize choices that support their physical and mental health. By selecting non-toxic, nutrient-dense, and environmentally considerate

Table 3.4 Elements of the ethical and moral perspective on responsible consumption

Elements of the ethical and moral perspective on responsible consumption	Definition	Example
Human dignity and rights	Ethical consumption emphasizes respect for human dignity, recognizing that each person involved in a product's lifecycle—from raw material extraction to manufacturing and distribution—deserves fair and respectful treatment. This includes supporting companies that uphold human rights, pay fair wages, and ensure safe working conditions.	Choosing products from companies certified for fair labor practices or avoiding goods linked to child labor respects the inherent dignity of all people. Consumers, therefore, take responsibility for understanding the human impact of their choices and ensure that they do not support practices that exploit or harm individuals.
Animal welfare and compassion	The ethical and moral perspective includes compassion for animals, opposing practices that inflict suffering on animals for the sake of profit. This aspect encourages consumers to be mindful of animal welfare in their purchasing decisions, choosing products that do not involve cruelty, exploitation, or unnecessary harm to animals.	Consumers might choose cruelty-free cosmetics, which are produced without animal testing, or opt for plant-based foods instead of animal products to reduce the demand for factory farming. By making compassionate choices, consumers can support brands and practices that respect animal rights and reduce animal suffering.
Environmental stewardship as a moral duty	Many view the protection of the environment as a moral obligation to future generations, emphasizing that current consumption should not harm the planet or deplete resources for those who come after us. This perspective calls for choices that minimize pollution, reduce carbon emissions, and conserve natural resources.	Ethical consumers seek products with a low environmental footprint, preferring sustainably sourced materials and goods that minimize waste and pollution. For instance, buying biodegradable household items, supporting renewable energy, or reducing single-use plastics reflects a commitment to stewardship of the planet as a shared resource for all life.
Promoting transparency and integrity in business practices	Ethical consumers value transparency and expect companies to be honest and forthright about their practices. This includes clear communication on sourcing, labor conditions, environmental impacts, and any social contributions. By supporting brands that embrace transparency, consumers reward companies that act with integrity and hold those accountable that do not.	Purchasing from companies that provide detailed sustainability reports or certifications shows an endorsement of integrity. Ethical consumption discourages "greenwashing" and promotes honest marketing, pushing businesses to live up to their ethical claims rather than using them solely as branding tools.

(continued)

Table 3.4 (continued)

Elements of the ethical and moral perspective on responsible consumption	Definition	Example
Supporting social equity and fair distribution of wealth	Ethical consumption also seeks to promote social equity, focusing on a fair distribution of wealth, opportunities, and benefits along the supply chain. This perspective urges consumers to choose products that support marginalized communities, fairly compensate laborers, and invest in local economies rather than concentrating wealth among corporations.	By purchasing fair-trade products or goods from social enterprises, consumers contribute to a more balanced and equitable economy. These choices help uplift underserved communities, foster social mobility, and reduce income inequality, which aligns with a moral commitment to fairness and justice.
Minimalism and intentionality in consumption	From an ethical and moral viewpoint, responsible consumption involves intentionality—buying only what is necessary and avoiding excessive consumption that leads to waste. This minimalist approach encourages consumers to focus on quality over quantity, purchase durable goods, and prioritize needs over wants.	Ethical minimalism promotes buying fewer, high-quality items that last longer, reducing the burden on both society and the environment. For example, investing in timeless, durable clothing instead of fast fashion reduces waste, conserves resources, and challenges industries built on disposability. This aligns with the moral principle of avoiding wastefulness and respecting the planet's limited resources.
Personal integrity and consistency with ethical beliefs	Responsible consumption, from an ethical standpoint, involves aligning one's purchases with personal values and moral beliefs. This means consumers actively consider whether their choices are consistent with their principles, whether they believe in social justice, animal welfare, or environmental protection.	An individual committed to environmental conservation might choose a hybrid vehicle over a conventional one, even if it requires a higher upfront cost, to stay true to their values. Responsible consumption, therefore, becomes a reflection of one's moral beliefs, allowing individuals to live with integrity and make choices that resonate with their ethical commitments.

Source: Created by authors according to Karimzadeh and Boström (2023), Stiefenhofer (2025)

products, individuals can enhance their own well-being while supporting broader health-focused and sustainable practices. This approach reflects a holistic understanding that personal health is interconnected with environmental and community health, highlighting the broader impacts of mindful consumption on quality of life.

Responsible consumption is a multifaceted concept that considers the ethical, social, environmental, economic, and health impacts of consumer choices. Each

Table 3.5 Elements of the personal health and well-being perspective on responsible consumption

Elements of the personal health and well-being perspective on responsible consumption	Definition	Example
Choosing products free from harmful chemicals	Responsible consumers, from a health perspective, prioritize products that are free from toxic substances, synthetic additives, and potentially harmful chemicals. This includes selecting natural, organic, or minimally processed products that reduce exposure to pesticides, artificial preservatives, and synthetic fragrances.	Buying organic fruits and vegetables or skincare products made from natural ingredients helps reduce the intake of chemicals associated with adverse health effects, such as hormone disruption, allergies, or even long-term chronic conditions. Such choices support the goal of minimizing toxic load in daily life, which contributes to both short-term and long-term health.
Supporting nutrient-dense and whole foods	Responsible consumption also involves choosing whole, nutrient-dense foods that support physical health and optimal nutrition. This means opting for foods rich in vitamins, minerals, and antioxidants rather than processed foods high in added sugars, fats, and artificial ingredients.	A diet centered around fresh vegetables, whole grains, lean proteins, and healthy fats supports immunity, energy levels, and mental clarity. For instance, choosing locally grown produce or sustainably sourced seafood not only provides a nutrient-rich diet but also often aligns with more sustainable and ethical food practices, bridging individual health with environmental consciousness.
Avoiding products linked to environmental pollution	Health-focused responsible consumption includes choosing products with minimal environmental pollutants, as pollution can directly affect community health. Avoiding products linked to air and water pollution, such as certain plastics, non-biodegradable items, and chemical-laden cleaning supplies, helps limit exposure to pollutants that may harm respiratory health, water quality, and ecosystems.	For instance, opting for biodegradable cleaning products reduces indoor air pollution and prevents toxic runoff into waterways, protecting both personal and community health. This approach reflects the idea that individual well-being is closely tied to a clean, healthy environment, which is vital for overall quality of life.
Prioritizing mental health and wellness	Responsible consumption from a health perspective also means choosing products and services that support mental well-being. This includes engaging in practices that reduce stress, promote mindfulness, and enhance overall life satisfaction.	For example, choosing experiences over material goods, such as spending on activities like nature outings, wellness retreats, or fitness classes, can provide meaningful, health-enhancing experiences. Such choices prioritize personal fulfillment and mental wellness over accumulation of goods, contributing to a balanced and mentally healthy lifestyle.

(continued)

Table 3.5 (continued)

Elements of the personal health and well-being perspective on responsible consumption	Definition	Example
Reducing consumption of ultra-processed foods	A health-conscious approach to consumption advocates for reducing or avoiding ultra-processed foods, which are often high in refined sugars, unhealthy fats, and sodium. Consuming these foods in excess is linked to an increased risk of lifestyle-related diseases such as obesity, diabetes, and cardiovascular issues.	By choosing minimally processed, whole foods over ultra-processed options, consumers can enhance their physical health, maintain better energy levels, and reduce the likelihood of chronic health issues. This approach aligns responsible consumption with nutritional well-being, reinforcing that health-promoting choices often go hand-in-hand with sustainable practices.
Opting for clean and safe personal care products	Responsible consumption extends to personal care products, where consumers seek options free from potentially harmful chemicals such as parabens, sulfates, and synthetic dyes. Health-conscious consumers may opt for organic or natural personal care items, such as soaps, shampoos, and cosmetics, which prioritize skin health and avoid exposure to irritating or toxic ingredients.	Using natural deodorants or organic skin creams helps reduce exposure to chemicals absorbed through the skin, enhancing both skin health and overall wellness. Such choices often support brands committed to safety and ethical sourcing, reflecting responsible consumption's alignment with health and ethical integrity.
Promoting physical activity and active lifestyles	A health-centered approach to consumption emphasizes products and services that encourage physical activity, which is essential for maintaining physical fitness, managing stress, and supporting mental clarity. This might include choosing active transportation options, such as biking or walking, or investing in fitness equipment or outdoor gear.	For example, purchasing a bicycle instead of a car for short commutes promotes both physical fitness and environmental sustainability. Similarly, supporting brands that promote active lifestyles—such as fitness centers, outdoor apparel companies, or eco-friendly sports equipment manufacturers—reinforces the connection between responsible consumption and holistic well-being.
Fostering healthier habits through intentional consumption	From a well-being perspective, responsible consumption involves fostering habits that promote balance, mindfulness, and reduced stress. This can mean choosing a minimalist lifestyle to avoid clutter, practicing mindful eating, or engaging in "digital detox" to minimize screen time and promote mental clarity.	For instance, intentional purchases that simplify life—such as limiting purchases to essentials, choosing quality over quantity, or prioritizing experiences over possessions—can reduce mental stress associated with materialism. This approach reinforces that responsible consumption can also contribute to a more peaceful and mentally enriching lifestyle.

Source: Created by authors according to Nhung Thang and Nguyen (2024), Arora et al. (2024)

perspective highlights unique aspects of how individuals can make conscious decisions that benefit not only themselves but also society and the planet.

The environmental perspective emphasizes selecting products that reduce pollution, conserve resources, and protect biodiversity. The goal is to minimize the ecological footprint and support practices that promote long-term sustainability. The economic perspective highlights the power of consumers to support fair trade, local economies, and sustainable business models. By choosing ethically produced goods, individuals encourage fair wealth distribution and innovation in sustainable practices. The social justice perspective focuses on fairness and equity, advocating for human rights, fair labor conditions, and support for marginalized communities. It challenges consumers to use their purchasing power to foster social equity and respect for workers worldwide. The ethical and moral perspective urges consumers to align their choices with compassion, integrity, and respect for life. This involves promoting animal welfare, transparency in business practices, and stewardship of resources for future generations. The personal health and well-being perspective encourages selecting products that support physical and mental health, emphasizing choices free from toxins, nutrient-rich foods, and products that enhance a balanced lifestyle.

Together, these perspectives illustrate that responsible consumption is about more than just buying—it's about making decisions that reflect one's values and contribute positively to the world. By choosing responsibly, individuals can drive industry changes, support fair practices, protect ecosystems, and foster personal wellness.

The concept of responsible consumption has evolved significantly over time, shaped by social, environmental, economic, and ethical changes. Early forms of responsible consumption were rooted in simple, frugal lifestyles, often out of necessity rather than choice. In agricultural societies, people prioritized efficient use of resources, often practicing forms of sustainable living to conserve food, fuel, and materials for future seasons. This conservation mindset, however, was largely circumstantial, driven by the need to survive in a world of limited resources.

The historical context of responsible consumption is shown in Figs. 3.1 and 3.2.

The historical evolution of responsible consumption reveals a shift from necessity-based frugality to a global movement driven by ethical, environmental, and social concerns. Today, responsible consumption reflects a commitment to using consumer power to advocate for sustainable and fair practices, with the understanding that individual choices contribute to broader systemic change. As awareness grows, responsible consumption continues to evolve, shaping a future where purchasing decisions reflect a shared commitment to a just, sustainable, and healthy world.

The concept of sustainable consumption has evolved significantly over time, adapting to societal changes, environmental challenges, and advancements in technology. Initially, sustainable consumption was primarily associated with resource efficiency—using resources sparingly to ensure their availability for future generations. Over time, it has expanded into a broader framework that incorporates environmental, social, and economic dimensions. Trends in the concept of sustainable consumption are shown in Table 3.6.

Industrial revolution and the rise of mass consumption

- The Industrial Revolution in the 18th and 19th centuries marked a shift toward mass production and consumerism. As goods became cheaper and more widely available, people in industrialized nations began to adopt more materialistic lifestyles. Consumption became a marker of wealth and social status, and efficiency in production often took precedence over environmental or social considerations. During this time, labor exploitation, environmental pollution, and the depletion of natural resources became widespread issues, setting the stage for future concerns about responsible consumption.

Early 20th century: emergence of ethical consumption movements

- By the early 20th century, social reform movements began to address the ethical issues associated with industrialization. The Progressive Era in the United States, for example, saw campaigns advocating for fair labor practices, child labor laws, and improved working conditions. The establishment of labor unions helped improve workers' rights, highlighting the need for fairness in production processes. Socially aware consumers began questioning the ethical implications of their purchases, laying the foundation for responsible consumption as a conscious choice.

Post-war consumer boom and environmental awareness

- After World War II, an economic boom fueled unprecedented levels of consumption in the Western world, especially in the United States. Mass-produced goods, convenience products, and disposable items became widespread. However, the 1960s and 1970s saw a growing awareness of the environmental and social costs of unchecked consumerism. Influential works like Rachel Carson's *Silent Spring* (1962) exposed the environmental damage caused by industrial chemicals, inspiring the modern environmental movement. This era marked the beginning of environmental consciousness as a key aspect of responsible consumption, with a focus on reducing pollution and conserving resources.

The rise of fair trade in the 1980s

- In the 1980s, the Fair Trade movement gained momentum, driven by concerns over exploitative practices in developing countries. Fair Trade sought to create a system where producers in poorer nations could receive fair wages and work under safe conditions. Coffee, chocolate, and handicrafts became symbols of ethical consumption, with Fair Trade certifications helping consumers identify products that supported fair labor practices and equitable economic development. This movement solidified social justice as a core component of responsible consumption, advocating for transparency and accountability in supply chains.

Fig. 3.1 The historical context of responsible consumption (1). Source: Created by authors according to Glavič (2021), Chan et al. (2018), Fuchs and Lorek (2005)

1990s: the birth of green consumerism

- The 1990s saw a surge in environmental awareness, with concepts like "green" and "sustainable" entering mainstream consumer culture. The rise of organic foods, biodegradable packaging, and eco-friendly products reflected a growing demand for goods that minimized environmental harm. Certifications such as "Organic" and "Energy Star" began to guide consumers in making environmentally conscious choices. Green consumerism made it clear that purchasing habits could impact the planet, and consumers began to expect companies to address sustainability as part of their corporate responsibility.

2000s: Corporate Social Responsibility (CSR) and ethical branding

- In the early 2000s, Corporate Social Responsibility (CSR) became a significant focus for businesses, as consumers increasingly demanded that companies act ethically and transparently. CSR initiatives included reducing carbon emissions, improving labor conditions, and supporting community projects. Companies began to build ethical branding around responsible practices, and consumers became more aware of concepts like "greenwashing"—misleading claims of environmental responsibility. Responsible consumption expanded to include not just product choice but also skepticism about corporate motives, reinforcing the need for accountability and transparency.

2010s: rise of minimalism and conscious consumerism

- The 2010s saw the rise of minimalism, zero-waste lifestyles, and conscious consumerism, driven by growing concerns over climate change, plastic pollution, and excessive waste. Documentaries like *The True Cost* (2015), which exposed the dark side of the fast fashion industry, fueled awareness of the social and environmental impacts of overconsumption. Many consumers began to adopt more mindful lifestyles, focusing on quality over quantity and prioritizing sustainable, ethical brands. The concept of a circular economy—designing products to be reused, repaired, or recycled—became more widely recognized as a solution to wasteful consumption patterns.

2020s: emphasis on systemic change and individual responsibility

- In the 2020s, responsible consumption has become a mainstream issue, with individuals, companies, and governments recognizing that systemic change is necessary to address global challenges like climate change and social inequality. Movements such as Fridays for Future and advocacy for Sustainable Development Goals (SDGs) have emphasized that responsible consumption is not just an individual choice but a societal imperative. Consumers today are more informed and expect companies to adopt sustainable practices, reduce emissions, and contribute to a fair economy. Responsible consumption now encompasses a holistic view, focusing on economic, social, environmental, and health impacts.

Fig. 3.2 The historical context of responsible consumption (2). Source: Created by authors according to Glavič (2021), Chan et al. (2018), Fuchs and Lorek (2005)

Table 3.6 Trends in the concept of sustainable consumption

<table>
<tr><td colspan="2">Early focus on resource efficiency</td></tr>
<tr><td colspan="2">In its early stages, sustainable consumption emphasized minimizing resource use and reducing waste. This was largely a reaction to concerns about finite natural resources, particularly during the energy crises of the 1970s. The focus was primarily on individual behaviors, such as conserving water and energy or reducing waste. While practical and accessible, this approach placed most of the responsibility on consumers without addressing the structural factors driving unsustainable consumption patterns.</td></tr>
<tr><td>Advantages</td><td>Disadvantages</td></tr>
<tr><td>Encouraged immediate, actionable steps individuals could take.
Highlighted the importance of conserving resources in everyday life.</td><td>Lacked systemic solutions to address broader industrial or corporate contributions to resource depletion.
Limited in addressing global inequalities, as wealthier nations consumed disproportionately more resources.</td></tr>
<tr><td colspan="2">Incorporation of environmental awareness</td></tr>
<tr><td colspan="2">By the 1990s, sustainable consumption began to include considerations of environmental impacts, particularly those related to climate change, pollution, and biodiversity loss. The idea of "green consumption" emerged, promoting eco-friendly products, renewable energy, and sustainable agriculture. Certifications like "organic" and "Fair Trade" helped consumers identify environmentally and socially responsible products.</td></tr>
<tr><td>Advantages</td><td>Disadvantages</td></tr>
<tr><td>Increased consumer awareness of environmental and ethical issues.
Created demand for greener alternatives, pushing companies to innovate.</td><td>This led to issues like "greenwashing," where companies exaggerated sustainability claims to attract eco-conscious consumers.
Often made sustainable choices more expensive and less accessible to low-income individuals.</td></tr>
<tr><td colspan="2">Shift toward systems thinking</td></tr>
<tr><td colspan="2">In the twenty-first century, sustainable consumption evolved to consider systemic factors. This shift acknowledged that individual actions alone cannot achieve sustainability without changes in production systems, government policies, and corporate practices. Concepts like the circular economy gained prominence, emphasizing reuse, repair, and recycling over linear consumption patterns. Consumers began to demand transparency in supply chains and greater corporate accountability.</td></tr>
<tr><td>Advantages</td><td>Disadvantages</td></tr>
<tr><td>Recognized the interconnectedness of production and consumption in achieving sustainability.
Encouraged innovation in business models, such as sharing economies and product-as-a-service models (e.g., renting instead of owning).</td><td>Systemic change requires significant time, coordination, and investment, often leading to slow progress.
Creates a knowledge gap for consumers who may not fully understand or trust complex supply chain claims.</td></tr>
</table>

(continued)

Table 3.6 (continued)

Holistic approach: social and ethical dimensions	
Today, sustainable consumption integrates social justice and ethical considerations alongside environmental and economic factors. It emphasizes reducing inequalities, promoting fair labor practices, and considering the well-being of communities affected by production. The Sustainable Development Goals (SDGs), particularly SDG 12 (Responsible Consumption and Production), exemplify this comprehensive approach.	
Advantages	*Disadvantages*
Combines sustainability with equity, aiming for a more just global system. Expands the focus from products to lifestyles, encouraging shifts like plant-based diets, minimalism, and reduced consumption overall.	The holistic approach can be overwhelming for consumers, as it requires navigating a multitude of criteria (environmental, social, and economic). Often requires systemic support (e.g., policy incentives, infrastructure), which may not exist uniformly across regions.
Current Trends and Future Directions	
Modern sustainable consumption increasingly emphasizes collective action and global cooperation. Movements like "climate strikes" and consumer-driven advocacy are putting pressure on governments and corporations to lead the charge toward sustainability. The rise of digital platforms enables greater transparency, but also risks reinforcing inequalities if digital access is unevenly distributed.	
Advantages	*Disadvantages*
Leverages technology and collective power to amplify the impact of sustainable practices. Encourages accountability across all levels, from individual to corporate and governmental.	Can create a false sense of progress if systemic issues, such as overproduction, are not addressed alongside consumption. Risks are excluded for marginalized communities that lack access to sustainable alternatives or digital tools.

Source: Created by authors

The evolution of sustainable consumption reflects a growing recognition of its complexity and interdependence with broader societal systems. While early efforts focused on individual behaviors, today's approach incorporates systemic, social, and technological solutions. However, achieving sustainable consumption remains a challenge due to barriers like accessibility, greenwashing, and the need for systemic transformation. Balancing individual responsibility with structural change is key to ensuring that sustainable consumption leads to meaningful progress.

3.2 The Linkages Between Consumption and Climate Change

The relationship between consumption and climate change is deeply intertwined, as the demand for goods and services drives a significant portion of global greenhouse gas emissions. Consumption patterns influence how resources are extracted, produced, transported, and disposed of, each stage contributing to emissions that exacerbate climate change. As societies grow wealthier and more urbanized, the scale and intensity of consumption increase, leading to higher carbon footprints and greater environmental degradation.

At its core, consumption impacts climate change through two primary mechanisms: direct and indirect emissions. Direct emissions stem from activities such as energy use in households or personal transportation. Indirect emissions, on the other hand, are associated with the production and supply chains of consumed goods, from the energy-intensive manufacturing of products to the emissions from transporting goods across the globe.

Climate change is further amplified by unsustainable consumption habits, including reliance on fossil fuels, overuse of natural resources, and the generation of waste. The cumulative effect of these activities contributes to rising global temperatures, extreme weather events, and ecosystem disruptions. Conversely, shifts toward sustainable consumption, such as adopting low-carbon lifestyles, reducing waste, and prioritizing eco-friendly products—can play a crucial role in mitigating climate change and achieving global climate targets.

Understanding the relationship between consumption and climate change is critical for effectively addressing the global climate crisis. Consumption patterns are a primary driver of greenhouse gas emissions, accounting for a significant portion of the carbon footprint associated with production, transportation, and waste. Recognizing this linkage enables governments, businesses, and individuals to identify opportunities for reducing emissions and aligning consumption behaviors with climate goals (Koide et al., 2021).

A key reason for understanding this relationship is its potential to inform policy and guide systemic change. Without addressing consumption, efforts to mitigate climate change—such as transitioning to renewable energy or improving industrial efficiency—will be insufficient. For example, even if energy production becomes fully renewable, unsustainable consumption patterns, such as excessive demand for non-recyclable goods or high-emission foods, will continue to place pressure on natural resources and exacerbate environmental degradation.

Moreover, addressing consumption helps to bridge the gap between individual actions and systemic solutions. Public awareness of how daily habits, such as food choices, energy use, and purchasing decisions, contribute to climate change fosters a culture of responsibility and empowerment. This understanding encourages consumers to adopt low-carbon lifestyles, driving demand for sustainable products and services, which in turn pushes businesses and policymakers to innovate and implement climate-friendly practices.

On a global scale, understanding consumption's role highlights the disparities between high- and low-income regions. High-consumption lifestyles in wealthier nations often disproportionately contribute to emissions, while lower-income countries bear the brunt of climate impacts. By identifying these inequalities, stakeholders can design fair and inclusive climate strategies that prioritize equitable resource distribution and ensure that the transition to sustainability benefits all.

Ultimately, recognizing the link between consumption and climate change is essential to achieving international climate targets, such as those outlined in the Paris Agreement and the United Nations' Sustainable Development Goals (SDGs). Addressing this linkage ensures that efforts to reduce emissions are comprehensive, encompassing not only energy and industrial sectors but also the behaviors and systems driving demand. By aligning consumption patterns with sustainable principles, humanity can take a significant step toward limiting global warming and fostering a resilient, equitable future.

Consumption is a primary driver of carbon emissions worldwide, as the demand for goods and services fuels activities across the supply chain, from production and transportation to usage and disposal. Each stage in this lifecycle contributes to greenhouse gas emissions, which accumulate and exacerbate global climate change. Understanding these processes reveals the systemic nature of consumption-related emissions and underscores the need for targeted solutions.

The extraction and processing of raw materials, such as metals, fossil fuels, and timber, are among the most carbon-intensive stages of the consumption cycle. These activities require significant amounts of energy, often derived from fossil fuels, and result in direct emissions. For instance, deforestation for agriculture or construction releases stored carbon into the atmosphere, while mining and manufacturing contribute through energy use and chemical reactions. Global demand for resources like steel, concrete, and plastics drives substantial emissions from these sectors.

Manufacturing processes across industries are energy-intensive and heavily reliant on fossil fuels. Factories producing consumer goods, electronics, clothing, and vehicles generate large quantities of carbon dioxide (CO_2) and other greenhouse gases (GHGs). For example, the fashion industry alone is responsible for approximately 10% of global emissions, driven by fast production cycles and resource-intensive practices.

The globalization of trade has significantly increased emissions from transportation, as goods are shipped across the world to meet consumer demand. International shipping and aviation, which depend heavily on fossil fuels, are major contributors to CO_2 emissions. Additionally, the rise of e-commerce has intensified local delivery networks, adding emissions from last-mile logistics.

The way consumers use products and services also drives emissions. For instance, residential energy use for heating, cooling, and lighting contributes significantly to global emissions. Similarly, the use of private vehicles powered by gasoline or diesel remains a leading source of GHGs in many countries. The carbon footprint of these activities is amplified in high-consumption lifestyles, where energy demand per capita is much higher than in low-income regions.

Agriculture, driven by global food demand, is a major source of methane (CH_4) and nitrous oxide (N_2O), potent greenhouse gases. Livestock farming, particularly cattle for meat and dairy production, generates significant emissions due to enteric fermentation (methane release during digestion) and deforestation for grazing land. Fertilizer use in crop production also contributes to emissions. Changing dietary patterns, especially in high-income countries, have exacerbated the climate impact of food consumption.

Consumption drives the generation of waste, much of which ends up in landfills or is incinerated, releasing methane and CO_2 into the atmosphere. Single-use plastics, electronics, and fast-fashion items exacerbate the problem by creating non-biodegradable waste. Improper disposal methods, such as open burning of waste, further contribute to air pollution and carbon emissions. Global disparities in consumption patterns significantly influence emissions. Wealthier nations and individuals typically have higher carbon footprints due to greater access to energy-intensive goods and services, frequent travel, and resource-intensive diets. In contrast, low-income communities contribute comparatively little to emissions but often suffer the most from climate change impacts.

Many products carry "embodied emissions," which are the GHGs released during their entire lifecycle, from raw material extraction to production and transportation. For example, purchasing a smartphone or a vehicle contributes not just the emissions from using the product but also those involved in its creation and eventual disposal.

Globally, consumption drives carbon emissions through interconnected systems of production, transportation, energy use, and waste management. Addressing these emissions requires a shift in both individual consumption habits and systemic structures, such as the energy grid, transportation networks, and global supply chains. By adopting sustainable practices, such as reducing waste, supporting circular economies, and transitioning to renewable energy, consumers and stakeholders can mitigate the impact of consumption on climate change.

Consumption-related emissions are a result of the complex processes required to extract, produce, transport, use, and dispose of goods and services. Understanding the key drivers behind these emissions is essential for identifying intervention points to reduce their impact. These drivers include resource extraction, energy use, transportation, waste generation, and specific patterns of consumption that vary across sectors and geographies. Key drivers of consumption-related emissions are shown in Fig. 3.3.

The extraction of raw materials, such as metals, fossil fuels, and timber, generates significant greenhouse gas (GHG) emissions. Mining, drilling, and logging activities consume large amounts of energy, often derived from fossil fuels. Industries such as steel and cement production are among the highest emitters. For instance, cement production accounts for approximately 7–8% of global CO_2 emissions due to the chemical processes involved. Land-use changes for agriculture, mining, or urban development release vast amounts of stored carbon, particularly in tropical regions.

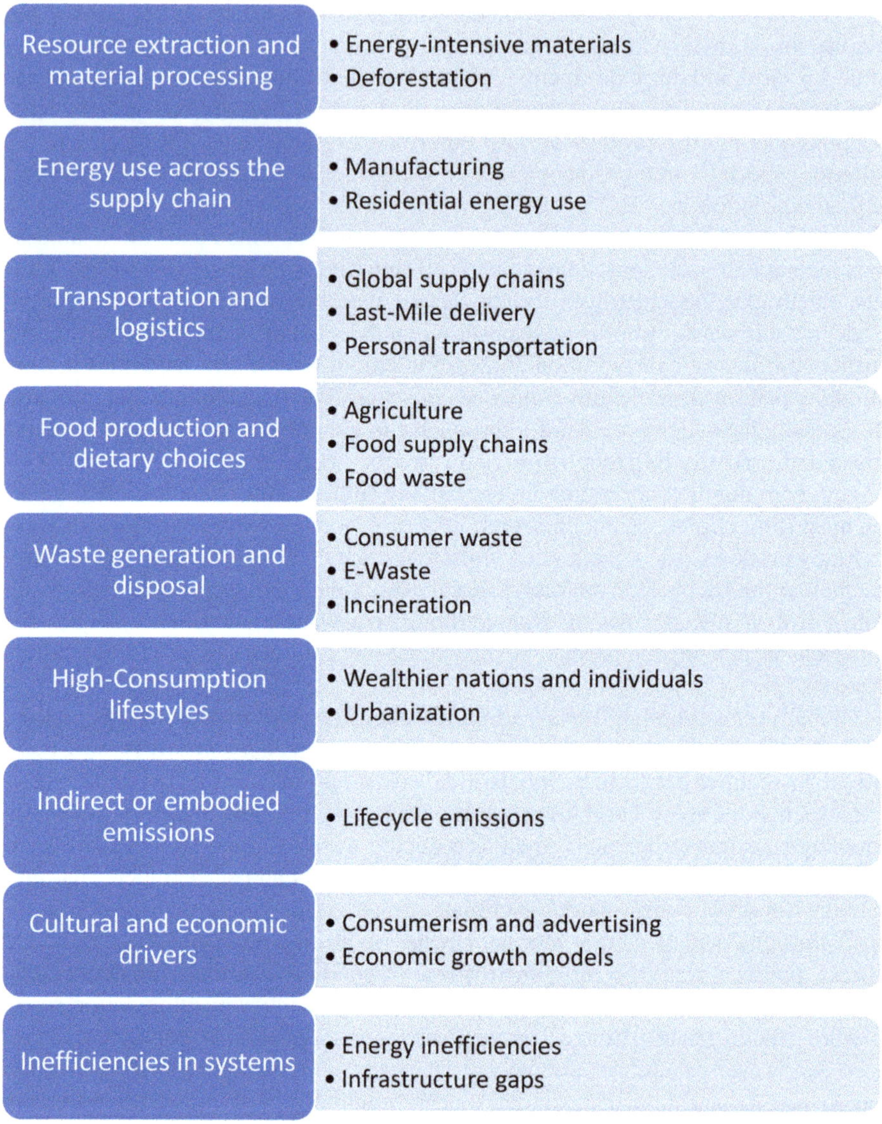

Fig. 3.3 Key drivers of consumption-related emissions. Source: Created by authors

Factories that produce consumer goods, clothing, electronics, and vehicles consume significant amounts of electricity and fossil fuels. Energy-intensive sectors, such as heavy industry, contribute a substantial share of global emissions. Consumers' direct use of electricity and heating in homes accounts for a significant portion of consumption-related emissions. The reliance on coal, oil, or natural gas for power generation intensifies this impact.

The globalization of production and trade has increased emissions from shipping, aviation, and trucking. Goods often travel thousands of kilometers before reaching consumers, with transportation emissions comprising a large share of the carbon footprint. The rise of e-commerce has intensified emissions from localized delivery networks, especially with just-in-time delivery systems and increased packaging waste. Consumer reliance on fossil fuel-powered vehicles adds significantly to consumption-related emissions, particularly in regions with inadequate public transport infrastructure.

Farming activities are major sources of methane (CH_4) and nitrous oxide (N_2O), potent greenhouse gases. Livestock production, particularly cattle for meat and dairy, is a leading contributor due to enteric fermentation and deforestation for grazing land. Transportation, refrigeration, and processing of food add further emissions. Imported foods, particularly those requiring long-haul transportation or cold storage, carry a higher carbon footprint. Roughly one-third of all food produced globally is wasted, leading to emissions from decomposition in landfills.

Packaging materials, single-use plastics, and disposable products create significant waste, much of which ends up in landfills. Decomposing organic waste emits methane, a greenhouse gas more potent than CO_2. Discarded electronics contribute to emissions during disposal and recycling, especially when toxic components are not managed responsibly. While incineration reduces landfill waste, it generates CO_2 and other pollutants if not powered by renewable energy.

High-income countries and affluent individuals tend to consume more energy-intensive goods and services, such as air travel, luxury vehicles, and large homes, resulting in disproportionately high emissions. Cities concentrate consumption and energy use, particularly in transportation, housing, and infrastructure. Urban lifestyles, characterized by increased energy demand and higher waste generation, intensify emissions.

Many products carry "hidden" or embodied emissions, which are the total GHGs emitted during the product's lifecycle. This includes emissions from raw material extraction, manufacturing, and disposal. A smartphone or vehicle's carbon footprint includes emissions from mining rare materials, assembly in energy-intensive factories, and eventual disposal or recycling.

Modern consumer culture, driven by advertising and social norms, promotes frequent purchases, often of resource-intensive goods, contributing to higher emissions. Economic systems that prioritize GDP growth over sustainability often encourage overproduction and overconsumption, intensifying the climate impact.

Many production and distribution systems still rely on outdated, energy-inefficient technologies, which amplify emissions. Inadequate infrastructure for recycling, renewable energy, or public transport exacerbates the carbon intensity of consumption.

The drivers of consumption-related emissions are deeply embedded in global economic systems and consumer habits. From resource extraction and energy use to transportation and waste generation, each stage of the consumption cycle contributes to the overall carbon footprint. Addressing these drivers requires systemic changes, such as transitioning to renewable energy, promoting circular economies, and encouraging sustainable consumption behaviors, alongside technological innovation and policy reform.

Consumption and climate change are interconnected through processes transforming natural resources into goods and services, ultimately driving greenhouse gas (GHG) emissions (Tian et al., 2024). Each stage of the consumption cycle—extraction, production, distribution, use, and disposal—contributes to emissions, making unsustainable consumption patterns a significant driver of climate change. Table 3.7 shows the primary linkages that illustrate this connection.

The linkages between consumption and climate change are systemic, encompassing every stage of the product lifecycle and influencing multiple sectors. Understanding these connections highlights the need for sustainable consumption patterns and systemic changes, such as transitioning to renewable energy, adopting circular economies, and reducing overconsumption. By addressing these linkages, we can make significant progress toward mitigating climate change and achieving global sustainability goals.

Resource extraction (Table 3.7 and Fig. 3.4) is a critical stage in the consumption cycle that directly connects consumer demand to climate change. The process of extracting raw materials—such as metals, fossil fuels, minerals, and timber—drives significant greenhouse gas (GHG) emissions, disrupts natural carbon sinks, and contributes to widespread environmental degradation. This linkage is rooted in the ever-increasing demand for goods and services, which requires vast quantities of resources to be harvested, mined, or drilled, often at a high environmental and climate cost.

The extraction of coal, oil, and natural gas is among the most carbon-intensive activities, as it not only requires significant energy inputs but also leads to emissions from associated activities like flaring and methane leaks. *Example*: Oil drilling and refining emit CO_2 and methane at every stage, from exploration to transportation, making it one of the largest contributors to climate change.

Extracting metals such as iron, aluminum, copper, and rare earth elements is energy-intensive. The use of heavy machinery, explosives, and chemical processes adds substantial emissions. *Example*: The production of 1 ton of aluminum generates up to 12 tons of CO_2 due to the high energy demands of smelting and refining.

Forests and natural ecosystems act as carbon sinks, absorbing CO_2 from the atmosphere. Resource extraction, particularly for agriculture, logging, and mining, often involves large-scale deforestation, releasing stored carbon and reducing the planet's ability to mitigate emissions. *Example*: Clearing forests for palm oil plantations in Southeast Asia releases millions of tons of CO_2 annually.

Consumer demand for products like soybeans and beef drives deforestation, particularly in tropical regions, which are some of the most carbon-dense ecosystems on Earth. *Example*: The Amazon rainforest is a major site for deforestation linked to cattle ranching, driven by global demand for beef and leather.

Methane, a potent greenhouse gas, is frequently released during oil and gas extraction through leaks or venting. Methane traps 25 times more heat in the atmosphere than CO_2 over a 100-year period, making its emissions particularly damaging. *Example*: Shale gas extraction (fracking) is associated with significant methane

Table 3.7 The linkages between consumption and climate change

Activity	Linkages	Explanation	Example
Resource extraction	Carbon-intensive processes	The extraction of raw materials, such as mining metals, drilling for oil, and logging timber, is energy-intensive and heavily reliant on fossil fuels, generating significant emissions.	The demand for palm oil leads to deforestation in tropical regions, releasing massive amounts of carbon stored in forests.
	Land-use change and deforestation	The clearing of forests for agriculture, urban development, or resource extraction releases stored carbon into the atmosphere and reduces the planet's capacity to absorb CO_2.	
Production and manufacturing	Energy use	Factories that produce goods require large amounts of energy, often generated from fossil fuels. Industries like cement, steel, and textiles are among the highest emitters.	The fashion industry contributes approximately 10% of global emissions due to resource-intensive textile production and energy use in factories.
	Chemical processes	Some manufacturing processes, such as those used in cement and fertilizer production, release GHGs through chemical reactions in addition to energy use.	
Transportation and distribution	Global supply chains	The movement of goods across countries by ships, planes, and trucks results in emissions from fossil fuel-powered transportation.	Shipping a product from a factory in Asia to a consumer in Europe involves emissions from ocean freight, trucking, and local delivery systems.
	E-commerce	The rise of online shopping has increased last-mile deliveries, which rely on fuel-intensive logistics networks.	
Consumer energy use	Residential emissions	The use of energy in homes for heating, cooling, lighting, and appliances contributes significantly to global emissions.	Suburban lifestyles that depend on private cars and large homes lead to higher energy consumption and emissions.
	Transportation choices	Personal vehicles powered by gasoline or diesel are a major source of CO_2 emissions, particularly in regions with limited public transport.	

(continued)

Table 3.7 (continued)

Activity	Linkages	Explanation	Example
Food consumption	Agriculture and livestock	The production of food, particularly meat and dairy, generates methane and nitrous oxide, two potent GHGs.	A high-meat diet has a carbon footprint several times larger than a plant-based diet due to emissions from livestock and feed production.
	Food supply chains	Emissions occur throughout the food system, from transportation and refrigeration to processing and packaging.	
	Food waste	Decomposing food in landfills releases methane, a greenhouse gas more powerful than CO_2.	
Waste generation and disposal	Landfills and methane emissions	Organic waste decomposes in landfills, producing methane.	Single-use plastics, heavily used in packaging, contribute to waste that often ends up in landfills or the ocean, exacerbating environmental and climate challenges.
	Non-biodegradable waste	Plastics and other non-recyclable materials persist in the environment, requiring energy-intensive disposal methods like incineration, which also emits CO_2.	
High-consumption lifestyles	Disproportionate impact	Wealthier nations and individuals often have significantly larger carbon footprints due to higher consumption of energy-intensive goods, services, and travel.	Frequent air travel, luxury vehicles, and large homes in affluent societies contribute disproportionately to global GHG emissions.
	Urbanization	Rapid urban development increases the demand for construction materials, energy, and transportation, leading to higher emissions.	
Embedded carbon in products	Lifecycle emissions	Many products have a hidden carbon footprint, encompassing emissions from extraction, production, transportation, and disposal.	A smartphone's carbon footprint includes emissions from mining rare earth metals, manufacturing components, and global distribution.
	Planned obsolescence	Products designed with limited lifespans require frequent replacement, increasing resource use and emissions.	

(continued)

Table 3.7 (continued)

Activity	Linkages	Explanation	Example
Feedback loops	Climate impacts intensify resource needs	As climate change causes more extreme weather events, energy and resources are required for rebuilding, cooling, and heating, further driving emissions.	Droughts caused by climate change require energy-intensive irrigation systems, adding to emissions from agricultural production.
	Resource scarcity	Depleting resources due to overconsumption leads to more intensive extraction practices, increasing emissions.	
Cultural and systemic drivers	Consumerism	Marketing and societal norms promote overconsumption, increasing demand for resource-intensive products and services.	Fast-fashion trends encourage frequent purchases of inexpensive, resource-intensive clothing that contributes to waste and emissions.
	Economic models	Systems that prioritize growth over sustainability perpetuate high consumption and emissions.	

Source: Created by authors

leakage, contributing to global warming. Methane is also emitted during coal mining, particularly in underground operations, where it is released from coal seams and surrounding rock strata.

Surface mining and strip mining disturb soil, releasing carbon stored in the soil into the atmosphere. This disruption also reduces the soil's future capacity to store carbon, further amplifying its climate impact. *Example*: Open-pit mining for coal or minerals can turn once-carbon-sequestering landscapes into sources of emissions.

Resource extraction is a key driver of the link between consumption and climate change, as it fuels the production of goods and services while generating significant emissions and environmental degradation. As global consumption grows, the pressures on resource-rich ecosystems intensify, exacerbating climate impacts. Transitioning to more sustainable practices in extraction, reducing demand for raw materials through recycling and circular economies, and preserving natural carbon sinks are essential steps in addressing this critical linkage. By tackling emissions at the extraction stage, we can make substantial progress in mitigating the climate impact of consumption.

Production and manufacturing are key stages in the consumption cycle that significantly contribute to climate change (Tables 3.7 and 3.8). Transforming raw materials into finished goods requires energy-intensive processes, which are often powered by fossil fuels. These activities not only emit large quantities of greenhouse gases (GHGs) directly but also involve indirect emissions from the infrastructure, machinery, and supply chains required to sustain production systems. As

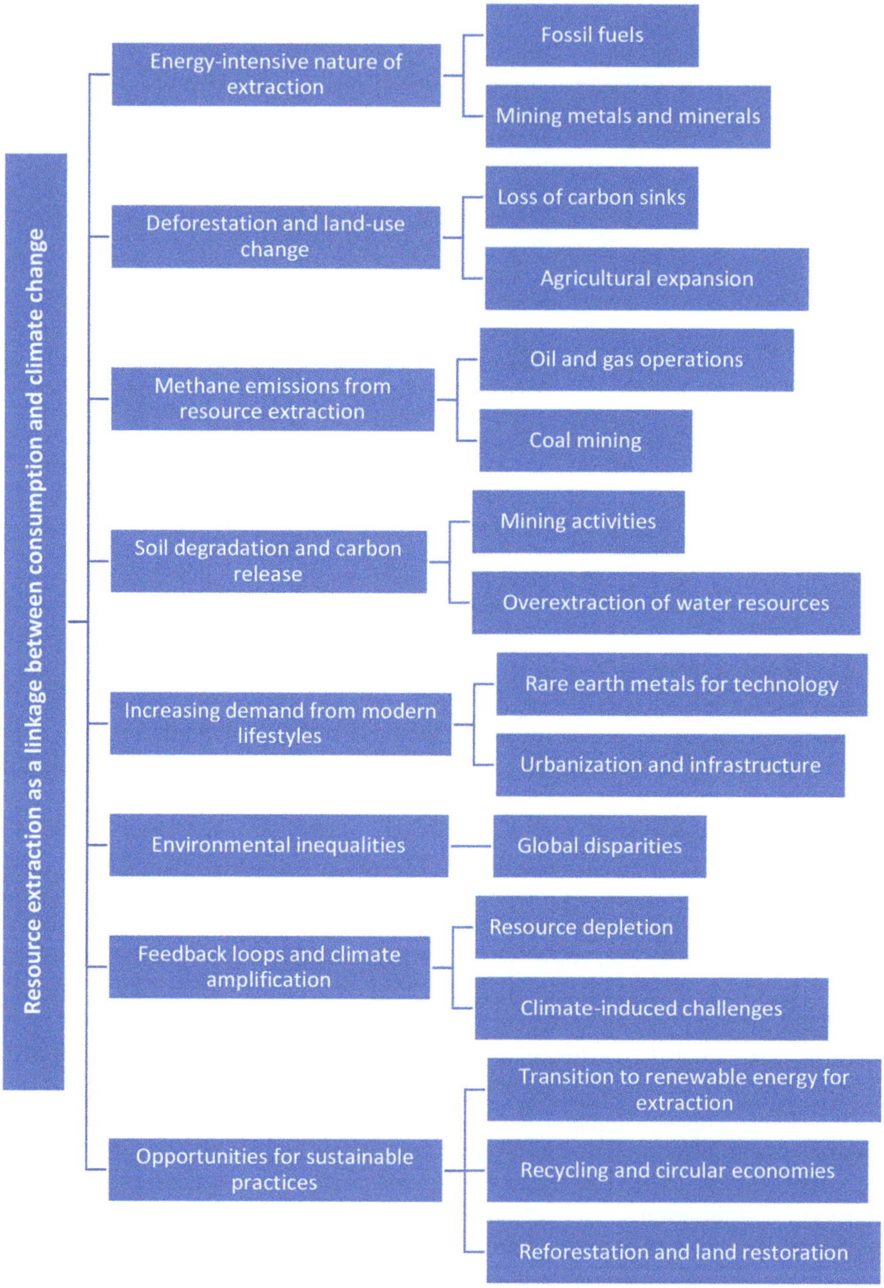

Fig. 3.4 Resource extraction as a linkage between consumption and climate change. Source: Created by authors

Table 3.8 Production and manufacturing as a linkage between consumption and climate change

Activity	Explanation	Example
Energy use in industrial processes	Manufacturing is one of the largest consumers of energy globally, much of which is derived from non-renewable sources. Factories rely heavily on electricity and heat, often generated by coal, oil, or natural gas, to power machinery and production lines.	Steel and cement production, which are foundational to infrastructure and construction, are among the most energy-intensive industrial processes. Cement alone accounts for approximately 7–8% of global carbon dioxide (CO_2) emissions due to the combination of high heat requirements and chemical reactions during production.
Emissions from chemical reactions	Certain manufacturing processes emit GHGs not only from energy use but also from chemical transformations involved in producing materials.	During cement production, limestone is heated to release calcium, a process that emits CO_2 as a by-product. Similarly, the production of ammonia for fertilizers generates substantial CO_2 emissions due to the chemical reactions involved.
Resource waste and inefficiency	Manufacturing systems often produce significant waste, including offcuts, defective products, and surplus materials. These waste streams represent embodied emissions, as they reflect the energy and resources used during extraction and processing.	In fast fashion, rapid production cycles lead to high levels of fabric waste and unsold inventory, which contribute to unnecessary emissions from production that ultimately results in landfill disposal.
Carbon-intensive industries	Certain industries are particularly carbon-intensive due to the scale of production and the nature of the goods produced.	The production of textiles and clothing generates emissions from energy use, chemical dyeing, and synthetic fiber manufacturing. Polyester, for example, a widely used synthetic fiber, is derived from fossil fuels and has a high carbon footprint.
Role of automation and technology	Advances in technology have accelerated production speeds, often at the cost of increased energy consumption. Automated factories, while improving efficiency, rely heavily on continuous energy inputs, amplifying emissions if powered by fossil fuels.	Robotics and AI-driven production lines in automotive and electronics industries enhance productivity but require high amounts of electricity, much of which is derived from non-renewable sources.
Globalized supply chains	Manufacturing is often spread across multiple countries, with different stages of production occurring in specialized regions. While this approach reduces costs, it amplifies emissions due to the need for transporting semi-finished goods between facilities.	A smartphone may involve raw materials from Africa, assembly in Asia, and final distribution to Europe or North America, with each step adding to its carbon footprint.

(continued)

Table 3.8 (continued)

Activity	Explanation	Example
Overproduction and short product lifecycles	Modern manufacturing systems are often designed for overproduction to meet fluctuating consumer demands, leading to excess inventory and waste. Additionally, short product lifecycles, driven by trends or planned obsolescence, require frequent replacement of goods, increasing the emissions associated with continuous production.	The fast-fashion industry produces billions of garments annually, many of which are worn only a few times before being discarded, perpetuating a cycle of production and waste.
Embedded carbon in products	The production process embeds carbon within products, which represents the emissions associated with their creation. These embodied emissions persist even if the products themselves are not directly carbon-intensive during use.	A single automobile embodies significant emissions from the production of steel, aluminum, plastic, and glass used in its construction, as well as the energy required for assembly.

Source: Created by authors according to Nicholson et al. (2023), Hu et al. (2024)

global consumption grows, the scale and intensity of manufacturing activities increase, deepening their impact on climate change.

Production and manufacturing form a vital linkage between consumption and climate change, serving as the engine that transforms raw materials into the goods consumers demand. Reliance on fossil fuels, inefficiencies in production systems, and globalized supply chains amplify these processes' carbon footprint. Transitioning to sustainable manufacturing practices and promoting circular economies are essential for reducing emissions and mitigating climate impacts. By addressing this critical linkage, industries can play a key role in achieving global climate goals.

Transportation and distribution (Table 3.7 and Fig. 3.5) form a critical link between consumption and climate change, as they facilitate the movement of goods from production facilities to markets and, ultimately, to consumers. These processes are heavily reliant on fossil fuels, making them a significant contributor to global greenhouse gas (GHG) emissions. As global trade and consumer demand continue to grow, transportation and distribution networks expand, intensifying their climate impact.

The modern global economy is characterized by highly interconnected supply chains, where raw materials and finished goods often travel thousands of kilometers before reaching consumers. Modes of transport such as cargo ships, airplanes, and trucks are essential to this system but generate significant emissions. Maritime shipping, responsible for moving about 80% of global trade by volume, is a major emitter of CO_2. Large container ships, powered by heavy fuel oil, release pollutants like sulfur oxides (SOx) and nitrogen oxides (NOx) in addition to CO_2. While air transport accounts for a smaller share of global goods movement, it has a disproportionately high carbon footprint per ton of goods transported due to the energy-intensive

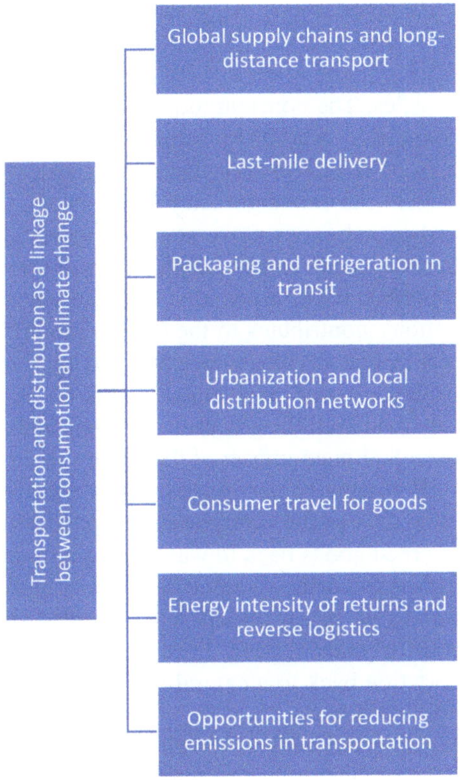

Fig. 3.5 Transportation and distribution as a linkage between consumption and climate change. Source: Created by authors

nature of aviation (Xie et al., 2023). *Example:* Shipping electronics from Asia to North America involves substantial emissions from container ships and the subsequent trucking required for distribution within the destination region.

The final leg of the supply chain, often referred to as "last-mile delivery," involves moving goods from distribution centers to consumers' homes or retail stores. This stage has become increasingly carbon-intensive with the rise of e-commerce and the demand for fast shipping. The use of delivery trucks and vans powered by diesel or gasoline adds significantly to urban traffic congestion and emissions. Consumer preferences for same-day or next-day delivery exacerbate emissions by reducing the efficiency of delivery routes, as vehicles prioritize speed over consolidation. *Example:* A single online order delivered via an express van can have a higher per-unit carbon footprint than multiple items shipped together in bulk.

Many goods, especially food and pharmaceuticals, require specific packaging and temperature controls during transportation. Refrigerated transport systems, often powered by fossil fuels, contribute additional emissions. Excessive packaging, often used to protect goods during transit, generates waste and embodied carbon, amplifying the climate impact of transportation. *Example:* Transporting fresh produce across continents requires refrigerated containers, which consume energy and produce emissions throughout the journey.

In urban areas, the growth of consumer markets has led to the proliferation of local distribution networks. While these systems aim to ensure quick and reliable delivery, they often involve inefficient routing and reliance on fossil fuel-powered vehicles. The concentration of deliveries in cities increases emissions from traffic congestion and idling vehicles, particularly in densely populated areas (Maxner et al., 2022). *Example:* Delivery trucks making multiple stops in congested urban centers can emit significant amounts of CO_2 and other pollutants.

Beyond goods movement, transportation emissions are also linked to consumer behavior, such as traveling to stores or markets to purchase items. Private car use for shopping trips, especially in suburban areas with limited public transportation options, contributes to the carbon footprint of consumption. Retailers that rely on car-dependent shopping malls and big-box stores indirectly encourage emissions from consumer travel (Li et al., 2016). *Example:* Driving to a large retail store in a suburban area for groceries or goods adds personal transportation emissions to the overall climate impact of the supply chain.

E-commerce has made product returns more common, adding another layer of emissions to the transportation system. Reverse logistics, which involves moving returned goods back to warehouses or manufacturers, can significantly increase the carbon footprint of online purchases. Inefficient systems for managing returns often lead to increased vehicle miles traveled and additional packaging waste (Cullinane and Cullinane, 2021). *Example:* Returning clothing bought online involves transportation back to a central warehouse, doubling the emissions associated with the original delivery.

Efforts to mitigate the climate impact of transportation and distribution include:

- Shifting to low-carbon fuels. Using biofuels, hydrogen, or electric vehicles for freight transport can significantly reduce emissions.
- Optimizing logistics. Improving delivery route planning and using advanced logistics software can increase efficiency and reduce unnecessary miles.
- Encouraging local sourcing. Promoting locally sourced goods reduces the need for long-distance transport, cutting emissions and supporting regional economies.
- Adopting green shipping practices. Companies can invest in technologies like wind-assisted ships or electrified container ports to reduce emissions from maritime transport.

Transportation and distribution are integral to modern consumption but remain significant contributors to climate change due to their reliance on fossil fuels and energy-intensive practices. The movement of goods across global supply chains, coupled with the rise of e-commerce and consumer expectations for fast delivery, has amplified emissions from this sector. Addressing these challenges requires systemic changes, such as transitioning to low-carbon transportation, optimizing logistics, and promoting local sourcing. By reducing the climate impact of transportation and distribution, we can make substantial progress toward achieving global sustainability goals.

Consumer energy use (Tables 3.7 and 3.9) is a critical link between consumption and climate change, as it directly drives greenhouse gas (GHG) emissions through

Table 3.9 Consumer energy use as a linkage between consumption and climate change

Activity	Explanation	Example
Residential energy consumption		
Heating and cooling	The largest portion of residential energy use typically goes toward heating and cooling homes. In regions with extreme climates, energy demand spikes, particularly during winter or summer, leading to increased emissions from fossil fuel-based electricity or heating systems.	In colder climates, natural gas furnaces and oil-based heating systems are significant sources of CO_2 emissions.
Lighting and appliances	Household appliances such as refrigerators, washing machines, and entertainment devices contribute to energy use. While energy-efficient models are becoming more popular, the growing number of devices per household offsets some efficiency gains.	A typical household in a developed country may use multiple televisions, game consoles, and smart devices, increasing overall electricity demand.
Personal transportation		
Urban congestion	In urban areas, traffic congestion worsens emissions as vehicles idle or operate at inefficient speeds.	Idling in traffic during peak hours in major cities contributes to localized air pollution and elevated CO_2 emissions.
The growing demand for energy-intensive devices		
Smart devices and electronics	The proliferation of energy-consuming devices, including smartphones, tablets, and home assistants, adds to household electricity demand. Many of these devices are used continuously or require frequent charging.	Constant charging of smartphones and laptops increases the overall energy consumption of a household, especially in regions where electricity is generated using fossil fuels.
Air-conditioning and heating systems	As living standards improve in warmer regions, air-conditioning use is rising dramatically. These systems are often energy-intensive and contribute to spikes in electricity demand, particularly during heatwaves.	The increasing adoption of air conditioners in emerging economies is projected to be a major driver of future electricity consumption.
Indirect energy use		
Embedded energy in products	Many consumer goods carry "embedded energy," representing the energy required for their production, transportation, and disposal. When consumers purchase and use such products, they indirectly drive the energy consumption of the entire supply chain.	The lifecycle of an electric vehicle battery involves significant energy inputs during production, which contributes to its overall carbon footprint, even if the vehicle itself emits no direct GHGs.

Source: Created by authors according to Goldstein et al. (2020), Hu and Milner (2020)

everyday activities such as powering homes, operating appliances, and using personal vehicles. These activities often rely on electricity and fuels derived from fossil energy sources like coal, oil, and natural gas, making them significant contributors to carbon emissions. As consumption patterns evolve, the demand for energy-intensive lifestyles grows, amplifying the climate impact.

Energy consumption patterns vary greatly by region and lifestyle. For example, households with higher incomes tend to consume more energy—they tend to live in larger homes, have more vehicles, and use more electronic devices. Meanwhile, households with lower incomes often limit themselves to basic energy needs, although their heating and lighting solutions may be less efficient.

Differences between countries are also evident—in developed countries, per capita energy consumption far exceeds that of poorer regions. This is partly due to the greater availability of modern technologies and amenities, such as district heating and air conditioning (Falchetta et al., 2024).

In addition, the source of electricity also has a significant impact on carbon dioxide emissions. In regions where renewable energy sources—such as wind, solar, and hydroelectric power—dominate energy production, the carbon footprint of residents is much lower. For example, a household that uses electricity from renewable sources for heating, cooling, and appliances contributes significantly less to climate change than one that relies on coal-fired power plants.

Opportunities to reduce emissions:

- Energy efficiency. Encouraging the adoption of energy-efficient appliances and systems can significantly reduce household energy demand.
- Behavioral changes. Small shifts in daily habits, such as turning off lights, unplugging devices when not in use, or using public transportation, can collectively lower emissions.
- Smart technology. Home automation systems that optimize energy use, such as smart thermostats or energy monitoring devices, can help consumers track and reduce energy consumption.

Consumer energy use is a significant linkage between consumption and climate change, encompassing residential electricity consumption, personal transportation, and the growing demand for energy-intensive devices. By addressing inefficiencies in energy use, transitioning to renewable energy sources, and adopting energy-efficient technologies, consumers can reduce their carbon footprint and contribute to mitigating climate change.

Food consumption (Tables 3.7 and 3.10) is the next link between consumption patterns and climate change. The global food system, encompassing production, processing, transportation, storage, and waste management, is responsible for a significant share of greenhouse gas (GHG) emissions. As consumer demand for food grows and dietary preferences evolve, the environmental impact of food systems becomes increasingly significant. This connection highlights the need for sustainable food choices to mitigate climate change while ensuring global food security.

Expanding agricultural land to meet food demand often results in deforestation, particularly in tropical regions. Clearing forests for grazing livestock or growing crops such as soy and palm oil releases large amounts of carbon stored in trees and soil. The industrial processing of food involves energy-intensive activities,

Table 3.10 Food consumption as a linkage between consumption and climate change

Activity	Explanation	Example
Agricultural production and emissions		
Livestock farming	Animal agriculture is one of the largest contributors to food-related emissions. Livestock, particularly cattle, produce methane (CH_4) through enteric fermentation during digestion. Methane is a potent GHG with a global warming potential significantly higher than carbon dioxide (CO_2).	The beef and dairy industries are among the highest emitters, driven by large-scale production and the resources required for feed cultivation and land use.
Crop production	Cultivating crops like rice, soybeans, and corn generates emissions through the use of synthetic fertilizers, which release nitrous oxide (N_2O), another potent GHG. Additionally, tilling practices can release stored carbon from soil.	Rice paddies emit methane due to anaerobic conditions in flooded fields, making rice cultivation a significant source of GHGs.
Dietary choices and climate impact		
Meat-intensive diets	Diets high in red meat and dairy have a significantly larger carbon footprint compared to plant-based diets due to the emissions associated with livestock farming and feed production.	A kilogram of beef can generate up to 60 kg of CO_2-equivalent emissions, far exceeding the emissions from most plant-based proteins like lentils or beans.
Plant-based and sustainable diets	Plant-based diets generally have a lower environmental impact, as they require fewer resources and produce fewer emissions. Incorporating seasonal and locally sourced foods can further reduce the carbon footprint.	A shift from a meat-heavy diet to a Mediterranean-style diet rich in fruits, vegetables, and legumes can significantly reduce GHG emissions.
Sustainable practices to mitigate food-related emissions		
Reducing food waste	Implementing strategies like better storage, meal planning, and redistributing surplus food can reduce waste and emissions.	Composting organic waste prevents methane emissions in landfills and creates nutrient-rich soil.
Shifting dietary patterns	Encouraging plant-based diets and reducing meat consumption can significantly lower emissions while improving health outcomes.	Public campaigns promoting "Meatless Mondays" have raised awareness of the environmental impact of diets and inspired reductions in meat consumption.
Local and seasonal eating	Sourcing food locally and consuming seasonal produce reduces transportation emissions and supports regional agriculture.	Choosing locally grown apples over imported avocados reduces food miles and the associated carbon footprint.

Source: Created by authors

including refrigeration, cooking, and packaging. The use of single-use plastics and non-recyclable materials in food packaging further exacerbates the carbon footprint.

Transporting food from farms to markets and consumers, often across long distances, adds to its carbon footprint. Energy-intensive refrigeration is required for perishable goods, and long-haul transportation relies heavily on fossil fuels.

Imported fruits and vegetables, such as berries shipped by air or refrigerated containers carrying seafood, generate significantly higher emissions compared to locally sourced alternatives.

Approximately one-third of all food produced globally is wasted, either during production, distribution, or consumption. Food waste in landfills decomposes anaerobically, releasing methane into the atmosphere. Discarded fruits and vegetables in landfills contribute to methane emissions, highlighting the climate impact of over-purchasing and improper storage by consumers (Gustavsson et al., 2011).

Overconsumption of food, particularly in wealthier nations, exacerbates the climate impact by increasing demand for high-emission products and contributing to food waste. Large portion sizes and the popularity of all-you-can-eat dining in high-income countries lead to unnecessary food waste and higher emissions throughout the supply chain.

Food consumption is a key driver of climate change, contributing to emissions through agricultural practices, land use, processing, transportation, and waste. The connection between dietary choices and environmental impact underscores the importance of adopting sustainable food systems and consumption behaviors. By reducing food waste, shifting to plant-based diets, and prioritizing local and seasonal foods, consumers can play a significant role in mitigating the climate impact of food consumption.

Waste generation and disposal form a critical link between consumption and climate change, as improper waste management, resource inefficiency, and overconsumption lead to significant greenhouse gas (GHG) emissions. Table 3.11 below provides examples of how waste generation and disposal contribute to climate change.

Waste generation and disposal are critical links between consumption and climate change, as they contribute significantly to greenhouse gas (GHG) emissions and environmental degradation. The demand for goods and services leads to increased production, packaging, and disposal of materials, all of which have climate implications. Every stage of the waste lifecycle—generation, collection, treatment, and disposal—produces emissions that exacerbate global warming.

Waste-related emissions primarily stem from two key processes:

1. Decomposition of organic materials (e.g., food, wood, and paper) in landfills, which releases methane (CH_4), a potent GHG.
2. Combustion and incineration of materials, such as plastics and textiles, which emit carbon dioxide (CO_2) and black carbon.

Furthermore, improper waste management practices, such as open burning, landfill mismanagement, and limited recycling, worsen the climate impact of consumption. This link is amplified in societies with high consumption patterns, where single-use items, e-waste, and overpackaging are prevalent. At the same time, low-income regions often lack the infrastructure to manage waste sustainably, further exacerbating emissions and pollution (Gómez-Sanabria et al., 2022).

Key challenges in waste generation and disposal:

Table 3.11 Examples of how waste generation and disposal contribute to climate change

Example	Explanation	Impact
Food waste in landfills	In high-income countries, consumers often purchase more food than needed, leading to significant quantities of food being discarded. When food waste ends up in landfills, it decomposes anaerobically (without oxygen), producing methane (CH_4), a greenhouse gas that is 25 times more potent than carbon dioxide (CO_2) over a 100-year period.	Globally, food waste accounts for roughly 8–10% of total GHG emissions. For example, discarded fruits, vegetables, and meat products in landfills contribute to both methane emissions and the embodied carbon footprint of production, transportation, and refrigeration that was wasted.
Single-use plastics and packaging	The increased use of single-use plastics, such as water bottles, shopping bags, and food containers, has created significant environmental and climate challenges. Plastics are derived from petrochemicals (fossil fuels), and their production and disposal release substantial GHGs. Improper disposal, such as open burning of plastics, further exacerbates emissions by releasing CO_2 and toxic pollutants into the atmosphere.	In 2019 alone, the production and incineration of plastics emitted over 850 million metric tons of CO_2 equivalent. Plastic waste that is not incinerated or recycled often ends up in oceans or landfills, where it persists for hundreds of years.
E-waste and electronics	Discarded electronic devices, such as smartphones, laptops, and appliances, contribute to growing electronic waste (e-waste). E-waste is often improperly disposed of in open dumps or incinerated, releasing CO_2 and toxic chemicals into the air. Extracting new raw materials (like metals) to replace discarded devices adds further emissions.	In 2022, global e-waste reached approximately 50 million metric tons, with only a fraction being properly recycled. Poor recycling practices lead to the loss of valuable materials like copper and aluminum, forcing additional resource extraction and increasing emissions.
Fast-fashion and textile waste	The fast-fashion industry promotes disposable clothing, leading to massive textile waste. Many garments are made from synthetic fibers like polyester, derived from petroleum. When discarded clothes end up in landfills, synthetic fibers release methane and microplastics as they degrade. If incinerated, they emit CO_2 and other pollutants.	The fashion industry contributes around 10% of global emissions, and approximately 92 million tons of textile waste are generated annually. This waste represents both the embodied carbon of production and the emissions from disposal.
Municipal solid waste and open burning	In many low- and middle-income countries, municipal solid waste (household and commercial waste) is often burned in open fields due to inadequate infrastructure. Open burning releases large amounts of CO_2, methane, black carbon, and toxic pollutants into the air, contributing to both climate change and air quality degradation.	Black carbon, a short-lived climate pollutant produced by incomplete combustion, is a major contributor to global warming. Its warming potential is hundreds of times higher than CO_2 over a short time frame.

(continued)

Table 3.11 (continued)

Example	Explanation	Impact
Landfills and organic waste	Organic waste, such as food scraps, yard trimmings, and paper, makes up a significant portion of landfill content. As this waste decomposes, it generates methane emissions. Large-scale landfills with poor gas capture systems contribute substantially to GHG emissions.	The U.S. Environmental Protection Agency (EPA) reported that landfills are the third-largest source of methane emissions in the United States, highlighting the need for better waste management practices like composting.
Construction and demolition waste	Construction and demolition (C&D) activities generate large amounts of waste, including concrete, wood, and metal. Improper disposal often involves incineration or dumping in landfills, which adds to emissions. Additionally, producing new construction materials to replace discarded ones requires energy-intensive processes.	For instance, cement production for new infrastructure is responsible for 7–8% of global CO_2 emissions. Recycling construction waste into usable materials can reduce emissions from new production.
Disposable products and lifestyle waste	The rise of disposable products, such as single-use coffee cups, utensils, and diapers, has increased waste volumes. These items are often non-recyclable, leading to their incineration or burial in landfills, which generates additional emissions.	For example, disposable diapers account for significant landfill waste, where synthetic components can take centuries to degrade, releasing emissions throughout the process.
Waste from overpackaging in logistics and e-commerce	The growth of e-commerce has led to a surge in packaging waste, including cardboard boxes, plastic wrapping, and foam materials. The production of these materials consumes energy, and improper disposal leads to emissions through incineration or decomposition.	A study found that packaging contributes up to 45% of e-commerce's carbon footprint, driven by both the materials and the emissions associated with waste disposal.
Agricultural residue burning	In agricultural regions, crop residues (like straw and stalks) are often burned to clear fields for the next planting season. This practice releases large amounts of CO_2, methane, and black carbon, contributing to both air pollution and global warming.	In parts of India, for instance, agricultural burning significantly contributes to regional air pollution and climate change, with emissions spreading far beyond local boundaries.

Source: Created by authors

1. Rising consumption and overproduction. Modern consumer culture promotes overconsumption, leading to increased waste generation. Fast-fashion, single-use plastics, and e-waste are prime examples where products are produced and discarded at alarming rates. Addressing the root cause of waste requires a shift in consumer behavior and business models that prioritize sustainability over profit-driven overproduction.

2. Methane emissions from landfills. Organic waste, including food scraps and agricultural residue, decomposes anaerobically in landfills, releasing methane—a GHG with a global warming potential far greater than CO_2. Many regions lack the infrastructure for composting or capturing landfill methane, particularly in developing countries.
3. Plastic pollution and its climate footprint. The production and disposal of plastics contribute heavily to GHG emissions, as plastics are derived from fossil fuels. Improper disposal—through incineration or open burning—further releases CO_2 and toxic pollutants. Despite growing awareness, reducing plastic consumption and improving recycling systems remain difficult due to their convenience and low cost.
4. E-waste mismanagement. Electronic waste (e-waste) is growing rapidly due to technological advancements and short product lifecycles. Improper disposal leads to emissions from burning, while valuable materials remain unrecovered, driving further resource extraction. Establishing circular systems for electronics is hampered by poor recycling infrastructure, high costs, and a lack of consumer awareness.
5. Inefficient recycling and circular systems. Recycling rates remain low globally, particularly for complex materials like plastics, textiles, and electronics. Additionally, products are often not designed for reuse or recycling, leading to significant waste. Building effective recycling systems requires investment, advanced technologies, and a shift toward product design that prioritizes durability and recyclability.
6. Waste inequality. Developing nations disproportionately bear the burden of global waste, often receiving exported waste from wealthier countries. These regions often lack the infrastructure to manage this waste sustainably, leading to emissions and pollution. Addressing the global waste trade requires international cooperation and policies to ensure equitable waste management solutions.

Opportunities to address waste generation and disposal:

1. Improving waste management infrastructure. Investing in advanced waste management systems, such as anaerobic digesters, methane capture technologies, and waste-to-energy plants, can reduce emissions from landfills while producing renewable energy. Countries can use captured methane from landfills to generate energy, creating a win-win solution for waste reduction and clean energy production.
2. Promoting composting and organic waste solutions. Expanding composting systems for food and agricultural waste can prevent methane emissions and create nutrient-rich soil, which supports sustainable agriculture. Cities can implement compost collection programs, reducing landfill contributions while supporting regenerative farming practices.
3. Transitioning to a circular economy. A circular economy reduces waste by reusing, repairing, recycling, and upcycling materials, thereby extending product lifecycles and reducing the need for virgin resource extraction. Businesses can design products for durability and recyclability, while governments can incentivize circular practices through policies and infrastructure development.

4. Scaling up recycling programs. Improving recycling technologies, creating incentives for consumers to recycle, and increasing the use of recycled materials in production can significantly reduce waste emissions. Innovations such as chemical recycling for plastics and closed-loop systems for electronics can tackle hard-to-recycle materials.
5. Reducing single-use plastics and disposable goods. Policies such as bans on single-use plastics, taxes on non-recyclable items, and incentives for reusable alternatives can drive reductions in plastic waste. Consumers and businesses can adopt reusable products, biodegradable alternatives, and minimal packaging to lower emissions.
6. Raising consumer awareness and behavioral change. Educational campaigns highlighting the link between waste, consumption, and climate change can encourage individuals to reduce waste, reuse materials, and support sustainable products. Behavioral changes, such as mindful consumption, meal planning to avoid food waste, and proper sorting of recyclables, can have significant cumulative impacts.
7. Technological innovations. Emerging technologies, such as AI-powered waste sorting, smart packaging, and bio-based materials, offer promising solutions to improve waste management and reduce emissions. Integrating smart systems into waste management can enhance efficiency, reduce emissions, and create economic opportunities.

Waste generation and disposal represent a significant link between consumption and climate change, driven by unsustainable production systems, inefficient waste management, and overconsumption. While challenges like methane emissions, plastic waste, and e-waste mismanagement persist, numerous opportunities exist to address these issues through improved infrastructure, circular economy practices, technological innovation, and consumer awareness (Wiedenhofer et al., 2025).

High-consumption lifestyles are a significant driver of climate change, as they lead to an outsized demand for resources, energy, and goods. These lifestyles are characterized by excessive consumption of energy-intensive products, frequent purchases of nonessential items, reliance on private transportation, and wasteful practices. The link between high consumption and climate change lies in the increased greenhouse gas (GHG) emissions generated at every stage of the consumption cycle—resource extraction, manufacturing, transportation, usage, and disposal. While the impact of consumption varies by region and income level, high-income nations and individuals disproportionately contribute to global emissions due to their elevated levels of consumption.

3.3 The Environmental Impact of Online Shopping

It is hard to imagine contemporary consumption habits without the convenience of online shopping. The past decade has seen not only a surge in e-commerce activity but also a shift in the way people think about consumption, time, and access. However, while digital commerce seems to offer a cleaner, more efficient alternative to traditional shopping, its environmental footprint is not as small or simple as it may appear.

At first glance, online shopping reduces the need for consumers to travel by car to brick-and-mortar stores. Fewer car trips could mean less fuel burned and fewer greenhouse gas emissions. That argument, repeated often in media and industry reports, is attractive—but not the whole story. Behind the interface of seamless deliveries and quick checkouts lies a complex and often overlooked chain of environmental costs.

Packaging is one of the most visible signs of this shift. Online goods, especially when delivered individually, are often overpackaged. A single item might arrive in a cardboard box, wrapped in plastic, with added cushioning material (Xie et al., 2021). Multiply that by millions of daily shipments, and the waste generated is significant—not just in terms of volume, but in terms of materials used, recyclability, and transport emissions related to handling larger shipment volumes.

Another issue is the logistics chain. Fast delivery options have led to an increase in "last-mile" emissions, with courier vehicles making more frequent, often less efficient trips to reach individual addresses. Unlike consolidated deliveries to stores, home deliveries rarely follow optimized routes. In urban areas, this leads to traffic congestion, while in rural regions, it increases the fuel required to reach dispersed homes.

There is also the problem of returns. Online shopping has normalized a culture of try-and-return, especially in sectors like fashion. Returned goods often travel back across long distances, are sometimes repackaged or even discarded if resale isn't economically viable. This not only doubles transport emissions in some cases but also contributes to overproduction and waste (Eriksson and Käck, 2023).

Moreover, the infrastructure behind e-commerce—server farms, digital platforms, warehouses—is energy-intensive. While not immediately visible to consumers, the digital side of shopping requires significant electricity, often sourced from non-renewable energy grids, particularly in regions with less sustainable infrastructure.

So while online shopping may seem more sustainable to individual consumers, especially when compared to driving to a distant store, the broader picture reveals a more nuanced, and in many ways problematic, environmental impact. As with many modern conveniences, the sustainability of online shopping depends less on the technology itself and more on the way it is used—and regulated.

Transport and Emissions

The environmental cost of online shopping becomes particularly visible when we look at transportation. While the idea of having goods delivered to one's doorstep suggests convenience and efficiency, the actual logistics tell a more complicated story.

In theory, centralized delivery systems could reduce emissions. A well-planned route delivering to multiple homes in the same area may emit less CO_2 per item than dozens of individuals driving separately to stores. But in practice, the reality of e-commerce logistics is far from optimized. Express delivery expectations, next-day shipping, and fragmented orders have pushed delivery systems to operate at suboptimal efficiency.

According to a study published by the World Economic Forum in collaboration with McKinsey and Company, demand for urban last-mile delivery is expected to grow by 78% by 2030, which could lead to a 32% increase in carbon emissions from urban delivery transport. In high-density cities, this translates not only into higher emissions but also more traffic congestion, air pollution, and noise—effects that are especially pronounced in poorer neighborhoods, which often lack infrastructure to absorb such pressure.

What's more, the increase in same-day and next-day deliveries contributes heavily to the inefficiency. Research by Van Loon et al. (2015) found that faster delivery options significantly increase the number of trips made and reduce the ability to consolidate packages into fewer, fuller loads. In other words, the faster the delivery, the less sustainable it becomes. Even electric vehicles, while helpful, do not fully resolve the problem—especially when electricity is not from renewable sources, and when vehicles are used inefficiently.

In suburban or rural areas, the environmental cost per package can be even greater. Deliveries to sparsely populated regions often involve longer driving distances for a single item. These trips, often with low drop density, consume more fuel and time, offsetting any potential gains from not driving to a store oneself.

Some cities are experimenting with solutions. Micro-fulfillment centers, bicycle couriers, and parcel lockers are being tested in European urban centers like Amsterdam and Berlin. While promising, these strategies are not yet widespread and tend to work only in areas with high population density and strong logistical coordination.

Another dimension is the increase in failed delivery attempts, which often leads to repeated trips. According to research by Allen et al. (2018), failed first delivery rates in some European cities reach up to 25%, further intensifying unnecessary vehicle miles and emissions. Although digital tracking and notifications help reduce this, they have not eliminated the problem. The transportation side of online shopping carries a growing environmental burden. It is shaped not only by how products are delivered but also by consumer behavior—our collective insistence on speed and convenience feeds an unsustainable logistical cycle. Addressing this challenge requires both technological innovation and cultural shifts in what we consider to be "fast" or "good" service.

When it comes to online shopping, the logistics behind "free shipping" often hide an environmental cost that many shoppers overlook. It's not just about convenience; it's about carbon.

A recent scenario: the World Economic Forum predicts a 78% growth in urban last-mile delivery by 2030, leading to 32% more carbon emissions from delivery vehicles alone. In other words, if we don't rethink how goods get to our doors, our cities will literally choke on more delivery vans.

What's driving that surge? Customers increasingly expect next-day or even same-day delivery—an expectation that shrinks delivery windows and fragments delivery routes. It's harder to optimize routes when packages rush out as soon as you click "buy." A 2023 peer-reviewed analysis from *Transportation research interdisciplinary perspectives* highlights delivery speed as a key factor: faster delivery options correlate with more-but-inefficient routes, eroding any carbon gains from shared deliveries.

In rural or suburban areas the situation worsens. Low-density deliveries mean vans travel long distances for single items, which is far less efficient than a personal shopping trip to a nearby store. According to a health and environment overview from Wikipedia, delivery vans average around 1.3 kg CO_2 per mile (roughly 7.8 mpg). Those miles add up fast when a parcel makes a 50 km round trip for one book.

Another wrinkle—air freight. Demand for speed has driven many parcels into planes. One Guardian analysis reports that greenhouse gas emissions from air freight grew 25% since 2019, propelled by a post-pandemic surge in parcel shipping. And it's not subtle—air freight can emit 80 times more CO_2 per km than sea or truck routes. But all hope isn't lost. Some logistics players are taking action. Take DHL in Germany: as of early 2024, they've rolled out 6100 e-bikes, 13,500 e-trikes, and 23,000 electric vans, cutting emissions by about 1 million tons of CO_2 in 2022. Those aren't small numbers—they're equivalent to removing around 223,000 gasoline cars off the road for a year. E-bikes can also deliver 60% faster than vans in dense urban settings, with a much smaller carbon footprint.

Still, electrifying vans alone won't suffice. Efficient routing is essential: UPS, for instance, eliminated left-turns in certain routes, cutting fuel use by 10 million gallons and CO_2 emissions by 22,000 tons per year. Add in consumer behavior—bulk ordering, flexible delivery times, or pick-up points—and you've got a fuller strategy. The environmental impact of online shopping isn't inevitable. It stems from a tangle of speed expectations, route inefficiencies, transport modality, and delivery density. Solutions are emerging—electric fleets, bikes, lockers—but they require smart design, supportive policy, and a willingness from consumers to rethink convenience.

If online shopping is here to stay—and by all signs, it is—then the challenge is not to reverse the trend but to shape it in smarter, less harmful ways. Reducing emissions in transport, especially in the last mile, won't come from one silver-bullet technology. It's a matter of piecing together many small, workable changes that depend on location, infrastructure, and how willing both businesses and consumers are to compromise.

One of the more promising ideas is parcel consolidation and delivery windows. Retailers can encourage shoppers to choose slower, grouped delivery options by offering incentives—discounts, loyalty points, or simply more honest information about environmental impacts. If five people on one street order separately and want everything "next day," that's five separate stops. But if those orders are batched over 2 or 3 days, the van makes just one efficient trip. The carbon math is simple.

Pick-up points and parcel lockers also make a real difference. Instead of scattering hundreds of packages across town, carriers drop them off at centralized locations—supermarkets, gas stations, residential building lobbies. This reduces failed deliveries and optimizes routes. A 2022 study in *Sustainable Cities and Society* found that using lockers could cut last-mile emissions by over 30% in dense urban areas (Li et al., 2022). Still, this requires consumers to take an active role—walking or cycling to collect their items, instead of defaulting to doorstep service.

Then there's the shift to electric and low-emission delivery vehicles, which has gained momentum but isn't a complete fix. Electricity has to come from somewhere, and in many regions, it still comes from fossil fuels. But when paired with route optimization and smart deployment—such as using e-cargo bikes in city centers or electric vans in suburban zones—the savings are measurable. Cities like Oslo and Amsterdam have started experimenting with zero-emission delivery zones, banning combustion vehicles from specific districts during working hours. These are early, imperfect trials, but they show what policy nudges can do.

More radical—but increasingly realistic—is the idea of urban consolidation centers. These are shared logistics hubs on the edge of cities where packages from different retailers are bundled and reloaded into clean vehicles for the last mile. It's a shift from competition to collaboration in logistics, something many companies have resisted. But pilot programs in Belgium and the Netherlands have shown they can work—if governments help with coordination and regulation.

And not everything has to be high-tech. Some of the most effective strategies are shockingly low-key: avoiding returns by improving product descriptions, sizing guides, and customer reviews. Every returned item is a transport event that might have been prevented. Likewise, better route planning—even something as simple as avoiding left-turns (as UPS famously did)—can reduce idling, improve fuel efficiency, and trim emissions at scale.

None of these approaches is without friction. They require a change in mindset: slower shipping, more patience, sharing infrastructure, and rethinking what "convenience" means. But emissions from last-mile logistics aren't some law of nature. They're the outcome of design choices—by companies, cities, and all of us.

Packaging Waste

Among the more visible consequences of online shopping is the sheer amount of packaging that arrives with every order. Boxes inside boxes, plastic wrap, air pillows, branded envelopes—it's all part of a logistics system designed for protection, not sustainability. But while the packaging may be necessary to ensure items arrive safely, the volume and type of materials used raise serious environmental concerns.

Unlike traditional retail, where goods are shipped in bulk to stores and displayed without additional wrapping, e-commerce relies on individualized, protective packaging for each shipment. That shift changes the scale of material use entirely. A 2023 report by the OECD estimated that e-commerce generates up to three times more packaging waste per product than in-store retail, primarily due to the need for protective padding and the lack of consolidation (OECD, 2023).

The most common materials—corrugated cardboard, plastic films, polystyrene, composite envelopes—are not equally recyclable. While cardboard is relatively easy to recover in many countries, plastic-based materials often aren't accepted by municipal recycling systems, especially when they are mixed or contaminated. Worse, many consumers don't know how (or don't bother) to separate materials properly. As a result, significant amounts of packaging end up in landfills or are incinerated.

There's also the issue of overpackaging, driven partly by logistics automation. Algorithms often match products to box sizes based on availability rather than efficiency. That's why a single pen can arrive in a shoebox filled with plastic padding. According to a 2022 analysis by Greenpeace Germany, up to 40% of Amazon's packaging space is unused air—essentially shipping empty space around the world (Greenpeace, 2022). The energy costs of transporting that space are real, and they add up quickly at scale.

The environmental impact isn't just in waste disposal. Producing packaging materials is itself resource-intensive. Paper production, for example, contributes to deforestation, water consumption, and chemical pollution, even when recycled content is used. Plastics, meanwhile, are fossil fuel-based and rarely recycled into new packaging. Instead, most "recycling" ends in downcycling—turning plastic wrap into lower-grade plastic that's unsuitable for reuse in e-commerce.

Several companies have begun to explore alternative packaging systems, including reusable containers, compostable mailers, or minimalist wrapping. But these efforts are far from mainstream. Reusable packaging works best in closed-loop systems—where customers return the packaging for future use—but the convenience-driven nature of e-commerce doesn't always support such loops. Return rates are low, and tracking reusable assets adds logistical complexity and cost.

Policy can help here. The EU's proposed Packaging and Packaging Waste Regulation (PPWR), currently under negotiation, aims to ban unnecessary packaging and set minimum recyclability standards across the bloc by 2030. If passed in its current form, it could force e-commerce giants to redesign packaging systems entirely. In countries like France, laws already require online sellers to offer plastic-free shipping options and label packaging recyclability clearly.

Still, meaningful change won't happen unless consumers shift their expectations. Fast, cheap, overprotected deliveries come with hidden costs. Choosing slower shipping, bundling orders, or even opting for click-and-collect instead of home delivery can reduce packaging waste substantially. But those are choices—ones that require awareness and a bit of patience.

If packaging waste is one of the most visible and tangible consequences of online shopping, it also offers some of the clearest opportunities for change. The challenge is not simply technical—many alternative materials and systems already exist—but structural and behavioral. What's needed is a shift in logistics design, consumer expectations, and regulatory pressure, all working together.

Possible solutions:

1. Smarter packaging design.

The first step is reducing what doesn't need to be there. A number of retailers are beginning to adopt right-size packaging algorithms, which better match box size to product dimensions. Companies like Zalando and IKEA have shown that simply optimizing packaging dimensions can cut material use by 20–30% and reduce shipping volumes at the same time (Zalando, 2023). This isn't revolutionary technology—it's just a matter of prioritizing efficiency over convenience in warehouse operations.

Other strategies include removing redundant layers, eliminating plastic fillers, and switching to flat-pack shipping when possible. Books, clothes, and other durable items don't need bubble wrap. They need a snug, minimal enclosure—and most of the time, that's achievable with cardboard and smart folding.

2. Shift toward reusable and returnable packaging.

More ambitious solutions involve reusable shipping containers. Companies like RePack (used by fashion brands in Europe) and Loop (focused on groceries and personal care) offer reusable mailers or boxes that customers send back after receiving their products. The environmental payoff comes with repetition: the more times the same package is used, the lower its footprint compared to single-use alternatives.

However, return logistics for reusable systems are complex. They require customer participation, strong return incentives, and efficient collection systems. They also work best in national or regional systems, not across continents. But in places like Finland, Germany, and parts of France, early trials show these systems can work—especially when tied to existing return habits like clothing returns or recycling drop-offs.

3. Compostable and recyclable materials.

Some companies are shifting to biodegradable or compostable mailers, often made from cornstarch, mushroom fibers, or paper pulp. These are typically better for lightweight, non-fragile items and can be disposed of in industrial composting facilities—if such infrastructure exists. That last point is key: compostable does not mean harmless if it ends up in a landfill. These materials still require proper sorting and processing, which varies widely between countries and municipalities.

Recyclable materials are another route—but here, transparency matters. Just because a material is *theoretically* recyclable doesn't mean it will be. Mixed materials, glossy coatings, and synthetic padding often make the process more difficult. Clear labeling, standardization, and simple, mono-material packaging designs could help reduce confusion and increase actual recovery rates.

4. Policy interventions and producer responsibility.

Voluntary action has its limits. Regulatory pressure is often what drives companies to innovate faster. As noted earlier, the EU's Packaging and Packaging Waste Regulation is pushing for bans on unnecessary packaging, stronger Extended Producer Responsibility (EPR) schemes, and clear recyclability standards. France already requires online sellers to minimize packaging volume and label all components by material—a practice that could be scaled across the EU and beyond.

Producer responsibility schemes shift the waste burden away from municipalities and toward the companies that generate it. In practice, this means higher fees for non-recyclable materials, incentives for innovation, and a clearer link between environmental cost and design choices. These policies don't solve everything, but they change the economic logic of waste.

5. Consumer behavior and cultural shifts.

Lastly—and perhaps most unpredictably—change also depends on us, the buyers. Choosing slower delivery options, bundling purchases, rejecting overpackaged items, or even leaving feedback when waste is excessive—all of these actions signal a market preference. If enough consumers speak up, companies notice. If regulation and innovation align with consumer pressure, change becomes not just possible, but inevitable.

Returns and Overproduction

Online shopping has normalized a pattern that would seem wasteful in traditional retail: ordering multiple items with the full intention of returning some—or most—of them. Whether it's buying three sizes of the same jacket or testing out a handful of gadgets with plans to send back what doesn't "feel right," the return culture has become a built-in part of the e-commerce model. (But behind that seemingly harmless convenience lies a chain of environmental consequences that are often invisible to the end user.)

The carbon cost of a return is rarely counted. Each returned item represents a second trip through the logistics system—transportation, repackaging, re-shelving (if it happens at all). According to a 2023 report by Optoro, a reverse logistics company, returns in the United States alone generated over 24 million metric tons of CO_2 in 1 year, equivalent to the annual emissions of more than 5 million cars (Optoro, 2023). And this is just one market.

Returns also fuel overproduction. Retailers must anticipate high return rates—especially in industries like fashion, where rates can reach 40%—and keep excess stock ready to replace items that don't "stick" with customers. In fast fashion, this often means manufacturing far more than what is ultimately needed, just to keep pace with churn. This overproduction has direct environmental consequences: more energy, more water, more textiles, and ultimately, more waste.

What happens to returned items is less sustainable than many assume. Some are restocked and resold, but a substantial number are destroyed, landfilled, or sent to secondary markets overseas—where they may displace local producers or end up as unregulated waste. According to a 2022 European Parliament briefing, as many as 30% of returned fashion items in Europe are never resold (European Parliament, 2022). The logistics cost of inspection, cleaning, and repackaging often outweighs resale value.

Electronics and cosmetics face similar problems. Hygiene standards, short product life cycles, or tamper concerns often mean returned items are discarded—even if unused. Add to this the packaging waste associated with returns, and the cycle becomes doubly unsustainable.

Some retailers are starting to address the problem. AI tools are being used to reduce return rates by offering better sizing recommendations, realistic product visuals, and personalized suggestions based on past purchases. Brands like ASOS and Zalando have experimented with "blacklist" systems that flag frequent returners, while others impose restocking fees or encourage in-store returns to reduce the logistical footprint.

But there's a fine line here. Penalizing returns can alienate customers, especially when fit or quality isn't consistent. The deeper issue is not just how people return, but why they feel the need to do it in the first place. That comes down to expectation management, product transparency, and responsible marketing. In other words: fewer surprises, fewer returns.

Ultimately, reducing returns is about slowing down the consumption cycle itself. It requires better design, more conscious buying, and some collective rethinking of what it means to shop "responsibly" in a digital world.

The return culture in online shopping didn't emerge by accident. It's the result of deliberate business models, consumer expectations, and digital convenience. Undoing its environmental harm doesn't mean eliminating returns altogether—people will always need to send things back. But it does mean rethinking how products are sold, returned, and—ideally—not returned in the first place.

Possible solutions:

1. Better product information and visualization.

One of the most effective strategies is also one of the simplest: improving product detail accuracy. Many returns happen not because the product is defective, but because it doesn't match expectations—wrong size, misleading photos, unclear specs. E-commerce platforms can reduce return rates by offering more detailed sizing charts, video demonstrations, customer-uploaded photos, and AI-based fit prediction tools.

Retailers like Amazon and ASOS already use machine learning to analyze return patterns and suggest sizing adjustments. When implemented carefully, these tools can significantly lower return rates in fashion and footwear sectors, where fit issues are common.

2. Virtual try-ons and augmented reality.

Emerging technologies like virtual fitting rooms and augmented reality (AR) apps offer consumers a better preview of what they're buying. From trying on glasses digitally to placing virtual furniture in your living room, these tools can help shoppers make more confident, accurate decisions. While not yet widespread, the tech is advancing quickly—and early adopters have seen reductions in return rates.

3. Incentivizing responsible ordering.

Some retailers are testing ways to nudge consumers toward more thoughtful purchases. This might include discounts for skipping return options, bundling orders to reduce repeat shipping, or adding friction to excessive multi-size purchases (e.g., showing environmental impact at checkout). Patagonia, for instance, includes sustainability messaging at various points in the buying process, encouraging customers to consider whether they truly need the item.

There's also the possibility of return fees for low-cost or fast-fashion items, especially when returns are frequent and avoidable. While controversial, such fees can discourage careless overordering and encourage consumers to think twice.

4. Repair, resale, and refurbishment.

Not all returns should go straight to resale or landfill. Some companies are investing in repair and refurbishment programs, giving returned items a second life. Zalando's Zircle program resells lightly used fashion items, and Back Market offers a growing market for refurbished electronics. These programs extend product life while reducing waste and avoiding unnecessary overproduction.

5. Smarter inventory planning.

Returns fuel overproduction, but part of that equation can be solved with better demand forecasting. AI and data analytics now allow retailers to predict more accurately what will sell, where, and in what volume. This reduces the need to overstock "just in case." For fast-moving industries like fashion or electronics, better inventory accuracy could mean fewer unsold items—and fewer returns sent straight to destruction.

6. Regulation of product destruction and returns handling.

Governments are starting to take notice of the link between returns and environmental harm. France passed a law in 2022 banning the destruction of unsold goods, pushing retailers to find reuse or donation pathways. Similar laws could be extended to returns, particularly in categories like clothing, electronics, and books, where the default is still disposal over reuse.

7. Educating consumers.

Finally, part of the solution lies in redefining what responsible consumption means in the digital era. Buying three pairs of shoes to test at home and returning two isn't just about convenience—it has a footprint. If consumers become more aware of the emissions, waste, and labor behind each return, many would likely adjust their behavior. But this requires transparency, not guilt trips. Retailers and platforms have a role to play in making these impacts visible.

Data Infrastructure and Energy Use

When we think about the environmental impact of online shopping, it's easy to focus on the visible: delivery vans, cardboard boxes, piles of plastic. But the digital infrastructure behind e-commerce—the data centers, algorithms, warehouse management systems, and payment platforms—consumes an enormous amount of energy, most of it invisible to the average shopper. The environmental footprint of online retail doesn't end when a product is purchased. In some ways, that's where it begins.

E-commerce is powered by vast cloud computing systems, many of which are operated by the same few companies: Amazon Web Services, Microsoft Azure, and Google Cloud. Every time a user scrolls through products, clicks an image, or receives a shipping update, that interaction passes through a network of servers located in energy-hungry data centers. While each individual interaction is tiny, the scale is staggering: Amazon alone handled over 5.6 billion product deliveries in

2022 (Amazon, 2024), supported by countless digital transactions, recommendation algorithms, and real-time inventory updates.

According to the International Energy Agency (IEA), data centers accounted for roughly 1.3% of global electricity demand in 2022, with total energy use expected to grow significantly due to AI integration and rising digital commerce (IEA, 2024). The rise of personalized shopping—suggested items, dynamic pricing, instant customer service via AI—further increases the computational load. More data equals more storage, more processing, and more cooling.

Cooling is a major issue. Data centers operate continuously and generate enormous heat. Maintaining stable temperatures, especially in older or poorly designed facilities, often requires air-conditioning systems that run 24/7, adding to electricity demand. While some providers are investing in liquid cooling and renewable-powered data centers, these practices are far from universal—especially in countries with weak regulatory frameworks or unreliable clean energy supplies.

Warehouses and distribution centers, too, are deeply dependent on energy-intensive digital systems. Automated picking robots, conveyor belts, surveillance and tracking technologies, lighting, heating—all of these are now managed by connected platforms that rely on continuous power. The smarter the warehouse, the more complex and energy-dependent it becomes. Some fulfillment centers operate with little human input, but their sustainability hinges on the source and efficiency of the energy they consume.

There's also the issue of planned obsolescence and device energy use. Smartphones, tablets, and computers—used by both consumers and employees—are part of the e-commerce chain. Their manufacture, charging, and regular replacement add another layer of emissions, often left out of official retail calculations. A consumer browsing on a phone is indirectly tied to a long supply chain of raw materials, assembly, and data transfer, all of which leave an environmental mark.

Unlike transport and packaging, which are slowly becoming visible sustainability targets, digital emissions remain largely invisible and unregulated. This creates a gap between perception and reality. A paperless, contactless, virtual shopping experience feels sustainable—but that feeling can be misleading. As more shopping shifts online and artificial intelligence becomes embedded in every stage—from predicting consumer behavior to routing trucks—this digital infrastructure will only grow more energy-intensive.

Unlike packaging or transport, where the environmental impact is immediate and visible, the energy used by data infrastructure is hidden—but no less urgent. Addressing this part of e-commerce's carbon footprint requires action at multiple levels: from global tech providers to individual retailers, from policy makers to everyday users.

Possible solutions:

1. Shifting to renewable energy sources.

The most obvious—but still under-implemented—solution is transitioning data centers to renewable electricity. Leading providers like Google and Microsoft have committed to 100% renewable energy operations, and Amazon Web Services claims it will reach that target by 2025. However, these commitments vary widely in transparency and scope. In some cases, companies purchase renewable energy certificates (RECs) without actually sourcing clean electricity locally.

The more meaningful shift involves location-based renewable sourcing and grid-level decarbonization. Data centers built in regions with strong solar, wind, or hydro power—such as parts of Scandinavia or Canada—offer a real opportunity to reduce emissions. But siting data centers responsibly also means weighing other factors, such as land use, water availability for cooling, and proximity to energy infrastructure.

2. Improving energy efficiency in data centers.

Energy use isn't just about what powers the servers—it's also about how efficiently that power is used. Many older data centers are notoriously inefficient, with high levels of energy wasted through poor cooling, idle server operation, or outdated equipment. Modern facilities are adopting advanced cooling systems (e.g. liquid immersion), AI-based load balancing, and modular designs that scale with demand rather than staying fully powered 24/7.

One key metric is PUE (Power Usage Effectiveness), which measures how much energy is used by computing equipment versus total facility energy. A typical data center might have a PUE of 1.8 or higher; state-of-the-art centers are getting closer to 1.1. Lowering this number means more of the electricity goes to actual computing rather than cooling or lighting.

3. Retailer and platform-level responsibility.

Large e-commerce platforms—whether they operate their own data centers or rely on cloud providers can take steps to monitor and reduce their own digital emissions. This includes choosing cloud partners based on sustainability performance, optimizing their websites and apps for lower energy usage, and avoiding unnecessary data collection or processing.

For example, compressing images, reducing auto-play videos, and minimizing unnecessary scripts can reduce the energy required to load a website—especially on mobile devices, where data transmission has a higher per-unit carbon cost. While these changes may seem minor, they scale rapidly across millions of users.

4. Consumer awareness and digital habits.

On the user side, solutions are more behavioral than technical. Turning off auto-updates, using energy-efficient devices, extending the life of electronics, and minimizing needless browsing can all contribute to reduced digital emissions. These actions won't fix the system, but they do help reduce demand—and build public awareness around the footprint of "the cloud."

Some sustainability-minded retailers already provide consumers with "digital impact" dashboards, showing estimated carbon emissions from website visits, cloud storage use, or order processing. While still rare, such tools could help create a more informed digital economy—where invisible emissions are brought into the light.

5. Regulatory standards and disclosure requirements.

At the policy level, governments and regulators can drive change by introducing mandatory disclosure of energy use and emissions for digital infrastructure. This includes setting minimum efficiency standards for data centers, requiring emissions reporting from cloud providers, and incentivizing investment in clean-powered facilities.

The European Union, for example, has proposed tighter regulations on energy transparency for cloud service providers as part of its broader Green Deal objectives. If adopted, these could form the basis for a digital carbon accountability framework—similar to the way fuel economy standards shaped the automotive industry (Commins & Irion, 2025).

Online shopping has been widely celebrated as one of the hallmarks of modern convenience. It saves time, offers endless choice, and fits seamlessly into digitally connected lifestyles. Yet, as this chapter has shown, that convenience comes with a complex and often hidden environmental price—a price distributed across packaging waste, transportation emissions, digital infrastructure, and the broader consequences of consumer behavior.

At first glance, e-commerce appears more efficient than traditional retail. The elimination of storefronts, the reduced need for personal travel, and the potential for optimized delivery systems all suggest a leaner, cleaner model. But reality is less tidy. In practice, online shopping has not replaced traditional retail so much as added to it, increasing total consumption while shifting emissions into less visible domains.

Transport and emissions illustrate this paradox well. While centralized delivery can theoretically reduce carbon emissions, the race for speed and individual delivery preferences undermines efficiency. Same-day shipping, fragmented routes, and high return rates drive up emissions—especially in the "last mile." The introduction of electric vehicles and cargo bikes offers a promising path, but only if paired with system-level changes in delivery logic and consumer expectations.

Packaging waste provides another layer of contradiction. Designed for product protection, much of today's e-commerce packaging is oversized, redundant, and poorly recyclable. Although sustainable materials and reusable systems exist, they remain niche, and most consumers lack clear guidance on disposal or alternatives. As packaging becomes a physical representation of environmental neglect, policy and regulation may need to take the lead where voluntary action falls short.

The issue of returns and overproduction further complicates the environmental equation. Online shopping has normalized a trial-and-error mindset, especially in fashion, where consumers routinely order multiple sizes or styles with little intention of keeping all of them. This return culture not only doubles emissions but feeds overproduction, unsold stock, and product destruction. Addressing this requires more than technical fixes—it demands a cultural shift in how we understand ownership, choice, and waste.

Perhaps most overlooked is the impact of data infrastructure and energy use. Every click, recommendation, and delivery is supported by vast networks of energy-intensive servers and logistics systems. These digital emissions are hard to quantify and easy to ignore. Yet they are growing—especially as artificial intelligence becomes embedded in every stage of the shopping process. A low-carbon future must grapple not just with physical goods, but with the digital architectures that support their consumption.

Across all these dimensions, one theme recurs: efficiency alone is not enough. Technological solutions can help reduce waste, emissions, and energy use—but they cannot fully address the deeper issue: the normalization of fast, frictionless, and disposable consumption. Unless expectations shift—both among consumers and in business models—many sustainability gains will be incremental at best, or canceled out by rising demand.

At the same time, the path forward is not bleak. The tools for change already exist: from smart delivery routing and reusable packaging to responsible returns policies and transparent digital systems. What is needed now is integration—bringing these solutions together through policy, industry standards, and public engagement. Governments can regulate waste and emissions. Companies can design for longevity and circularity. Consumers can slow down, ask questions, and expect more from "convenience."

In short, making online shopping sustainable is not about rejecting technology or reverting to the past. It is about redesigning systems that align speed and access with environmental responsibility—not as an afterthought, but as a core value. The environmental impact of online shopping is not an accident. It is the result of choices. And it can be changed by them.

3.4 Policies and Measures to Promote Responsible Consumption

It is often assumed that consumption is a matter of personal choice—something shaped by individual values, habits, and preferences. But this assumption overlooks the powerful role of structure: the systems, incentives, and rules that frame those choices in the first place. Prices, availability, advertising, infrastructure, and even social norms are not accidental. They are built and maintained through policy, whether explicitly or by default.

If we are serious about promoting responsible consumption—not just as a personal ethic, but as a societal shift—then policy must be part of the conversation. Voluntary change has its limits. While many consumers express concern about climate change, waste, or overconsumption, their everyday decisions are shaped by affordability, convenience, and access. Without supportive frameworks, even the most well-intentioned individuals find it difficult to consistently act in environmentally and socially responsible ways.

This chapter explores how governments, institutions, and regulatory bodies can influence consumption patterns through targeted interventions. These measures range from economic instruments like taxes and subsidies, to legislative actions such as product bans or labeling requirements, to broader strategies like public awareness campaigns and infrastructure investments. In each case, the aim is not to control behavior, but to reshape the context in which consumption takes place—making responsible choices easier, more visible, and more widely available.

It is also important to recognize that policy does not operate in a vacuum. Measures that promote sustainability must also consider equity, inclusion, and practicality. Policies that work in one region may fail in another; a tax on high-impact products might reduce emissions but also disproportionately affect low-income households. The success of policy depends not only on its design but on the political, economic, and cultural context in which it is implemented.

This chapter does not present a blueprint or a single model. Instead, it examines the variety of tools available to policymakers and the challenges they face in aligning economic systems with environmental goals. As responsible consumption becomes increasingly urgent in the face of climate change and ecological degradation, the question is not whether governments should act, but how—and how effectively.

Promoting responsible consumption isn't just about asking people to change their habits. It also means changing the rules of the game. Policies that shape consumption typically fall into two broad categories: regulatory instruments (sometimes called "command-and-control" measures) and economic instruments. Each has its strengths, limits, and political trade-offs.

1. *Regulatory Instruments*

Regulatory tools are the most direct form of state intervention. They include bans, standards, mandatory labeling, and restrictions that limit or prohibit specific products, materials, or behaviors deemed harmful to the environment or society.

One of the clearest examples is the ban on single-use plastics, now in place in many EU countries following Directive (EU) 2019/904. These bans target products like plastic cutlery, straws, and foam containers—items with a short useful life but long environmental legacy. In this case, regulation does not rely on market incentives or consumer education; it simply removes certain options from the table.

Other regulations include eco-design standards, which mandate that products meet specific criteria for energy efficiency, repairability, or recyclability. The EU's Ecodesign Directive and the Right to Repair legislation are prime examples, aiming to make more sustainable products the default rather than the exception.

Regulations can also promote responsible consumption indirectly—through mandatory transparency measures, such as carbon footprint labeling or origin disclosure. These instruments don't forbid behavior, but they empower consumers with better information. However, their impact depends on literacy, trust, and how the information is presented. A label that says "climate neutral" without a clear explanation may confuse more than it helps.

The main strength of regulatory instruments is clarity and enforceability. They create hard boundaries and legal certainty. But they can also provoke resistance, especially from industry groups, and may be seen as paternalistic or inflexible.

Poorly designed regulations can backfire—shifting environmental harm to other areas, or creating compliance burdens that disproportionately affect small businesses or low-income consumers.

While economic tools work through incentives and market adjustments, regulatory instruments (Fig. 3.6) operate by establishing rules—clear boundaries that define what is acceptable, what is not, and under what conditions consumption can take place. These "command-and-control" approaches may sound rigid, but they are often essential where urgent action is needed, market signals are weak, or social norms have yet to evolve.

Regulations can ban, limit, or mandate, and they often do so in ways that reach across entire industries or sectors, forcing structural change rather than relying on voluntary shifts. While sometimes criticized as inflexible or bureaucratic, well-designed regulations have the power to rapidly transform markets and set new expectations—not just for businesses, but for consumers as well.

- Product bans and restrictions

One of the most direct regulatory tools is the outright ban or phase-out of harmful products or materials. These measures tend to be used when the environmental or health risks are high, alternatives are available, and voluntary reduction efforts have failed.

The EU Directive on Single-Use Plastics (2019/904) is a prominent example. By banning items like plastic straws, cutlery, cotton buds, and certain food containers, the regulation didn't just reduce waste; it also pushed innovation, forcing producers to develop biodegradable or reusable alternatives. Similarly, several countries have banned microbeads in cosmetics, due to their role in water pollution—another case where voluntary reform proved too slow.

However, bans are not always universally welcomed. In some regions, enforcement capacity is limited, and substitutes may not be accessible or affordable. In

Fig. 3.6 Regulatory instruments. Source: Created by authors

Kenya, one of the strictest plastic bag bans globally was implemented in 2017, but it led to black markets and enforcement tensions in poorer areas (UNEP, 2018).

Key insight—bans can be powerful, but must be accompanied by transitional support, public education, and viable alternatives to avoid unintended consequences or social backlash.

- Minimum standards and mandatory design criteria

Rather than outlawing entire product categories, governments can also set minimum environmental standards—defining how products must be designed, produced, or disposed of.

The EU Ecodesign Directive is a leading example. It requires that household appliances meet energy efficiency criteria and, more recently, includes provisions for durability, reparability, and recyclability. The aim is to make sustainable products the default, not the niche (Barkhausen et al., 2022).

These kinds of regulations are often technology-forcing: they create predictable conditions under which manufacturers must innovate or lose market access. Over time, they can shift global standards. For instance, energy labels like A+++ have now become part of consumer expectations—not because consumers demanded them, but because regulation made them visible and standardized.

Still, minimum standards are only as strong as their enforcement and updating mechanisms. If thresholds remain too low or outdated, the regulatory effect can flatten out, and companies may design just to the legal minimum rather than pushing beyond it.

- Mandatory information and labeling

Regulation can also operate through mandatory disclosure—forcing companies to share clear, standardized, and verifiable information about their products. Labels and certifications may seem less forceful than bans or standards, but when mandatory, they create transparency, reduce greenwashing, and give consumers the tools to make more informed choices (Nipper et al., 2025).

Examples include:

- Nutrition labeling on food, which has become standard in most developed countries.
- Energy labels on appliances and buildings.
- Carbon footprint labeling (voluntary in most cases, but increasingly discussed as a regulatory option).
- Country-of-origin and supply chain disclosures, especially in textiles and electronics.

France's Anti-Waste Law for a Circular Economy (AGEC) mandates environmental labeling on certain products, including clothing and electronics, requiring data on repairability, recyclability, and environmental impacts. The law goes beyond vague symbols, aiming to make sustainability claims auditable and comparable.

But labeling isn't a silver bullet. For consumers to act on information, they need trust, clarity, and relevance. Overload is a risk: too many labels, with inconsistent metrics, can confuse rather than guide.

- Extended producer responsibility (EPR)

One of the most transformative regulatory concepts in consumption policy is Extended Producer Responsibility. Under EPR laws, producers are legally responsible for the full lifecycle of their products—including post-consumer waste. This shifts the burden of disposal, recycling, and recovery upstream to those who design and profit from products, rather than leaving it to municipalities or individuals.

EPR systems are now common in Europe for packaging, electronics, batteries, and vehicles. They often require producers to finance or manage waste collection and recycling systems, incentivizing them to design products that are easier to disassemble, reuse, or recycle (Siuta-Tokarska et al., 2022).

France's EPR system for textiles, for instance, mandates that apparel brands contribute to a national fund used to support reuse and recycling infrastructure. The aim is not just to pay for cleanup—but to reshape production logic toward circularity.

However, implementation varies. In some countries, EPR has become more about compliance paperwork than genuine design reform. Without clear performance targets, public accountability, and proper enforcement, the transformative potential of EPR can fade.

While regulatory instruments are essential, they face real-world barriers:

- Political resistance, especially from powerful industries or lobbies.
- Administrative complexity, especially in low-capacity states or fragmented governance systems.
- Equity concerns, if regulations increase costs for vulnerable consumers.
- Policy fragmentation, where overlapping rules create confusion or legal loopholes.

To be effective, regulation must be context-aware, phased, and responsive. It must involve consultation with affected stakeholders and be embedded in broader strategies that include public communication, infrastructure investment, and complementary economic and behavioral tools.

Regulatory instruments often occupy an uneasy space in public discourse around consumption. They are seen as necessary but unpopular—tools of last resort when markets or individuals fail to self-correct. Yet as this chapter has shown, regulation is not just about control or restriction. At its best, it acts as a framework that redefines what is normal, acceptable, and viable within a given society.

In the context of responsible consumption, regulation plays several vital roles. First, it creates boundaries that protect public goods—limiting the use of harmful materials, setting minimum standards for durability or efficiency, and holding producers accountable for waste. These boundaries are essential when environmental degradation is systemic and cumulative, not easily visible or priced.

Second, regulation can level the playing field. In unregulated markets, companies that invest in sustainability often compete at a disadvantage against cheaper, less responsible alternatives. By setting baseline requirements—on emissions, packaging, labeling, or lifespan—governments ensure that ethical practices are not just optional add-ons, but structural expectations.

Third, regulation sends long-term signals to markets, guiding investment, innovation, and consumer culture. Banning microbeads, requiring repairability, or enforcing supply chain transparency tells both businesses and consumers: this is where we are going. Over time, such signals shape product design, business models, and everyday norms in ways that voluntary action rarely achieves.

That said, regulation is not a one-size-fits-all solution. It must be carefully designed, well-timed, and socially attuned. Poorly implemented rules risk backlash, enforcement problems, or unintended social harm. A plastic ban that works in Copenhagen might create hardship in rural Indonesia if alternatives are unavailable. A repair mandate that boosts circularity in France might bankrupt small producers in countries with weaker service sectors. In short: rules matter, but so does context.

Equally important is the political dimension of regulation. Resistance to change is often not about the content of a policy, but about who pays for it, who enforces it, and who gets left out. For regulation to shape consumption systems effectively, it must be developed transparently, with input from a wide range of stakeholders—not just industry voices or technocrats (Ansell et al., 2025).

In the long run, regulatory approaches will be indispensable for making responsible consumption more than a lifestyle choice. They are the invisible architecture that shapes what's on the shelves, what's in the ads, what's in the landfill, and what's in the minds of consumers. While no single rule will fix an unsustainable system, a coherent, flexible, and forward-looking regulatory framework can do what market forces alone often cannot: draw a line between what is profitable and what is permissible—and in doing so, help steer consumption toward responsibility.

2. *Economic instruments*

Economic tools, by contrast, influence behavior through pricing, incentives, or financial penalties. Rather than banning a product outright, these instruments make harmful consumption more expensive—or sustainable choices more affordable.

Examples include eco-taxes, such as carbon pricing, landfill levies, or taxes on sugary drinks and plastic bags. These aim to internalize environmental or social costs that are usually left out of market prices. When designed well, they can drive innovation, shift demand, and generate public revenues that can be reinvested in sustainability programs (Pindyck, 2012).

Subsidies and incentives represent the flip side. Governments may offer tax breaks, rebates, or grants for energy-efficient appliances, organic farming, or repair services. These make sustainable choices more competitive, especially in markets where they might otherwise lose out on price. Germany's "repair bonus" scheme, for instance, reimburses up to 100 euros per person annually for fixing old devices instead of replacing them.

Economic instruments are generally more flexible than regulations. They allow market actors to adapt in their own ways. But they also come with risks: regressive effects (e.g., fuel taxes that disproportionately affect rural or low-income communities), or market loopholes that allow companies to comply on paper while avoiding real change.

Moreover, their success often depends on the elasticity of demand. If a price increase on fast fashion doesn't change purchasing habits—because trends or status override cost—then the tool loses effectiveness. That's why price instruments work best in tandem with education, access, and cultural shifts.

Economic instruments (Fig. 3.7) are not a new invention in environmental policy—but their application to consumer behavior, especially in the context of responsible consumption, is becoming more sophisticated and urgent. In essence, these tools seek to correct market failures by aligning prices with social and environmental realities. They recognize that consumption choices are not made in a vacuum; they're shaped by affordability, availability, and perceived value. And when prices fail to reflect real costs—such as pollution, carbon emissions, or resource depletion—market behavior tends to follow the wrong incentives.

- Eco-taxes and environmental pricing

One of the clearest examples of economic correction is the eco-tax, a mechanism that puts a price on environmentally harmful behavior. These can take many forms: carbon taxes, plastic bag levies, landfill charges, or airline ticket taxes. The goal is to internalize externalities—to make sure that environmental damage is reflected in the final cost to the consumer (Aldy & Stavins, 2012).

The classic case is carbon pricing. By attaching a financial cost to greenhouse gas emissions, carbon taxes or cap-and-trade systems aim to discourage carbon-intensive consumption—from electricity to meat to imported goods. Sweden, for example, has maintained one of the world's highest carbon taxes (currently over €100/ton CO_2) and has simultaneously achieved strong economic growth and declining emissions (World Bank, 2022). While the carbon price alone isn't

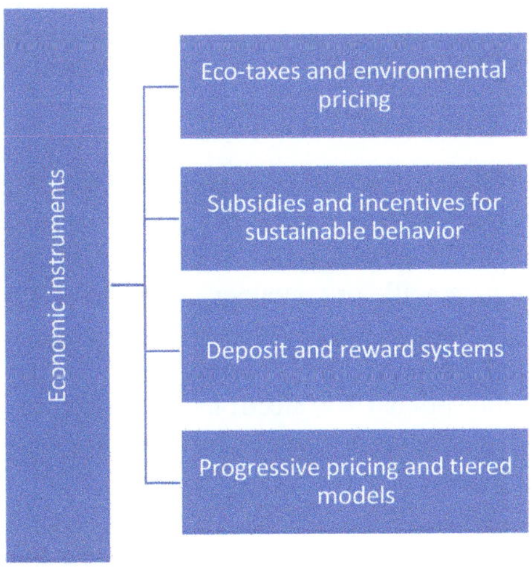

Fig. 3.7 Economic instruments. Source: Created by authors

responsible, it sends a market signal that ripples across production, consumption, and innovation.

However, carbon pricing has a political downside. It is often unpopular—seen as a "green tax" that hits households rather than industries. Without proper compensation mechanisms, it can be regressive, disproportionately affecting lower-income or rural populations who rely more on fuel and heating. That's why more recent designs include revenue recycling, where the money collected from the tax is redistributed to citizens through rebates or public investment.

- Subsidies and incentives for sustainable behavior

While taxes discourage harmful behavior, subsidies and incentives reward sustainable practices. These can include:

- Purchase subsidies for energy-efficient appliances, electric vehicles, bicycles, or water-saving devices.
- Support for sustainable agriculture, such as organic farming, agroecology, or shorter supply chains.
- Incentives for repair and reuse, like Austria and Germany's public reimbursement schemes for electronics repair.
- Tax deductions for home insulation, solar panels, or car-sharing memberships.

These instruments not only lower the price barrier for more sustainable choices, but also help signal what types of behavior are socially valued. In many countries, the success of rooftop solar adoption was not simply a result of environmental awareness—but of feed-in tariffs, installation grants, and net metering policies that made solar energy financially appealing.

That said, not all subsidies promote responsible consumption. In fact, one of the biggest challenges today is the persistence of harmful subsidies—such as those for fossil fuels, intensive agriculture, or fast transport infrastructure. According to the International Monetary Fund (2023), global fossil fuel subsidies still exceeded $7 trillion in 2022 when factoring in both direct support and unpriced externalities. Reforming these subsidies is often politically difficult but remains essential to shifting long-term consumption patterns.

- Deposit and reward systems

Another important class of economic tools includes deposit-return schemes and reward-based systems, designed to promote circular behavior like reuse and recycling. In these systems, consumers pay a small deposit when purchasing a product (e.g., a bottle or container) and receive it back when the item is returned.

Countries like Germany, the Netherlands, and some US states have achieved high recycling rates through such schemes. More recently, deposit systems are being piloted for electronics, textiles, or even packaging in e-commerce deliveries—creating a financial incentive for consumers to return goods instead of discarding them.

Some cities have tested positive incentives: points or credits for recycling, taking public transport, or bringing reusable bags. These "nudges with teeth" use small economic rewards to reinforce sustainable habits, especially when combined with gamification or community recognition.

- Progressive pricing and tiered models

In the water and energy sectors, tiered pricing has been used to discourage overconsumption. Households pay a basic rate for essential use, and higher rates for excessive use—creating an incentive to conserve. This model could be extended to consumer goods, especially those with high carbon or resource footprints. Imagine a clothing retailer that raises the price of each additional item bought in a short timeframe—or gives discounts for purchasing second-hand or recycled garments.

While such systems are still experimental, they hint at a future where pricing is personalized, transparent, and dynamic—not just to increase profit, but to guide behavior toward collective goals.

As societies face growing ecological stress, economic inequality, and social fragmentation, the promotion of responsible consumption has become a policy priority in many parts of the world (Mont et al., 2022). But promoting responsibility in markets shaped by convenience, disposability, and profit-maximization is no simple task. The tools available to policymakers—economic, regulatory, and increasingly behavioral—each offer different leverage points, with distinct strengths and limitations.

Regulatory instruments are the clearest in intent. They draw firm lines around what is acceptable: banning harmful products, mandating sustainability standards, enforcing transparency, or extending producer responsibility. They are essential when risks are high, market failures are persistent, or when social consensus supports clear legal boundaries. But regulation can be politically sensitive, especially when poorly communicated or implemented without equity in mind. Its success depends on legal infrastructure, enforcement capacity, and the presence of viable alternatives for both producers and consumers.

Economic instruments, in contrast, work through price signals. They aim to correct distortions in the market by making harmful choices more expensive (taxes) and sustainable ones more attractive (subsidies, incentives). They offer flexibility—allowing market actors to adjust behavior without coercion—and can generate public revenue for reinvestment in sustainability (Mottershead et al., 2021). However, their effectiveness relies on careful design. Price-based measures must account for social impacts, avoid regressive effects, and be supported by complementary infrastructure and education. A carbon tax alone cannot reduce emissions if public transport is underdeveloped or energy alternatives are unaffordable.

What both policy types share is the recognition that individual behavior is shaped by structural conditions. People rarely consume in a vacuum. They respond to what is available, affordable, and socially normalized. If the default options are cheap, wasteful, and invisible in their impacts, no amount of awareness will fix the problem. Policy must therefore go beyond nudging—it must reshape the systems that make sustainable behavior realistic and accessible.

Equally important is the integration between instruments. Economic tools work better when embedded in a regulatory framework that sets clear goals and boundaries. Regulations are more effective when supported by market signals and incentives. No single approach can deliver responsible consumption on its own. The task is not to choose between carrots and sticks, but to combine them intelligently, with attention to timing, context, and long-term alignment.

While regulatory and economic instruments operate by setting rules or shifting incentives, informational and behavioral tools (Fig. 3.8) take a subtler approach. They don't ban, tax, or subsidize. Instead, they work by influencing perception, awareness, and decision-making—the psychological and social space between knowing something and doing something.

These tools have gained popularity in recent years for one clear reason: even when people *want* to make more sustainable choices, they often don't. Sometimes it's due to habits, lack of information, or time pressure. Other times, it's because the default option is easier, cheaper, or simply more visible. Informational and behavioral interventions try to bridge that gap—by making responsible consumption clearer, simpler, and more socially supported.

- Awareness campaigns and public information.

The most traditional form of informational policy is the public awareness campaign: media messaging that informs people about the environmental or social impact of their consumption habits. From water conservation ads to anti-food waste initiatives or "Buy Less" campaigns during shopping holidays, these interventions aim to shift attitudes and cultural norms.

In some cases, they work—especially when the message is specific, emotionally resonant, and delivered through trusted channels. For example, the UK's "Love Food, Hate Waste" campaign contributed to a 21% drop in avoidable food waste over 5 years. But general awareness is rarely enough. People often *know* what's right—they just don't act on it.

This is where behaviorally informed approaches come in.

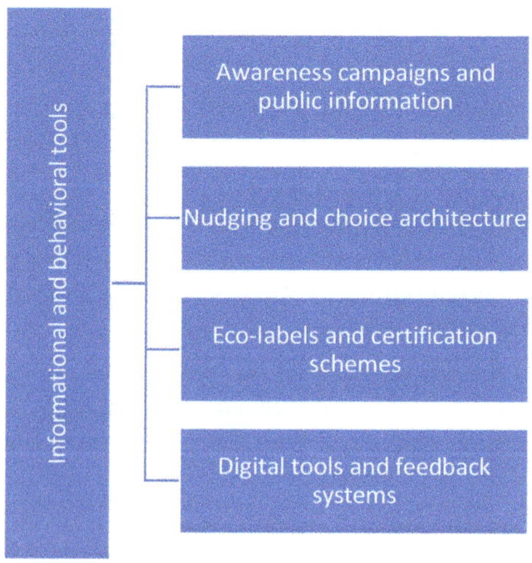

Fig. 3.8 Informational and behavioral tools. Source: Created by authors

- Nudging and choice architecture.

A "nudge" is a subtle design intervention that alters the way choices are presented—without restricting options. Developed from behavioral economics, the concept assumes that small changes in context can lead to large changes in behavior.

Examples include:

- Default green options—making paperless billing or slower shipping the default, requiring users to opt out rather than opt in.
- Visual cues—placing sustainable products at eye level in stores or marking them with simple color-coded symbols.
- Social norms messaging—telling consumers "most people in your area recycle" or "your neighbors use 30% less energy" to encourage conformity with positive behavior.
- Pre-commitment tools—allowing consumers to set personal goals (e.g., "no new clothing for three months") and receive reminders or rewards.

The power of nudging lies in its non-intrusiveness. It doesn't tell people what to do. It just makes some options easier to choose. But nudging also has limits. It works best when barriers are small. It does not solve affordability, access, or deep-rooted habits. And critics argue it can sometimes feel manipulative or symbolic—a distraction from the need for stronger structural change.

- Eco-labels and certification schemes.

Eco-labels are a form of structured information—offering consumers a shortcut for understanding the environmental or social profile of a product. Labels like Fair Trade, EU Ecolabel, Rainforest Alliance, or Energy Star have become widely recognized, especially in food and household goods.

Research shows that clear, credible labels can influence purchasing behavior—especially when consumers are already motivated by ethical or environmental concerns. But the market is crowded. There are now hundreds of overlapping labels, some rigorous, others self-declared or poorly monitored. This can lead to confusion or skepticism.

For labels to work, they must be:

- Standardized and verifiable.
- Easily understood (not overloaded with technical jargon).
- Trustworthy, with independent third-party certification.
- Supported by education and visibility.
- Digital tools and feedback systems.

As consumption becomes increasingly digital, so do the tools to influence it. E-commerce platforms, smart devices, and mobile apps now allow for real-time feedback on purchasing decisions, carbon footprints, or energy use.

For example:

- Apps like Joule Bug or Olio offer tips and gamified tracking for sustainable habits.

- Platforms like Ecosia turn web searches into tree planting, blending behavior with visible impact.
- Some retailers now show carbon scores at checkout, nudging users toward lower-impact items.

These tools can personalize the sustainability journey—but they also risk digital fatigue and uneven access. Not everyone has the time, interest, or digital literacy to engage. Still, for tech-savvy users, they offer new ways to connect consumption with consequence.

Informational and behavioral instruments do not replace economic or regulatory policies. They support them. They help make structural changes visible, acceptable, and personally meaningful.

Their greatest value lies in shaping social norms and cultural expectations—creating the feeling that responsible consumption is not only possible, but normal. Over time, they can shift habits, build trust in sustainable products, and reduce friction in everyday choices.

But they cannot carry the weight of transformation alone. When used in isolation, these tools often produce limited, short-term, or uneven effects. When embedded in a larger policy mix—with incentives, standards, and infrastructure—they become more than just tools of persuasion. They become part of the system itself.

The transition toward more responsible consumption is one of the defining challenges of our time. It sits at the intersection of environmental urgency, economic inequality, and cultural inertia—where everyday decisions by individuals are shaped by systems that often reward excess, convenience, and invisibility over sustainability, fairness, and accountability.

Across the different policy domains—regulatory, economic, informational, and behavioral—a common thread emerges: individual responsibility is important, but insufficient when the system itself remains unchanged. If the least sustainable option is the cheapest, most visible, and most accessible, then it is also the most likely to be chosen—regardless of personal values or environmental awareness. The role of policy, then, is to shift the baseline: to make responsible choices easier, fairer, and more structurally supported.

Regulatory instruments remain essential for setting hard boundaries. Bans on harmful products, minimum sustainability standards, and extended producer responsibility schemes send a clear signal: certain practices are no longer acceptable. Regulations not only reduce harm; they create predictability and trust, allowing businesses and consumers alike to plan within a framework that favors sustainability.

Economic instruments complement this by adjusting incentives. Taxes on wasteful or polluting behavior, and subsidies for sustainable goods and services, help to internalize external costs and reward socially desirable outcomes. But their success depends on careful design. They must be progressive, transparent, and paired with social protections—otherwise, they risk reinforcing inequalities or generating political resistance.

Informational and behavioral tools work at a different level. They recognize that knowledge, norms, and habits matter. Even when price and regulation are aligned with sustainability, people still need clarity, motivation, and social reinforcement to act differently. Nudges, feedback tools, eco-labels, and awareness campaigns all help make sustainability more tangible and personally relevant. They can shift mindsets and build public support—but they are rarely enough on their own.

What emerges from this chapter is not a checklist of isolated tools, but a policy mix—an understanding that sustainable consumption requires coordinated efforts across sectors and levels of governance. It requires governments to regulate and invest, businesses to redesign and disclose, and citizens to engage and demand better options. The most effective policies are not only well-crafted individually but mutually reinforcing, creating an environment where the right choices are no longer the hardest ones.

Finally, a successful policy for responsible consumption must be context-sensitive and adaptive. What works in one country or sector may fail in another. Cultural norms, institutional capacity, and market structure all shape outcomes. Policies must be inclusive, consultative, and flexible—able to evolve as new challenges and innovations emerge.

Promoting responsible consumption is not just a technical task. It is a political, cultural, and ethical one. Policies must not only guide behavior, but also reflect the kind of society we want to build—one where sustainability is not a niche concern, but a shared responsibility embedded in the way we live, produce, and consume.

Conclusions

Responsible consumption is more than a personal choice—it is a response to the broader social, environmental, and economic consequences of unchecked consumerism. While individual actions matter, the concept must be understood within a systemic context, where responsibility is shared among consumers, producers, and institutions. Embedding this perspective into everyday life requires cultural change, policy support, and structural conditions that enable sustainable decisions to become the default, not the exception.

As environmental challenges intensify and social inequalities persist, the meaning of responsible consumption continues to evolve. It now reflects not only an awareness of one's impact, but a growing commitment to fairness, sufficiency, and long-term well-being. The future of consumption lies not in promoting more ethical versions of the same patterns, but in reshaping values, systems, and expectations—toward a model that is both ecologically viable and socially just.

Modern consumption patterns—particularly in high-income societies—are a major driver of greenhouse gas emissions, with impacts embedded across global supply chains. From food systems to fashion, transport to electronics, the choices made by individuals and institutions are directly linked to resource extraction, energy use, and carbon output. Addressing climate change requires confronting not only how we produce, but also how and how much we consume.

A significant share of climate-related emissions is "outsourced" through global trade, making the carbon footprint of consumption less visible to end users. This disconnect highlights the need for greater transparency, accountability, and shared responsibility between producers and consumers, as well as across nations. Climate policies must recognize these cross-border dynamics to drive meaningful reductions in consumption-based emissions.

Technological efficiency alone cannot offset the environmental impacts of growing consumption. A deeper transformation toward *sufficiency*—consuming less, more consciously, and with longer-lasting value—will be necessary to stay within planetary boundaries. Climate mitigation strategies must therefore include behavioral and cultural shifts that support more sustainable lifestyles, alongside structural and policy-level interventions.

One of the key takeaways from this chapter is that the environmental consequences of online shopping are not always where we expect to find them. While the packaging and delivery vehicles are highly visible, much of the carbon footprint is hidden—in returns that never get resold, in data centers that run silently behind the interface, and in the overproduction cycles fueled by convenience-based consumer behavior. This invisibility makes it harder for consumers, and sometimes even businesses, to grasp the full picture.

Bringing environmental costs into view—through better data, clearer regulation, and transparent digital interfaces—can empower smarter decisions across the supply chain. Awareness alone won't fix the problem, but it is a necessary starting point for more responsible design and consumption patterns in the e-commerce sector.

Efforts to reduce the environmental footprint of e-commerce have so far focused heavily on efficiency: lighter packaging, faster electric vehicles, smarter AI-powered logistics. But while these are necessary, they are not sufficient. The core issue is not how efficiently we consume online, but how much and how often—and how normalized disposability has become in digital retail.

Sustainable online shopping will require a cultural and structural transition: from speed to durability, from volume to value, and from passive consumption to informed participation. Solutions already exist, but their impact depends on uptake. Real progress lies not just in optimizing systems, but in rethinking what kind of consumption the system is designed to support.

Efforts to promote responsible consumption are often scattered—relying on isolated campaigns, subsidies, or bans. Yet the scale of environmental and social challenges linked to unsustainable consumption demands more than piecemeal solutions. This chapter has shown that policy must operate as a coherent system, not a patchwork.

Effective intervention requires integrating regulatory, economic, and behavioral tools—each addressing different parts of the consumption ecosystem. Regulations can establish limits and expectations, economic instruments can shift incentives and signal priorities, while informational and behavioral tools help shape social norms and habits. When aligned, these instruments don't just reduce harm; they redefine what is normal, viable, and desirable in the marketplace.

The most transformative policies are those that don't treat consumption as a matter of individual virtue, but as a structural outcome—something shaped by price signals, infrastructure, cultural expectations, and political choices. Building such policies is neither simple nor quick, but it is necessary if responsible consumption is to become the rule, not the exception. The notion of "responsible consumption" often falls too heavily on individuals, as if better choices can emerge from willpower alone. But this chapter reminds us that true responsibility is a collective construction, shaped by institutions, markets, and the cultural messages we absorb every day.

Policies have the power to shift responsibility upstream—to producers, advertisers, and regulators—and to build systems where sustainability is not a sacrifice, but a default. That means making the responsible choice the affordable, visible, and socially supported one. It means designing policies that work not just for the ideal consumer, but for the real one—navigating constraints of time, money, access, and information. Ultimately, promoting responsible consumption is not about restriction. It is about enabling better lives within planetary boundaries—through shared responsibility, systemic design, and a policy environment that makes doing the right thing both easier and more meaningful.

References

Aldy, J. E., & Stavins, R. N. (2012). The promise and problems of pricing carbon: Theory and experience. *The Journal of Environment & Development, 21*(2), 152–180.

Allan, S., Browne, M., & Woodburn, A. (2018). Unlocking the failed delivery problem? Opportunities and responses. *Transportation Research Interdisciplinary Perspectives, 2*, 100018.

Amazon. (2024). *Amazon logistics statistics*. https://capitaloneshopping.com/research/amazon-logistics-statistics

Ansell, C., Sørensen, E., & Torfing, J. (2025). Theorizing the political dimension of collaborative governance. *Perspectives on Public Management and Governance*, gvaf007.

Arora, N., Gandotra, R., & Dhiman, N. (2024). Consumer happiness and sustainable consumption. *Global Business and Organizational Excellence, 43*(6), 59–73. https://doi.org/10.1002/joe.22258

Arora, N. K., & Mishra, I. (2023). Responsible consumption and production: A roadmap to sustainable development. *Environmental Sustainability, 6*, 1–6. https://doi.org/10.1007/s42398-023-00266-9

Barkhausen, R., Durand, A., & Fick, K. (2022). Review and analysis of ecodesign directive implementing measures: Product regulations shifting from energy efficiency towards a circular economy. *Sustainability, 14*(16), 10318.

Brož, D., Čábelková, I., Hlaváček, M., Smutka, L., & Procházka, P. (2023). It starts from home? Explaining environmentally responsible resource and waste management. *Frontiers in Environmental Science, 11*, 1136171. https://doi.org/10.3389/fenvs.2023.1136171

Çam, S., Tuna, M. F., & Bayır, T. (2025). Understanding green consumption: Exploring the role of socially responsible attitudes in sustainable buying behavior. *Discover Sustainability, 6*, 372. https://doi.org/10.1007/s43621-025-01223-8

Chan, S., Weitz, N., Persson, Å., & Trimmer, C. (2018). *SDG 12: Responsible consumption and production. A review of research needs*. Technical annex to the Formas report Forskning för Agenda 2030: Översikt av forskningsbehov och vägar framåt. Stockholm Environment Insitute, Stockholm. https://www.sei.org/wp-content/uploads/2018/11/sdg-12-responsible-consumption-and-production-review-of-research-needs.pdf?utm_source=chatgpt.com

Commins, J., & Irion, K. (2025). Towards planet proof computing: Law and policy of data centre sustainability in the European Union. *Technology and Regulation, 2025*, 1–36.

Cullinane, S., & Cullinane, K. (2021). The logistics of online clothing returns in Sweden and how to reduce its environmental impact. *Journal of Service Science and Management, 14*(1), 72–95.
De, T., Singh, N., Ibrahim, B. S. K. S. M. K., et al. (2025). Mindful, responsible, and sustainable consumption: A hybrid review of evolving research trends. *Discover Sustainability, 6*, 512. https://doi.org/10.1007/s43621-025-01343-1
Eriksson, S., & Käck, J. (2023). Sustainable reverse logistics in fast fashion e-commerce: A literature review-Impact of sustainable practices on customer satisfaction.
European Parliament. (2022). *Environmental impact of textile and clothing industry: What consumers need to know*. Briefing. https://www.europarl.europa.eu
Falchetta, G., Cian, E. D., Pavanello, F., & Wing, I. S. (2024). Inequalities in global residential cooling energy use to 2050. *Nature Communications, 15*(1), 7874.
Fuchs, D. A., & Lorek, S. (2005). Sustainable consumption governance: A history of promises and failures. *Journal of Consumer Policy, 28*, 261–288. https://doi.org/10.1007/s10603-005-8490-z
Glavič, P. (2021). Evolution and current challenges of sustainable consumption and production. *Sustainability, 13*(16), 9379. https://doi.org/10.3390/su13169379
Goldstein, B., Gounaridis, D., & Newell, J. P. (2020). The carbon footprint of household energy use in the United States. *Proceedings of the National Academy of Sciences, 117*(32), 19122–19130.
Gómez-Sanabria, A., Kiesewetter, G., Klimont, Z., Schoepp, W., & Haberl, H. (2022). Potential for future reductions of global GHG and air pollutants from circular waste management systems. *Nature Communications, 13*(1), 106.
Grant, L. K. (2011, Fall). Can we consume our way out of climate change? A call for analysis. *Behavior Analyst, 34*(2), 245–266. https://doi.org/10.1007/BF03392256
Greenpeace Germany. (2022). *Unboxing the waste: The environmental cost of Amazon's packaging practices*. https://www.greenpeace.de
Guilbert, A. (2024). Energy sufficiency and recognition justice: A study of household consumption. *Buildings and Cities, 5*(1), 489–505. https://doi.org/10.5334/bc.458
Gustavsson, J., Cederberg, C., Sonesson, U., Van Otterdijk, R., & Meybeck, A. (2011, May). *Global food losses and food waste*.
Hu, L., Hu, X., Li, B., Guo, L., Chen, D., Yang, Y., et al. (2024). Carbon dioxide emissions from industrial processes and product use are a non-ignorable factor in China's mitigation. *Communications Earth & Environment, 5*(1), 800.
Hu, M., & Milner, D. (2020). Visualizing the research of embodied energy and environmental impact research in the building and construction field: A bibliometric analysis. *Developments in the Built Environment, 3*, 100010.
International Energy Agency. (2024). *AI is set to drive surging electricity demand from data centres while offering the potential to transform how the energy sector works*. https://www.iea.org/news/ai-is-set-to-drive-surging-electricity-demand-from-data-centres-while-offering-the-potential-to-transform-how-the-energy-sector-works?utm_source=chatgpt.com
International Monetary Fund (2023). IMF Annual Report 2023. https://www.imf.org/external/pubs/ft/ar/2023/
Karimzadeh, S., & Boström, M. (2023). Ethical consumption in three stages: A focus on sufficiency and care. *Environmental Sociology, 10*(1), 1–11. https://doi.org/10.1080/23251042.2023.2277971
Koide, R., Lettenmeier, M., Akenji, L., et al. (2021). Lifestyle carbon footprints and changes in lifestyles to limit global warming to 1.5 °C, and ways forward for related research. *Sustainability Science, 16*, 2087–2099. https://doi.org/10.1007/s11625-021-01018-6
Li, J., Lo, K., Zhang, P., & Guo, M. (2016). Consumer travel behaviors and transport carbon emissions: A comparative study of commercial centers in Shenyang, China. *Energies, 9*(10), 765.
Li, C., Song, M., & Xie, Z. (2022). Optimizing parcel locker systems to reduce carbon emissions in last-mile delivery. *Sustainable Cities and Society, 81*, 103837. https://doi.org/10.1016/j.scs.2022.103837

Maxner, T., Dalla Chiara, G., & Goodchild, A. (2022). Identifying the challenges to sustainable urban last-mile deliveries: Perspectives from public and private stakeholders. *Sustainability, 14*(8), 4701.

Mont, O., Lehner, M., & Dalhammar, C. (2022). Sustainable consumption through policy intervention—A review of research themes. *Frontiers in Sustainability, 3*, 921477.

Mottershead, D., Watkins, E., Gore, T., Andersen, M. S., Pedersen, A. B., Whiteoak, K., ... & Chewpreecha, U. (2021). Green taxation and other economic instruments: Internalising environmental costs to make the polluter pay.

Nhung Thang, T. H., & Nguyen, C. H. (2024). Does customers' well-being lead to their sustainable consumption? Exploring the mediating role of online shopping. *Journal of Global Marketing, 38*(2), 133–155. https://doi.org/10.1080/08911762.2024.2424839

Nicholson, S. R., Rorrer, N. A., Uekert, T., Avery, G., Carpenter, A. C., & Beckham, G. T. (2023). Manufacturing energy and greenhouse gas emissions associated with United States consumption of organic petrochemicals. *ACS Sustainable Chemistry & Engineering, 11*(6), 2198–2208.

Nipper, M., Ostermaier, A., & Theis, J. (2025). Mandatory disclosure of standardized sustainability metrics: The case of the EU Taxonomy Regulation. *Corporate Social Responsibility and Environmental Management, 32*(2), 2171–2190.

OECD. (2023). *Packaging and the environment: Trends, impacts, and policy responses*. Organisation for Economic Co-operation and Development. https://www.oecd.org/content/dam/oecd/en/publications/reports/2023/02/development-co-operation-report-2023_be7899d0/f6edc3c2-en.pdf

Optoro. (2023). *The hidden environmental costs of returns*. https://www.optoro.com

Pindyck, R. S. (2012). Uncertain outcomes and climate change policy. *Journal of Environmental Economics and Management, 63*(3), 289–303.

Siuta-Tokarska, B., Thier, A., & Hornicki, K. (2022). The concept of extended producer responsibility in the field of packaging industry and the energy sector in the light of the circular economy—The example of Poland. *Energies, 15*(23), 9060.

Stiefenhofer, P. (2025). *The role of ethical consumption in promoting democratic sustainability: Revisiting neoclassical economics through Kantian ethics*. https://arxiv.org/pdf/2504.01138v1

Tian, P., Zhong, H., Chen, X., et al. (2024). Keeping the global consumption within the planetary boundaries. *Nature, 635*, 625–630. https://doi.org/10.1038/s41586-024-08154-w

UNEP (2018). Annual Report 2018. https://www.unep.org/resources/annual-report-2018

Van Loon, P., Browne, M., & Allen, J. (2015). Reducing the environmental impact of last-mile delivery: The role of consolidation and delivery time windows. *Transportation Research Procedia, 12*, 171–182.

Wahlen, S., & Stroude, A. (2023). Sustainable consumption, resonance, and care. *Frontiers in Sustainability, 4*, 1013810. https://doi.org/10.3389/frsus.2023.1013810

Wiedenhofer, D., Wieland, H., Leipold, S., Aoki-Suzuki, C., Watari, T., Aguilar-Hernandez, G. A., et al. (2025). The circular economy and climate change: The state of national and global evidence on mitigation potential. *Annual Review of Environment and Resources, 50*.

World Bank (2022). The World Bank Annual Report 2022 : Helping Countries Adapt to a Changing World. https://documents.worldbank.org/en/publication/documents-reports/documentdetail/099030009272214630

Xie, G., Huang, L., Apostolidis, C., Huang, Z., Cai, W., & Li, G. (2021). Assessing consumer preference for overpackaging solutions in e-commerce. *International Journal of Environmental Research and Public Health, 18*(15), 7951.

Xie, W., Li, Y., Yang, Y., Wang, P., Wang, Z., Li, Z., et al. (2023). Maritime greenhouse gas emission estimation and forecasting through AIS data analytics: A case study of Tianjin port in the context of sustainable development. *Frontiers in Marine Science, 10*, 1308981.

Zalando (2023). Annual Report 2023. https://corporate.zalando.com/en/investor-relations/annual-report-2023

Chapter 4
Global Crises and Their Influence on Responsible Consumption

Abstract This chapter explores how major global crises have shaped the understanding and practice of responsible consumption from the 1970s to the present day. It examines four critical moments—the 1973 Oil Crisis, the 2008 Global Financial Crisis, the COVID-19 pandemic, and the Russo-Ukrainian War—each of which disrupted established consumption norms and revealed new forms of awareness and adaptation. The discussion begins with the oil shocks of the 1970s, when rising energy prices exposed the fragility of industrial societies built on cheap fossil fuels. What started as a geopolitical conflict evolved into a turning point for energy-conscious behavior, encouraging efficiency, restraint, and the first serious discussions about sustainability. The analysis then moves to the financial collapse of 2008, which challenged consumer confidence and values more than material access itself. As jobs and savings disappeared, consumption slowed, and many people began to question habits of excess. In its aftermath, local exchange networks, solidarity economies, and fair-trade movements gained ground, suggesting a moral reorientation toward fairness and sufficiency. The COVID-19 pandemic brought another rupture—one that redefined what was "essential." Lockdowns reshaped consumption geographically and psychologically: from global supply chains to local stores, from abundance to resilience, from convenience to care. Digitalization accelerated, but so did reflections on fragility, interdependence, and the meaning of responsible living. The chapter concludes with the ongoing effects of the Russo-Ukrainian war, which reignited debates about energy dependence and ethical consumption across Europe. As households faced soaring costs, conservation became not only practical but also civic—a form of solidarity tied to democratic values and energy autonomy. Taken together, these crises show that responsible consumption rarely emerges from comfort or prosperity; it often grows out of disruption. Each shock forced societies to reconsider the relationship between need and want, between individual action and collective survival. The chapter argues that crises, while destabilizing, also open moral and structural spaces where responsibility, restraint, and cooperation can take root—and perhaps endure.

A. Mikalauskienė et al., *Climate Change and Responsible Consumption*, Springer Climate, https://doi.org/10.1007/978-3-032-16218-2_4

4.1 The 1973 Oil Crisis: The Birth of Energy-Conscious Consumption

Few events in the twentieth century reshaped global consumption habits quite like the 1973 Oil Crisis. It didn't begin as an energy issue per se—it began as war. In the wake of the Yom Kippur War (Rolef, 1999; Rabinovich, 2007), OAPEC imposed an embargo that caught Western economies off guard, quadrupling oil prices in a matter of months (Bini et al., 2016). The impact hit quickly and showed up in everyday life. Drivers sat in idling cars, sometimes for hours, just to get a few liters of fuel. In industrial districts, machines went quiet—not because of strikes or supply issues, but simply because the energy wasn't there. Governments were slow to react. Some issued public service announcements. Others tried price controls or rationing schemes. None of it felt coordinated. What had long been assumed to be permanent—cheap and readily available energy—was abruptly exposed as fragile, with immediate and far-reaching economic consequences. But maybe the deeper shock was existential: a moment when modern society looked in the mirror and saw how exposed it really was. For many, this was the moment energy stopped being invisible. It became part of the political conversation, the household budget, the daily routine. People didn't just cut back; they began to reflect. How did we get so dependent on oil? And more importantly, was there a way out of it? The scale and severity of the crisis can be best understood by examining the dramatic rise in oil prices within a single year (Table 4.1).

It's hard to overstate how severe the price shock really was. In just 1 year, the cost of a barrel of oil in the United States jumped from $3.89 to $6.87—that's a 76.61% increase. Numbers like that don't just rise; they slam into systems that aren't ready. This wasn't a gradual shift—it was a jolt, triggered directly by the OAPEC embargo, and it sent shockwaves through global markets. Prices continued to rise after that, though the pace slowed somewhat: $7.67 in 1975, $8.19 in 1976, edging up to $9 by 1978.

Then came another spike—but this one felt different. It wasn't just about markets anymore. The Iranian Revolution in 1979 and the Iran–Iraq War in 1980 added a new layer of volatility, and oil prices responded fast. In those 2 years, crude surged again: by 40.44% in 1979 and an astonishing 70.81% in 1980, reaching $21.59. The climb didn't stop until 1981, when the average price hit its peak at $31.77 a barrel.

After that, the momentum broke. Prices eased down to $28.52 in 1982 and then to $26.19 in 1983. It wasn't just one thing—more supply came online, demand softened, and people began adjusting to the new price reality. Even after prices began to fall, the sense of disruption stuck around. It showed up not just in the news but in daily conversations—in homes, in offices, even in government memos. People weren't just thinking about oil as a commodity anymore. It had become something more uncertain, more fragile. That earlier confidence—that energy would always be there, cheap and ready—wasn't holding up so well. Inflation was rising, yes, but something else was shifting too: people were starting to realize that energy security might not be as solid as they'd assumed. It felt like the rules had changed, and nobody had quite figured out what came next.

Table 4.1 Crude oil domestic first purchase price in the United States, 1973–1983 (USD per Barrel)[a]

Year	Average price (USD/barrel)	Annual % change
1973	3.89	–
1974	6.87	76.61
1975	7.67	11.64
1976	8.19	6.78
1977	8.57	4.64
1978	9	5.02
1979	12.64	40.44
1980	21.59	70.81
1981	31.77	47.15
1982	28.52	−10.23
1983	26.19	−8.17

Source: EIA, U.S. Energy Information Administration (2025)

[a]The average domestic first purchase price represents the average price at which all domestic crude oil is purchased. Crude oil domestic first purchase prices were derived as follows: for 1949–1973, weighted average domestic first purchase values as reported by state agencies and calculated by the Bureau of Mines; for 1974 and 1975, weighted averages of a sample survey of major first purchasers' purchases; for 1976 forward, weighted averages of all first purchasers' purchases

The economic damage didn't build slowly—it came fast and left a mess. Production lines stalled, prices climbed, and more people were out of work. In countries that relied a lot on foreign oil, the problems hit even harder (Vázquez-Fariñas, 2023). Governments couldn't afford to wait. Across Europe, North America, and Japan, officials scrambled for solutions. Some launched public awareness campaigns. Others shifted policies or dusted off energy contingency plans (Lin, 1984). The old model—fossil-fueled growth at low cost—wasn't holding. Bit by bit, a new logic took shape: use less, spread risk, and tighten efficiency.

But the bigger shifts, the ones that stuck, didn't necessarily begin with policymakers. They started at home—around kitchen tables, in how people drove to work, or how they used appliances. As fuel prices spiked and shortages made headlines, energy went from background noise to something people noticed. In some places, they talked about it daily. It wasn't just a bill anymore; it had become unpredictable—something you couldn't quite count on (Clô, 2000). In the United States and parts of Western Europe, this led to a broader questioning of postwar consumption norms. Large, fuel-hungry vehicles—once symbols of prosperity—started to feel like liabilities. Slowly, people began looking for alternatives (Urry, 2013).

Japan felt the pressure even more than most. With more than 90% of its energy coming from abroad, the country didn't have much room to maneuver. The situation was tense. The government didn't wait—they jumped in fast, pushing for better efficiency in factories and encouraging people to rethink their everyday choices. One of the biggest changes happened in how people got around. Smaller, fuel-efficient cars became a real alternative, and the public responded. The shift wasn't just about saving money—it was also about coping, adapting. And Japanese carmakers were ready. Companies like Toyota and Honda didn't just serve their home market; they started sending these new vehicles overseas. Western buyers, who were facing their own energy problems, picked them up quickly. It wasn't planned as a grand strategy at first, but looking back, that's what it became. Japan found a way to align technology, consumer habits, and national interest—all under the pressure of crisis (Yamakoshi, 1986; Haghirian, 2011).

India got hit hard too, though things played out differently there. The oil crisis didn't just raise prices—it squeezed India's foreign exchange reserves, which were already stretched thin. The government didn't have a lot of options, but it had to respond somehow. So, priorities shifted. Not with grand reforms, but with whatever was possible at the time—more reliance on domestic coal, and the first steps, small ones, toward nuclear energy (Power, 1975).

For most people, though, the changes were even more immediate. In the cities, fuel was harder to come by. So people adjusted. They started using whatever was available—buses, bikes, shared rickshaws, even walking more. It wasn't a big shift in values; it was just what worked. In rural areas, the story was different but familiar. As diesel got expensive and petrol became unreliable, many stuck to what they knew: cooking with firewood, using animal labor, and farming the way their parents had. It wasn't a push toward sustainability. Not really. People didn't choose low-energy living because it sounded better—they just didn't have a lot of alternatives (Reddy, 1981).

When you look across countries, the differences in how people responded to the energy crisis really stand out. Some adjusted through new technology. Others just had to make do with less. And in a lot of cases, it was a mix—people doing whatever they could with what they had. In the United States, where cars were deeply woven into daily life, one of the clearest signs of change showed up in fuel efficiency. People didn't stop driving, but they started paying closer attention to what they were driving. The numbers reflect that shift. You can see it in the next table—how both government policies and consumer choices started nudging fuel economy upward (Table 4.2).

Table 4.2 Average fuel economy of new passenger cars in the United States, 1970–1985 (mpg)

Year	Average fuel economy (mpg)	Annual % change
1970–1975	13.5	–
1976	14.2	5.19
1977	15.1	6.34
1978	15.8	4.64
1979	15.9	0.63
1980	19.2	20.75
1981	20.5	6.77
1982	21.1	2.93
1983	21	−0.47

Source: U.S. Environmental Protection Agency (2024)

The table tracks how fuel efficiency changed in new passenger cars in the United States from 1970 to 1985. It's one way to see how the 1973 oil crisis started to shape what people drove—and what carmakers built. At the start of the decade, there wasn't much happening. Fuel economy held steady at around 13.5 miles per gallon (mpg), which made sense in a market still dominated by big, fuel-thirsty cars.

But that started to shift by the mid-1970s. In 1976, there's a noticeable bump—a 5.19% increase—and from there, the trend moves upward year after year. Then in 1980, something big happened: fuel economy jumped by 20.75%, the largest spike in the data. That coincides with the second major oil shock at the end of the '70s, suggesting that prices were doing what policy often struggled to—forcing change. By 1982, average efficiency had reached 21.1 mpg. That's about a 56% improvement compared to the average between 1970 and 1975. It's a dramatic shift in a relatively short span.

Things level off a bit after that. In 1983, there was even a slight dip—0.47%. That might reflect some stabilization in oil markets, or maybe the limits of how far efficiency could be pushed with the technology available at the time. Either way, what we see in the numbers isn't just about engineering. It's also about changing expectations, shifting regulations—like the introduction of CAFE standards in 1975—and a growing public interest in making cars that didn't burn through fuel so quickly.

Governments didn't just leave it to markets. Faced with the energy crisis, a lot of countries stepped in with direct interventions—some of them quite visible. Car-free Sundays, public campaigns about energy use, new speed limits, even rationing in some places—all of it was aimed at reducing demand (Baumeister & Kilian, 2016). In the Netherlands, for instance, the first car-free Sundays weren't about cutting emissions. They were about fuel—conserving it, and doing it fast. But those Sundays stuck in people's minds. They were strange, quiet days. And over time, they started to shift how people thought about cars, roads, and even public space. The policies didn't look like much at first, but they opened the door to later environmental thinking—and maybe a deeper sense of shared responsibility (Glazener et al., 2022).

Denmark took a different path, but the turning point came at the same time. In 1973, the country was getting more than 90% of its energy from oil—most of it imported. When prices surged, it wasn't just a shock; it was a wake-up call. The government moved quickly with awareness campaigns and subsidies for energy-saving appliances. They also started encouraging district heating—getting people to share heat, not just electricity, as a way to lower household demand. But the real shift came with the wind. The oil crisis didn't just prompt savings; it pushed Denmark to start investing in wind power seriously for the first time. The push for wind in Denmark didn't start as a long term master plan. It was a reaction—urgent, probably messy—but it turned out to matter. Some would later point to it as the moment Denmark began to rethink its whole energy future (Wang et al., 2019). And it wasn't just about energy. The oil crisis raised questions that hadn't been asked publicly before—about how people lived, what kind of economy they wanted, and whether total dependence on oil made any real sense (Rüdiger, 2019).

Table 4.3 Change in primary energy consumption by source, 1973–1980 [% change (1973 TWh–1980 TWh)]

Energy source	United States	Japan	France	Germany (FRG)
Oil	–2.09 (9655–9453)	−12.23 (3271–2871)	−13.08 (1506–1309)	−8.46 (1927–1764)
Gas	−10.12 (5938–5337)	+375.47 (53–252)	+60.51 (157–252)	+73.58 (352–611)
Coal	+18.91 (3611–4294)	+2.73 (659–677)	+12.32 (341–383)	+1.17 (1625–1644)
Nuclear	+201.2 (249–750)	+735.71 (28–234)	+314.29 (42–174)	+364.71 (34–158)
Renewables[a]	+3.5 (886–917)	+33.33 (198–264)	+44.52 (146–211)	+29.17 (48–62)

Source: International Energy Agency (2024), Our World in Data (2025)
[a]Includes hydro, geothermal, biomass

Of course, not every country followed Denmark's lead. Some turned to coal or nuclear, others leaned harder into gas. It all depended on where they started and what resources they had to fall back on. What's clear, though, is that the crisis forced choices. The table that follows looks at how energy use changed across several OECD countries in the years that followed. It gives a snapshot of who moved away from oil, what they turned to instead, and how fast those transitions happened (Table 4.3).

The table shows how the energy mix changed between 1973 and 1980 in four major OECD countries: the United States, Japan, France, and West Germany. It gives a sense of how each country tried to reduce its reliance on oil after the first big price shock. One pattern is obvious right away—oil use dropped across the board. In the United States, the decline was modest, just 2.09%. But in France and Japan, it was much steeper—13.08% and 12.23%, which makes sense since both were more dependent on imported oil before the crisis.

To make up for that drop, countries turned to other sources. Nuclear power, for one, expanded rapidly. Japan saw a massive jump—over 735%—while France wasn't far behind at 314%. It was a big bet on something more stable and home-grown. Natural gas also took off in some places, especially Japan (+375.47%) and Germany (+73.58%). But in the United States, gas use actually fell. That might've been due to infrastructure limits or supply issues—it's hard to say from the numbers alone.

Coal made a comeback too, though not dramatically. The United States increased coal use by nearly 19%, probably falling back on what was already available. And renewables—hydro, biomass, and a bit of geothermal—saw steady gains. France added about 44%, Japan 33%, while the United States and Germany grew more slowly.

The oil crisis made energy visible in a way it hadn't been before. People noticed it more—at home, at work, on the street. It was no longer this background system you didn't think about. Now it was part of the news, part of dinner table conversations. Some people started wondering where it all came from. Others worried about whether there'd still be enough, or if the next shock was just around the corner. There was uncertainty, for sure. But more than that, there was this sense—hard to describe—that something so basic might not be reliable after all. That's when energy stopped being just a technical thing. It started to feel like something tied up with politics, with economics, and with everyday life in ways that weren't so easy to ignore.

The oil crisis didn't just shake up prices or trade. It started to seep into how people were thinking—about energy, about where it came from, how it fit into daily life. It stopped feeling like just a background system. More and more, it was showing up in public discussions. It felt messier. Some people even started to ask whether there was a moral side to all this. The idea that your daily choices—how you heated your home, what kind of car you drove—could affect national stability became part of everyday conversations (Buell, 2012). It was the start, in a way, of something like energy citizenship: the sense that individuals were connected to broader systems, not just as users, but as participants.

Of course, most of this was driven by pressure—by price hikes and shortages—rather than ecological enlightenment. But even so, something changed. The crisis didn't create the environmental movement—but it gave it more room to speak. People who had been warning about resource limits and overuse for years found a new audience. What they were saying suddenly felt more real. Ideas like waste, depletion, and ecological pressure—they didn't seem like distant scenarios anymore. They started to land. Books like The Limits to Growth got more attention. And even though "sustainability" hadn't become a mainstream word yet, it was beginning to surface—in schools, in newspapers, in government talk (Ekins, 1993; Lifset, 2014).

In Sweden, things played out a little differently. Because the country had a broader mix of energy sources, it wasn't hit quite as hard. Still, it got people thinking. The government launched media campaigns—not just about using less energy, but about what that meant. They didn't only talk about saving energy—it was also about something else. Not just the numbers, but the reasons behind them. Things like fairness came up, and responsibility—toward others, maybe even toward the future. It wasn't framed as policy. It felt more grounded, something closer to everyday choices. People weren't told what to do exactly, but the message was there: pay attention, do what you can, even if it's not much. Schools picked it up too. Kids started learning about where energy comes from, and why it matters over the long run. And local officials—architects, planners, city workers—they began to rethink how buildings used energy, how spaces could be made more efficient (Bösch & Graf, 2014). In Sweden, where public trust and social support already ran deep, that kind of message didn't feel out of place. If anything, it sounded familiar. It fit. Bit by bit, the memory of the crisis sank in—not in a dramatic way, but in how people talked, planned, and imagined what it meant to live responsibly in a shared society.

It's easy to look back now and see the oil crisis as a turning point. It shook things up, for sure. Cheap energy didn't feel like a given anymore. And even if not all the behavioral changes lasted, some of them left a trace. They gave people a sense—just a glimpse, maybe—of what a different future could look like. The oil crisis didn't solve anything, but it rehearsed something. It showed how people might respond when systems falter. And it left behind a simple lesson that still holds today: when the conditions shift, when the pressure builds, people change.

4.2 The 2008 Global Financial Crisis: Economic Downturn and Consumer Ethics

The financial crisis of 2008 didn't just happen in banks or on trading screens. It reached much further—into housing markets, job markets, and eventually into the way people thought about their own money. The headlines started with Wall Street, sure. But it hadn't come out of nowhere. For years, lending practices had become more aggressive, and oversight wasn't keeping pace. Some parts of the financial system, maybe more than people realized at the time, had started drifting into risk without much pushback. The signs were there—just not always easy to read. And by the time it became visible, a lot of the damage had already been set in motion (Qin, 2023). And once it did start breaking down, it didn't just stay in one corner of the economy. It spread quickly. It didn't just shake institutions—it rattled households, spending habits, and broader conversations about what kind of consumption actually made sense.

Then came the crash. When Lehman Brothers went under in September 2008, markets around the world plunged. Credit all but disappeared. Businesses stopped hiring. Investments were put on hold. Layoffs followed fast (Wiggins & Metrick, 2019). And by 2009, global GDP had shrunk. That kind of contraction hadn't been seen in a long time—and for a lot of people, it felt like the ground had shifted.

People didn't just stop spending because they had less money. For some, the crisis also raised uncomfortable questions—about what really mattered, what was essential, and what could be let go. That kind of shift showed up clearly in Southern Europe, where the downturn was deeper and dragged on longer than in other regions. In Greece, for example, the austerity rules that came with EU and IMF bailouts weren't only about cutting public budgets. They ended up triggering something broader. You could hear it in conversations—on sidewalks, in newspapers, in everyday talk. People started questioning how much their way of life had depended on debt, on chasing things they maybe didn't need. In Athens, Thessaloniki, and other cities, a lot of households began looking elsewhere for basics. Some joined barter groups. Others got food from neighborhood co-ops or nearby farms that delivered straight to the community (Visvizi, 2012).

What drove those choices wasn't always clear-cut. Part of it was survival, no doubt. But part of it felt like something else—like people trying to pull away from systems they no longer trusted. It wasn't a movement, exactly, but it had momentum. Over time, researchers started calling it "resilient localism"—a kind of everyday economy grounded in local ties, mutual support, and doing more with less.

Table 4.4 Real GDP growth and private consumption growth in selected economies, 2007–2009 (% change)

Country	GDP growth (2009)	Private consumption growth (2009)
United States	−2.6	−1.3
Euro Area	–4.5	–1.2
United Kingdom	–4.2	–3.3
Japan	–5.4	–2.0
OECD Average	–3.4	–1.5

Source: Organisation for Economic Co-operation and Development (OECD) (2010)

In Spain, similar things were happening. People brought back time banks, organized swap events, and reopened repair shops. It was about saving money, sure, but also about leaning on each other (Valor Martínez & Papaoikonomou, 2016).

Still, none of this happened in a vacuum. It all unfolded in the middle of a bigger economic collapse. To get a sense of the scale, the next table shows GDP and household consumption drops across advanced economies in 2009. Those numbers help explain why so many people started questioning the old model (Table 4.4).

The table shows how sharply the 2008 financial crisis hit some of the world's biggest economies. 2009 was the low point, and by then, every country listed had seen drops in both GDP and private consumption. Japan took the hardest hit in terms of output, with GDP falling by 5.4%. The Euro Area saw a drop of 4.5%, and the UK followed closely at 4.2%. In the United States, the hit was a bit smaller—about 2.6%—but given how central it was to the unfolding crisis, that decline carried weight.

Spending didn't hold up either. Private consumption dropped pretty much everywhere, though not always in lockstep with output. The pattern wasn't identical across countries, but the overall pullback was clear. In the United States, for instance, consumption fell by 1.3%. In the UK, it dropped more steeply—around 3.3%. That drop wasn't only about having less income. A lot of people were unsure about what was ahead. Jobs felt uncertain, the news was full of bad signs, and personal plans were suddenly put on hold. People stopped spending the way they used to—not necessarily out of strategy, but more out of hesitation. Some were being cautious; others just didn't want to make things worse. It wasn't always a conscious decision. It felt more like a mood that crept into daily life.

The numbers in the table don't tell the whole story, but they point toward something bigger. When stability disappears, people don't just change what they spend—they change how they think about spending. You could see that shift in the choices they made. Fewer upgrades, more savings, fewer risks. It wasn't just an economic slowdown—it was a kind of pause. A moment where the old habits didn't feel right anymore, but the new ones hadn't quite taken shape either.

The OECD average—down 3.4% in GDP and 1.5% in private consumption—shows that this wasn't just a series of isolated downturns. It was something broader, a kind of shared retreat. For a time, at least, the crisis didn't just shrink what people could afford—it shifted what they were willing to spend it on.

After 2008, when jobs were lost and savings felt uncertain, people didn't just spend less because they had no choice. For some, it sparked something more personal—a kind of reassessment. They looked again at how they had been living, how often they were buying, and what sort of goods filled their homes. Before the crash, it had been easy to fall into a cycle of fast spending and fast replacement. Short product lifespans, constant upgrades, and easy access to credit had shaped daily consumption. But in the aftermath, those habits began to feel less secure—and in some cases, less satisfying.

A quiet shift began. There was more interest in scaling down, in slowing things, in finding value that didn't rely on speed or excess. Words like "voluntary simplicity" and "downshifting" started appearing more—sometimes in academic papers, sometimes in blog posts, and sometimes in conversations that wouldn't have included those ideas before. Not everyone used those terms, of course, but the spirit behind them resonated. It wasn't just about budgeting. It was about stepping back. The crisis gave space—maybe not deliberately, but effectively—for older concerns to return. Concerns about where things came from, about labor conditions, about environmental harm. Buying started to feel more connected to ethics again (Panizzut et al., 2021).

In Latin America, this shift looked different. The region already carried deep inequalities, and the global crisis made many of them more visible. In Argentina, the financial trauma of 2001 was still very close, especially in the working-class neighborhoods of Buenos Aires and Rosario. So when the effects of the GFC reached them, it didn't exactly surprise people—it reminded them. But this time, some of the responses were more organized. Community gardens, food cooperatives, and neighborhood barter systems grew—not just as emergency fixes, but as tools people already knew how to use. Civil society groups helped connect these practices to bigger ideas: not just getting by, but stepping away from a system that felt distant, extractive, and indifferent (Veltmeyer, 2018).

Brazil was also home to grassroots efforts that gained momentum during the crisis. The idea of *economia solidária*—a solidarity-based economy—had been developing long before 2008, but the crisis made it more visible. It wasn't about resisting capitalism in sweeping terms, and it wasn't centered on protest. Instead, it grew through networks of small cooperatives, mutual credit systems, and alternative markets. What it offered wasn't only material support—it gave people another way to relate to work, trade, and need. It asked whether economic participation could be more inclusive, more democratic, and more respectful of social and ecological limits (de Barros, 2010).

Beyond Latin America, subtler signs of change appeared elsewhere too. One of the clearest was the rising interest in second-hand goods. It wasn't just about used clothes—it extended to tools, electronics, furniture, and kitchenware. Some of it was driven by cost, of course. But for others, it was a shift in preference. People began looking for alternatives to buying new—less waste, less pressure to keep up. Peer-to-peer platforms were part of that. Sites like eBay and Craigslist weren't new, but their role grew. People turned to them more. Later, Airbnb, tool libraries, and ride-sharing services—all carried a similar idea: make use of what's already there, and rely more on others nearby (Miguel et al., 2022).

At the same time, some consumers became more interested in how goods were produced—not just what they cost. Brands that marketed organic, fair trade, or low-impact products found new audiences. Certifications that had once been overlooked started to carry weight. This didn't mean every shopper changed their habits, but something shifted in what people noticed. The questions started to change, even if the answers weren't always clear (Tee et al., 2017).

Beyond Latin America, the 2008 financial crisis also reshaped how people consumed in parts of Asia—but not in one uniform way. The shifts were layered, sometimes coming from government policy, other times from the ground up. In some cases, older cultural habits merged with new environmental goals, producing patterns that weren't always labeled "green," but often had sustainability at their core.

In South Korea, for example, the government took an unusually active role. As part of its response to the crisis, it launched what became known as a "Green New Deal." This wasn't just a budget item—it included public investment in energy-efficient technologies, support for new infrastructure, and direct efforts to stimulate green industries. Alongside that, there were public awareness campaigns tying the idea of sustainability to national renewal. It gave environmental language a role in the story of recovery. Over time, people began responding—not just with political support, but with small shifts in how they shopped and lived. More attention was paid to green labels. Eco-certifications became familiar terms. Lifestyle minimalism started to appeal—not always as a philosophy, but as a way to simplify, save money, or reduce waste. What began as a top-down stimulus effort slowly wove itself into parts of everyday life, and the influence of those years has lingered (OECD Korea, 2017).

India's response wasn't defined by policy in the same way, but something equally significant unfolded. When formal jobs dried up and credit became harder to access, many families leaned on habits they already knew. Fixing what was broken, handing things down, reusing before replacing—these weren't framed as ecological acts. They were just what made sense. Especially in communities with fewer resources, these everyday routines were practical and necessary. But they also, in hindsight, carried a kind of environmental logic. The crisis didn't spark these behaviors, but it made them more visible, more central to survival again (UNDP India, 2009).

Seen side by side, these two examples speak to different ways people meet uncertainty. One involves a government-led push for green industry and behavior change. The other reflects how long-standing informal systems step back in when official ones become unreliable. Neither of them fits cleanly into textbook definitions of ethical consumption. But both, in their own way, show how people adapt—not just by spending less, but by reshaping what it means to consume in the first place.

Meanwhile, in the Global North, another kind of shift was gaining ground. Some consumers started seeking out purchases that felt more aligned with personal ethics, however loosely defined. Labels like Fair Trade began to show up more often—not just in specialty stores, but in major retailers as well. These certifications gave

Table 4.5 Growth of fair trade certified products in Europe and North America, 2007–2011 (% annual growth)

Product category	2007	2008	2009	2010	2011
Fair Trade Coffee	12	22	10	14	18
Fair Trade Chocolate	20	34	15	18	21
Fair Trade Bananas	11	16	9	13	17

Source: Fairtrade International Monitoring Report (2012)

products an added layer of meaning. They suggested a supply chain that paid attention to fairness, worker rights, or environmental limits. That mattered to some shoppers. Maybe not always enough to change every decision, but enough to pause, to consider. The idea of responsible consumption wasn't new, but during and after the crisis, it gained traction in more structured forms. People wanted to feel like their choices counted—even if only in small ways, even if imperfect (Table 4.5).

This table demonstrates the evolving consumer orientation toward ethical consumption in the aftermath of the 2008 Global Financial Crisis (GFC), using the growth of Fair Trade certified products as a proxy for changing values and purchasing priorities. Across three product categories—coffee, chocolate, and bananas—the data reveal consistently positive annual growth rates from 2007 to 2011, even as overall economic conditions remained volatile. Fair Trade coffee, for example, grew by 12% in 2007 and reached a high of 22% in 2008, the very year the financial crisis deepened. Despite economic contraction, this upward trajectory persisted, with growth rebounding from 10% in 2009 to 18% in 2011.

One of the clearest examples of this shift can be seen in the case of Fair Trade chocolate. Sales grew sharply in 2008—by 34%—and kept gaining ground in the years that followed. Even bananas, usually seen as a low-margin and heavily commodified product, showed consistent annual growth. That kind of pattern suggests something more than niche appeal. It hints at a wider willingness among consumers to support ethical sourcing, even during financial uncertainty.

It's easy to assume that recessions drive people toward the cheapest available option, no matter how it's made. But here, the numbers tell a more complicated story. Instead of pulling away from value-driven purchases, many buyers seemed to lean in. That might have had something to do with the times. The crisis left a lot of people frustrated—with corporate behavior, with broken systems, with the feeling that ordinary choices had no real impact. Fair Trade labels and the values attached to them may have offered something that felt more grounded. A way to opt out, even just slightly, of the parts of the global economy that had come to feel inaccessible or unjust.

Of course, the numbers alone don't explain exactly why people made those choices. But they do raise questions. Maybe concerns about fairness and sustainability didn't disappear when budgets tightened—maybe they shifted, or took on new weight. It's possible that, for some, those values became more visible in a moment when trust in larger systems was already fading. Ethical products, in that context, might have felt like a small way to hold on to something that still made sense.

Not everyone reacted the same way when the crisis hit, and not all responses took the form of protest or organized resistance. Some of the shifts were smaller, more personal—almost invisible from the outside. A few people started putting money into funds that claimed to invest more responsibly. Others paid closer attention to what companies were doing behind the scenes, or talked more often about what it means to make decent choices when buying things. None of this followed a straight line, and most of it didn't feel especially coordinated. But taken together, these gestures pointed to something—maybe a kind of quiet unease with how things had been working. Or maybe just a wish for something that felt less empty (Ritzer, 2012).

This turn toward more value-driven behavior didn't only take shape in the Global North. In other regions—where consumer culture had long been shaped by different norms—people turned to traditions and frameworks that had been there all along. These weren't necessarily called "sustainable" or "ethical" in the language of policy or branding, but they carried their own kinds of guidance. In many communities, especially across parts of Asia and the Middle East, ideas about fairness, moderation, and responsibility were already embedded in daily life. And during times of economic uncertainty, those values became easier to reach for—more relevant, more trusted.

In Indonesia and Malaysia, where Islamic teachings are deeply woven into economic life, that turn was especially visible. The principles of Islamic finance—transparency, shared risk, and the rejection of exploitation—offered a kind of ethical compass at a time when conventional markets seemed unsteady. These weren't abstract doctrines. They shaped how people thought about debt, about savings, and increasingly, about consumption too. After the crisis, more attention was paid to whether goods were halal, but also whether workers had been treated fairly or whether production had caused harm. These weren't always new concerns, but they were more openly discussed, and they entered into people's choices in tangible ways. The result wasn't a rejection of markets—but a recalibration. Many families didn't just ask what they could afford, but what they could justify—morally, socially, and spiritually (Bashir, 2010; Kayed & Hassan, 2011).

What ties these varied responses together—whether from consumers in Western cities or families in Southeast Asia—isn't a single ideology or solution. It's the fact that crisis made the act of consuming visible again. Suddenly, choices that once felt automatic came under scrutiny. Some turned to labels. Others turned to scripture. Some leaned into activism; others into memory or tradition. But across these very different settings, the same question kept surfacing, in one form or another: how do we live, and spend, in ways that still make sense when the world feels unstable?

Not everything about the post-crisis response was visible on the surface. While people were adjusting in their own ways—within communities, families, habits—something quieter was happening in the background. Institutions, both national and supranational, started to treat the crisis not just as a disruption, but as a kind of reset button. An opening. A way to rethink what economies were supposed to do. And maybe, just maybe, how consumption could work differently, too. The tone was different from the grassroots. More technical. More formal. But still, the intention was clear enough: align people's everyday spending with bigger goals—ecological, social, sometimes moral. Governments didn't shout about it, but they acted. Frameworks were rewritten. Budgets were redirected. There was a sense—subtle, not always stated—that consumption shouldn't just bounce back. It should evolve.

In the European Union, that shift took form through the Europe 2020 Strategy. The language was polished—talk of "resource efficiency," "inclusive growth," and "green innovation" (European Commission, 2010). But behind the policy jargon was something real: an attempt to make recovery mean more than just numbers going back up. Other OECD countries followed suit. Some countries—many, in fact—rolled out what they later called green stimulus plans. It sounded clean, modern. Forward-looking. These were public investments, yes, but directed not just at economic recovery in the usual sense. The money flowed toward things like energy-saving technologies, better insulation, and transport systems that didn't rely so heavily on fossil fuels (Kempa & Tyagi, 2025). Officially, it was just fiscal policy. Another measure filed, debated, and passed—one of many. That's how it looked. But standing back, something else seeped through. Not loud, not written down anywhere, but still there—like a hum in the background. Maybe it wasn't even meant that way. Still, people felt it. It didn't tell anyone what to buy. Didn't preach. It was more like… a pause. A quiet tug at the edge of things. Like: hold on. What are we doing with this money? What direction are we taking, even if we don't say it out loud? These weren't questions people planned to ask. They just sort of emerged. Not about cost, really—but about meaning. Futures, even (Table 4.6).

The table shows how different countries chose to bring environmental goals into their fiscal responses after the 2008 financial crisis. It compares overall stimulus spending with the share that went to "green" efforts—things like clean energy, better energy use, low-carbon transport, and related infrastructure. South Korea stood out, putting 80.6% of its $38.1 billion plan toward green goals—a bold, clear move to tie economic recovery to ecological renewal. That wasn't accidental; it was a strategy, and a signal, showing where the country wanted to head. China, which spent far more in total—$586 billion—still managed to put 37.7% toward green investments, especially in transport and renewables, though that share was more balanced with other priorities. The United States, meanwhile, took a different tack. Out of its $787 billion package, just 14.2% went to green projects, suggesting a more traditional focus: jobs, consumption, economic speed—though still with some environmental intent. The EU, surprisingly, was even lower. Only 7.9% of its $278 billion plan was green, which stood in contrast to its usual leadership in

Table 4.6 Green stimulus spending as share of total economic recovery packages (2008–2010)

Country	Total stimulus (USD billion)	Green spending (USD billion)	% Green stimulus
South Korea	38.1	30.7	80.6
China	586	221	37.7
United States	787	112	14.2
European Union	278	22	7.9

Source: HSBC Global Research (2009)

sustainability rhetoric. These contrasts make something else clear too: even among wealthy states, priorities varied widely when it came to recovery. But the table does more than compare. It raises a question about whether crises can be turned into turning points. Where governments saw that chance, green investments became more than economic tools; they became seeds for something longer term. And where that chance was missed, the result was less transformation—and more of the same.

These stimulus efforts were meant to lay the groundwork for a greener kind of recovery. And they did, in part. But whether they actually reshaped what people do in the long run—that's less clear. The systems were in place, yes. The investments happened. But lasting change? That's still up for debate.

It's worth asking how much of what shifted during the crisis really stayed shifted. In the beginning, yes—there was a moment. People paid more attention to what they bought, how much, and why. When credit returned and growth followed, familiar patterns did too. Quietly. But not all of it slipped back. Some things—ideas like slowing down, using again, thinking different about money—they stayed. Not just in laws or white papers. In talk. In the cracks where newer ways could take root (Sharma & Sonwalkar, 2013).

So even if not all behaviors stuck, the memory did. Something about that period stayed behind—in values, in language, in the shape of institutions that didn't exist before. The outlines of what responsible consumption could mean didn't disappear. They kept evolving, slowly.

Looking back, the financial crash wasn't just a break in the system—it was a kind of jolt to public thinking. It knocked loose the belief that endless consumption was normal. And it made space for different kinds of questions. Not everyone changed course, of course. Still, the crisis shook something loose. Ethics—turns out they move. Pressure, fear, not knowing what comes next—that's when they shift. And maybe, when the ground gives way, that's when values step out. So no, the GFC didn't just break things. It made something visible.

4.3 The Covid-19 Pandemic: Health Crisis and the Reshaping of Consumption

When COVID-19 first appeared in late 2019, no one quite knew what it would become. But by early 2020, it had reshaped nearly everything—a health crisis, yes, but also a turning point in how people thought about consumption. It wasn't like the other crises—those that hit finance or politics. This one was everywhere at once. It broke supply chains. It kept people home. It shifted how we met, worked, and moved through the world. Suddenly, the things people bought—and how they bought them—looked different. Not just in rich countries or poor ones, but across the board. And for many, it brought tough questions. Not just what to consume, but why. And what it might mean later on (Leal Filho et al., 2022; Hu et al., 2022).

Italy was among the first in Europe to feel the full weight of the pandemic—and when it hit, the shift in how people consumed was sharp and sudden. In those early weeks of 2020, the country seemed to pause. Streets emptied. Movement slowed to almost nothing. Buying patterns changed fast. But even in that stillness, something new began to stir. Online shopping took off. So did neighborhood stores, small co-ops, food that didn't travel far—things people could trust, close by. The idea of "essential" goods took on a new meaning, not just in policy, but in daily life. People started asking what really mattered. What they actually needed. And even when the rules eased, some of those habits didn't go away. Studies found people holding on—to quality, to things that last, and to the feeling that buying local meant something more (Cervellati et al., 2022; Sorrentino et al., 2022).

Italy's early story showed how consumption could change close to home—on streets, in shops, in daily life. But further out, the bigger picture was shifting too. In the United States, broad trends began to tell their own version of the crisis. Numbers, sales, patterns—they showed the blow and how the system tried to recover.

The data that follows make it plain. 2020 saw a drop in retail activity the United States hadn't experienced in years—maybe decades. Stores with doors and aisles struggled to stay afloat. Online sales, by contrast, took off. It was the first time in over 10 years that total retail actually fell (Table 4.7).

The table looks at how retail sales changed in the United States between 2018 and 2021—a stretch that included both a shock and a strong rebound. Before COVID hit, things were steady. Growth in 2018 reached +4.6%, and in 2019 it slowed a bit to +3.4%—still solid, still normal. And then, 2020 arrived. Things dipped—by −2.8%. First time in over a decade that happened. There were lockdowns, rules, confusion. People stayed put. Stores were open less, or not at all. Clothes? Travel stuff? In-store shopping? They took the brunt. But that downturn didn't stick. In 2021, retail snapped back. Fast. Sales rose +7.1%—more than before COVID. Why? Hard to pin it on one thing. Maybe it was people catching up. Maybe it was the checks. Or just the relief of things slowly feeling… okay again. One other thing shifted too: how people shopped. Physical stores gave ground to online ones. That trend, already underway, sped up. It shows up even more clearly in the e-commerce numbers. These figures don't just show up-and-down movement. They reflect how deeply a crisis can shake habits. Not just how much people buy—but where, and how. Some of those shifts? They don't snap back.

Table 4.7 Retail sales growth in the United States, 2018–2021 (%)

Year	% Growth
2018	+4.6
2019	+3.4
2020	–2.8
2021	+7.1

Source: Trading Economics (2025a)

Table 4.8 Growth in E-commerce sales in the United States, 2018–2021 (%)

Year	$ Billions	% Growth
2018 Q1	122	4.27
2018 Q2	125	2.46
2018 Q3	128	2.4
2018 Q4	132	3.13
2019 Q1	132	0
2019 Q2	138	4.55
2019 Q3	146	5.8
2019 Q4	153	4.79
2020 Q1	159	3.92
2020 Q2	212	33.33
2020 Q3	215	1.42
2020 Q4	221	2.79
2021 Q1	232	4.98
2021 Q2	240	3.45
2021 Q3	235	−2.08
2021 Q4	244	3.83

Source: Trading Economics (2025b)

The pandemic made regular shopping harder—but at the same time, it pushed people online faster than anyone had expected. E-commerce didn't just grow—it leapt ahead of the old forecasts by a wide margin.

To get a clearer sense of when and how this happened, the next table zooms in on e-commerce sales by quarter. It lets us see the shift not just in numbers, but as it unfolded—in real time, from the first wave to the peak months (Table 4.8).

This table tracks how e-commerce grew in the United States, quarter by quarter, from early 2018 through the close of 2021. It gives a close-up look at just how quickly digital shopping sped up during COVID. From 2018 to 2019, growth was there—but it was steady, slow. Mostly between 2% and 6% each quarter. A gradual shift, part of retail's long move online. Then came the shock. In Q2 of 2020, e-commerce jumped from $159 billion to $212 billion in just one quarter—a 33.33% leap. That kind of spike hadn't happened before. It was lockdowns, store closures—people had little choice but to go online, even for basics. After that, things calmed a bit. The big surge faded, but sales stayed up—much higher than before. That wasn't a one-time thing. It looked like a reset. By the last quarter of 2021, numbers reached $244 billion—almost double where they'd been in early 2018. The quarterly pace went up and down—Q3 2021 dipped by −2.08%, then picked up again—but that seemed more about seasons and supply chains, not a step backward. So the trend held. And it meant more than sales. It meant the pandemic had pushed digital buying into a new gear—one that changed not just habits, but the systems underneath. And that change matters. For packaging. For emissions. For how long do products last? All of it reshaped by a world that now buys more for speed, for ease.

This shift wasn't just about easier access or faster delivery—it started to change the retail system itself. And not in small ways. Emissions, packaging, transport, the carbon cost of what we buy—all of that began to look different, long term. In homes, not much stayed the same. Some routines vanished altogether. Others got bent out of shape. People paused—jobs weren't secure, health was up in the air, income felt fragile. So they pulled back, quietly. They started counting again, watching where the money went. Travel… yes, that went quiet. Eating out, same story. It wasn't just less—it was gone. And in its place? Not one big thing, but lots of little ones. Fixing things at home. Subscribing to something new. Just... staying in. Familiar, nearby, low-risk. The shift was fast. Some parts of the economy just froze. Others, oddly, were overwhelmed—couldn't deliver fast enough (Das et al., 2022).

In low-income countries such as Kenya, the COVID-19 crisis forced a shift in consumption that exposed long-standing weaknesses—structural, institutional—but also brought other layers to the surface. The ones less visible. The ones already embedded in daily routines. Jobs were lost or suspended. Supply chains—erratic, delayed, then silent. Faced with that, many households reached for what still worked. Mobile money platforms—M-Pesa most of all—became lifelines. Not just for convenience, but survival. It wasn't the state that organized the response. In many places, it was the community. Sometimes through apps, sometimes through the church or a neighbor. Aid moved by proximity, not hierarchy. Goods flowed, if unevenly. The informal economy didn't plan. It moved. It filled in, adjusted, stepped where there was space. People adapted—not because they chose to, but because they had to. And within that space, they made decisions. They chose, even with few options. So maybe what we're seeing here isn't just a reactive model. It's something else—built on connection, not coordination. These systems aren't often labeled as resilient. But in moments like these, they function. That's what matters (Mugume & Bulime, 2022; Wachira & Njuguna, 2023).

Meanwhile, countries like the United States—more formalized, more regulated—shifted differently. Spending patterns changed too, but along institutional lines. The following table reflects how that process unfolded, category by category (Table 4.9).

The table presents how consumer spending patterns shifted in the United States during 2020—the first full year of the COVID-19 pandemic—compared to the year before. Behind the numbers lie clear signals of changed behavior, shaped by

Table 4.9 Change in consumer spending categories in the United States, 2020 vs. 2019 (%)

Category	% Change
Transportation	–26.0
Restaurants	–19.5
Health care	–9.0
Groceries	+11.2
Home improvement	+14.0
Digital services (e.g., streaming, cloud software)	+28.4

Source: McKinsey & Company (2021)

lockdowns, limits on movement, and growing concern over health and financial stability. Transportation spending fell the most, dropping 26.0%. With fewer commutes, grounded flights, and canceled trips, the entire mobility sector contracted sharply. Restaurants followed, with a 19.5% decline, as bans on indoor dining and strict capacity rules made social eating difficult or impossible. Health care spending also declined—down 9.0%. At first glance, this might seem contradictory during a health emergency. But delays in non-urgent care and the suspension of elective procedures made the drop more understandable. At the same time, categories tied to home life and digital routines saw substantial growth. Grocery spending rose by 11.2%, as more meals were cooked at home. Home improvement grew 14.0%, perhaps reflecting the new centrality of domestic spaces—for work, rest, and everything in between. The biggest leap came from digital services, which surged by 28.4%. Streaming platforms, video calls, paid online services—suddenly, these weren't optional add-ons. They became part of daily life, without much time to consider alternatives. What people spent their money on began to look different. It wasn't just about adapting to circumstances—it was also, in part, a reassessment. What do we really need? What keeps us going when the outside world slows down? Many answers pointed inward: toward basics, toward home, and toward the digital space. But even these shifts came with trade-offs. Travel dropped, and so did emissions—for a while. Yet new pressures surfaced. Deliveries increased. More packaging, more data use, more electricity. Sustainability took on a different form—less visible, perhaps, but no less complex.

Beyond the visible shifts in how people spent their money, the pandemic touched something older—quiet habits of thought, ethical reflexes that weren't written down but lived, passed on, assumed. In parts of East Asia, change didn't come just because it was ordered. It came because it fit—with ideas people already held close. There was no need for sweeping mandates when cultural memory did the work. Restraint, modesty, caring about how your actions ripple outward—that was already in the air, waiting.

Japan is a clear example. The state didn't push hard. No strict lockdowns. Still, behavior shifted. Not slowly, either. People cut back. They stayed put. They focused on what was essential. Not because someone told them to—but because it felt right. The word jishuku—self-restraint—started appearing again, carrying more than just politeness. Purchases dropped, especially the nonessential kind. Savings grew. Support for local producers quietly strengthened. And even small acts—like cooking more, or skipping a purchase—took on another meaning. It wasn't just consumption anymore. It was care. These values weren't invented by crisis. They were already there, folded into daily life. COVID just turned up the volume (Wright, 2021; Borovoy, 2022).

And those shifts—what people chose to buy, what they let go—mattered beyond the home. At first glance, less flying and driving meant lower emissions. That sounded like a silver lining. But then came the surge online. Everything went digital: shopping, shipping, returns. And with that, a different weight settled in—cardboard, plastic, vans on the road, and electricity behind the screens. The fix wasn't clean. What seemed like progress brought its own clutter. The frictionless promise of convenience was suddenly heavy with consequences. The pandemic didn't offer neat lessons—it exposed the trade-offs we live with. Every solution tugs at something else. Every adaptation leaves a mark. And for a moment, we were forced to see it.

Beyond just what people bought or skipped, the pandemic touched something subtler: how consumption itself was understood. Mortality wasn't abstract anymore. Risk felt near. And the sense of being tied together—not just through markets, but through air, water, and food—became harder to ignore. In different parts of the world—Europe, North America, Asia—surveys from 2020 and 2021 started picking up a change in tone. People were thinking differently. They weren't just asking, "Can I afford this?" but "Where does it come from?" or "Who made it—and under what conditions?" The words began to shift too. "Resilient consumption," "local sourcing," "essentialism"—once fringe terms—started popping up. Not everywhere, not always clearly, but more often. And for some, those words began turning into choices. Not necessarily cheaper ones. But ones that felt, in a quiet way, more in line. Closer. Less extractive. Less anonymous. Even if it meant paying a bit more (Leal Filho et al., 2022; Sijabat, 2024).

Elsewhere, the pandemic peeled open older questions—about justice, belonging, and what it means to live well without leaving others behind. In places where inequality had long shaped daily life, the crisis didn't introduce new problems—it made old ones harder to ignore. Consumption, in those settings, began to take on another role: not just a transaction, but a kind of reflection. Of history. Of wounds. Of what needs healing.

In Canada, that reflection found different voices. For some, it echoed in small shifts: farmers' markets that sold out before noon, co-ops that doubled in size, local supply chains patched together out of necessity. But it also came from deeper wells. Indigenous communities—long sidelined—brought forward ideas they had always held: that land isn't a resource, that enough is a value, that taking without giving back eventually hollows a place out. These weren't new teachings. But now, more people were listening. Especially in cities like Vancouver or Toronto, interest in where things came from wasn't just about carbon footprints. It was about the process. And people. And whether something had been made with care, or just made fast. Labels that hinted at fairness or traceability started to carry more weight—not for everyone, but for enough to notice (Bernauer & Slowey, 2020; Carolan, 2021).

The pandemic didn't just reveal gaps—it widened them. Low-income households, informal workers, people already pushed to the edges—they bore the brunt. Not evenly, not quietly. And as those inequalities became harder to look past, they began to shape how people responded. Some looked inward, changed habits. Others looked outward—toward businesses they knew, places they trusted. Support shifted. Small stores, neighborhood cooperatives, social enterprises—they began to matter more. Not just economically, but symbolically. Buying from them felt different. It felt like showing up. In that light, responsible consumption stopped being only about the planet or public health. It turned into something else too—a civic gesture, a moral stance in the face of systems that had faltered (Das et al., 2022; Ryan & Nanda, 2022).

At the same time, governments moved. Big plans, big money. Stimulus packages rolled out across continents—some traditional, others trying something new. A few, like the EU's €750 billion recovery program, chose to link recovery not just to growth, but to change. The Green Deal sat at the heart of that plan, tying climate action to jobs, to infrastructure, to everyday decisions. And while not every euro shifted behavior, the tone was different. There was intent. A kind of nudge—not loud, not commanding, but present. Toward efficiency, toward renewables, toward choices that aligned with a different kind of economy. Whether people noticed in the moment or not, the signals were there. They opened a space. A chance to make responsible consumption not just personal, but structural (Bäckstrand, 2022; Urios et al., 2022).

Looking back, it's hard to pin the pandemic to a single role. Was it a break? A push? Probably both. It disrupted habits that had seemed stable—what we bought, how it moved, where it came from. But it also sped up what was already on the rise: digital shopping, local production, and ethical questions that had been simmering below the surface. With everything on pause, there was time—finally—to ask what all this consumption was for. Whether those questions will last, no one can say for sure. But something shifted. Not just in numbers, but in perception. Risk now feels closer. Resilience isn't just a word in reports—it's something people think about. And responsibility, once a niche concern, has started to matter more in how futures are imagined. What comes next will depend on whether that awareness stays in the room.

4.4 The Russo-Ukrainian War: Energy Crisis and Ethical Consumer Choices

No one expected the war to feel this close. When Russia sent tanks into Ukraine in early 2022, it was, yes, a geopolitical shock—but not only that. Pretty soon, the consequences started creeping into everyday places. Not with a bang, but with a kind of slow unease. Energy was one of the first things to shake. Not as an idea, but as a real-life issue. Radiators that didn't come on when they should've. Bills that tripled without warning. People asking questions they hadn't asked in years, maybe ever. How did we end up here? Who supplies our gas? Why did no one fix this sooner?

In Europe, these thoughts weren't entirely new. The dependence had been tolerated—managed, maybe, but never really solved. Russia, by then, was providing over 40% of imported gas to the EU (European Central Bank, 2022). It had been convenient. Familiar. And suddenly, it was politically toxic. The taps didn't just close gently. There were cuts, restrictions, and sanctions flying both ways. In a matter of weeks, what used to seem like a stable arrangement had become a mess no one could ignore.

It wasn't just officials scrambling. Households felt it first. And hardest. Everything that used to run in the background—heating, appliances, long showers, even the light in the hallway—was up for negotiation again. This wasn't about abstract models anymore. It was about choices, sometimes tough ones. Do we heat the whole flat

Table 4.10 EU natural gas imports from Russia (2021–2023)

Year	EU gas imports from Russia (bcm)	Share of total EU gas imports (%)
2021	150.2	44.93
2022	78.8	23.59
2023	42.9	14.80

Source: Council of the European Union (2025)

tonight, or just the bedroom? What's the price of comfort now? And underneath that, something quieter: a broken trust. That sense that someone, somewhere, should have seen this coming—and didn't (Tsekeris, 2025; Cui et al., 2023) (Table 4.10).

This table does more than list figures. What it really shows is the pace at which Europe's energy system began to unstick itself from a dependency that had felt immovable for years. Between 2021 and 2023, the drop in Russian gas imports wasn't just steep—it was disruptive. In a short window of time, supply chains shifted, new terminals were rushed into use, and infrastructure plans once stuck in paperwork found sudden momentum. Sanctions played a role. So did politics, urgency, and the fear of exposure. It wasn't clean or coordinated at every step, but the direction was unmistakable.

At the same time, something quieter began to shift. Public conversations started to pick up—about security, about who holds power in the energy relationship. These weren't just policy debates. You could sense it even if no one said it outright: consumption had stopped being neutral. The question wasn't only how to keep the lights on—it was who gets to decide how, and at what cost.

When that break in supply hit, the effects came fast. Prices at the wholesale level spiked, and it didn't take long for those costs to find their way to households. Bills jumped. People noticed. Governments moved to soften the blow—capping prices, offering subsidies, trying to stretch social safety nets that were already under pressure. Still, many felt the weight. Some made small changes—turning down the heat, shifting appliance use to off-peak hours. But for others, it became a turning point.

That's when longer-term thinking began to surface—not just among policymakers, but in kitchens, living rooms, apartment blocks. Should we install solar? What about insulating the walls? A heat pump instead of that old gas boiler? These weren't always technical decisions. Often, they carried something else—an urge to feel less exposed, less dependent. In that sense, the crisis didn't just raise prices. It raised awareness. And for many, it marked the first time energy wasn't just something you used. It was something you had to think about. Maybe even take back some control over (Huebner et al., 2023).

Across the EU, consumer responses to the energy crisis did not follow a single path. Patterns varied—not only by policy, but also by geography, infrastructure, and even climate. Northern Europe, where heating needs dominate energy demand for much of the year, faced challenges that were both technical and social in nature. Among these, Finland stood out.

There, the impact of the Russo-Ukrainian War made itself felt quickly—not just through energy prices, but through public messaging, social norms, and the quiet recalibration of daily routines. In a country where winter temperatures regularly fall below freezing, the call to reduce household energy use was never going to be simple. Yet the response was swift. National campaigns asked residents to lower room temperatures, delay sauna use, and avoid peak-hour consumption. And people listened. These were not seen only as cost-cutting steps. For many, they became something else—acts of alignment, of shared purpose. Gestures that said: we are part of this too (Matschoss et al., 2025).

Municipalities supported the shift. "Energy saving weeks" were launched. Households received insulation kits, thermal curtains, advice. The messaging mattered. These efforts weren't framed as burdens or sacrifices—they were framed as contributions. As responsibilities. In that way, the Finnish response reveals something crucial: that under geopolitical pressure, even the most technical forms of consumption—heating, lighting, timing—can take on ethical weight. The crisis did not just shift behavior. It recast it, tying everyday domestic choices to broader narratives of solidarity and civic duty (Farghali et al., 2023) (Table 4.11).

The table lays out the numbers—but what they show is pressure. Uneven, sharp, and hard to avoid. From 2020 to the first half of 2024, electricity and gas prices across the EU didn't just fluctuate—they convulsed. In 2020, electricity prices were

Table 4.11 Change in consumer energy prices in the EU (2020–2022)[a]

Year		
	Electricity price (EUR/kWh)	*Electricity Price Increase (%)*
2019-S2	0.1280	–
2020-S1	0.1269	−0.86
2020-S2	0.1282	1.02
2021-S1	0.1341	4.6
2021-S2	0.1515	12.98
2022-S1	0.1934	27.66
2022-S2	0.2401	24.15
2023-S1	0.2393	−0.33
2023-S2	0.2226	−6.98
2024-S1	0.2187	−1.75
	Natural gas price (EUR/kWh)	*Natural gas price increase (%)*
2019-S2	0.0498	–
2020-S1	0.0430	−13.65
2020-S2	0.0475	10.47
2021-S1	0.0411	−13.47
2021-S2	0.0546	32.85
2022-S1	0.0629	15.2
2022-S2	0.0980	55.8
2023-S1	0.0916	−6.53
2023-S2	0.0891	−2.73
2024-S1	0.0802	−9.99

Source: Eurostat (2024a, 2024b)

[a]Excluding taxes and levies, European Union—27 countries

steady. Then, in the second half of 2021, they jumped: +12.98%. In 2022, things broke loose. Prices rose 27.66% in the first half, then climbed another 24.15% in the second. At the peak: €0.2401 per kilowatt-hour. That wasn't just inflation—it was something else. Supply chains had buckled. Russian imports were shrinking. Global markets spun. From 2023 on, prices dipped a little. But not enough. Not to where they had been. The baseline had shifted.

Gas moved similarly. Early 2020 saw a drop—13.65%. After that, the direction changed. Slowly at first. Then, in late 2022, a spike: +55.8%. Price per kWh hit €0.0980. It wasn't abstract. People felt it. Budgets stretched. Some cracked. So they adapted. Not just by turning down the heat or switching off lights. Many started thinking longer-term. Energy-efficient fridges. Better windows. Smaller steps with bigger meaning. Some could afford solar panels, insulation, heat pumps. Others just used less. And underneath it all—conversation. About what's fair. What's fragile. Where energy comes from, and what happens when it doesn't. That's what this table holds, quietly. Numbers, yes. But also a signal. That geopolitical disruption reaches the meter, the wallet, the mind.

The pressure from rising prices did more than squeeze household budgets. It also stirred reflection—quiet, complicated, and often overdue. For many, energy consumption became harder to think about in neutral terms. It wasn't just about what something cost anymore, but where it came from, who it funded, and what kind of future it implied. The public conversation began to shift. Not quickly, but unmistakably. Questions of energy independence, national resilience, and sustainability moved into the foreground. Words like "ethical sourcing" and "fossil fuel divestment" were no longer confined to policy circles. They began showing up in public debate, in news coverage, and even in daily choices.

In that sense, the war acted less like a one-time shock and more like a trigger—bringing to the surface questions that had long been present but easier to ignore. Energy, once treated mostly as a technical or economic issue, began to carry ethical weight. The term "ethical energy" started to circulate. And not just in the narrow sense of carbon metrics. It broadened—to include human rights, democratic alignment, global equity (Huhta, 2023). Some measures, like the boycotts of Russian gas and oil, were led by governments. But they didn't move in a vacuum. Across much of Europe, consumer sentiment supported them. People accepted trade-offs. Not always easily, and not always without resistance—but often willingly, when framed as acts of solidarity. Reduced indoor comfort. Higher monthly bills. These things became, at least for a time, expressions of civic alignment and shared values (Huhta & Reins, 2023).

Of course, that shift in sentiment didn't play out identically everywhere. Local conditions, institutional capacity, and historical memory shaped what it looked like in practice. Some countries leaned into it—connecting ethically framed consumption with a larger European narrative. Others moved more cautiously, driven by domestic priorities or political skepticism. The case studies that follow explore this variation. They offer a view of how one crisis can splinter into different consumption pathways, depending on where it lands.

In the Baltic States—Lithuania, Latvia, and Estonia—the war landed close. And it changed more than energy bills. What followed was a groundswell of consumer interest in energy autonomy, unlike anything seen before. In 2022 alone, residential solar panel installations doubled. Heat pump orders surged—so much so that supply chains struggled to keep pace. But this wasn't just about reacting to prices. For many, the deeper trigger was memory. The kind that lingers. During the Soviet era, energy dependency had come with other kinds of dependency. That history hadn't faded.

In Lithuania, surveys showed a clear pattern. People were ready to endure short-term hardship if it meant reducing reliance on Russian energy. That willingness wasn't framed as sacrifice—it was moral alignment. Municipalities and cooperatives began working together, channeling public will into practical solutions. Rooftop solar. Decentralized heating. The technical and the symbolic started to blur. You couldn't separate personal energy choices from the broader story of resistance (Genys et al., 2024; Grigolienė et al., 2024). And somewhere along the way, the idea that consumption was just private lost traction. It became collective. Political. Part of who we are.

Elsewhere, the landscape looked different. Turkey, for instance, faced the same global price hikes—but the narrative that followed took another shape. Yes, households adapted. There was a visible uptick in low-energy appliances and rooftop kits, especially in rural and suburban areas. But here, affordability came first. Ethics stayed in the background. There was no sweeping consensus about where energy should come from or what it should stand for. The state kept buying from Russia. At the same time, it expanded its renewable sector. A balancing act—not just in supply strategy, but in public discourse too (Dastan, 2023). The result was a kind of fragmentation. People adjusted, yes—but not always with shared direction or shared meaning.

These contrasts matter. They show how crisis does not guarantee convergence. What people do with disruption depends on the frames available to them: history, politics, identity. Even when prices rise everywhere, the stories people tell—and the actions they take—can pull in different directions (Table 4.12).

The table tracks how public opinion inside the EU shifted between 2019 and 2024—a period that didn't just change energy systems, but the way people thought about them. The most striking movement is in one number: the share of consumers putting affordability first. In 2019, it was 27%. By 2024, it had climbed to 40%. That's a 13-point jump. And it maps closely onto the cost-of-living anxiety that

Table 4.12 EU27 consumer views on energy policy (2019 vs. 2024)

Indicator	2019 (%)	2024 (%)	Change (pp)
Ensuring more affordable energy prices for consumers	27	40	13
Investing in innovative energy technologies	24	33	9
Decreasing energy consumption across Europe	28	30	2
Coordinating European countries on energy matters	22	27	5

Source: European Commission (2019, 2024)

spread after energy prices shot up—when Russian gas stopped flowing and bills started doubling. But that wasn't the only signal. Support for investment in new technologies—solar, batteries, smart grids—also grew. It moved from 24% to 33%. Maybe not headline-grabbing, but meaningful. It points to something deeper: a sense that quick fixes wouldn't be enough. That resilience had to be built, not just hoped for. Smaller changes show up too. A two-point uptick in the number of people backing lower energy consumption. A five-point rise in support for better EU-wide coordination. Not dramatic, but steady. And maybe more important than they seem. They hint at a growing sense that energy isn't just a personal matter. It's shared. Contested. Political. Put together, these shifts mark a kind of reorientation. Under pressure, people began to look not just at what they were paying—but at where it was all heading. The short term and the long term, side by side. Price and policy. Survival and strategy. This matters. Because policies like REPowerEU don't just need money or engineering. They need legitimacy. Public buy-in. And that only comes when people see energy for what it really is: not just wires and tariffs, but something tied to fairness, sustainability, and the democratic project itself (Aliyev, 2023).

These changes didn't come only as reactions. There was something more intentional about them. Surveys and market data pointed to a marked rise in interest toward decentralized energy—especially rooftop solar and small-scale wind. Not huge shifts overnight, but visible ones. And the concern didn't stop with electricity. More products—especially those tied to fossil fuel financing, authoritarian regimes, or unsustainable supply chains—started drawing scrutiny (Ahmed et al., 2024). At the same time, pressure mounted on companies to be clearer. About where their energy came from. What their carbon footprints looked like. Whether they were tangled up with conflict economies. The bar had been raised. Quietly, but firmly (Lee et al., 2023).

Outside Europe's immediate orbit, and far from the calculus of middle-power diplomacy, there were other kinds of responses. In places like India, the war didn't trigger sanctions—but it still left a mark. Not politically, but economically. Energy prices went up. So did public anxiety. And that, too, can shape what people care about. Not from high-level declarations—but from how life gets lived.

In India, urban middle-class households felt the pinch directly. True, the government kept importing discounted Russian oil. But within cities, especially among youth and climate-conscious groups, something else was happening. Ethical consumption became part of the conversation. Not abstractly, but practically. Electric scooters. Solar lamps. Off-grid systems. The kinds of things people could see, buy, use. On social media and in civil society circles, energy-saving tips began circulating. Small hacks, household experiments. Even without a strong geopolitical stance, there was momentum. Groups reframed ethical consumption not just as climate action—but as national interest. As self-preservation (Warren & Ganguly, 2022; Saur Energy, 2021). That distinction matters. It shows that consumer awareness doesn't always flow from top-down foreign policy. Sometimes it emerges laterally—from need, from values, from vulnerability.

Policy didn't stand still. In May 2022, the European Commission launched REPowerEU—an ambitious, €300 billion push to speed up energy independence and the shift toward renewables (Aliyev, 2023; Kanapiyanova, 2023). National governments followed suit, expanding support for things like heat pumps, insulation, and home electrification. These programs weren't just about infrastructure. They changed how people calculated their choices. Suddenly, cleaner options didn't just seem virtuous—they made financial sense. They became easier to want. But it's important not to oversimplify. These changes weren't accessible to everyone. Many people—especially in lower-income brackets, renters, or those living in old, inefficient buildings—had few real options. Switching to greener tech isn't always a question of will. Sometimes, it's about what's even possible. For them, cutting back could mean real discomfort. Or risk. So while the war pushed ethical awareness into the mainstream, it also made visible something else: that fairness matters. That sustainability without access isn't much of a solution.

Taken together, the Russo-Ukrainian War altered how conflict and consumption are understood. It forced a reckoning—not just with supply chains, but with the assumptions beneath them. Every day, energy use becomes geopolitical. And ethical behavior, often seen as slow or niche, got a jolt of urgency. Crisis sped things up. Not just out of choice, but necessity. That transformation won't vanish easily. People have started asking harder questions—about where power comes from, who profits, and who's left behind. They're not only looking for low-carbon answers, but for systems that feel transparent, resilient, just. In that sense, the war's imprint might last longer than the war itself.

4.5 The Climate Crisis: An Ongoing Emergency Shaping Consumer Decisions

Unlike the shocks of war or economic collapse, the climate crisis doesn't erupt. It builds. Slowly, then faster. It isn't local, and it doesn't pass. It accumulates—across borders, across decades. That's what makes it hard to grasp, but impossible to ignore. It seeps into markets. It shifts ecosystems. It alters how people think about what they buy, and why. The signs are all around now. Hotter years. Fires that don't stop. Crops that fail. Water that dries up or floods in. Species vanish. And somewhere along the way, public awareness has started to shift. Not perfectly. Not everywhere. But more people are connecting the dots—between what they consume and what it costs the planet. That reckoning, quiet but growing, is as much ethical as environmental (Thøgersen, 2021; Habib et al., 2021).

The science, meanwhile, has been clear for a while. To stay within climate limits, emissions have to fall—and fast. Especially from fossil fuels. Diplomacy has tried. So has innovation. But emissions kept rising. The only real dip came during the 2020 lockdowns. That drop didn't last. By 2021, they were climbing again. 2022 followed the same path. Which says something. About inertia. About the strength of the systems already in place. And about the limits of behavior change when it's driven only by crisis—or left up to individual choice (Table 4.13).

The table tells a story in numbers—but the story is unmistakably human. Between 2015 and 2024, global CO_2 emissions from fossil fuels climbed from 35.5 to 37.4 gigatons. Despite policies, targets, and summits, fossil fuels continued to dominate the global energy mix. A brief pause came in 2020, during the height of the COVID-19 lockdowns—emissions dropped by 4.6%. But the rebound in 2021 and 2022 erased that dip almost entirely. The system held steady. And that's part of the problem. Emissions from land-use change barely budged either. They hovered between 4.0 and 4.2 $GtCO_2$ for most of the decade, dipping slightly to 3.7 $GtCO_2$ in 2023. Maybe it was conservation. Maybe deforestation just slowed, temporarily. But nothing pointed to structural change.

In the atmosphere, the trend was even clearer. CO_2 concentration rose from 400.8 ppm in 2015 to 422.5 ppm in 2024. Carbon accumulation outpaced absorption. Natural sinks—the forests, soils, and oceans that buffer the system—were doing what they could. They held steady for a time: 2.9, maybe 3.2 GtC per year. But in 2023, even the land sink slipped to 2.3 GtC. Stress, drought, heat—it adds up. Then there's the carbon budget. In 2015, the world still had 810 $GtCO_2$ left to emit if it wanted to stay under 1.5 °C. By 2024, that had dropped to just 235 $GtCO_2$. That's nearly 71% gone in one decade. The implications are stark. Temporary disruptions aren't enough. The crisis isn't waiting. Still, something is shifting. Climate

Table 4.13 Global CO_2 metrics (2015–2024)

Metric	2015	2016	2017	2018	2019	2020	2021	2022	2023	2024
Fossil CO_2 Emissions ($GtCO_2$)	35.5	35.7	36	36.2	36.6	34.9	36.3	36.6	36.8	37.4
Land-Use Change Emissions ($GtCO_2$)	4.1	4	4.1	4.2	4.2	4	4	4.1	3.7	4.2
Total Anthropogenic Emissions ($GtCO_2$)	39.6	39.7	40.1	40.4	40.8	38.9	40.3	40.7	40.6	41.6
Atmospheric CO_2 Growth Rate (GtC)	5	5.1	4.8	5	5.2	4.9	5.1	5.3	5.9	6.1
Atmospheric CO_2 Growth Rate (ppm)	2.29	2.38	2.24	2.36	2.44	2.33	2.42	2.5	2.79	2.87
Atmospheric CO_2 Concentration (ppm)	400.8	404.2	406.5	408.5	411	414.2	416.5	418	419.3	422.5
Ocean Sink (GtC)	2.9	2.8	3	2.9	2.9	2.9	3	2.9	2.9	3
Land Sink (GtC)	3.2	3.1	3.3	3.3	3.4	3.2	3.1	3.3	2.3	3.2
Carbon Budget Imbalance (GtC)	0	−0.1	−0.3	−0.1	0	0.1	0.2	0	−0.02	0
Annual Fossil CO_2 Emissions Growth (%)	0.6	0.6	0.8	0.6	1.1	−4.6	4	0.8	0.5	0.8
Remaining Carbon Budget for 1.5 °C ($GtCO_2$)	810	760	710	660	610	570	530	480	440	235

Source: International Energy Agency (2023), Global Carbon Budget (2024)

change is no longer abstract. Consumers are starting to feel implicated—and, in some cases, empowered. Surveys show growing concern, especially among the young, the urban, and those who've lived through fire, flood, or record heat (McKinsey & Company, 2023). Concern is turning into action—or at least intention.

Nowhere is this more visible than in Australia. After the 2019–2020 "Black Summer" fires, climate awareness took on a new texture. The damage wasn't distant. It was everywhere—across ecosystems, into cities. People responded. They bought differently: more plant-based food, fewer throwaway goods, more products that showed their footprint. Slogans like "buy for a burning world" began to circulate. Retailers took note, advertising with carbon labels. Local governments built emissions inventories that tracked not just production, but consumption. And suddenly, responsible consumption wasn't just a climate idea—it was a survival response (Xu et al., 2023; Abram et al., 2021; Kemter et al., 2021) (Table 4.14).

The numbers in this table may look small—but they signal something deeper: a shift in how people think about climate responsibility, and who should lead. Between 2021 and 2022, belief that personal inaction would harm future generations dropped slightly—from 73% to 70%. Not a collapse, but a pause. A rebalancing, maybe. The same goes for how people see businesses: support for the idea that they carry climate responsibility fell from 71% to 68%. At the same time, something else ticked upward—belief in government responsibility rose from 65% to 68%. Taken together, these aren't wild swings. But they hint at changing expectations. Individuals and businesses still matter. But more people are turning their eyes toward the state. Maybe because the problem feels bigger now. Maybe because action—real action—seems to demand more than good intentions. Regulation. Investment. Coordination. The kind of scaffolding only governments can build.

That idea gained some traction, too. In 2021, only 31% believed their government had a clear climate plan. By 2022, it was 39%—an eight-point rise. Still a minority, but a growing one. Maybe driven by bold moves like the European Green Deal, the U.S. Inflation Reduction Act, or pledges under the UN climate framework (Domorenok & Graziano, 2023; Bang, 2025). These aren't just policies—they're signals. And signals shape belief.

What all this shows is that concern hasn't faded. But the way people channel that concern is shifting. Responsible consumption doesn't happen in a vacuum. It

Table 4.14 Public agreement on responsibility and climate action planning (2021 vs 2022)[a]

Indicator	2021 (%)	2022 (%)	Change (pp)
Agree: If individuals do not act, we will fail future generations	73	70	−3
Agree: If businesses do not act, they are failing employees/customers	71	68	−3
Agree: If government does not act, it is failing the people	65	68	3
Agree: Government has a clear plan to tackle climate change	31	39	8

Source: IPSOS (2022)

[a]Global average based on 29 comparator countries surveyed in both 2021 and 2022 (Feb–Mar)

grows—or stalls—based on whether people trust the systems around them. Whether governments seem capable. Whether businesses are transparent. Whether sustainable options feel real, or just symbolic. And in that sense, these numbers are more than opinion—they're context. They shape the conditions under which ethical choices are even possible (Table 4.15).

This table pulls together country-by-country data from 2022 and tries to answer a simple but loaded question: how worried are people—really—about climate change? Not in theory, but in a way that sticks. The numbers are clear, though not always easy to interpret. Colombia sits at the top with 71% of respondents saying they're either "very" or "fairly" concerned. Chile follows close behind, then Italy, also at 69%. That's Latin America and Southern Europe showing high levels of concern—probably not a coincidence, given the weather extremes they've faced recently. Floods. Heatwaves. Droughts. When those become part of daily life, climate worry stops being abstract. But in richer parts of Europe, the figures look different. In France, the number drops to 45%. In Germany, it slides even further to 36%. China? Just 28%. And that's despite major state messaging on environmental issues. Somehow, the message isn't sticking—or perhaps it's not framed in a way that creates urgency. Across all countries in the sample, the average lands at 48%. Not terrible. But not reassuring either.

Dig deeper, and another number jumps out. The group of people who say they're "not worried at all" is tiny in Chile and Colombia—between 5% and 8%. But in Germany and China, it's triple or more: 24% and 26%, respectively. What's going on here? Media framing, probably. Institutional trust, maybe. Or just whether people think the threat is far off, or already on their doorstep. Either way, it matters. Because when concern is low, so is the chance of changing behavior. And for anyone trying to shape policies or public campaigns around responsible consumption, this variation is a real constraint. Still, even where worry runs high, responses vary. In countries with strong economies, the shift toward responsible consumption often rides on access—rooftop solar, plant-based diets, insulation upgrades. These are changes made possible by choice, sometimes even framed as lifestyle improvements. But in low-income regions, the story is something else entirely. Climate disruption doesn't arrive as a debate—it's already the context. And the responses

Table 4.15 Level of public concern about climate change by country (2022)[a]

Country	% Worried (Great deal/fair amount)	% Not worried at all
Colombia	71	8
Chile	69	5
Italy	69	8
Global Average	48	15
France	45	18
Germany	36	24
China	28	26

Source: IPSOS (2022)
[a]Base: 22,033 (2022) and 20,511 (2021) online adults aged 16–74 across 29 countries, Feb–Mar

that emerge aren't cushioned by subsidies or green consumer markets. They're improvised, daily, and very often overlooked.

Sub-Saharan Africa brings this into sharp focus. In Kenya, Ethiopia, Namibia—places where drought isn't a news item but a seasonal given—households have been pivoting out of necessity. Solar cookers replace firewood when forests thin. Drip irrigation gets installed not as an innovation, but as a survival. Waste isn't wasted; it's turned into goods through circular micro-enterprises—metal scraps become tools, textiles get a second life, plastic finds function (Xie et al., 2021; Falchetta et al., 2023). These aren't consumer trends. They're lived adaptations. And here's the thing: they're rarely held up as models. Yet they should be. Because in their stripped-down efficiency, they hold something that's missing in wealthier debates—resilience without excess. More and more, NGOs and youth networks are starting to push this point. These aren't signs of underdevelopment. They're templates for how low-emission living can look when you start with constraint instead of abundance. When responsible consumption isn't about privilege—but about doing what you must, with what you have (Table 4.16).

This table offers more than just figures—it shows how people around the world think responsibility for cutting greenhouse gas emissions should be shared. And what's striking isn't just the overall concern, but how evenly it's spread. Three numbers stand close together: 77% say governments should take responsibility, 76% say businesses, and 74% point to individuals. That near-parity doesn't happen by accident. It reflects an emerging public sense that climate change isn't one group's burden to carry—it's structural. And everyone is implicated.

The fact that governments are just slightly ahead in this perception isn't surprising. They write the rules, after all. People still expect state actors to lead: to pass laws, fund infrastructure, set targets that go beyond soft commitments. But the barely smaller number for businesses—76%—speaks volumes too. There's growing awareness that corporate decisions ripple outward: what's produced, how it's shipped, what ends up on shelves or in landfills. Supply chains, marketing choices, disclosure practices—they all shape emissions, and the public increasingly sees that. And individuals? Still very much in the frame. With 74% assigning responsibility to themselves and others like them, there's clearly a widespread belief that change isn't only top-down. It's in habits, purchases, diet, travel. The personal realm matters, even if people know it can't fix the problem alone.

What emerges here isn't just a list of numbers—it's a pattern. A shared expectation. One that recognizes this crisis doesn't sort neatly into roles or boundaries. It

Table 4.16 Public perception of responsibility for reducing emissions (2022)[a]

Actor	% Agree they bear responsibility
Governments	77
Businesses	76
Individuals	74

Source: IPSOS (2022)

[a]Base: 22,534 online adults aged 16–74 across 30 countries, Feb–Mar 2022

asks for government frameworks, yes—but also corporate shifts, and individual decisions made differently, more consciously. And the fact that people view these responsibilities as overlapping is telling. It hints at readiness for integrated approaches—where policy, business incentives, and behavioral shifts don't compete but co-evolve. In that sense, the table is more than a snapshot—it's a kind of mandate. A reminder that tackling climate change is ethically complex, but not paralyzing. If anything, the data show a public willing to act—if all the players are at the table, and no one pretends the job belongs only to someone else.

While the Gulf States often project sustainability through ambitious, top-down initiatives—think glittering eco-cities or bold national campaigns—other advanced economies have gone another way. South Korea, for instance, doesn't just talk about greening its image. It has leaned into something more personal: helping citizens change how they live, one decision at a time. This isn't about spectacle. It's about quietly turning everyday behavior into a form of climate action.

The country's model is built on infrastructure, yes—but of a different kind. The government has rolled out a network of digital platforms that let people track their carbon emissions, get nudges on how to cut back, and even earn points for greener habits. These tools aren't floating in isolation; they're wired directly into utility bills, shopping apps, school curricula. It's not just about saving energy—it's about teaching people to see their choices as part of something bigger. Over time, the message has landed: that managing your household footprint is a civic act, part of what it means to contribute to national goals. The strategy works not because it scolds, but because it connects incentives, information, and identity in a way that feels actionable. As Kim (2019) and the World Bank Group Korea Office (2022) suggest, what makes this approach stand out isn't the technology itself, but the ecosystem around it—the subtle but steady pressure to align daily life with climate responsibility.

The story looks different when we focus on resource-heavy countries, especially those whose economies are still tied to carbon. Here, responsible consumption gets tangled with something larger—energy wealth, political image, and global expectations. Change doesn't always come from public demand or everyday scarcity. It often arrives dressed up as futuristic projects, as if technology and branding alone can carry the weight of transformation. It can look impressive from a distance, but up close it raises uncomfortable questions. How much of this is structural, and how much is just a narrative of progress?

The Gulf States show this tension in sharp relief. Nations like the United Arab Emirates and Saudi Arabia have started pouring billions into green infrastructure while trying to reshape their public image. Think of Masdar City or NEOM—ambitious eco-cities marketed as glimpses of a sustainable future. People are being encouraged to switch to electric cars, to save water drawn from energy-hungry desalination plants, to use apps that monitor household energy use. All the tools and messages are there, and yet the numbers tell another story: per capita carbon emissions remain among the highest in the world. That gap between the story and the substance is hard to miss. Scholars such as Yusuf and Abdulmohsen (2022) and Aldegheishem (2024) have pointed out that this approach leans heavily on technological solutions rather than on changes in behavior. It keeps the economic model largely untouched. Responsible consumption, in this framing, isn't so much a collective shift in values as it is a polished narrative of modernization—an attempt to balance fossil fuel wealth with the language of ecological responsibility. Whether this balance can hold, or whether it will be seen as surface-level adjustment, is still up for debate (Table 4.17).

This table breaks down how people assign responsibility for cutting emissions across different economic sectors. And the pattern is pretty clear: energy companies top the list, with 82% of respondents pointing to them, followed closely by car manufacturers at 80%. These are not surprising figures—both industries are front and center in the climate conversation. They're seen as not only massive contributors to global emissions, but also as emblematic of the fossil fuel era itself. People aren't just reacting to the pollution; they're responding to what these sectors represent—centralized power, carbon-heavy systems, and decades of environmental cost largely passed down to the public.

What the numbers suggest is that the public doesn't view the climate crisis as something evenly distributed across society. They expect the biggest shifts to come from the biggest players. And that makes sense, given how upstream decisions in energy and transport shape everything downstream—from the cars people buy to the electricity that powers their homes. There's also a kind of implicit demand embedded in this perception: these sectors are seen as having both the tools and the responsibility to lead. Whether it's through innovation, regulation, or market shifts, the public seems to believe these industries are where the most meaningful change could—and should—begin.

Public transport providers and airlines don't escape scrutiny either—77% of respondents say they should shoulder a "great deal" or at least "a fair amount" of responsibility for cutting emissions. And it's easy to see why. Trains, buses,

Table 4.17 Sector-specific responsibility for reducing emissions (2022)[a]

Sector	% Responsibility (Great deal/fair amount)
Energy companies	82
Car manufacturers	80
Public transport providers	77
Airlines	77
Household goods manufacturers	74
Tech/electronics companies	74
Clothing/fashion brands	68
Online retail	55
Financial services	53

Source: IPSOS (2022)
[a]Base: 23,577 online adults aged 16–74 across 31 countries, Feb–Mar 2022

planes—they move millions every day, and their environmental footprint is anything but light. The call for cleaner, smarter, and more efficient transit isn't just coming from activists anymore; it's becoming a mainstream expectation.

That same 74% of people pointed to both household goods and electronics companies speaks volumes. It's no longer just about what fuels our cars or powers our homes—attention is shifting to what sits in our kitchens, on our wrists, and in our pockets. People are starting to recognize the hidden climate costs behind everyday objects: the raw materials pulled from the Earth, the factories that shape them, and the e-waste that piles up when we're done. The environmental story of a product now runs far deeper than the box it comes in.

Fashion brands are on the radar too, though slightly fewer people—68%—assign them serious responsibility. That might seem lower, but it's still significant. The fast-fashion industry churns out trends at breakneck speed, guzzling resources along the way. The public may not yet grasp the full scale of its emissions, but growing awareness of the ecological cost of cheap clothes is pushing the industry into the climate conversation, whether it likes it or not.

Then come financial services and online retail—sectors that don't burn fuel or make gadgets, yet still shape how the world works. With 53% and 55% of respondents assigning them climate responsibility, it's clear that people are beginning to connect the dots. These industries might seem abstract, but the money they move, the investments they back, the purchases they enable—they all influence emissions. The public is catching on: climate action isn't just about switching lightbulbs or buying electric cars. It's about shifting the deeper systems behind what we buy and why.

This broader awareness is changing the terrain for companies. Even if people don't always act on their climate intentions—because greener options cost more, or old habits are hard to shake—the marketplace is shifting. There's been a sharp rise in climate-conscious products, and consumers are asking tougher questions. Labels that list emissions, promises of carbon neutrality, packaging that tells an ecological story—these aren't just for the eco-elite anymore. They're edging toward expectation. Whether it's a t-shirt, a smartphone, or a bag of coffee beans, the backstory now matters as much as the price tag (Table 4.18).

Looking at sales data from 2018 to 2022, a clear pattern emerges: products carrying Environmental, Social, and Governance (ESG) labels have been gaining traction—not just in reputation, but in real economic terms. Over that 5-year stretch, ESG-claiming products saw cumulative sales climb by 28%, outperforming their conventional counterparts, which rose by 20%. The advantage holds even when you factor in growth rates year over year. On average, ESG-tagged items grew at a compound annual growth rate (CAGR) of 6.4%, while non-claiming products clocked in at 4.7%.

But perhaps the more telling figure is this: ESG-linked goods accounted for over half—56%—of total category growth. In other words, while they didn't make up the majority of products on the shelf, they were responsible for most of the expansion. That's more than just solid performance—it's influence. These products aren't just keeping pace; they're setting the pace.

Table 4.18 Market growth and consumer loyalty linked to climate- and ESG-labeled products in the U.S. Consumer Packaged Goods Sector (2018–2022)[a]

Metric	ESG-claiming products	Non-claiming products
Cumulative Sales Growth (2018–2022)	28%	20%
Compound Annual Growth Rate (CAGR)	6.4%	4.7%
Share of Total Category Growth Attributed to ESG-Claiming Products	56%	44%
Growth Differential—Low-Prevalence Claims (e.g., "carbon zero")	+8.5%	–
Growth Multiplier with Multiple ESG Claims	Up to 2.5× vs. single claim	–
Brand Loyalty (Repeat Purchase Rate)	34% (brands with >80% ESG-labeled sales)	27% (brands with <20% ESG-labeled sales)

Source: McKinsey & NielsenIQ (2023)
[a]Data reflect sales performance in the U.S. consumer packaged goods (CPG) market (2018–2022) across 600,000 SKUs in 32 product categories. ESG-related claims include environmental, social, and governance themes such as "carbon zero," "eco-friendly," "plant-based," and "biodegradable." Figures represent correlations, not causal effects; the study does not control for variables such as marketing spend or distribution

The data also reveal a telling pattern in how consumers respond to sustainability claims. Products featuring less common labels—such as "carbon zero"—showed a notable edge, generating an 8.5% higher growth rate compared to similar items without such claims. This suggests that specificity in climate messaging may carry real weight with shoppers. Interestingly, the effect appears to intensify when multiple ESG claims are combined. In fact, products with several overlapping environmental or social indicators grew up to 2.5 times faster than those carrying just one, highlighting consumer interest not only in green branding, but in perceived thoroughness.

Brand loyalty, too, seems to follow this trend. Companies whose sales are predominantly tied to ESG-labeled products—those with over 80% of offerings marked accordingly—saw a 34% repeat purchase rate. Meanwhile, brands where these products made up less than 20% of the catalog lagged behind at 27%. The contrast here hints at something deeper: when consumers sense a consistent commitment to ethical or climate-conscious production, they're more likely to return. Together, these figures challenge any lingering assumption that climate-aware purchasing is still confined to the margins. What we're seeing is a broader shift—responsible consumption is no longer just rhetoric. It's showing up in the numbers. Consumers are increasingly factoring environmental and ethical considerations into their everyday shopping habits, and in doing so, they're helping to reshape the market landscape.

Of course, some caution is warranted. Correlation doesn't equal causation, and other forces—like marketing budgets or product visibility—likely influence the results. Still, the patterns are hard to dismiss. For firms navigating a changing marketplace, the lesson is increasingly clear: weaving sustainability into product portfolios and brand messaging isn't just about public image anymore—it's becoming a strategic business imperative.

The climate crisis has gradually reshaped how many people think about their role in the world—not just as citizens or workers, but as consumers. For a growing number, responsibility for the climate doesn't stop at voting or recycling. It has become a matter of personal ethics. People are starting to ask themselves harder questions: Is what I'm buying doing harm somewhere else? Does it add to the problem or help solve it? And are my everyday choices fair—not just to the planet, but to future generations, or to people who didn't cause this crisis but will suffer the worst of it? (Spijkers, 2018). This shift is showing up in all sorts of ways. It's not just about swapping out one product for another. For some, it's a deeper rethinking of how they live—how often they fly, what kind of food they eat, how their homes are heated, even whether they need as much stuff in the first place. It's about stepping back and asking whether one's lifestyle is compatible with what the planet can handle.

Digital tools have started to play a role in nudging these shifts along. Carbon calculators, product-scanning apps, browser extensions that flag sustainable choices—these might sound small, but they give people a way to see the impact of their habits in real time (Hoffmann et al., 2024). Some of it is about information, yes, but some of it is about agency. It's easier to change when you can measure what matters.

Governments, too, have begun to explore more nuanced ways of shaping consumer behavior. Instead of just regulating from above, many are turning to behavioral strategies—what some call "green nudges." These are subtle but intentional tweaks in how choices are presented: making renewable electricity the default option on bills; offering rebates for energy-efficient fridges or electric heat pumps; taxing carbon-heavy products to make the real costs visible (Carlsson et al., 2021). It's not always obvious that you're being steered—but often, you are.

What's more interesting, though, is how these policies are starting to reframe who the consumer is. It's no longer just about buying power or price sensitivity. Increasingly, national plans—like the European Green Deal—speak to the consumer as a participant in something larger: a societal transition, a collective reimagining of what progress means (Gray & McArdle, 2025). That framing matters. It suggests that fighting climate change isn't just about big technology or global agreements. It's also about small choices made millions of times over—across grocery aisles, power bills, and commute routes. Not everyone can afford to act the same way, and not all actions have equal weight. But the idea is catching on: consumption isn't neutral anymore. It's political. It's ethical. And more than ever, it's consequential.

Still, good intentions run into hard limits. Much of what we call climate-relevant consumption—especially in housing or transport—is not easily changed by personal willpower alone. You might want to insulate your home or ditch the car, but that depends on whether the options exist, whether they're affordable, and whether the system around you supports the shift. Roads, public transit, zoning rules, energy prices—these set the stage for what's even possible. So while behavior matters, structure shapes behavior more than we often admit.

And then there's the slippery issue of trust. Over the past decade, companies have learned that consumers care about sustainability—but some have also learned how to fake it. "Greenwashing" is no longer a fringe concern; it's a real, growing problem. Brands promise carbon neutrality or eco-friendliness, but the proof often lags behind the marketing (de Freitas Netto et al., 2020). The result? People who care about climate action are left guessing which claims are credible and which are just clever packaging. Without stricter rules on disclosures and third-party verification, this confusion will keep weakening the force of responsible consumption.

But despite all these barriers, something deeper has started to shift. The climate crisis, unlike past disruptions, is not a storm we weather and forget. It lingers. It alters the backdrop of everyday life. And over time, it has begun to rewire how people think about consumption—not just what they buy, but why they buy it, and what it means. The motives are changing. So are the stories we tell ourselves about what matters.

Previous crises—economic crashes, pandemics, wars—often changed habits in the short term. But climate change is more persistent, more existential. It's fostering a slow but steady shift in values. People are beginning to weigh not just cost or convenience, but alignment: does this choice sit right with my sense of fairness? With the future I want for others? With the kind of world I believe in?

That shift doesn't make the consumer powerless. On the contrary, it redefines their role. More and more, consumption is not just a market act—it's a moral one. And with that comes a kind of agency. Responsible consumption, in this light, becomes not a burden, but a way of participating in something larger. The climate crisis asks us to move beyond passive consumption toward something more deliberate—more self-aware, more attuned to consequences. Not perfect. Not always possible. But aimed in the right direction.

References

Abram, N. J., Henley, B. J., Sen Gupta, A., Lippmann, T. J., Clarke, H., Dowdy, A. J., et al. (2021). Connections of climate change and variability to large and extreme forest fires in southeast Australia. *Communications Earth & Environment, 2*(1), 1–17.

Ahmed, S., Ali, A., & D'angola, A. (2024). A review of renewable energy communities: Concepts, scope, progress, challenges, and recommendations. *Sustainability, 16*(5), 1749.

Aldegheishem, A. (2024). Factors affecting ecological footprint in Saudi Arabia: A panel data analysis. *Frontiers in Environmental Science, 12*, 1384451.

Aliyev, I. (2023). REPowerEU: Feasibility of fast renewable energy growth under a crisis.

Bäckstrand, K. (2022). Towards a climate-neutral union by 2050? The European green deal, climate law, and green recovery. In *Routes to a resilient European Union: Interdisciplinary European studies* (pp. 39–61). Springer International.

Bang, G. (2025). The US Inflation Reduction Act: Climate policy as economic crisis response. *Environmental Politics*, 1–22.

Bashir, M. S. (2010). Islamic finance and its contribution to solving the current financial crisis. *International Journal of Management Studies, 17*, 85–99.
Baumeister, C., & Kilian, L. (2016). Forty years of oil price fluctuations: Why the price of oil may still surprise us. *Journal of Economic Perspectives, 30*(1), 139–160.
Bernauer, W., & Slowey, G. (2020). COVID-19, extractive industries, and indigenous communities in Canada: Notes towards a political economy research agenda. *The Extractive Industries and Society, 7*(3), 844–846.
Bini, E., Garavini, G., & Romero, F. (Eds.). (2016). *Oil shock: The 1973 crisis and its economic legacy*. Bloomsbury.
Borovoy, A. (2022). The burdens of self-restraint: Social measures and the containment of Covid-19 in Japan. *Asia-Pacific Journal: Japan Focus, 20*.
Bösch, F., & Graf, R. (2014). Reacting to anticipations: Energy crises and energy policy in the 1970s. An introduction. *Historical Social Research/Historische Sozialforschung*, 7–21.
Buell, F. (2012). A short history of oil cultures: Or, the marriage of catastrophe and exuberance. *Journal of American Studies, 46*(2), 273–293.
Carlsson, F., Gravert, C., Johansson-Stenman, O., & Kurz, V. (2021). The use of green nudges as an environmental policy instrument. *Review of Environmental Economics and Policy, 15*(2), 216–237.
Carolan, M. (2021). Practicing social change during COVID-19: Ethical food consumption and activism pre-and post-outbreak. *Appetite, 163*, 105206.
Cervellati, E. M., Stella, G. P., Filotto, U., & Maino, A. (2022). How COVID-19 changed Italian consumers' behavior. *Global Finance Journal, 51*, 100680.
Clô, A. (2000). Energy crises: Perception and reality. In *Oil Economics and Policy* (pp. 99–124). Springer US.
Council of the European Union. (2025). *Where does the EU's gas come from?* Retrieved March 26, 2025, from https://www.consilium.europa.eu/en/infographics/where-does-the-eu-s-gas-come-from/
Cui, L., Yue, S., Nghiem, X. H., & Duan, M. (2023). Exploring the risk and economic vulnerability of global energy supply chain interruption in the context of Russo-Ukrainian war. *Resources Policy, 81*, 103373.
Das, D., Sarkar, A., & Debroy, A. (2022). Impact of COVID-19 on changing consumer behaviour: Lessons from an emerging economy. *International journal of consumer studies, 46*(3), 692–715.
Dastan, S. A. (2023). The predicaments of the Turkish natural gas market between supply shortages and price hikes. *Resources Policy, 82*, 103566.
de Barros, J. R. M. (2010). *The impact of the international financial crisis on Brazil (ARI). International Cooperation & Development*.
de Freitas Netto, S. V., Sobral, M. F. F., Ribeiro, A. R. B., & Soares, G. R. D. L. (2020). Concepts and forms of greenwashing: A systematic review. *Environmental Sciences Europe, 32*, 1–12.
Domorenok, E., & Graziano, P. (2023). Understanding the European Green Deal: A narrative policy framework approach. *European Policy Analysis, 9*(1), 9–29.
EIA, U.S. Energy Information Administration. (2025). *Statistical review. Historical data*. https://www.eia.gov/totalenergy/data/browser/index.php?tbl=T2
Ekins, P. (1993). 'Limits to growth' and 'sustainable development': Grappling with ecological realities. *Ecological Economics, 8*(3), 269–288.
European Central Bank. (2022). The impact of the war in Ukraine on euro area energy markets. *ECB Economic Bulletin*, Issue 2/2022. https://www.ecb.europa.eu/press/economic-bulletin/focus/2022/html/ecb.ebbox202204_01~68ef3c3dc6.en.html
European Commission. (2010). *Europe 2020: A strategy for smart, sustainable and inclusive growth*. https://eur-lex.europa.eu/LexUriServ/LexUriServ.do?uri=COM:2010:2020:FIN:EN:PDF
European Commission. (2019). *Eurobarometers on energy, Eurobarometer 492, EB492 Tables, QB1*. https://europa.eu/eurobarometer/surveys/detail/2238

European Commission. (2024). *Eurobarometers on energy, Eurobarometer 555, EB555, QC1.* https://europa.eu/eurobarometer/surveys/detail/3229
Eurostat. (2024a). *Electricity price statistics.* https://ec.europa.eu/eurostat/databrowser/view/nrg_pc_204/default/table?lang=en
Eurostat. (2024b). *Natural gas price statistics.* https://ec.europa.eu/eurostat/databrowser/view/nrg_pc_202/default/table?lang=en
Fairtrade International. (2012). *Monitoring the scope and benefits of Fairtrade: Sixth edition 2012.* 2012-Monitoring_the_scope_and_benefits_of_Fairtrade.pdf
Falchetta, G., Semeria, F., Tuninetti, M., Giordano, V., Pachauri, S., & Byers, E. (2023). Solar irrigation in sub-Saharan Africa: Economic feasibility and development potential. *Environmental Research Letters, 18*(9), 094044.
Farghali, M., Osman, A. I., Mohamed, I. M., Chen, Z., Chen, L., Ihara, I., et al. (2023). Strategies to save energy in the context of the energy crisis: A review. *Environmental Chemistry Letters, 21*(4), 2003–2039.
Genys, D., Krikštolaitis, R., & Pažėraitė, A. (2024). Lithuanian energy security transition: The evolution of public concern and its socio-economic implications. *Energies, 17*(4), 971.
Glazener, A., Wylie, J., van Waas, W., & Khreis, H. (2022). The impacts of car-free days and events on the environment and human health. *Current Environmental Health Reports, 9*(2), 165–182.
Global Carbon Budget. (2024). *Carbon labelling update: Global market trends.* https://globalcarbonbudget.org/gcb-2024/
Gray, E. K., & McArdle, R. (2025). Communities and the European Green Deal: Opening 'sites of struggle' for a democratic energy transition. *Journal of European Integration*, 1–23.
Grigolienė, R., Kiyak, D., Šimanskienė, L., Labanauskaitė, D., Župerkienė, E., & Mishenina, H. (2024). Household energy consumption tendencies: The Baltic States context. *Journal of Business Economics and Management, 25*(6), 1202–1219.
Habib, R., White, K., Hardisty, D. J., & Zhao, J. (2021). Shifting consumer behavior to address climate change. *Current Opinion in Psychology, 42*, 108–113.
Haghirian, P. (2011). The historical development of Japanese consumerism. In *Japanese consumer dynamics* (pp. 3–17). Palgrave Macmillan UK.
Hoffmann, S., Lasarov, W., Reimers, H., & Trabandt, M. (2024). Carbon footprint tracking apps. Does feedback help reduce carbon emissions? *Journal of Cleaner Production, 434*, 139981.
HSBC Global Research. (2009). *A climate for recovery: The colour of stimulus goes green.* https://www.vivideconomics.com/wp-content/uploads/2020/05/A-Climate-for-Recovery.pdf
Hu, P., Bhuiyan, M. A., Rahman, M. K., Hossain, M. M., & Akter, S. (2022). Impact of COVID-19 pandemic on consumer behavioural intention to purchase green products. *PLoS One, 17*(10), e0275541.
Huebner, G. M., Hanmer, C., Zapata-Webborn, E., Pullinger, M., McKenna, E. J., Few, J., et al. (2023). Self-reported energy use behaviour changed significantly during the cost-of-living crisis in winter 2022/23: Insights from cross-sectional and longitudinal surveys in Great Britain. *Scientific Reports, 13*(1), 21683.
Huhta, K. (2023). Conceptualising energy justice in the context of human rights law. *Nordic Journal of Human Rights, 41*(4), 378–392.
Huhta, K., & Reins, L. (2023). Solidarity in European union law and its application in the energy sector. *International & Comparative Law Quarterly, 72*(3), 771–791.
International Energy Agency. (2023). *CO_2 emissions in 2022.* https://www.iea.org/reports/global-energy-review-co2-emissions-in-2022
International Energy Agency. (2024). *World energy balances overview.* https://www.iea.org/reports/world-energy-balances-overview
IPSOS. (2022). *Earth Day 2022: Global attitudes to climate change, 2022 report.* https://www.ipsos.com/en-uk/earth-day-2022-global-attitudes-climate-change
Kayed, R. N., & Hassan, M. K. (2011). The global financial crisis and Islamic finance. *Thunderbird International Business Review, 53*(5), 551–564.

Kanapiyanova, Z. (2023). END OF FOSSIL DEPENDENCY–"REPOWEREU" PLAN. *Farabi Journal of Social Sciences, 9*(2), 30–34.

Kempa, K., & Tyagi, A. (2025). Climate and environmental impacts of green recovery: Evidence from the financial crisis. *World Development Sustainability, 6*, 100194.

Kemter, M., Fischer, M., Luna, L. V., Schönfeldt, E., Vogel, J., Banerjee, A., et al. (2021). Cascading hazards in the aftermath of Australia's 2019/2020 Black Summer wildfires. *Earth's Future, 9*(3), e2020EF001884.

Kim, Y. (2019). Global citizenship education in South Korea: Ideologies, inequalities, and teacher voices. *Globalisation, Societies and Education, 17*(2), 177–193.

Leal Filho, W., Salvia, A. L., Paço, A., Dinis, M. A. P., Vidal, D. G., Da Cunha, D. A., et al. (2022). The influences of the COVID-19 pandemic on sustainable consumption: An international study. *Environmental Sciences Europe, 34*(1), 54.

Lee, J., Serafin, A. M., & Courteau, C. (2023). Corporate disclosure, ESG and green fintech in the energy industry. *The Journal of World Energy Law & Business, 16*(6), 473–491.

Lifset, R. D. (2014). A new understanding of the American energy crisis of the 1970s. *Historical Social Research/Historische Sozialforschung*, 22–42.

Lin, C. Y. (1984). Global pattern of energy consumption before and after the 1974 oil crisis. *Economic Development and Cultural Change, 32*(4), 781–802.

Matschoss, K., Laakso, S., & Rinkinen, J. (2025). Disruptions and energy demand: How Finnish households responded to the energy crisis of 2022. *Energy Research & Social Science, 121*, 103977.

McKinsey & Company. (2021). *Survey: US consumer sentiment during the coronavirus crisis*. https://www.mckinsey.com/capabilities/growth-marketing-and-sales/our-insights/survey-us-consumer-sentiment-during-the-coronavirus-crisis

McKinsey & Company. (2023). *Consumers care about sustainability—and back it up with their wallets*. McKinsey & Company. https://www.mckinsey.com/industries/consumer-packaged-goods/our-insights/consumers-care-about-sustainability-and-back-it-up-with-their-wallets

McKinsey & NielsenIQ. (2023). *Consumers care about sustainability—and back it up with their wallets*. https://nielseniq.com/global/en/insights/report/2023/consumers-care-about-sustainability-and-back-it-up-with-their-wallets/

Miguel, C., Avram, G., Klimczuk, A., Simonovits, B., Balázs, B., & Česnuitytė, V. (2022). The sharing economy in Europe: From idea to reality. In *The sharing economy in Europe: Developments, practices, and contradictions* (pp. 3–18). Springer International.

Mugume, R., & Bulime, E. W. (2022). Post-COVID-19 recovery for African economies: Lessons for digital financial inclusion from Kenya and Uganda. *African Development Review, 34*, S161–S176.

OECD Korea. (2017). *OECD environmental performance reviews: Korea 2017*. OECD Publishing. https://www.oecd.org/content/dam/oecd/en/publications/reports/2017/03/oecd-environmental-performance-reviews-korea-2017_g1g742d0/9789264268265-en.pdf

Organisation for Economic Co-operation and Development (OECD). (2010). *OECD economic outlook, Vol. 2010 Issue 1*. https://www.oecd.org/en/publications/2010/05/oecd-economic-outlook-volume-2010-issue-1_g1ghbb3a.html

Our World in Data. (2025). *Primary sub-energy source – world energy production by source*. https://ourworldindata.org/grapher/primary-sub-energy-source

Panizzut, N., Rafi-ul-Shan, P. M., Amar, H., Sher, F., Mazhar, M. U., & Klemeš, J. J. (2021). Exploring relationship between environmentalism and consumerism in a market economy society: A structured systematic literature review. *Cleaner Engineering and Technology, 2*, 100047.

Power, P. F. (1975). The energy crisis and Indian development. *Asian Survey, 15*(4), 328–345.

Qin, M. (2023). Subprime crisis and regulatory responses. *BCP Business & Management, 46*, 140–145. https://doi.org/10.54691/bcpbm.v46i.5089

Rabinovich, A. (2007). *The Yom Kippur War: The epic encounter that transformed the Middle East*. Schocken.

Reddy, A. K. N. (1981). A strategy for resolving India's oil crisis. *Current Science, 50*(2), 50–53.

Ryan, J. M., & Nanda, S. (2022). *COVID-19: Social inequalities and human possibilities*. Routledge.

Ritzer, G. (2012). "Hyperconsumption" and "hyperdebt": A "hypercritical" analysis. *A Debtor World: Interdisciplinary Perspectives on Debt*, 60–80.

Rolef, S. H. (1999). The domestic fallout of the Yom Kippur War. *Israel Affairs, 6*(1), 177–194.

Rüdiger, M. (2019). From import dependence to self-sufficiency in Denmark, 1945– 2000. *Energy Policy, 125*, 82–89.

Saur Energy. (2021). *Self-sustaining off-grid options in remote areas can lead to technological as well as social changes*. Saur Energy. https://www.saurenergy.com/solar-energy-conversation/self-sustaining-off-grid-options-in-remote-areas-can-lead-to-technological-as-well-as-social-changes

Sharma, V., & Sonwalkar, J. (2013). Does consumer buying behavior change during economic crisis?.

Sijabat, R. (2024). Impact of the COVID-19 pandemic on sustainability knowledge and sustainable purchase decisions: The application of the theory of stimulus–organization–response. *Cogent Business & Management, 11*(1), 2327134.

Sorrentino, A., Leone, D., & Caporuscio, A. (2022). Changes in the post-covid-19 consumers' behaviors and lifestyle in Italy. A disaster management perspective. *Italian Journal of Marketing, 2022*(1), 87–106.

Spijkers, O. (2018). Intergenerational equity and the sustainable development goals. *Sustainability, 10*(11), 3836.

Tee, E., Asare, L. B., Opoku, R. T., & Tabitha, O. D. (2017). The effect of the 2008 financial crisis on corporate social responsibilities: Evidence from multinational companies. *Research Journal of Finance and Accounting, 8*(16).

Thøgersen, J. (2021). Consumer behavior and climate change: Consumers need considerable assistance. *Current Opinion in Behavioral Sciences, 42*, 9–14.

Trading Economics. (2025a). *United States retail sales*. https://tradingeconomics.com/united-states/retail-sales

Trading Economics. (2025b). *United States e-commerce retail sales (mil of $) q sa Fed data*. https://tradingeconomics.com/united-states/e-commerce-retail-sales-mil-of-$-q-sa-fed-data.html

Tsekeris, T. (2025). Transformations in the European gas supply network due to the Russia–Ukraine conflict. *Energies, 18*(7), 1709.

U.S. Environmental Protection Agency. (2024). *EPA Automotive Trends Report: Summary*. https://www.epa.gov/automotive-trends/download-automotive-trends-report#Summary

United Nations Development Programme (UNDP) India. (2009). *Global financial crisis and India's informal economy: Review of key sectors*. https://www.undp.org/india/publications/global-financial-crisis-and-indias-informal-economy-review-key-sectors

Urios, J., Casert, C., Gore, T., Foulds, C., & Afghani, N. (2022). Behavioural, cultural and social issues in EU Green Deal policy documents.

Urry, J. (2013). *Societies beyond oil: Oil dregs and social futures*. Bloomsbury.

Valor Martínez, C., & Papaoikonomou, E. (2016). Time banking in Spain. Exploring their structure, management and users profile.

Vázquez-Fariñas, M. (2023). Major economic recessions in the last quarter of the 20th century: The oil crisis (1973–1980). In *The Age of Global Economic Crises* (pp. 56–81). Routledge.

Veltmeyer, H. (2018). The social and solidarity economy in Latin America. In *Co-operativism and local development in Cuba* (pp. 29–50). Brill.

Visvizi, A. (2012). The crisis in Greece and the EU-IMF rescue package: Determinants and pitfalls. *Acta oeconomica, 62*(1), 15–39.

Wachira, G., & Njuguna, A. (2023). Enhancing growth and productivity through mobile money financial technology services: The case of M-Pesa in Kenya. *International Journal of Economics and Finance, 15*(12), 1–91.

Wang, C. J., Han, X., Xin, S., Liu, D. H., Xu, M., Ma, J. Q., & Yu, Y. (2019). An empirical analysis of Denmark's energy economy and environment and its sustainable development policy. *Journal of Sustainable Development, 12*(2), 29–38.

Warren, S. A., & Ganguly, S. (2022). India–Russia relations after Ukraine. *Asian Survey, 62*(5–6), 811–837.

Wiggins, R. Z., & Metrick, A. (2019). The Lehman brothers bankruptcy h: The global contagion. *Journal of Financial Crises, 1*(1), 172–199.

World Bank Group Korea Office. (2022). *Greening digital in Korea: Korea case study for greening the ICT sector*. World Bank. https://thedocs.worldbank.org/en/doc/08165a76ca0f1ef688d2782dfaab3406-0400072022/related/Greening-Digital-in-Korea-Korea-Case-Study-for-Greening-the-ICT-Sector.pdf

Wright, J. (2021). Overcoming political distrust: The role of 'self-restraint' in Japan's public health response to COVID-19. In *Japan Forum* (Vol. 33, No. 4, pp. 453–475). Routledge.

Xie, H., Ringler, C., & Mondal, M. A. H. (2021). Solar or diesel: A comparison of costs for groundwater-fed irrigation in sub-Saharan Africa under two energy solutions. *Earth's Future, 9*(4), e2020EF001611.

Xu, R., Yu, P., Liu, Y., Chen, G., Yang, Z., Zhang, Y., et al. (2023). Climate change, environmental extremes, and human health in Australia: Challenges, adaptation strategies, and policy gaps. *The Lancet Regional Health–Western Pacific, 40*.

Yamakoshi, A. (1986). *A study on Japan's reaction to the 1973 oil crisis* (Doctoral dissertation, University of British Columbia).

Yusuf, N., & Abdulmohsen, D. (2022). Saudi Arabia's NEOM project as a testing ground for economically feasible planned cities: Case study. *Sustainability, 15*(1), 608.

GPSR Compliance
The European Union's (EU) General Product Safety Regulation (GPSR) is a set of rules that requires consumer products to be safe and our obligations to ensure this.

If you have any concerns about our products, you can contact us on

ProductSafety@springernature.com

In case Publisher is established outside the EU, the EU authorized representative is:

Springer Nature Customer Service Center GmbH
Europaplatz 3
69115 Heidelberg, Germany

www.ingramcontent.com/pod-product-compliance
Ingram Content Group UK Ltd.
Pitfield, Milton Keynes, MK11 3LW, UK
UKHW021614260926
475829UK00010B/43

* 9 7 8 3 0 3 2 1 6 2 1 7 5 *